AN INTERPRETATION OF THE LOGIC OF HEGEL

Errol E. Harris

UNIVERSITY
PRESS OF
AMERICA

LANHAM • NEW YORK • LONDON

Copyright © 1983 by

University Press of America,™ Inc.

4720 Boston Way
Lanham, MD 20706

3 Henrietta Street
London WC2E 8LU England

Library of Congress Cataloging in Publication Data

Harris, Errol E.
    An interpretation of the logic of Hegel.

    Bibliography: p.
    Includes index.
    1. Hegel, Georg Wilhelm Friedrich, 1770–1831–
Logic. 2. Logic–History–19th century. I. Title.
B2949.L8H29   1983   160'.92'4   83–17112
ISBN 0–8191–3543–7 (alk. paper)
ISBN 0–8191–3544–5 (pbk. : alk. paper)

TABLE OF CONTENTS

PREFACE

The purpose of this commentary is to render Hegel's Logic intelligible to the uninitiated and to dispel the numerous misconceptions which have accumulated around it and around Hegel's philosophy generally. No attempt has been made to trace historically the development of the Logic through its various versions, or to give a biographical account of Hegel's philosophical development. This has been done by other writers with whom I have no desire to compete. My object has been only to grasp the kernel of Hegel's thought and to penetrate, so far as I can, the obscurities of his writing, as well as, where necessary and practicable, to explain and sort out some apparent anomalies in the arrangement of the material.

Misconceptions and misrepresentations of Hegel are so numerous, so varied and so widespread that one can hardly hope to list or to combat every one of them; but if I have been able to present correctly the main Hegelian position and if I have properly identified and successfully communicated the essential principles on which Hegel's thought is founded, most of the misapprehensions and confusions should become obvious and the errors of interpretation will be dispelled. Oddly enough, some of these are committed even by sympathetic and astute commentators, like Walter Kaufmann, in his Reinterpretation[1], who, in a commendable attempt to defend Hegel against charges of rigidity, stuffiness and restriction of outlook (charges which any intelligent reader of Hegel's works would hardly contemplate), tends to go much too far. He alleges, for instance, that the dialectic is so far from being fundamental to Hegel's thought that it is at best peripheral, or even non-existent, and that it was never intended to be 'scientific' (though Kaufmann does not explain in what sense he is using that word), 'at most a method of exposition'.[2] The account I have given of the dialectic will, I hope, make the error of these judgements apparent, although I am in full agreement with much of what Kaufmann says when he rejects the allegations made by many of rigidity and mechanism in the three-step of thesis, antithesis and synthesis. Also, I consider his criticism of McTaggart to be fully justified. Yet it seems incredible that one who understands Hegel as well as Kaufmann obviously does could maintain that the arrangement of the Greater Logic is no more than the result of a struggle 'to impose some order on excess and abundance', producing a spurious and deceptive appearance of excessive neatness.[3] It is equally surprising that anybody with the least grasp of the dialectic should interpret the Idea as 'a "third section" which naturally became the place for leftovers' (ibid.), or misconceive the Doctrine of the Concept as a different kind of work from the first two Parts of the Logic intended merely to treat the traditional subject matter of logic as a sort of adjunct to 'objective logic', the substitute for traditional metaphysics. How could Kaufmann have missed Hegel's explicit statement that the whole of the Logic is really the theory of the Concept, though we cannot begin with its developed form and must first treat of its moments, Being and Essence? The antithesis of subjectivity to objectivity, which Kaufmann dismisses as mere afterthought, is fundamental to virtually everything Hegel wrote, and it is the major goal of his whole philosophy to demonstrate their identity and reconciliation. Nobody could think otherwise who knows its historical background and understands its development from Kant, Fichte and Schelling.

Of McTaggart I have said very little in the course of my commentary (and that mostly in footnotes) because his consistent failure to understand what Hegel is doing becomes obvious as soon as the structure and principle of the dialectic and the unfolding of the exposition are clearly set out. Mure's remark, that McTaggart seems to have conducted himself like a schoolmaster correcting Latin verses which occasionally fail to scan,[4] is surely apt, if rather too gentle. McTaggart will quote a superb passage from Hegel, carrying conviction in every line, and follow it with the comment, 'I cannot regard this as satisfactory'; and it is not improbable that he is in large measure responsible for the bad reputation that Hegel has acquired among many English speaking writers, because he transforms Hegel's dialectical procedure, for the most part, into a texture of incoherent (not to say incomprehensible) nonsense which no sane person would wish to countenance. It is perhaps indicative of how little McTaggart realizes what either he or Hegel is about that towards the end of a Commentary obstensibly and professedly on the Logic, which is essentially the theory and practice (in one) of dialectic, he should write: 'To discuss the dialectical method would, however, be beyond the object I have proposed to myself in this book.' (p. 309).

The perceptive reader soon becomes aware that McTaggart's thinking is persistently at the level of the understanding -- the constant tendency to think apart of things that go together, and so to falsify. In fact, despite occasional glimmers of insight, his understanding of Hegel is so clouded and myopic, and his mistakes so numerous and often so gross that detailed criticism, had I entered upon it, would have swelled this volume to double its size, with little compensating profit. Consequently, rather than indulge in extensive polemic, I have thought it more fruitful to try to make clear what Hegel actually intended, in the hope that once that is achieved, errors and misunderstandings like those of McTaggart will become easily apparent.

In an interesting and original book, Gotthard Günther has alleged that Hegel did not properly understand the logical significance of his own dialectical method, which, he maintains, is quite independent of Hegel's metaphysics and his general philosophical system -- although the method is used in its construction. He claims that the method has a validity of its own irrespective of its application in Hegel's philosophy. Gunther has insight of sorts into Hegel's way of thinking, yet at the same time he has a curious blindness to its integrity and to the solid coherence of Hegel's doctrine. It is quite impossible (as I hope the sequel will make clear) to drive a wedge between the dialectic and the system, if only for the reason that the dialectic precisely is the logic of system -- the self-developmental movement of the whole (or of wholeness as such). Moreover, to speak of the logical validity of the dialectic as something distinct from its structure and categorical forms is to miss the whole point of Hegel's demonstration of the identity of form and content, sustained throughout the exposition of the Logic and cogently driven home at its conclusion. If fault is to be found with Hegel's position in this regard it ought to be argued (not merely affirmed) and if it could be established it would undermine the whole structure of the Logic and completely demolish any claim to validity made on behalf of the dialectic. Validity and truth in Hegel's logic are not separable, because the truth is the whole and only that is valid which the structural principle of the whole necessitates.

In what follows I have dealt with some other interpretations, but only so far as seemed necessary to remedy misunderstanding; and, again, I have not sought to ferret out every mistake made by every other commentator, but have been concerned chiefly to follow the course of Hegel's exposition and to render it as clear, as consistent and as coherent as possible, for consistent and coherent I am convinced that it is.

By its very nature the Hegelian dialectic returns one constantly to concepts and relationships presented and discussed before in preliminary and inchoate forms. Some repetition in the commentary is, therefore, scarcely avoidable, if only to remind the reader of essential points made earlier upon which later claims are based. I have striven so far as possible to avoid undue repetition save where necessary to clarify and emphasize the movement of the dialectic. Bernhard Lakebrink[6] pursues the opposite policy and is willing tirelessly to repeat, moving forward by slow and overlapping steps in the argument lest any connexion should be missed. Possibly his procedure is the more persuasive, but it runs the risk of becoming long-winded and tedious, so I have not adopted it but have trusted the reader to bear in mind the earlier phases of the argument and to relate them wherever relevant and applicable to later developments.

My hope is that this book may persuade those who give careful attention to its argument that Hegel's work is worth close study and consideration, and that, if properly understood, has much to recommend it as a philosophy supported, even today, by sufficient evidence to make it credible and acceptable, if not always in the form presented by Hegel. Just how it might be adapted to suit contemporary needs I have not discussed here, though I have made some attempt to suggest it elsewhere.

The present intellectual milieu in the English-speaking world is such that the odds against success for any such undertaking as this are enormous, but unless they are faced no beginning can be made. Hegel's writings have so long been shunned and despised, and his theories so commonly ridiculed as mere fantasy and paradox, that few are likely to approach with tolerance any attempt to rehabilitate him. The term 'Hegelian' applied to any philosophical essay has become one of opprobrium and almost of abuse in some philosophical circles, and many academic philosophers would shrink from research into, or serious criticism of, Hegel's philosophy, as endangering their professional reputations. It is part of my purpose to show that such attitudes are the result of either ignorance or misunderstanding, or both, one born of the other.

Nevertheless, there are some encouraging developments to mitigate the bleakness for the Hegelian commentator of this intellectual climate. On the continent of Europe Hegel studies have never flagged. Interest has been kept alive not only by Marxist scholars but by a whole range of historical and philosophical research. In America, for the past twelve years, a flourishing Hegel Society has been active, and its members have produced, and are currently producing, new translations and excellent studies of Hegel's works. In Britain a similar society has recently been founded, and Oxford University has appointed to an important Chair a scholar whose reputation was established by a full length, sympathetic and appreciative study of the entire Hegelian system. Professor Charles Taylor is not, however, the first nor the only one to have taken the plunge. Professor John Findlay redirected the attention of the philosophical public to Hegel as a significant thinker some twenty years earlier. And throughout the long period of eclipse the work of Geoffrey Mure and Sir Malcolm Knox had kept the torch of Hegelian scholarship alight in Britain. If I can add some small contribution to the slowly brightening dawn of the Hegelian revival, my object will have been gained.

To the uninitiated, and even to many who are more fully acquainted with Hegel's writings, the intricacies and obscurities of the dialectic often seem virtually impenetrable. The aim of this commentary is to make Hegel's views and his manner of thinking intelligible and credible to those who are willing and patient enough to study the text but who need an explanation of the texture of Hegel's thought and an overview of his system to help them to grasp his meaning, to become aware of the objective towards which he is moving and to appreciate the method by means of which he seeks to reach it. With the current revival of interest in Hegel's philosophy and the recent spate of translations, new editions and scholarly studies of his works, there will be a growing demand for some such guide to the perplexed. But the attention of contemporary scholars has been directed predominantly to the Phenomenology of Spirit and (to a lesser extent) to the Philosophy of Right, while the Science of Logic has remained largely neglected. Yet the Logic is in important respects the key to the whole system and the epitome of Hegel's thought, even though the Phenomenology retains its fascination as the staggering (if somewhat bewildering) tour de force of a young philosopher's 'voyage of discovery', hammering out the shape and ramifications of a vast and incredibly comprehensive system of philosophy.

Nevertheless, the Logic is the first clear statement of the principles that govern at once the method and the structure of the entire philosophical enterprise to which Hegel devoted his life. Once the central concept is mastered, one has the key to the rest of the system and the antidote to the errors of interpretation into which all too many commentators have fallen. The general principle of the dialectic, so often and so variously misreprensented, is the fundamental holism which grounds it and of which it is the expression, and when this is clearly and firmly grasped, many difficulties and obscurities melt away, and what (at first sight) seem arbitrary connexions and transitions are seen to be in place. It is insight into this principle with which I have sought to provide my reader as the sure guide to understanding and interpretation of Hegel.

I have used the text of the Logic in the Encyclopaedia of Philosophical Sciences to set the course of the discussion and have made reference to the Science of Logic wherever it seemed necessary to clarify the argument and progression of the later, more compact and abbreviated version. In fact, I have tried to use each text to elucidate the other wherever passages of special difficulty occur. The Encyclopaedia Logic is referred to throughout as the Lesser Logic, and the Science of Logic as the Greater Logic. References to the German text (unless otherwise indicated) are to the Suhrkamp Werkausgabe as the handiest and most easily obtainable for students, and the English translations used are those of William Wallace of the Encyclopaedia version (as revised by Miller and Findlay) and of A.V. Miller of the Science of Logic.

NOTES: Preface

1.   Hegel, A Reinterpretation (New York, 1965).

2.   Op. cit., pp. 160, 162.

3.   Op. cit., p. 214.

4.   Cf. G.R. Mure, A Study of Hegel's Logic (Oxford, 1950), pp. 366-67.

5. Grundzüge Einer Neuen Theorie des Denkens in Hegels Logik (Hamburg, 1978).

6. Cf. Kommentar zu Hegels Logik, Freiburg/Munchen, 1979.

BOOK I

PROLEGOMENA

PART I

INTRODUCTION

PART I

INTRODUCTION

Chapter 1

Hegel's Conception of Logic

What nowadays is understood by the name 'Logic' is a highly abstract and formalized science more mathematical than philosophical, and even what is called the philosophy of logic tends to coincide with the philosophy of mathematics. No exponent of contemporary logic would recognize as any part of his discipline what Hegel wrote under that title. Hegel's Logik, he would say, if perchance he were to take any notice of it, is not logic at all, but an old-fashioned, obsolete and (in respectable scientific circles) discredited conglomeration of epistemology and metaphysics. Certainly it is more than a century and a half since the Wissenschaft der Logik was written, and since then rivers of ink have flowed under the philosophical bridges. What was once called logic has meanwhile changed almost beyond recognition. But whether Hegel's thought is obsolete or still has something to teach us today, the reader may judge for himself as he works through the following pages and the texts which they seek to explain. The description of the Logik as metaphysics and epistemology would not much have troubled Hegel, although he would have repudiated what he called dogmatic metaphysics; for he himself maintained that logic, properly understood, covered the same ground and performed the same function as was intended by the metaphysicians of earlier times. How and why this should be so will appear in what follows.

Why then did Hegel call the subject 'logic' if its content was really metaphysical? The answer that he would probably have given is that it is the theory of the Concept, which has been the concern of logic ever since its systematic exposition was first given by Aristotle. But what this theory under Hegel's hand reveals is that the Concept is the ultimate principle, not merely explanatory, but constituting the essential nature, of all reality; so that the theory of the Concept is just as much a metaphysic as it is logic.

The main topic of the traditional formal logic, from Aristotle onward, had been the principles of valid scientific inference. And Kant had expressed the opinion that in his day it was a perfected and complete science to which nothing further could be added. But mere validity of reasoning does not ensure truth or the objectivity of knowledge, which is, or should be, the distinguishing characteristic of science; and Hume's analysis of empirical knowledge had destroyed the basis of objectivity -- namely, the necessity and universality of empirical laws. For Hume had argued that universality was only an assumption based on a subjective psychological propensity to believe with

3

confidence that what has been frequently experienced will always recur, and he showed that the connexion between experienced facts was never necessary but always contingent. Kant, therefore, declared the need for a new sort of logic: one that would investigate the conditions under which alone any experience could be objective. This he called transcendental logic, which, as he expounded it, developed the theory that knowledge could be objective (or scientific) only if and so far as experience conformed to certain categories or concepts, imposing on it universal and necessary rules.

Transcendental logic was thus obviously a theory of the Concept, but not just of the abstract concept irrespective of its specific content. It was a theory of the Concept (or concepts) as the indispensable prior condition of the experience of objects. 'It concerns itself,' Kant wrote, 'with the laws of Understanding and Reason solely so far as they relate a priori to objects.'[1]

As the theory developed in Kant's hands it became clear that these concepts were the conditions of any objective knowledge whatsoever. Although Kant maintained that concepts were only formal, the matter of experience being provided solely by sensuous intuition, his account of their application and function made it apparent that without them, as principles ordering and synthesizing the material of experience, no objects of any kind could be cognized, not even the a priori forms of intuition, space and time.[2] They proved, therefore, to be principles as much of the objective nature of what is known as of thinking or Understanding.

Kant, however, alleged that the categories of the Understanding were applicable only to objects as they appeared to us and not to things in themselves which remain for ever beyond our reach. Nevertheless, in transcendental logic concepts were treated as conditions and principles of objectivity, not simply of the formal consistency of subjective thinking. This kind of logic, therefore, turned the attention of philosophers to the relation between the categorical forms of knowledge and its content. It was a logic that tended to be less abstract than the traditional formal logic, and it was the beginning of a new philosophical approach to the subject.

After Kant the development of Logic bifurcated, for despite his opinion that formal logic had reached its zenith, the interests of mathematicians in the general principles of their method led, at a later date, to a new system of formalization involving yet greater abstraction and more elaborate symbolic apparatus. Logic developed in the direction rather of algebra than of epistemology, enunciating axiom sets corresponding to principles of inference, and constructing formal deductive systems in the form of uninterpreted calculi. As wholly distinct from and independent of psychological considerations, this logic is 'objective' in one sense, but it abstracts entirely from the subject

4

matter of the thinking and the knowledge to which it might be applied. That can be whatever you please without affecting either the doctrine or the method of the logic, which is concerned only with the formal relations between elements which are purely logical (or in a special sense, linguistic). In consequence, logic turns out to be purely analytic. Its theorems are tautological, so that it can originate no new knowledge, and in this sense it has no objective bearing. Laws to which the objects of knowledge are subject are held by contemporary logicians to be empirical, and logic can pronounce upon nothing beyond their self-consistency and the validity of the arguments used to establish them and to deduce their consequences. This line of development has become dominant in our own day and excludes from the field any other claimant to the title of logic. In fact, if today one suggests that there might be an alternative logic to the one currently in vogue, contemporary logicians understand the suggestion only as a reference to an alternative algorithm within the present discipline.

Hegel's logic belongs to the other prong of the bifurcation and is a direct development from Kant's transcendental logic through the work of Fichte and Schelling. Fichte, however, dropped the title 'logic' and called the subject Wissenschaftslehre, explicitly theory of knowledge, or science, and that is equally an appropriate name for Hegel's doctrine; in fact he himself called it Wissenschaft, but he used the term (as did Fichte) in a wider sense than we today use the word 'science'. For him it was 'absolute knowledge',[3] and is, perhaps, better translated 'philosophy'. About Wissenschaft we shall have more to say in what follows.

Unlike Kant, Hegel did not regard formal logic as a perfected and completed science; rather he thought it typical, at best, of an intermediate level of thinking, that which he attributed to 'sound common sense' or 'understanding', the insights of which are mostly half-truths entangled with errors, quite incapable of and unsuited to philosophical speculation. In effect, in Hegel's view, formal logic was a kind of empirical science. He called it 'the natural history of finite thought',[4] taking examples from common discourse and empirical science and classifying forms of expression and argument much as the natural sciences classify species of butterflies or fish. He criticizes formal logic as insufficiently self-critical and as unaware of its own tacit assumptions and of implications in its doctrine which, when revealed, are seen to be in contradiction with its own avowed principles. This position is not very unlike that adopted later by Edmund Husserl in Formal and Transcendental Logic, but Husserl retained formal (apophantic) logic as a legitimate science in much the same way as Kant, whereas Hegel limited its justifiable applicability strictly to the understanding and considered its failure at the philosophical level more important than its admissibility at the level of common sense. Even here he thought its validity was subject to reservations.

5

Gotthard Günther (cf. op. cit.) correctly asserts that formal logic is applicable only at that level of thought which takes its object to be an external and independent reality. This is the level identified by Hegel as understanding. But Günther speaks of the traditional logic as 'objective logic' and as 'the logic of being' and these titles are misleading if attributed to Hegel; for, although he did, in the Greater Logic, call the Doctrines of Being and of Essence 'Objective Logic', they are by no means to be identified with formal logic, and, as we shall see, objectivity means for him something very different from mere giveness and externality.

In its proper place we shall have to give some attention to Hegel's critique of formal logic, which has been widely misunderstood and misrepresented; we shall have to consider whether, directed though it is mainly against the somewhat decadent form which in his day was taught in the schools, it has any significance in reference to the sophisticated logical theories of our own time.

There are, Hegel taught, more fundamental principles underlying not only those of formal logic but all forms of thinking, which, like Kant's categories, are the principles both of knowledge and of the objectively real. And knowledge, to be worthy of the name, must grasp the truth, and cannot be, as Kant alleged, merely phenomenal -- and so subjective -- it must apprehend reality itself (die Sache selbst). Hence the principles of knowing, or the determinations of thought (Denkbes-timmungen), will be at the same time principles of reality. Despite the element of subjectivity in his doctrine, Kant showed that they were principles of objectivity, conditions of the possibility of the experience of objects; but Hegel goes further and denies that objects are only phenomena (mere appearances). The principles must be the determina-tions of things as they actually are, or else they could not be principles of truth. Accordingly, they are just as much metaphysical as logical and epistemological principles, just as objective as they are subjective.

The identity of thought and being, of subject and object, is asserted firmly at the outset of the Logic. Hegel felt that he was entitled to make this assertion because he claimed to have demon-strated it in his Phänomenologie des Geistes. But the whole of the Logic is a demonstration in extenso of the same thesis, and the claim in the introduction must be treated as Hegel says we must view all introductory remarks, as provisional and unsatisfactory until established in the body of the science. They must be taken as preliminary explanations to ease the approach of the reader to the real starting point, otherwise they are apt to mislead and to be misunderstood.

Nevertheless, this initial claim carries with it a consequence which will also appear unshakably established at the end, that in logic and in philosophical knowledge generally form and content are insepar-able, are in fact ultimately identical. It is largely because formal logic assumes and is founded on their separability that it is inadequate to truth and is fundamentally misleading. Already in Kant's transcendental logic the mutual dependence of intuition and conception (content and form) had become apparent, even for empirical knowledge; and for Hegel the forms and procedures of thought are precisely those of its object in a way which will presently become clear. But not only is the form the same for both; it determines the very being and nature of the content, which, especially in logic, is its own form, the form of thought. The doctrine has many aspects and applications, for at every level of adequacy the form of thinking determines the nature of its content, yet it also proves to be the case that the nature of the content dictates the form of the knowledge of which it is the object. In perceptual thinking the object is immediate; in reflective thinking it is abstract and relational, and in speculative (philosophical) thinking the object is self-specifying; and each is as it is because the form of the thinking is what it is. Just how this is the case the body of the science will establish.

Formal logic denies the mutual interdependence of form and content and claims to abstract entirely from the latter without detriment to either. This, Hegel avers, is because it operates on the reflective level of the understanding, which makes hard and fast distinctions and then elevates them into separations or dichotomies which a higher reason shows to be unwarranted. Hence the presumed independence of logic from metaphysics, which the formal logician alleges, and which even in his own practice proves to be false, results from too absolute a separation between thinking and its object, between the form and the content of thought, and between the real and our knowledge of it.

Right up to the present day formal logicians have claimed that logic makes, and can make, no metaphysical assumptions, and that it is wholly independent of metaphysics. Any and every metaphysics must bow to its authority, and sound logic is held to be compatible with a variety of metaphysical doctrines, so long as each is internally self-consistent. Yet even in quite recent times at least two very eminent mathematical logicians have set out a metaphysical doctrine which they declare logic -- the only sort of logic they recognize as legitimate -- must reflect. Bertrand Russell propounded a theory of metaphysical pluralism which he called 'logical atomism' according to which propositions reflect facts which are mutually independent and atomic. In Principia Mathematica it is expressly stated that the language and procedure of logic presupposes the atomicity of facts.[5] Wittgenstein in the Tractatus Logico-Philosophicus declared that the world divides into facts any one of which may be the case or may not be the case without making any difference to the rest.[6] These mutually indifferent atomic facts can be stated in similarly atomic propositions which 'show forth' their form.[7] This hardly bespeaks an independence of form from content, nor yet of logic from metaphysics. Moreover the metaphysic has vital consequences for the logic itself; for it follows from the doctrine that atomic propositions (as the epithet entails) are logically independent for their truth or falsity. They cannot be derived or deduced one from another, and the doctrines and procedures of symbolic logic reflect this fact. p and q represent propositions each independent of the other for its truth value. Either may be true or false without making any difference to the other. They may be conjoined, p·q, or alternated, p v q, or negated ~p· ~q. Strictly speaking these are the only operations this logic permits, for all others can be reduced to these. So Quine tells us[8] that logical formulae are in normal form when they consist solely of literals, either posited or negated, either conjoined or alternated. The essential implicative relation of deduction is then reduced to conjunction or alternation of the truth values of atomic propositions:

$$p \supset q \equiv \sim(p. \sim q) \equiv \sim p \; v \; q.$$

I have shown elsewhere that this can be maintained only on the presupposition of a radically pluralistic metaphysic postulating atomic particulars in external relations,[9] and that it is so is born out by the teachings, not only of Russell and Wittgenstein, but also of Frege, Gustav Bergmann, and Quine.[10]

For Hegel, on the other hand, no propositions can possibly be atomic, because for him the real is a system which comprises all facts. It is die Sache selbst, and all facts and concepts are systematically interrelated within it as a single whole. They are mutually dependent in their very essence, so that there can be no atomic facts or propositions. From this, as we shall shortly see, it follows that both reality and thought, both logic and nature, are dialectical in form, and logic and metaphysics, which, despite the denials of the formal logician, are inseparable even for him, become for Hegel identically one.

A similar dichotomy between sense and thought, which has troubled philosophers ever since Plato, Hegel refuses to countenance. Kant, while he argues convincingly that intuition (or perception) without concepts is blind, still maintained that concepts without sensuous intuition were empty, and he strove to treat the two as separable sources (or even kinds) of experience. But Hegel takes seriously the interdependence of sense-perception and conceptual thinking. Thought for him is integral to all experience, as well as to reality itself, in a manner presently to be explained. He protests that thoughts are not just phantasms or fabrications of the brain (Hirngespinste) but are the actual principles of the structure of reality. In its more explicit forms thinking is what, in particular, distinguishes human activity from the purely animal and instinctive, even though at the levels of perception, sentiment and practical precept, as well as in the higher forms of experience such as art and religion, it is not always explicitly aware of itself as thought -- i.e., of its own conceptual nature. Nevertheless, in all experience, Hegel maintains, concepts are involved -- categories,

Denkbestimmungen, determinations or specifications of thought. This, of course, follows from Kant's analysis, although Hegel frequently accuses Kant of treating ideas (in particular the 'ideas of reason') as mere Hirngespinste. But in the common forms of human experience the categories are 'put to use' while they go unrecognized.[11] It is only in reflection that they begin to be identified as such. For example, in ordinary, every-day perception we 'use' the concepts of thinghood, of space and time, of actuality, and the like, without taking notice of them as special categories or considering what they are as pure concepts. In morality we judge actions to be good or bad, right or wrong, without examining the precise meanings of these concepts. In science, perhaps slightly more reflectively, we make use of ideas such as force, polarity, cause and law; but we do not grasp them as concepts pure and simple, or their mutual conceptual relations. Nevertheless, they are concepts and, as such, are the special subject-matter of logic, the function of which is to identify them in their purely conceptual character and to trace their development, at the various levels of self-consciousness, in our thinking.

For human experience ranges through a whole gamut of levels, varying from one to the next in sophistication and self-awareness; and these, for Hegel, are differing degrees of truth,[12] advancing from immediate sense-perception, through reflective understanding, to science and philosophy. They form a scale of continuous increase in degree of self-awareness, in the course of which the categories, or concepts (thought forms) which are implicit in the lower stages become progressively more explicit, until at the final stage they reach complete consciousness of themselves and are made the direct object of thinking. In short, thought becomes its own object, it develops itself as essentially concept; and this self-thinking of the concept is logic.

Logic is thus the thinking study of thought; but because thought is immanent in all experience and in all its objects -- that is, in reality itself -- logic is also (as is all philosophy) the thinking study of things.[13] It is with this description that the Encyclopaedia Logic begins; but the introduction to the Encyclopaedia is in many respects tantalizing and bewildering, for in it Hegel makes important and often paradoxical statements which he explains, if at all, only very partially, and which are left without supporting argument almost as obiter dicta. The reason for this has already been mentioned, that in an introduction what is said is provisional and dogmatic because the demonstration of these preliminary affirmations can only be given in the proper place and in the right order in the systematic exposition of the science itself. Little can be done therefore by way of commentary to make them intelligible and acceptable without anticipating much that is to come later.

He begins by declaring that the object of philosophy is Truth 'in that supreme sense that God and God only is the Truth', and is therefore

9

the same as the object of religion. Still more provocatively, he says in the Greater Logic, that the realm of pure reason, which logic grasps as the Truth, is 'the presentation of God in his eternal essence before the creation of Nature and the finite spirit.'[14] Today this claim must be shocking to many professing philosophers as well as to most theologians, and in Hegel's own day it would have been (and was) hotly contested by many. In our times the exact and the empirical sciences are, for the most part, elevated to the pinnacle of knowledge, and truth is believed to belong to them, while the philosophers strive to emulate the scientists, to work, as Professor A.J. Ayer once said, as journeymen, at special technical problems, rather than to make pretentious pronouncements as pontiffs (like Hegel); and religion is either made sacrosanct beyond the pale of philosophical criticism, or else its claim to truth is thought to have been for ever demolished by philosophical analysis. But the tradition that God is Truth and that philosophy and religion alike seek the same end is a very ancient one, which is traceable right back to Plato and Aristotle, was affirmed by Augustine in plain terms, was repeated by Anselm, reaffirmed by Maimonides and Aquinas and yet again by Spinoza. That religion seeks God and his Word as the supreme truth few (even who reject religion) will seek to deny, and that the love of wisdom should exclude this search for an ultimate truth would surely be strange. To allege that it does is surely perverse. If in these days philosophy has ceased to be the love of wisdom, though it continues to be called by that name, it has ceased to be philosophy and should be designated otherwise. But for Hegel it certainly was still what it professed to be, and as Hegel's system unfolds the meaning of his opening claim becomes progressively clearer until its final establishment is inescapable.

It will be necessary later to return to this issue. We shall see that for Hegel 'the truth is the whole' and is no piecemeal correspondence between propositions and 'facts'. It had become already apparent, after Kant's demonstration of the involvement of concepts in every fact, that any such notion of correspondence must be drastically modified. Concepts had been shown to be principles of order and unification (or, as Kant demonstrated, of 'synthesis'). Knowledge, in consequence, came to be seen as a unified system -- a whole -- in which, for Hegel, the truth ultimately resides; and where, as in Hegel's thought, concepts are the very constitutive principles of reality, our ideas of truth and falsehood need thorough revision. Just how they must be revised can be explained only when we have given fuller accounts of dialectical systems, and this is why Hegel in his introduction leaves his statement to be taken at its face value as something to be more fully substantiated later. It is also why little can be done at this stage to confirm its cogency. We can however, even here at the outset, see in a general way that if the whole is taken to be the truth and is identified as the Absolute -- i.e., what exists independently, in its own right and by its own power -- it will be what many thinkers, philosophers and theologians, have conceived God to be; and if this is what philosophy is about, we can understand, at least in a preliminary way, what Hegel is getting at when he says that its object is truth in the sense that God and God only is the truth, and that logic presents God in his eternal essence.

A few remarks may not come amiss about some of the more difficult and provocative statements made by Hegel in the opening paragraphs of the Encyclopaedia, if only to promise fuller discussion of them later; for the restriction on the philosophical possibilities of an introduction affects all preliminary claims. The remainder of this chapter may, however, be treated as a sort of appendix, and if the reader finds it obscure or unprofitable, no harm will be done if it is omitted until the main body of Hegel's argument has been mastered. It offers comment on what is purely introductory in the text and is there left unexplained, so that it might deter an uninitiated student, either through incredulity or incomprehension, from proceeding further unless some slight encouragement is provided.

In Section 1 Hegel says that thought will be satisfied with nothing short of showing the necessity of its content. By this he means that no explanations will render the facts fully intelligible short of a thorough-going development of the system to which they belong, in which they are enmeshed and out of which they emerge. What this system is and how it is constructed we shall discover later, but the mistake must be avoided at once of taking Hegel to mean that it is a purely mechanical system and that the facts are all and always inevitably fixed and determined, in particular by efficient causation, for this we shall find him denying emphatically and it is certainly not what he means here. Nor does he mean that empirical facts can or ought to be deduced by means of some kind of formal calculus from postulated first principles (or, as Frege and Russell claim for mathematics, from the axioms of logic).[15] Hegel's insistence in this introduction and elsewhere on necessity in philosophy derives from Kant's demand that scientific connexions must be necessary and universal, but Hegel's view is not the same as Kant's. He understands the phrases a priori and a posteriori in a new and more enlightened sense, which (as we shall see later) entails their mutual interdependence so that all knowledge proves to be both at once, and 'deduction', for him, is not what it is for formal logic.

He returns to this topic in Sections 9-12 where he discusses briefly the relation of philosophy to the empirical sciences, the distinction between their objects as infinite and finite, and the a posteriori and a priori aspects of knowledge, but here too he gives no clear or final account of any of these matters and in Section 10 explicitly defers the explanation to a later stage 'which falls within the scope of the science itself.'

In Section 2 he alludes to the current tendency to oppose thought to feeling and intuition and associate religion with the latter, and to consider thought as an antagonistic and destructive influence. This tendency is still potent in our own times and much that Hegel says about it, not only in this context, is still significant and applicable to modern experience. At this point he attributes the hostility to thinking and to philosophy, especially in its speculative phase (which in recent decades has been despised and repudiated by so many professing philosophers), to the identification of thought with 'after-thought' (Nachdenken). This he says is 'reflective' thinking and identifies it with raisonnement. Failure to observe the distinction between this kind of thinking and speculative reason is, he says, the source of crude objections and reproaches against philosophy as well as of mistakes by old-fashioned metaphysics about the alleged importance of demonstration in religious matters. All this is to be made much clearer in the sequel. The distinction is that, to which he constantly returns, between understanding and reason, which is dealt with more fully in Chapter 4 below.

In Section 3 he refers to the difference between 'ideas' as generalized images or figurative representations (Vorstellungen) and 'concepts,' or 'categories' (Begriffe, Gedanke), saying that the common complaint of the unintelligibility of philosophy is due to prevalence of the former in common reflection and the ordinary person's preference for Vorstellungen. The difficulty of philosophy is due to lack of practice in thinking pure thoughts (Begriffe). This distinction also will constantly recur and has been systematically worked out in the Phenomenology. It corresponds almost exactly to Spinoza's distinction between imagination and conception,[16] except that much, if not all, of what Spinoza includes under Ratio (which is conceptual) Hegel is inclined to regard as products of the understanding. Nevertheless, even the categories of the understanding are Denkbestimmungen, so the distinction made in this Section is at least close to Spinoza's.

Section 6 opens with a difficult but deeply pregnant passage:

...Philosophy should understand that its content is no other than that structure which, originally produced and producing itself in the confines of the living mind, has become the world, the external and internal world of consciousness.

He leaves this statement unexplained, saying only that we call our first awareness of this content 'experience' (Erfahrung). But how, we may ask, does actuality produce itself originally within the confines of the living mind? This kind of remark has laid Hegel open to frequent accusations of subjective idealism. But that is due to misunderstanding. The full understanding of the statement becomes possible only to one who grasps Hegel's conception of the relation of Nature to mind to which some attention is given in the following Chapter. Actuality, as Nature, begets, from inorganic and organic moments, living organisms capable of sentience and perception. Thus it produces itself, in the precincts of the mental life, as the perceived world which is both inward (as experienced, erlebt) and outward (as Gegenstand and Erfahrung). Thus do we become aware of it, at first, in what we call experience.

The quotation in the next paragraph of Section 6 from the Preface of the Rechtsphilosophie is explained in Chapter 3.

In Section 7 Hegel suggests that modern philosophy is more empirical and 'positivistic' than was ancient. His reference is to the powerful influence of the natural and empirical sciences since the Copernican revolution. But of course the Greeks were anything but unscientific in their approach, as Hegel well knew and they by no means neglected observation of nature least of all of the heavens. But Hegel's point here is that the Greeks treated science as metaphysics and made no distinction between them, as we do. The moderns, he somewhat sarcastically remarks, use the term 'philosophy' indiscriminately, to apply to 'Mineralogy, Mechanics, Natural History, Agriculture and Arts' (to say nothing of 'Preserving the Hair'), as well as to economics and politics. But Hegel is far from wishing to decry the importance of the empirical or of natural science. Empiricism he regarded merely as the obverse of Rationalism (cf. Section 8) and in Section 9 he declares quite explicitly that speculative Wissenschaft in no way neglects empirical facts as contained in the special sciences. It merely raises the categories they employ to a higher dialectical plane. Just how it does so will appear anon. The same continuity between empirical science and philosophy is reaffirmed in Section 12, where formalism is charged against the type of philosophy which never gets beyond the universality of ideas and contents itself with abstract formulae like 'In the absolute all is one' and 'Subject and object are identical'. These are Hegel's own beliefs but he claims to specify them -- or better, to show how they specify themselves. The critical dig here is at Schelling whom Hegel had accused in the Phenomenology of offering us in the end only an absolute 'night in which all cows are black'. The self-specification of the universal is of paramount importance in Hegel's logic, as will later become apparent. Here he makes cryptic reference to it simply as 'the development of thought out of itself.'

This development of thought out of itself, we are presently to see, is a dialectical development manifesting itself in several different forms, one of which, Hegel suggests in Section 13 is the history of philosophy. That history is not what an American Professor once described as 'a shooting match' between diverse, disconnected, capricious and mutually conflicting theories of individual thinkers, but the continuous development of a single philosophy passing through dialectical (i.e., logical) phases each conditioned by and incorporating its predecessors. He attributes this process to the direction of 'the one living Spirit, whose thinking nature it is to bring to self-consciousness that which it is.' It is this Spirit, immanent in both Nature and man, which is 'God in his eternal essence', that Truth presented by logic in its purely conceptual form. As philosophy is the love of wisdom, philosophers pursue this truth, and as it develops itself dialectically, the history of philosophy proceeds as a dialectical discussion between both contemporary and successive thinkers in whose thinking 'the whole' which is the truth is immanent. Hegel so presented it in his own lectures on the History of Philosophy, and he repeatedly illustrates throughout the logic the correlation between the logical categories and the theories put forward by the great philosophers from ancient to modern times.

In short, the history of philosophy is a dialectical system, just as the philosophy of every thinker worthy of the title philosopher, is such a system; for the entire content of philosophy is a system, not constructed around some one narrow principle, but developing out of itself all special principles (i.e., Denkbestimmungen) in dialectical series and relationship.[17] An unsystematic philosophy, says Hegel, is not scientific and only gives expression to personal peculiarities of mind with no principle regulating its content (a prophetic indictment of such writers as Nietzsche, Camus and a number of others who have repudiated all systematization, Hegel's above all).

Further, the dialectical system, we are told in the next paragraph (Section 15), is not simply a whole but is also a closed circle. This is because the Idea is immanent and developing itself throughout, and is therefore both beginning and end. It will become clear later how this is so, and also how, in the nature of the case, the total circular progression reveals itself in subordinate circles each of which leads dialectically to the next. So that it is a circle of circles, a whole of wholes, and each one of them is in specific form a self-manifestation of the Idea.

For this reason it is difficult to know how or where to begin a philosophical science (Section 17). One may not simply postulate a given subject matter, for the subject matter is the very process of thought in which it is being presented 'by a free act.' This was the difficulty faced, as we are told in Section 10, by Kant and Reinhold, but not satisfactorily solved by either of them. Kant professed to examine and criticize reason or thought as the instrument of knowledge in order to determine whether it was capable of dealing with the essential subject matter of metaphysics, the infinite and unconditioned. But, Hegel points out, the instrument is already being put to use in this critique, which must therefore beg its own question in order to begin. Reinhold, perceiving this difficulty, proposed to begin with a tentative hypothesis which would later be justified by systematic derivation, but this leaves unanswered the question how we are to reach 'the primary truths' (Urwahren), as Reinhold promises, by which our initial hypothesis is to be established.

14

The truth is that philosophy is always thought thinking itself, discovering itself. It is Spirit becoming conscious of what it really is in itself. Accordingly, the outcome or end of the science is already present and immanent in its beginning, and wherever we begin, we start in medias res. It follows also that thought, in its self-reflective progress is always self-critical. It recognizes the short-comings of its own forms in the light of the whole immanent in them, which figures in each as what it aspires, but fails, to be; yet it redeems itself from that failure by becoming aware of it, and corrects it by developing its own implications to reach a higher stage. To this question of starting-point we shall address ourselves again in the next Chapter, and yet more fully in Book II, and we shall see how a beginning may be determined which, in one sense, presupposes nothing, and yet, in another, presupposes the whole development of nature and consciousness; a beginning which is sheerly immediate and yet is mediated by the whole which is the final result of its own systematic development.

Much of which Hegel speaks in the next six sections of the Encyclopaedia, entitled Vorbegriff, we have already touched upon, and much else only becomes clear at a later stage. In the first Zusatz to Section 19 he discusses inconclusively the question whether to claim ability to know the truth is intolerable arrogance, or whether it is not rather false modesty to repudiate the claim. He gives clear examples of cases which are false modesty, such disclaimers as mask indolence and complacency, but then he seems to side-step the main issue with a tu quoque to his opponents by accusing contemporary intellectual society of encouraging the belief, especially in the young, that the complete truth is immediately attainable in ingenuous and intuitive experience. He then instances Pilate's scepticism ('What is truth?'), and the 'timidity' of those who claim (as Wittgenstein has done in our own day) that philosophy should 'leave everything as it is' (soll uns so lassen wie wir sind), which, he says, give the result that instruction can lead to a certian competence in routine matters but not to 'the higher life'. Just what that is, however, is left unexplained, nor is the claim to know the absolute truth justified and one must wait until the end of the Logic to discover its significance and its legitimacy.

In the second Zusatz he tells us that feeling can take possession (sich bemachtigen) of the concrete content, though its form is not suited to it. This is an obscure reference to what is only plainly unfolded in the Geistesphilosophie, where feeling is shown to be the epitomization and registration of all natural processes as they affect the organism (i.e., 'the concrete content') and the matrix from which explicit awareness and knowledge is developed.[18] So it takes possession of the concrete content which yet needs further articulation in more explicit and developed consciousness.

The third Zusatz refers to the apparent, and indeed the really, subversive effect of thought upon religion, morality and politics, which

15

led the people of Athens to condemn philosophers for 'corruption of the youth.' The task of justifying philosophical reflection, Hegel says, remains a special interest of philosophy to the present day, alluding to the Kantian attempt more rigorously to assess its claims. But the answer to the question of their validity is left to later sections.

Section 20 begins an interesting discussion of universality as the hallmark of thought, and again distinction is drawn between Vorstellung (figurative ideation) and Gedanken (thoughts). The penetrating remark is made that, though we tend to explain sensation in terms of the sense organs, pointing to them throws no light upon what we apprehend through them. That, we are reminded, is always individual in character, the appearance of individual things beside one another and in succession. Universal connexions do not appear in sense-perception but are only revealed by thought. Vorstellung, while it comprises mostly sensuous material, does also include universal elements, but it persists in individualizing and holding apart the moments of universal concepts (e.g., law, morality and religion), as is typical of the understanding. But thought is free and self-reflective, it is epitomized in the 'I think', which is essentially universal and pervades all forms of consciousness in which I am aware of the experience as my own. Hegel returns to this point in Section 23, adverting to the subjectivity and 'ownness' of my thinking activity, while insisting that objectivity is ensured only in the suppression of idiosyncracy and the submersion of thought in the universality (for all subjects) of the object.

All these matters are treated more fully and systematically in the sequel and, except as allusions to Kant and contemporary philosophers with whose work Hegel's students were familiar, his introduction of them thus briefly at this stage is somewhat bewildering to the uninitiated, serving mainly to stimulate the reader's thought and wonder and perhaps to whet his appetite for what is to come.

The nature of reflection is broached once more in Section 21. The examples in the Zusatz anticipate the categories to be developed in the Doctrine of Essence, the second main division of the Logic, and will be better treated in comment upon that. The subject is continued in Section 22 where we are told that 'after-thought' changes something in the way in which the content has been presented in sense-perception and only through such alteration is the true nature of the object brought to consciousness; for the true nature is only revealed by thought. The full significance of these assertions requires the whole of the logic for its clarification, and the statement here does no more than shock the empirically inclined whose faith rests in the solid truth of what is immediately presented. Hegel, however, has already demonstrated in the Phenomenology the volatile and ephemeral nature of sense-certainty and its nisus to understanding and reason; and he loses no opportunity to stress that the truth of the content emerges only at the end of the dialectical process, as will presently be demonstrated more at length.

So the introduction ends with the insistence on thought as objective and on Logic as coincident in consequence with metaphysics, for the reasons we have already adumbrated above. That the forms of thought cannot be alien and wholly external to things must be apparent from the outset, for thought strives to construct concepts of the things themselves and to grasp their universal (essential) nature. This is what is meant by calling knowledge 'objective', which is itself a claim that reason prevails in the world.

This must not, however, be understood as pan-psychism, for consciousness and thought is what distinguishes men from inanimate things. The claim is that the forms of thought (Denkbestimmungen) are equally the forms of things and so Hegel adopts Schelling's description of Nature as 'petrified intelligence' to express the doctrine he is advocating.[19] He supports it here by arguing that the universal, while it is not perceptible apart from its embodiment in the individual, is indispensable to it. Remove animality from a dog, he says, and we cannot tell what it is.

Accordingly logic is not, as is commonly held, a purely formal study. The categories are the very substance of things but it is only when they are cognized in their purity that the mind is truly free, because then it is operating in its own native element and is at home with itself (bei sich selbst). But because the categories are already in use in common thinking and ordinary language they are, in one way, familiar elements of our experience. However, what is most familiar is usually taken for granted and most frequently overlooked.

In logic we ask whether these categories are 'true', an unusual question, for we tend to think of truth as some sort of correspondence with fact, whereas actually it is self-consistency of thought, and more properly agreement with concept. This, again, is an obscure reference to Hegel's fundamental doctrine that the truth is the whole, and the whole, as we shall later see, is the concept, or concrete universal.

This, being immanent in all experience, can be discerned by great minds (like Goethe) in many different contexts, but philosophy seeks it in its pure form because it discovers the inadequacy and failure of every other. As a rule we find immediate experience the most convincing and appealing and we advocate unsophisticated ingenuousness in preference to reflection. But it is man's destiny to wonder, to inquire and to reflect and naivete is bound to give way to knowledge and rational enlightenment.

The Zusatz ends with an elaborate interpretation of the Mosaic myth of the Fall, as depicting man's development from innocence to the knowledge of his spiritual destiny. As he remains in bondage to the flesh he lives in 'original sin', which is his animal nature, and the law of the spirit is an imposition upon him from without. But so far as he reaches spiritual maturity and lives according to its principles he is free and no longer 'in bondage under the law.'

NOTES: Book I, Part I, Chapter 1

1. Kritik der reinen Vernunft, A57, B82.

2. Cf. Kritik der reinen Vernunft, B202-203, 220-221; A183, B223, B226; A194, B239; A200, B245; and my Nature, Mind and Modern Science, Ch IX, Section ii; Fundamentals of Philosophy, Ch. XXXI.

3. See below, pp. 22-23 and 27ff.

4. Cf. Vorlesungen über die Geschichte der Philosophie, I, 1, Kap. IIIB4, Werke (Suhrkamp) Vol. 19, p. 229. Trans., Lectures on the History of Philosophy, Haldane and Simson (London/New York, 1968), Vol. II, p. 211.

5. 2d. ed., Vol. I, p. xv.

6. Tractatus, 1.2, 1.21.

7. Op. cit., 2.172.

8. Cf. W.V.O. Quine, Methods of Logic (New York, 1972), p. 61.

9. Cf. 'The End of a Phase', Dialectica, Vol. 17, no. 1, 1963.

10. Cf. Frege, Grundlagen der Arithmetik; Gustav Bergmann, Realism (University of Wisconsin Press, 1967); W.V.O. Quine, Word and Object, M.I.T. Press (Cambridge, Mass., 1960).

11. Cf. Wissenschaft der Logik, Preface to the 2d. ed.

12. The objection frequently made that there can be no degrees of truth, that beliefs, propositions, etc., are either true or false, cannot really be taken seriously. Even those who raise it will maintain at the same time that there can be degrees of probability and that all human knowledge is merely probable (certainty being unattainable and even unnecessary). If by 'probability' they do not mean approximation to truth, it is difficult to say what they do mean. And they are the very people, as a rule, who insist that no opinion or belief can rank as knowledge unless it is true. Yet if all knowledge is only probable in

some degree, are we not forced to admit degrees of truth, or else to renounce every pretence to know?

13. Cf. Enzyklopadie der Philosophischen Wissenschaften, Sections 1-2. In future references, Enz.

14. Wissenschaft der Logik (hereafter W.L.), Introduction (Suhrkamp ed., 1969), p. 44; A.V. Miller's translation (London, 1969), p. 50.

15. McTaggart seems to make this mistake when he objects (in his Commentary on Hegel's Logic, Section 5) that Hegel refuses to contemplate the possibility of alternative dialectical routes between a given category and some other more advanced category. Just what sort of alternative routes McTaggart has in mind it is not always easy to divine, but the implication seems to be that Hegel treated the dialectic as a rigid mechanical deduction of each category from its predecessor, and that is entirely mistaken. It is an idea quite foreign (one may even say repulsive) to Hegel. The process of the dialectic (as will shortly appear) is that of a developing whole, and its 'necessity' is similar to the necessity of the path of ontogenesis in an organism.

16. Cf. Ep. XII; Ethics II, Prop. XL, 52.

17. Enz., Section 14. Cf. also R.G. Collingwood, An Essay on Philosophical Method (Oxford, 1933, 1965), Ch. IX.

18. See below, pp. 54, 209f, 257f, 280.

19. Enz., Section 24, Zus. 1.

19

developed natural forms precede in time the emergence of conscious beings, that this is so is a late discovery in the course of the reflective activity of such minds. To assume at the outset of our theorizing (as Marx does) that we know and fully understand the material nature of mankind, and that we can take for granted our own status in the scheme of things, is to assume without warrant far more than is justified. Hegel realized that to begin with a Philosophy of Nature would be to make too many unsupported assumptions, taking as given what ought first to be systematically established, as he would say, in the body of the science.

Apart from a conscious mind reflecting upon its experience, at least on the level of empirical science, there is no conception of Nature, for Nature is an idea or concept. The term connotes a unified system of physical entities, the motions and interrelations of which are subject to general laws. Any such conception is possible only for a thinking mind. It does not, of course, follow that apart from human theorizing nature does not exist; but what does follow is that until we have developed a theory of the Concept and examined its relation to finite consciousness, we are not in a position to appreciate the significance of the concept of Nature, or to understand aright the place in the dialectical scale of natural forms. For until we have grasped the essential nature of the Concept we do not rightly understand what a dialectical scale is or how dialectic operates. And this is precisely the source of the Marxist error, which is to assume the primacy of material nature as well as the efficacy of dialectic without demonstrating the necessity of the first or how, if the first is true, the second is possible. Hegel's view, which in its contrast to Marx will presently become clearer to us, is that 'the external world is the truth implicitly (an sich)':[2] it is real, but what is true of it and actual in it emerges only in and as the consciousness of the knowing mind which develops out of it -- for what the process produces is what was all along immanent in the prior phases.

So Hegel begins with the forms of consciousness and traces their development one from another in the Phänomenologie des Geistes. The simplest and most immediate of these is sensuous awareness, which by the nature of its own content (the 'this', the 'here' and the 'now') and its inadequacy to its own intention develops to more universal forms involving more reflection and greater comprehension. From perceptual awareness the dialectic moves to sound common sense and scientific understanding, which, at the rational level, becomes observational reason or empirical science. Then the development proceeds through all the phases of human experience, theoretical and practical, until it eventually culminates in 'absolute knowing', the absolute reflection-into-self which is philosophy. This is the reflection of consciousness upon consciousness, and its object embraces the entire prior process of which it is the result.

22

In the Phenomenology absolute knowing is the final and the highest form of consciousness. In itself it is νόησις νοήσεως, thought thinking itself, or, as Hegel also calls it, 'pure knowledge'; and as this is the outcome of the dialectic it is immanent in all the various forms of consciousness through which the development has been traced. As Hegel says in the Encyclopaedia (Section 2):

> As religion, law and morality pertain to man, and indeed only because he is a thinking being, so in the religious, the legal and the moral, be it as feeling and faith or imaginative representation (Vorstellung), thought has not been inactive; its activity and products are present and retained within them.

This implicit thought is, however, not aware of itself as such in these forms of experience, and becomes so only when it grasps its own nature as concept. For the determinations of thought (Denkbestimmungen) are concepts, and consequently the primary form of absolute knowing is the theory of the Concept -- namely, Logic. It extracts from the forms of consciousness hitherto examined the categories which operate in them 'unconsciously', or which in them have been 'put to use'.[3]

The Logic accordingly presupposes the whole course of the dialectic in the Phenomenology, and not only this but the entire range of experience on which the Phenomenology reflects, including common sense and empirical science, as well as much else. Hence there are two ways in which logic may be regarded: one as a form of experience -- the culmination of the dialectic of consciousness (as traced in the Phenomenology), by which the philosophical attitude is engendered; the other as an independent science developing its own subject matter; and in this aspect it makes a fresh start, without presuppositions, which, as we shall see, Hegel goes to some lengths to explain and to justify.

At the conclusion of the Phenomenology the knowing subject recognizes itself as identical and at one with what all along it had viewed as an external and alien object. It has now become clear that what consciousness is in and for itself is just its own content, whether perceptual, conceptual, practically objective, or philosophically self-reflective. The object has revealed itself as the subject's own activity projected as its other, set over against itself as an opposite, which is now seen to be nothing but its own self. The subject is now 'at home with itself in its other'. This acknowledgement of self-identity in and with its other is pure and thorough-going self-consciousness, and is the level of philosophical science (Wissenschaft) proper.

Recognizing itself in its object, the mind becomes aware that in the object its own principle of universality is immanent and operative. This universal principle is thought, or the Concept, the Kantian unity of apperception, the principle of organization and wholeness. Its first task

23

on this philosophical level is, accordingly, to work out the theory of the Concept, or rather to allow the Concept (thought) to work out the theory of itself, as the thinking study of thought -- or logic. Logic is the science of the pure Concept implicit in the forms of consciousness. It traces the dialectic of the Concept's own self-specification into categories, from the most abstract (Being) to the most concrete (absolute Idea). Subject and object are both themselves categories, or specifications of the Concept, in this series. They are 'at work' in the forms of consciousness generating themselves in the phenomenological process, and were there shown to be united in absolute knowing, which is logic. So logical thought is throughout both subjective and objective at the same time. In the course of its dialectic both sides of the polarity are developed and are seen finally to be identical in the absolute Idea.

So in effect the Logic goes over the same ground as the Phenomenology from a higher vantage point and presents as a dialectic of categories what the latter pursued as a scale of experiential forms. Logic, therefore, is a rediscovery of the identity of subject and object through a return upon and reflection over the prior forms of experience from a logical point of view.

The subjective concept is the thinking mind or ego. The objective Concept is the 'external world' which is the object of scientific knowledge; and their union occurs in the living organism, epitomizing the natural world in its action and adaptation to its environment, and its consciousness both of the world and of itself as knower. It is a product of nature as conceived by the empirical sciences; and thus nature, which empirical science treats as an external object opposed to the knowing subject, now transpires as no more nor less than that process of dialectical development through which life and mind are generated. Just as the whole course of the logical dialectic is nothing but the self-development of the Idea which emerges at the end, so life, which is the Idea as the union of subject and object, is what the entire process of Nature develops. The Idea thus 'passes over into' Nature and reveals it as the spatio-temporal deployment of its own system and the process of its own generation.

The Idea in which the logical process culminates is not a mere subjective abstraction. As Plato declared in the Parmenides, it is not simply 'in our heads'. It is immanent in the world of Nature and must be so if life and mind are to develop out of that world. 'The external world is implicitly the truth for the truth is actual and must exist.'[4] The truth is the absolute Idea, and the next phase of self reflection must be the philosophical return to Nature to demonstrate just how the truth is actual, and to develop in detail the dialectical progression through natural forms which brings into existence life and finite minds.[5]

24

The view-point of the Philosophy of Nature, the next science in Hegel's Encyclopaedia, is far in advance of that of natural science, (which looks upon the world of Nature as external and 'closed' to mind),[6] because it requires a degree of self-consciousness several orders above that operative at the empirical level. Science is a reflection upon common experience, and the Logic, following on the Phenomenology, has reflected upon that reflection to bring us to a grade of self-awareness at which Nature is rediscovered as the self-external embodiment of the Idea developing itself through the natural process. It is as such that the Philosophy of Nature treats it, not rejecting, or attempting to contradict, or even to improve upon, the findings of the natural sciences, but accepting them and using them, giving them a philosophical interpretation in the light of the discovery in the Phenomenology and the Logic of the identity of subject and object. This identity is now revealed through Nature as the Idea in the form of other-being, returning to itself out of the physical world (through mechanics, physics and organics) as life and ultimately conscious spirit.

The last science of the Encyclopaedia is then the Philosophy of Spirit, which traces the re-emergence of the Idea from Nature in the form of a living, self-conscious being developing itself into full-blown personality, both subjectively as a rational thinker and objectively as a responsible member of a community of persons, through the institutions of the family, civil society and government, and finally transcending its own finite form in the arts, in religion and in philosophy. Of all these the content is the same, the Absolute Idea, which is the totality and the Truth. This is what religion represents as God and art depicts in diverse imagery. It is the subject-matter of Logic in the pure form of universal concept, of Naturphilosophie in the form of externality as particular instantiation, and of Geistesphilosophie in the form of individual personality. Each of these is a presentation of the whole and each flows over into the other two: the pure Idea into the external other-being of Nature and that into the individual, self-conscious living subject. Thus, despite an appearance of linearity, the Encyclopaedia comes full circle, ending with Philosophy, which at the outset we encountered as phenomenology and to which the Philosophy of Spirit has returned enriched by the insights of the Logic and the Philosophy of Nature. Strictly, the Phenomenology was propaedeutic -- Hegel called it his voyage of discovery -- for without it we could not establish or justify the viewpoint of 'pure' knowing, from which the whole system is elaborated. This pure knowledge Hegel calls Wissenschaft, the first phase of which is the Logic, not, as Aristotle would have said, 'first to us', but first (logically prior) in the nature of things: 'God in his eternal essence before the creation of Nature and finite spirit', the pure universal Idea which is prior to, immanent in and the final result of the dialectical process.

Logic, then, the first of the triad of philosophical sciences, presupposes all the forms of common experience, the reflection upon them which constitutes empirical science (on the one hand) and morality (on the other) as well as the further reflection upon all of these in phenomenology. But logic begins afresh in its own right and relative to its own subject matter, the Concept. In doing so it presupposes the Phenomenology only in being that level of consciousness which has developed through its dialectic, founding its claim to be 'pure' or 'absolute' knowing upon its immanence in and its fulfilment of the demands of all the lower levels of consciousness. It is the culminating form of thought thinking itself and so generating its own categories. With respect to these it makes no presuppositions whatsoever, in that it is the Concept specifying itself by its own inherent activity. It presupposes (as we shall later understand more fully) only itself, seeking a sheer beginning in the wholly abstract and the totally unmediated.[7]

NOTES: Book I, Part I, Chapter 2

1. Cf. Enz., Section 81, Zusatz.

2. Enz., Section 38, Zus.

3. Cf. W.L., Preface to the 2d. ed.

4. Enz., Section 38, Zus.

5. Cf. my papers 'The Philosophy of Nature in Hegel's System', Review of Metaphysics, IV, 1949, and 'Hegel and the Natural Sciences' in Beyond Epistemology (ed., F. Weiss), The Hague, 1974. And see pp. 302-306 below.

6. Cf. A.N. Whitehead, The Concept of Nature (Cambridge, 1964), Ch. I.

7. See below, Book II, Introduction.

Chapter 3

Science and System

In the Preface to the Phenomenology Hegel writes:

The truth is the whole, but the whole is only the essential reality fulfilling itself through its development. One may say of the Absolute that it is essentially outcome (Resultat), that it is only at the end that it is what it is in truth; and its nature consists in precisely that -- to be actual subject, or self-developing (Sichselbstwerden).[1]

From this it is immediately obvious that any talk of truth as correspondence between ideas, or propositions, and self-existent facts must fall woefully short of the mark, and we have already seen some of the reasons why. First, no pure facts separable from ideas can be discovered to serve as the measure of such correspondence, and if any purely sensible datum could be identified its content would be wholly unintelligible and so hardly suitable as a criterion. Secondly, no such 'facts' as we commonly envisage are ever self-contained or self-complete; they are always so mutually connected and involved that description of them is always provisional and liable to modification as more is discovered about their dependence upon one another and upon new facts hitherto unknown. Even if they could be used as a criterion, therefore, it would be constantly shifting and alterable.

Similarly, any attempt to identify truth with some general principle, and to state it in an abstract formula, must fail, because the statement, until its meaning and implications have been set out in full, will be as unintelligible as would a mere sensuous datum. So Hegel writes further in the same context:

...knowledge is only real and can be expounded only as science or system; further, a so-called fundamental proposition or principle of philosophy, even if it is true, is also false, for the very reason and just so far as it is merely a fundamental proposition or principle.[2]

Thus it is only the whole system which is true and is actual knowledge or science (Wissenschaft), not merely because all facts are interconnected and interdependent,[3] but for the more far-reaching and significant reason that the various forms and differing grades of knowledge are continuously interfused. The Absolute, Hegel says, is essentialy result, or the outcome of a process, but even a conclusion lacks its full meaning unless it is seen as the conclusion from just this precise demonstration. It has to be seen perspicuously as the development of its premisses. The whole process must be summed up and held, as it were, in suspension within the final outcome. In consequence,

Hegel maintains that 'the true form in which the truth exists can only be the scientific system of that truth.'[4]

But the whole which is the truth in its true form, as the self-developed system of science, is knowledge of the real, which is itself the process or system of self-development that produces this knowledge. The natural world, as we saw in the last chapter, is a continuous development from physical to biological process generating sentient and conscious beings, the content of whose consciousness is an awareness of the world and of themselves and the knowledge that they are part of the world. This knowledge, as Kant taught, because it is synthesized and grasped as the single experience of a unitary subject of consciousness, is systematized by concepts and is a whole. Hegel shows that this system is constructed as a dialectical series of graded forms (Denkbestimmungen) and that it has the same structure (though in a higher degree of systematic integrity) as the world through which it has been brought to consciousness, and of which it is the knowledge. Accordingly, the true form of the whole is at once the form of the real, and the form of knowledge, and is the outcome of the evolution in the world, which is the knowledge of itself in its own true form.

It is not just that science (or knowledge) systematically set out represents or corresponds to the system of the world. There is a modicum of truth -- half-truth -- in that description. But more correctly, the developed system, which is science and knowledge, is the outcome, as well as the explicit form, of the total development which is the system of the real and of experience as a continuous whole, a development in which this outcome is immanent and implicit in every prior phase. It is the truth of the world -- what it is in truth -- 'the true form in which the truth exists'. Thus, what the real is in its truth is knowledge, or self-awareness. What is ultimately real, what is truly substance, is subject, or Spirit.

It follows that the truth which is the whole is not a lump, not a 'block universe'; nor is it merely a collection of particulars -- everything that happens to exist (be they 'facts' or 'things')[5]. Nor yet is it a blank unity into which all the differences and distinct individuals are absorbed without trace. It is not 'the night in which all cows are black'. It is a single, complete, unified, yet articulated system, so ordered and integrated that everything comprising it is what it is because of its precise place in the system and its relations to everything else. In short, the principle of order and unity is immanent in every element or 'part', determines its nature and its inter-relations with the rest.[6] This is why it is nothing in itself. Apart from its self-differentiation as system, this principle is a mere abstraction and is virtually unintelligible. It is actualized fully only in the articulated whole.

Further, it is not a static given whole, like a spatial pattern, but a dynamic system perpetually working itself out through a discursive activity. Yet it would not be correct either to think of it as a temporal process (although every temporal succession is a manifestation or expression of it in some specific form), for although it is, as Hegel says, 'infinite restlessness', it is also in principle, and in its truth or actuality, eternally complete and fully realized -- or absolute.

The sense in which it is active (or restless) is the Aristotelian sense of ἐνέργεια. It is a timeless activity or discursus, at once unified and differentiated, which does not require temporal lapse, although all temporal lapse involves just such an activity, in as much as any succession, in order to be a succession, must be one continuous whole of differences, which, as a whole, is not successive. The timeless activity is the perpetual and unremitting activity of thought as it grasps instantaneously and without lapse the nexus between distinct yet mutually implicated elements (like the equality of the angles of an equilateral triangle). Hence 'the true form in which the truth exists' is not a simple fixed system, but a constantly active discursus, which in its fully developed phase is self-consciousness -- the whole system at once, aware of itself as whole and as its own self-conscious content. In short, once again, it is Spirit.

The truth, then, is the whole articulating itself as a scientific system, which is the concrete universal, or Idea -- the truth of the Concept. The activity of self-differentiation of the whole, set out as the scale or series of moments into which it is specified, is the process of the dialectic. It presents itself in various forms and phases of which the most important are: (1) the series of natural forms, the dialectic of Nature as unfolded in the Naturphilosophie; (2) the forms of consciousness, traversed in the Geistesphilosophie and the Phäno-menologie; and the scale of categories or Denkbestimmungen exempli-fied and expressed in both (1) and (2), which are the self-specification of the Concept proper, or the pure Idea -- the system of the Logik.

Dialectic

The whole is system, and system cannot be anything but whole, for its systematic character implies completion. Moreover, what is systematic is not simply one, but consists of a variety of elements each of which is adapted to every other so that they fit together to form a unity. Thus it is a unity of differences, and because it is nothing over and above its elements, it is a unity in and through its differences. Both aspects (unity and difference) are equally essential to system. That is why it cannot be anything but whole. Accordingly, the nature of the elements and the way in which they are mutually adapted is determined by the principle of organization which unifies them. A simple and straightforward example of this is a jigsaw puzzle; but because it is only a spatial pattern and does not obviously involve dynamic flow, it is no more than an approximation to the true character of wholeness, which is typical of the higher reaches of the scale we are about to describe, and which approximate progressively more closely to the essential form (while they are at the same time phases, or moments) of the absolute Idea.

As each element is determined by -- in Hegel's terminology, is a determination (Bestimmung) of -- the universal organizing principle, each is an expression, or an exemplification, or an application -- a manifestation -- of the unifying principle of structure which governs the universal order within the whole. The universal principle is thus immanent in every element, and every element is, in some sense, or in a specific form, a representation of the whole. Hegel says of the categories of the Logic that each is a provisional definition of the Absolute, and to this aspect of the differentiation of the whole as a series of premonitory wholes we shall return presently. But any element prior to the last, as a mere element or factor in the totality (like one piece of a jigsaw) is only a partial and inadequate expression of the universal principle, whose full realization requires all the other elements as well in their proper order and arrangement. Taken alone, therefore, and in isolation, any partial factor demands supplementation; and what supplements it both differs from it and contrasts with it, as well as fits in with and completes it. The two are in one sense in opposition to each other, while in another they also supplement each other.

What each partial element omits is both other than, or 'outside' it, thus being the negation of it -- its opposite -- and at the same time it is necessary to it as its supplement. Neither can exist without the other nor be what it is apart from the whole; so each is necessary to the other; and because they are complementaries each defines the other and determines what the other is and does. Further, each viewed in isolation, because and in so far as it is incomplete and inadequate to its own nature (which is determined by the principle of wholeness), contradicts itself. It cannot, therefore, rest in its separation and false self-sufficiency. Its very partial nature calls forth what it lacks -- its other -- to supplement it, and any endeavour to maintain it within its own limits results in its revulsion into its own opposite, because the whole is immanent in it and asserts itself within the part. So its difference from and opposition to its other is emphasised as well as its dependence on and identity with it. This identity in difference, when the two opposites are taken together and seen in their proper mutual supplementation, constitutes a new and more adequate version of the whole, a fresh and a higher stage in its self-development.

Accordingly, each finite element calls forth, and opposes itself to, another, with which it then merges, and we have the famous formula of the triad: thesis, antithesis and synthesis. This formula, however, is not Hegel's invention and he does not explicitly enunciate it, except to criticize it as unduly restrictive and straightlaced.[7] It was Fichte who declared that without synthesis there could be no antithesis and without

30

antithesis no synthesis. Thesis he reserved for that absolute posit of the one whole without which neither antithesis nor synthesis was possible.[8]

In logic, however, we are not dealing with spatial patterns (or jigsaws) but with concepts, and these are more highly developed, more fluid and more subtly interpenetrating, even than organic and living systems, which form an intermediate stage between the merely spatial and physical and the conceptual. We must therefore be careful not to place too much reliance upon the simpler and more abstract examples, illuminating though they may be in some respects, lest they prove misleading in others.

The higher phase which emerges with the reconciliation and unification of the earlier inadequate and partial opposites, resolves the conflict between them and the contradictions which revealed themselves within the isolated parts; but it does not abolish the differences, which remain essential to their mutual supplementation. The new whole, therefore, includes and preserves within it the earlier phases, though in their new unity they are transformed and assume a new aspect and a new character. This preservation and transformation, which is at the same time a cancellation of earlier inadequacies and conflicts, Hegel designates by the German word, aufheben, exploiting its notorious ambiguity. There is no single English word by which we can properly translate aufheben. Commonly it means 'cancel', but it also means 'retain' and 'preserve', as it were, stored up. It also has the sense of raising up to a higher level, and this sense is indispensable to Hegel's usage, which always carries the implication of transformation or transfiguration. It is not surprising that translators have endless difficulty with this word. The most versatile of them, and perhaps the most successful, is William Wallace, yet even he sometimes fails to convey exactly and completely what is required in passages containing 'aufheben'. Sometimes he uses 'suspend', at others 'absorb', sometimes 'absolve', at others 'supersede', and occasionally the more literal 'cancel'. Each of these equivalents may serve in the appropriate context, yet none of them is wholly accurate, for 'aufheben' is used by Hegel to suggest them all. G.R. Mure uses 'sublate' as the English equivalent, and he has been followed by a number of more recent translators of Hegel's works. This word, according to the Oxford English Dictionary, does mean 'to remove' or 'take away', as well as 'to exalt', and this combination conveys very well much of what Hegel intends.[9] But unfortunately the word is little used in English and in current usage is almost unknown. Nevertheless, in conveying and explaining Hegel's arguments, it can be very helpful, as one can include and emphasize by its use at least two essential aspects of the meaning of aufheben. What is aufgehoben is held in suspension, thus cancelled yet preserved; the inadequacies are superseded and the contradictions resolved, yet the differences prompting them are retained, although what is sustained is nevertheless in the new context transformed.

31

Dialectical relations are therefore always highly complex; their tendency is always developmental, and what the development produces always carries with it and encompasses what it has in the process of development left behind. Accordingly, end and process are never separable and are finally seen to coincide.

The new phase -- or, in logic, the new category -- is a new specification of the universal principle: a new definition of the Absolute, at a higher grade or degree of realization. It is the opposite of its predecessor in the sense that truth is the opposite of error, yet it is also identical with it, for it is more truly what its predecessor claimed to be. It presents more fully what in its predecessor was only partially and inadequately expressed. So Hegel says that it is 'the truth of' its predecessor. But short of the Absolute itself even this more adequate expression is only finite and needs further supplementation. So the process repeats itself, generating another and still further developed phase. This process, through negation and opposition to reconciliation and unity at a higher stage, is the dialectical process; and as it continues, its own character develops and is transformed, so that the very principles of transition from one stage to the next are modified in the later phases and differ from those in the earlier. The simple triadic form, which is characteristic of the elementary phases, while preserved, or aufgehoben, in the later, is transformed and becomes more subtle and complex. What at first appears as mere transition, becomes reflection and reciprocal interaction, and that again is 'sublated' in a more complicated relationship where each moment and the totality is at one and the same time both a phase or moment and the whole system.

As each category in the series is a provisional definition of the Absolute, each is, in its own right, a whole of sorts, despite its partial and provisional character. This may sound paradoxical, but it does so mainly because of the examples we have been using. It is here that the image of a spatial pattern or a jigsaw is misleading, for the fragments of such a structure seem obviously not to be whole in their own right, but, at best, to demand completion and to imply the whole. Even in their case, however, if we wished to study it more closely, we should find reason to affirm some element of wholeness presented by each part. But I shall not pursue that claim immediately. In the case of categories there can be no doubt that we are dealing with universals from the start. Our subject in logic is the concept, and every specific concept is an exemplification, a differentiation or a particular case, of the Concept proper. Moreover, as the Concept is, in the last resort, the whole, of which the system is the specification, it is immanent (as already attested) in every specific form. Accordingly, each category, each specification of the universal, is itself universal and is a whole. The defect of the lower forms is not (as in the case of the jigsaw) simply the omission of parts, or pieces, co-ordinate in status with what is being affirmed. It is more correctly conceived as a sort of vagueness or indeterminacy characteristic of the more primitive and rudimentary, a lack of and need for further definition. Better, perhaps, than a jigsaw, the analogy to be used should be that of the optical projection of a transparency which begins out of focus but becomes progressively more distinct, more articulate and more coherent, as the focus sharpens. The dialectic, then, traverses a series of wholes, each a more adequate presentation than the last of the ultimate system. The categories, each of which is a specific exemplification of the Concept, thus form a scale of degrees increasing in completeness, in self-sufficiency and in truth. Their relation to one another is threefold: they are mutually opposed, they are alternative specifications of the universal Concept, and they are successive grades or degrees of truth in the manifestation of the whole, each being a more adequate presentation of the universal principle than its predecessor.

The progression, as we have seen moves from thesis, through antithesis, to synthesis; or from affirmation to negation and opposition and thence to reconciliation. But it is besides a movement from the immediate to the mediated and back to the immediate, now with mediation aufgehoben. Or again, it proceeds from a primitive and generalized unity to differentiation, analysis and discrimination, and thence once more to unity, but now a unity of differences systematically integrated. Of immediacy and mediation there will be much more to be said in what follows. Here we may note simply that the immediate is what is (at least apparently) not derivative from anything else, but is directly presented. The mediate, on the other hand, is so derived, it involves relations to and distinctions from something other, and it points beyond itself for explanation and for the justification of its asserted character. The first moment of the triad, therefore, is (relatively at least) underived; it presents its content as a whole and without specification. But clearly, if what has been said is taken seriously, that the mere assertion of a principle is meaningless without its particular applications, specification (what has initially been neglected) is demanded; and that is the second phase. The third shows the first two unified into a single whole in which they are identical, for the whole is nothing but the specific or particular differences which it unites.

Hegel is apt to maintain that the first and the third moments are more properly said to be provisional definitions of the Absolute because they are more rightly whole than the second moment, which is restricted more typically to the finite and particular, and is thus dissipated and partial. But this is not so without qualification and is only relatively true; for the second moment of the triad, that of mediation and differentiation, also comprises the whole concept, and also involves a form of infinity, even if of an inadequate and spurious kind.

33

The dialectical scale of categories which thus constitutes the logical form of the Concept is at the same time the actual form of the developing world. The culmination of the logical dialectic is the absolute Idea, and this, we have said, is immanent in each of its specific lower and less adequate forms. Because it is immanent in them it develops out of them, and only on this condition. Likewise it is the form of consciousness in which its categories are 'at work': and which advances through stages dialectically generated. The Idea is therefore immanent also in every phase of experience. It is immanent in Nature and in natural forms, the process of which is evolutionary and consequently dialectical. To repeat, the logical form of the Concept is equally the form of the world, and it brings itself to consciousness through the processes of Nature and finite experience. The logical form, the Idea, is 'the true form in which the truth exists' -- the truth at once of Nature and of conscious experience.

Those, therefore, who imagine that the Hegelian dialectic is simply a logical method, 'subjective' as opposed to 'objective' facts, to which it may be 'applied' in various approximative ways,[10] have simply failed to grasp Hegel's meaning. So have those who, like Karl Marx and Gotthard Günther, allege that the method can be divorced from the philosophical system, or the logic from the ontology.[11]

The Real and the Rational

In the light of the foregoing we may now see what Hegel means by the widely quoted, but little understood, declaration, which, in the Introduction to the Encyclopaedia, he quotes from his Preface to the Rechtsphilosophie: 'What is reasonable is actual, and what is actual is reasonable'.[12] Both the rational and the actual (in the full sense of both words) are the Truth, which is the whole. But the whole is Resultat, the outcome of the dialectical discursus, without which it is a merely abstract end-state. For the Absolute, besides being neither a blank unity nor a block universe, is not 'pure perfection' divorced and floating loose from the imperfect and defective. Any such purely 'perfect' state or being is just as abstract as either of the other two misconceptions of the whole. The Resultat which is the truth holds within itself the entire dialectical process, without which it is less than whole and far from perfect.

At the same time, any partial or provisional phase in the dialectic, as is obvious, must also be abstract in some degree and at best an inadequate manifestation of the truth. It is therefore neither real nor rational (actual nor reasonable) in full measure. Mere existents picked out more or less arbitrarily by sense-perception are such partial and imperfect entities; so they are not in themselves and apart from their connexions and relations with other finites, properly speaking real, or true, or rational. Similarly, what is distorted or depraved, wicked or deformed, evil or ugly, is always incidental to and the consequence of finiteness and defect. Nothing of that kind, therefore, can be true or real in Hegel's sense of those words, and any such is obviously irrational. As incidental to lower phases in the dialectical scale, however, they are actual in their proper context, as necessary and inevitable stages in the development which makes up the totality. But, if regarded, as we commonly view them as self-subsistent and existing in their own right, in isolation from that process of development, they are mere appearances, neither rational nor real. They are then misrepresentations of the truth, and if we insist upon their self-contained sufficiency, we fall into error and illusion. Their truth is what they become when dialectically developed. It is what they are potentially or implicitly (an sich), and when it is made explicit they are transformed into something new, something better and more complete, in which actuality is more apparent and rationality asserts itself more fully.

On the other hand, however, abstractions and appearances cannot be written off as mere illusions or non-entities. They have to be explained and not explained away. As phases of the dialectic, which in truth they are, they are properly accounted for, and, as such, they participate in the reality of the whole. But that whole, we must insist, is not separable, as a presumably 'perfect being' divorced from the process of its own gestation. It absorbs and transfigures the memories of its own birthpangs, sublating them in a totality which includes the whole process. The actual which is the reasonable, therefore, is the complete series of appearances and partial manifestations, in their varying and progressively increasing degrees of truth; but they are real only as moments in the dialectical series, aufgehoben as a whole in the final outcome, in the infinite restlessness of the Absolute Idea, which is reason. Only here is their full truth and actuality realized; but to this realization their partial and provisional manifestations are necessary as the phases and moments of its own self-generation.

Accordingly, everything is what it ought to be and yet nothing, short of the Absolute, is what it ought to be. The finite, taken in isolation and held to be self-sustaining (which it is not and cannot be) is never what it ought to be. But as a phase in the dialectically developing whole, it is precisely what it ought to be. Only so far as it is becoming what in potency it actually is, is it as it ought to be. Just so far is it actual; and just so far as it is becoming more rational, is it truly reasonable. And so far as it is reasonable it is real.

This identification of the reasonable with the real and the real with the reasonable is no justification of reaction in practice or of conservatism in politics, as it is so frequently alleged to be by Hegel's critics. It is not an expression of complacency with things as they actually are, nor a repudiation of reform and striving to improve the lot of human beings. Any such interpretation is sheer misunderstanding, and to accuse Hegel of accepting and condoning evils is gross misrepresentation. On the contrary, the dictum is the affirmation of a ubiquitous dynamism and a persistent nisus towards perfection (in the proper etymological sense of completion), for it declares all things to be actual and reasonable only so far as they are perpetually striving to overcome deficiency and remedy defect in themselves by actualizing the perfections implicit in them. The actual which is reasonable and the reasonable which is actual is, then in the last analysis, only Absolute Spirit comprehending and sublating as necessary moments of its totality every phase of the process of which it is the result.

NOTES: Book I, Part I, Chapter 3

1.   Phänomenologie des Geistes (Jubiläumsausgabe, Lasson, Leipzig 1907), p. 14; Miller's translation, p. 11; Baillie's trans., p. 81f. Hereafter abbreviated Phen.

2.   Op. cit., p. 16; Miller, p. 13; Baillie, p. 85.

3.   Kant had already declared that knowledge is always a whole of connected and related elements (Vorstellungen). Cf. Kritik der reinen Vernunft, A 79.

4.   Op. cit., p. 5; Miller p. 3; Baillie, p. 85.

5.   Cf. Wittgenstein, Tractatus, 1.1.

6.   The category of whole and part, we shall discover later, is a finite category not fully adequate to the truth, or the Absolute.

7.   Cf. W.L., Zweite Teil, III Abs., III Kap., Suhrkamp (Vol. II), p. 564; Miller's trans., pp. 836-37.

8.   Cf. G. Fichte, Grundlage der Gesamten Wissenschaftslehre, Iste Teil, Section 3 (Felix Meiner Verlag, Hamburg, 1961), p. 35.

9.   In the remark at the end of the first chapter of the Greater Logic (W.L., I, p.114; Miller, p. 107), Hegel mentions the similar ambiguity of the Latin word 'tollere', but he says that 'it does not go so far' as that of aufheben.

10.   Cf. McTaggart, op. cit., Sections 5-9.

11.   Cf. also Charles Taylor, Hegel (Cambridge, 1975), p. 237f.

12.   Enz., Section 6; Wallace, p. 10.

Chapter 4

Understanding and Reason

Hegel ends the long introduction to the Encyclopaedia Logic (Sections 79-83) with a discussion of the three 'sides' or 'moments' of logical form, the abstract, the dialectical (or negative-rational), and the speculative. But as his extensive criticism of his predecessors, which, in the text, precedes this discussion, relies heavily on much that he explains in these later sections, it will be expedient to deal first with these three aspects of scientific thinking. They are, Hegel tells us, not separable parts or branches of logic, but are moments of every 'logical-reality' (Logisch-Reellen). In other words, they are three aspects of all thought and of all actuality. They are also, in effect, attitudes, or casts of mind, typical of three different theoretical positions.

Understanding

The first moment is typical of the Understanding, and Hegel forthwith applies that term exclusively to it. By 'understanding' he means the capacity of reflective interpretation, using the word in the same sense as Kant used it, and much as did Locke and Hume before him. Understanding is what we commonly have in mind when we speak of thought, and is also the more usual form of thinking, or the frame of mind in which reflection and empirical science are generally carried on. It has two main characteristics, which are intimately connected with each other, abstraction and sharp, rigid distinction. If we treat the three moments of logical form under this aspect, Hegel says, we separate them and hold them apart. But so conceived they are not grasped or dealt with in their true character (in ihrer Wahrheit).

Hegel has already remarked in an earlier section (section 9) that the universal of the special sciences is abstract, that is, indeterminate, or purely general, and (as he puts it) unconnected with its particulars, which are contingently related to (subsumed under) it. It is an abstract quality or property, the common character of the group or class of particulars that happen to possess it. The understanding distinguishes rigidly between, nay separates, universal from particular and keeps the relation between them purely external, for its principle is that enunciated by Hume:

> Whatever objects are different are distinguishable, and whatever objects are distinguishable are separable by thought and imagination. And we may add, that these propositions are equally true in the inverse, and that whatever objects are separable are also distinguishable, and that whatever objects are distinguishable are also different.[1]

Thus understanding insists on a strict separation and division between distincta, whether they be objects of sense, thought or imagination, or extra-mental existents; and, of course, this strict separation is maintained between all of these classes, especially the last two -- the mental, or ideal, and the real. The principle is alternatively expressed in Bishop Butler's words: ' A thing is what it is and not another thing'.

This is the attitude of mind typical of Empiricism, but also, to some extent, of Rationalism, at least as it is represented by Descartes, with his insistence on clearness and distinctness as the marks of certainty. And it is equally characteristic of the empirical sciences, and eminently of the so-called 'exact' sciences. Its mark is what Hegel often refers to as 'raisonnement', reasoning as a means of deriving conclusions from given premises, reasoning as an instrument or 'tool'; but not reason as the originative source of truth.[2] That, for Empiricism, is sensation, which alone gives us contact with reality and to which reason, whether in theory or practice, is merely ancillary. In fact, as Hegel remarks in Sections 2 and 19 (Zus.), reason in this form falls into disrepute when it attempts to analyse the more concrete and valued interests of society. Its segregation and separation of aspects and elements from the quickening influence of the whole leaves the disjecta membra worthless and dead. It 'murders to dissect'. The true test of values is then seen as feeling or immediate intuition: 'The heart,' wrote Pascal, 'hath its reasons of which reason knows nothing'. Reason is held to be incapable of assessing ends or of constructive and definitive decision. At best it can discover the means to attaining the objects of desire, or the analytic consequences of opinions held on ground of inclination or experience. It is firmly held by the prudent to an instrumental role; as Hume uncomprisingly proclaims, where morality and practical affairs are concerned, 'reason is and ought only to be the slave of the passions.'[3]

The ideal of the understanding is precision -- sharp and exact differentiation made on the principle of strict identity. Frege requires 'that it should be determinate for any object whether it falls under a concept or not.'[4] The range or extension of each concept must be precisely defined so that it is definitely determinable to which concept any object belongs, and which objects belong to each concept. But the identity on which such distinctions rest is abstract identity, sheer sameness with self -- 'die einfache beziehung auf sich' (simple relation to self) -- without any internal difference. In accordance with its own ideal of precision and principle of distinction, the understanding unrelentingly separates identity from difference and allows neither to contaminate the other.

This form of thought is said to be abstract because it abstracts, or separates, each identifiable object or content from everything else with which it may be connected, and holds them apart as mutually independent and self-sustaining. It abstracts ('draws out') common properties

38

from the individuals that have them and sublimates them into abstract concepts. It abstracts particulars from universals, and holds them to be bare unqualified particulars externally related not only to one another but equally to their qualities and properties, which are, as it were, attached to them from the outside; so they are also externally related to the concepts, or universals, under which they are subsumed. It abstracts one concept (e.g., identity) from every other (e.g., difference, similarity, opposition, etc.). Everything, for the understanding, is identical with itself and different from everything else, and each is precisely what it is regardless of what others may be. 'The world divides into facts. Any one can either be the case or not be the case, and everything else remains the same.'[5]

Hegel points out that this mode (this aspect or moment) of thought is essential to all science, in his own sense of that word, as well as in every legitimate sense of systematic thinking, and to any sophisticated treatment of any subject. Without precision there can be no genuine science or philosophy. Without clear and definite distinctions there is only vagueness and confusion, against which Hegel is as implacably averse as any empiricist. Critics habitually accuse him and his followers of woolly thinking, but he was accutely aware of its dangers and was unremitting in his condemnation of it. The critics, however, are those who never proceed beyond the level of the understanding and so fail to grasp the operation or the significance of speculative reason, which appears to them only as muddle-headed perversity. They stick to and swear by the precision of abstract rationalism, which, when pressed to extremes, turns out to be the most flagrant irrationalism (as Hegel is presently to argue), and they fail to recognize that strict and rigid differentiation is but one moment, however necessary, of constructive scientific thinking.

Hegel insists, nevertheless, that precise distinctions and clear differentiations are indispensable to all science, and are especially important in philosophy: 'Above all things it belongs to philosophizing that each thought be grasped in its full precision and that one should not leave it vague and indeterminate.' (Enz., Section 80 Zus.). But not merely is differentiation one moment of thinking, it also belongs to the very nature of things that their parts and elements be sharply distinguished, in the physical and biological realms, for instance. Physical and chemical properties have their characteristic differences and exact relationships, which are expressible in precise mathematical formulae. In the living body, the functions of the organs, however complexly related one to another, are precisely differentiated. And much the same is true in the social sphere, in law, politics and economics. In art too, the various elements of the aesthetic object must be clearly discernible, and they must serve precise functions in the whole (even if the function is one of deliberately introduced vagueness, as in some of Leonardo da Vinci's paintings), so that the structure and balance of the work is determined. Even in religion, distinctions and differentiations

39

are indispensable, and Hegel praises the definition of conception of the Greek divinities as compared with the vagueness of those of Nordic mythology. But true as all this may be, we must always remember that Hume is, in fact, wrong, and that what is distinguishable, however, precisely, is not always separable and in some sense may never be, for the very reasons that precise definition is always in terms of what contrasts with and limits the definiendum.

The understanding, however, restricts itself to the finite, and its thinking is always finite thinking. Hegel often calls it finite reason. That is why its objects are always abstract and separated from the matrix in which they are, in truth, actually embedded as moments of an infinite process through which an infinite whole develops itself. We must, however, be careful to distinguish the infinite whole from the infinite regress, for the latter is a false infinite generated by this very finite thinking. Much will be said later about the distinction between the true and the spurious infinite, of which Hegel treats at length, and which recurs at various stages of the dialectic in the body of the science. The true infinite, which is the truly concrete universal, appears to the finite understanding as a contradiciton in terms. At this level of thinking the concrete cannot be grasped, for the abstract is its medium and its genre. The thought of the understanding, therefore, is opposed on the one hand to sense-perception and feeling (which are always concerned with individuals and make no distinction between universal and particular), and on the other hand to speculative reason, which overcomes and reconciles the oppositions generated by the abstraction of the understanding. It is to these that we shall next turn our attention.

Dialectic

The distinction and precise determination of things characteristic of the thought of the understanding depends upon negation. A thing is what it is just because and so far as it is not another thing. Omnis determinatio est negatio. But this negativity is not simply, not only, external. The very nature and conception of the determinate requires what negates it and what it negates to establish its own identity. A is A precisely in that it is not not-A, and neither A nor not-A can be distinctly conceived without the other. What each is in itself involves its relation to the other, and there is always some internal feature as the basis of the distinction and the relation. Yet what is internal and what is external are so intimately dependent upon one another that they cannot be separated. Light is red if and only if its wavelength is 4×10^{-5} cms., that is, if it is not more and not less, and it is not yellow or infra-red for precisely the same reason. What it is determines what it excludes, and what it excludes defines what it is. Consequently, if one attempts (as the understanding invariably does) to assert and maintain either independently of the other and to insist on its isolated self-sameness, it turns into its opposite in its own self-assertion. If you try to treat 4 as if it were independent of 1, 2 and 3, you must assume that it is not 2 x 2, nor 3 + 1. Similarly, in the more complex and concrete sphere of politics, the claim to freedom, regarded as complete absence of restraint, if pressed to its extreme, becomes anarchy, in which each struggles for his own exclusive interest against all the rest. But in such a dispensation the strongest prevails, might becomes indistinguishable from right, and the alleged freedom turns into tyranny, which is its opposite. Or again, free will, understood as complete absence of determination, even by the motives of the agent, becomes sheerly contingent behaviour over which not even the agent has any control, so it is utter indecision, arbitrariness, incapacity and helplessness -- the opposite of freedom. Law applied strictly according to the letter becomes injustice -- summum jus, summa injuria. Shylock's implacable demand for his legal right is tantamount to attempted murder. So the letter killeth but the spirit giveth life, and the understanding always insists upon the letter. In logic, Hegel points out, to regard the universal in total abstraction from the particular makes it just another particular (the basis of the so-called 'third man argument' of Aristotle against the Platonic theory of Forms, which Plato had himself anticipated in the Parmenides).

Hegel therefore maintains that the finite carries its own negation in itself and tends of its own motion to go over into its other, to perish and to change into what it is not (Cf. Enz., Section 81, Zus.). This is the dialectic of the negative, or negative reason. In incomplete and abortive form it displays itself as Sophism and as Scepticism. Sophistry is the art of making every proposition or argument contradict itself, and Scepticism renounces truth because of the success of Sophistry. In the history of Ancient Philosophy the arguments of the Sophists invariably led to some form of Scepticism, best illustrated, perhaps, by the negative doctrines of Gorgias and the utter relativism of Protagoras' teaching, as demonstrated by Plato in the Theaetetus. The later Sceptics based their denial of truth on their failure to find any theory free of contradiction. But Hegel maintains that such dialectic is abortive because it remains stuck with negation and is blind to its positive significance. Omnis negatio est determinatio is just as true as its converse.

The scientific form of dialectic, on the other hand, is what brings out the immanent wholeness and connexion of things and is the moving principle of scientific progress. It is the true form of philosophical discussion, the history of which goes back to Socrates and Plato, and even to Zeno and Parmenides. In Plato's Socratic dialogues a definition is sought; and when one is offered, Socrates, by judicious questioning forces his interlocutor to confess that by implication it contradicts itself and is the opposite of what he first intended. So another definition is sought, which will avoid the contradiction, and the process is repeated. In the earlier dialogues as a rule no satisfactory conclusion is reached and the matter at issue is left undecided with a mere plea of ignorance, Socrates contenting himself with having deflated the complacency of the self-styled expert who thinks he knows what he is talking about. But in the Theaetetus and the Sophist Plato's treatment of philosophical method is more thorough and his discussion of negation is more penetrating. The method is shown to be one of 'division' in which the definition of a term is reached through the differentiation of a genus and by distinction of specific forms marking off what the definiendum is from what it is not. Negation is seen to be positive in its significance as indicating what is other than the negated term.

But for Hegel dialectic is not confined to philosophical method. It does indeed direct the movement of thought, but thought and consciousness, we must not forget, are the outcome and consequence of a dialectical movement immanent throughout nature. The dialectical movement of conscious thought is no more nor less than the coming to self-awareness in the human mind of the dialectic already at work in the world at large. Dialectic, says Hegel, 'is the principle of all movement, all life and all activity in the actual world (in der Wirklichkeit), as well as being 'the soul of all truly scientific knowledge' (Section 81, Zus.).

Speculative Reason

Accordingly, reason cannot rest in the barely negative, for, as we have seen, negation is always significant negation. It does not issue in mere nonentity but always has some positive import. The other into which the finite goes over is always a positive other. What negates is always something determinate; so, as Hegel insists, negation always issues in a result, bringing with it and carrying in itself that from which it has emerged, sublated (aufgehoben), preserved within it although also cancelled in its original finite formulation. The result is thus more concrete, more complete and comprehensive, than the first abstract finite, and holds within it both the opposites that negate each other, now become moments in the larger whole, still in their mutual distinction and contrast, but with the opposition now reconciled and the contradiction resolved. The negation is thereby negated.

Let us return to some of the examples given above of abstract concepts which generate contradiction. Political freedom seen as the legal recognition and enforcement of rights is the reconciliation of the opposition between licence and coercion. Moral freedom as willing conformity to the moral law is the reconciliation of doing what one likes with obedience to rule as one ought ('the service of God is perfect freedom'). Justice, as equity, is the application of the law and also consideration for the litigants' welfare. The concrete universal, as particularizing itself, 'has the particulars in itself' and so reconciles the opposites.

42

This last example is the key to all and is the principle and the foundation of dialectic and all speculative reason. The universal is the concrete concept, or whole, the principle of structure, which is logically prior to the parts and which determines the nature of the particulars. Elements which derive their character from the structure of the system and whose activity is determined by it cannot exist apart or be maintained in isolation. Their mutual exclusion is mutual negation, but their complementarity negates the negation and binds them together in mutual dependence, so that they are revealed as moments of a more inclusive whole, and the earlier attempt to maintain them in isolation as the root of error. 'To think apart of things which go together,' wrote Collingwood, 'is to falsify, and to say that it makes no difference is to elevate falsification into a principle.'

Properly to understand the finite, therefore, we must re-establish the system, we must develop the implications of the 'given' fragment, or better let them develop themselves, into the whole to which they belong and the structural principle of which is immanent in them. This wholeness which resolves contradiction and identifies opposites is what the understanding cannot understand. The apprehension of the whole, is the function and achievement of speculative reason, a reason more genuinely rational than understanding, because it reveals the contradictions in the finite which wreck the logic of the understanding, and shows the contradictories to be complementary components necessarily differentiating a concrete whole. The whole, moreover, is rational through and through, because it is systematically ordered.

Because the understanding fails to comprehend this holism it either scoffs at speculative reason as mystification (or in its politer moods, as 'mysticism'); or in a more relenting attitude it embraces 'intuition' as the incomprehensible and ineffable truth, rightly placed beyond the reach of finite raisonnement, but accepted therefore dogmatically and uncritically, or treated as an impenetrable mystery. Holism, however, is neither incomprehensible nor egregious. The more closely we study nature and mind the more prevalent we find holism to be. Whatever is genuinely rational and fully intelligible is and must be systematic, and a system cannot but be a whole, a whole moreover the principle of whose organization determines its constituents down to their last detail. The principle of such wholeness is the concrete universal, the self-specifying or self-particularizing concept, the universal that has its particulars in itself.

Such a principle is no mere common property abstracted from concrete individuals. It is a principle of order or structure, which by itself is nothing, but is actual only as embodied in the system of its particulars. Thus, in determining them and their inter-relations, as well as the processes by which these relations are established both in time and in space, the universal ordering principle is specifying itself, or, in other words, manifesting itself or giving itself palpable shape.

43

This is the essential character of a principle of organization: that it distinguishes and specifies itself, determining the elements of the system that it organizes; and they are the specific (and only) ways in which it makes itself manifest. Thus, in specifying its elements, it specifies itself. We shall see this principle of self-specification repeatedly exemplified throughout the Logic. Here it may help to adduce a few examples from other spheres by way of illustration.

(1) In physics, the unified field theory establishes (or seeks to establish) a fundamental equation of motion that determines the curvature of space-time, and that again specifies the various laws of motion and electro-magnetism, the physical constants and, generally, the laws that govern the physical world;[6] so that it becomes true to say that the physical world is nothing more nor less than the self-specification of the fundamental equation -- the universal field.

(2) Another example is the development of the fertilized ovum into an adult organism. Here the genetic code in the DNA provides the principle of organization, which then generates the specific parts and organs of the embryo and, through its development, of the complete organism. That, as a whole, is the product of the self-specification of the genetic code.

(3) The development of a scientific theory from the statement of a general law is yet another example. Newton's theory of celestial motion is deduced from his law of gravitation, which specifies itself in the various theorems that define the structure of the solar system. Every orbit is a specific exemplification of the general law and is the way in which the law manifests itself. The system as a whole is the law in operation.

(4) More eminently, a philosophical theory is the self-specification of a universal principle: e.g., Plato's theory of knowledge as represented by the Divided Line.[7] The universal principle is the activity of knowing, and each of the divisions, conjecture (ἐιϰασία), belief (πίστις), science (διάνοια) and philosophy (ἐπιστήμη), is a variety of knowing. The whole gamut constitutes the content of knowledge, and the activity itself is what gives rise to each in turn and in its appropriate place. The whole schema is generated by philosophical thinking which is itself both the final specific form and the comprehensive over-view of the whole series, involving each and all of its prior phases (which are both presupposed by and contained in it). Knowledge, as an activity, specifies itself as the divided line and is constituted by it, especially in its final and most developed form.

In each case the universal principle 'holds its particulars in itself' and generates the system by developing them out of itself -- in short, by specifying itself. This is the structure of the concrete universal, or what Hegel calls the Concept. The Logic is precisely its self-specification through the process of the dialectic into particular concepts, on successive levels of concreteness, which, as a series, constitute the system of the science. The process of the dialectic is the process of self-development, as we described it in this and the last chapter, in which the immediate given (whose character is determined by the system in which it is integral) shows itself in abstract isolation to be inadequate to that character. This is so for the very reason that the part implies, as it is defined by, what it excludes; and because of its inadequacy and the spuriousness of its own professed self-sufficiency, it makes what is implicit explicit by developing the whole immanent within it. The entire process is, in consequence, the self-development or self-specification of the universal (Concept) -- the organizing principle of the system.

NOTES: Book I, Part 1, Chapter 4

1.   Treatise of Human Nature, Book I, Part I, Section vii. (Selby-Bigge, p. 18).

2.   Cf. Enz. Section 19 and Zus., and Section 52.

3.   Op. cit., Book II, Part III, Section iii. (Selby-Bigge, p. 415).

4.   Cf. 'Function and Concept', The Writings of Gottlob Frege, Translated by Geach and Black, Blackwell (Oxford, 1952), p. 33.

5.   L. Wittgenstein, Tractatus Logico-Philosophicus, 1.2, 1.21.

6.   Cf. W. Heisenberg, Physics and Philosophy (London, 1959), p. 60; Sir Arthur Eddington, The Expanding Universe (Cambridge, 1933), p. 103, New Pathways in Science (Cambridge, 1935), p. 227 and passim, The Philosophy of Physical Science (Cambridge, 1939), Ch. XI.

7.   Republic, VII, 533d-534a.

45

PART II

HEGEL'S CRITICISM OF HIS PREDECESSORS

PART II

HEGEL'S CRITICISM OF HIS PREDECESSORS

Chapter 1

Introductory Comments

Objectivity, Hegel tells us, or 'objective thought', is truth; but truth is for him, as we have already seen, the absolute whole, and he says that it is to be the absolute object of philosophy, not something beyond its reach at which it aims with ever unavailing effort. The attitude which a philosophy adopts towards this ultimate object gives it its character and indicates the level of reasoning the dialectical stage which it represents. Hegel divides the major philosophies prior to his own into three main types, each characterized by its attitude to objectivity. These three attitudes do not form a typical dialectical triad (if such a phrase is permissible), although, like all other successive phases in a continuous development, it is always possible so to represent them. The third is not properly the reconciliation of the opposition between the first two, but is more nearly a continuation of the second in a more extreme form. If the first is Rationalism and the second Empiricism the third, Intuitionism, is more a form of irrationalism than a concrete conceptualism such as Hegel himself is recommending. It does, however, represent that return to mediated immediacy which, according to Hegel, is the form assumed by the reconciliation of abstract antitheses in a more concrete concept. Actually, the Critical Philosophy of Kant seems a more effective reconciliation of Rationalism and Empiricism; but, again, it is only the first stage of that reconciliation, and in itself it is only a half-way house. It develops through the Idealism of Fichte and the Intuitionism of Jacobi to the Identity Philosophy of Schelling, which Hegel rounds out into a fully systematic account of what he regards as 'objectivity', that is Wissenschaft, science set out in systematic detail in the body of the Logic itself.

The three attitudes to objectivity discussed in the introduction to the Encyclopaedia are:

(1) The metaphysical philosophy of the 17th century Rationalists, inherited from the Mediaevals and secularized by Descartes, Spinoza and Leibniz. It was represented in Hegel's day chiefly by Christian Wolff, who had digested and simplified Leibniz' thought. In Wallace's translation, this is referred to as 'pre-Kantian Philosophy.' Hegel's critique does not apply in detail to the great 17th century Rationalists, nor does he refer to them here by name. He is criticizing a type of philosophy and an attitude to truth rather than the views of any individual thinker.

(2)   The second attitude is that of Empiricism as we find it in the British Empiricists, and somewhat surprisingly Hegel, while he distinguishes between the Empiricism of the main stream and the Critical Philosophy, brackets Kant with the very thinkers Kant took himself to be refuting. The reason for this will appear, and is by no means trivial.

(3)   The third attitude is that of the Intuitionists of Hegel's own time, whom he vigorously opposed and of whom the most eminent representatives were Jacobi and Schleiermacher.

Gotthard Günther, in this book, Grundzüge einer neuer Theorie des Denkens in Hegels Logik, alligns these three attitudes to objectivity with the three main Parts of the Logic (Being, Essence and Concept), but this is at best misleading.   Hegel undoubtedly intends them to represent the transition from understanding through dialectic to speculative reason.   He does not, however, consider his immediate predecessors to have reached the last stage in more than vague premonition, although in his earlier writings he does commend them for adopting a genuinely speculative attitude.   Here and later in the Logic he pays similar tribute to Kant.   But he regards these writers as taking only the first step towards that 'absolute knowing' the exposition of which he believes himself to be giving in his own work.

Günther characterizes the first attitude to objectivity as that in which the object is regarded as external to and independent of the subject, resulting in what he calls 'objective logic'; and this again he identifies with the traditional formal logic.   But in the relevant chapter in the Encyclopaedia, Hegel gives little, if any, indication that these positions are adopted by those he is criticizing.   Indeed, the kind of metaphysic he describes was accompanied by the traditional formal logic, and that logic does assume the externality and independence of the object.   But in his chapter on the first attitude Hegel seems less interested in these facts than in other features.   He emphasizes the rationalistic faith of Mediaeval philosophy and its immediate successors in the competence of thought to grasp the truth of its object, while at the same time he objects to their too confident reliance on finite categories.   Günther's identification of the first attitude with 'objective logic', though to some extent justifiable, does not seem to be what Hegel intended.

The second attitude to objectivity, according to Günther, is that in which the dependence of the object on the activity of thought is recognized and the corresponding logic is subjective.   This attitude is represented by Empiricism and the Critical philosophy of Kant and Fichte.   There is more agreement here with Hegel's account of this attitude, for he does say that the Empiricists and Kant adopt it, and he does accuse Kant (in particular) of subjectivism.   And, of course, Berkeley and Hume are notoriously subjectivist, while Locke, although he strove to sustain some sort of realism, confessed that ideas of secondary qualities were mind-dependent and was forced in the end to admit that we could know only our own ideas. Nevertheless, Hegel's emphasis is much more upon the restriction, by these thinkers, of experience to a sensuously given content, which limits knowledge to the finite, on their denial of the supersensible and of any possible knowledge of the infinite. He has almost nothing to say about the sort of logic typical of such a position, but devotes his attention throughout mainly to metaphysical issues. It is true, as we shall see later, that the transcendental logic of Kant provides much of the content of the Doctrine of Essence in Hegel's logic, so that Günther's attempt to identify that doctrine with the second attitude to objectivity has some foundation, but what he contends further is much more dubious.

He goes on to say that the proper logic required by the Kantian advance in epistemology was never really developed by Kant, nor by Fichte, nor even by Hegel. It is a logic, he holds, of mediation, to which Hegel pointed the way but (according to Günther) never elaborated. Kant failed, he says, because he held too rigidly to the traditional logic; Fichte because, despite his efforts to avoid it, he reinstated the traditional laws of thought in his final conclusion, and Hegel because he was led astray by his metaphysical absolutism. The necessary advance in logic, Günther maintains, would recognize the coalescence of the objective with the subjective attitudes as moments in one self-reflective unity of thought. This he calls 'absolute mediation' and identifies with the third attitude to objectivity. At first it is not apparent how this position is supposed to differ from Hegel's, and as Günther does not himself develop the appropriate logic we are left merely with the allegation that Hegel was mistaken in asserting that mediation is aufgehoben in the final phase and immediacy reestablished. This is a mistake, says Günther, because immediacy implies externality of the object, which, after the second stage of the development, cannot be reaffirmed.

Until we have discussed Hegel's view of mediation and immediacy in Chapter 4 below we cannot properly assess Günther's criticism. But we shall find it to be misguided as a judgement upon Hegel, as it is also unhelpful as a proposal for the advancement of logical theory. Günther is quite right to recognize Hegel's advance beyond formal logic and to say that Hegel saw its inadequacy as an exhaustive definition of rationality; but he has little right to reject Hegel's final account of reason as dialectical and speculative (for that seems to be his submission), unless and until he can provide a better account of his own.

Chapter 2

The First Attitude to Objectivity:
PreKantian Metaphysics (Dogmatism)[1]

Hegel commends pre-critical metaphysics for its firm confidence in the efficacy of thought to encompass the truth and to cope with infinite objects. It is not, he says, aware of the contradictions in thought or the opposition of thought to itself, and it takes the categories to be the fundamental laws of things. This indeed is the essence of rationalism, that it accepts as real whatever reason accredits and only what reason can approve. Thus, for Descartes, whatever is clearly and distinctly (i.e., rationally) conceivable is true and can be and is created by God. The clear and distinct is not derogated as merely subjective and for that reason incapable of revealing the nature of things as they are.

In his Lectures on the History of Philosophy, Hegel comments upon the dualism maintained by Descartes between Thought and Extension and in consequence between soul and body. Here he does not credit Descartes with any naive unconsciousness of the opposition between subjective and objective, but attributes his failure to reconcile that between Thought and Extension to his limitation to the level of the understanding. In these sections of the Encyclopaedia, however, he is not commenting directly upon Descartes, but on pre-critical metaphysics generally, and could perhaps afford to ignore the wedge driven by Descartes between the subjective and the objective which subsequent philosophy found it so difficult to dislodge. The apparent oversight may be justified by the fact that Spinoza and Leibniz were not victims to the dualism, and the pre-Kantian metaphysic which Hegel here has chiefly in mind is the Wolffian version with its strong Leibnizian flavour. The dualism reasserts itself in Locke's Empiricism and it also vitiates the philosophy of Kant (who nevertheless points the way to surmount it) and to these Hegel is presently to turn.

Having mentioned what he commends as the merits of this first attitude to objectivity, Hegel points out that in what he calls its extreme form it is apt to remain at the level of the understanding, and in this inferior form it has defects against which we must be warned. The concepts it espouses are taken in disconnection one from another and are applied to the subjects of its investigation as mere unexplained predicates. These subjects too are simply accepted, taken over without examination from common sense, and the predicates attached to them externally irrespective of their adequacy or truth, into which no inquiry is made. The predicates, moreover, are held in rigid opposition, so that they are thought either to apply to their subjects or not, in accordance with the habitual 'either-or' argumentation of the understanding. Accordingly, its categories remain finite and inappropriate to the infinite objects which it rightly takes to be the proper subject-matter of metaphysics: the world, the soul, and God.

In answer to those who declare that man's thought is finite and cannot, in any case, apprehend infinite objects, Hegel explains briefly, in the Zusatz to Section 28, how thought can be infinite. What is finite is limited by something else external to it -- something other --, whereas what is infinite is self-determining, that is, it is not determined or defined by anything other than itself. Thought directed upon an external object is limited by that object (as Fichte and Schelling had insisted). But thought the sole object of which is itself has no such limitation, is entirely self-determined and is therefore infinite. Its object is aufgehoben, is absorbed into itself 'and elevated to an idea'.[2]

Later there will be much more to be said both on the matter of infinity and on the identity of thought with its object. On the former it is noted here that infinity is not 'an away and away for ever and ever', as the finite understanding conceives it. That is the false infinite of which we are to hear more in the systematic treatment of the logic. On the latter something has already been said. The bourne of self-consciousness is the discovery that its other -- its object -- is nothing but itself, and that object and subject are one. The Phenomenology has established this and the Logic will do so afresh, while from the start it refuses to see its object as anything but itself, for it is the thinking study of thought. The essential point is that the object, the natural world which is object par excellence, brings itself to consciousness through the dialectical process, and its consciousness of itself is its own essence. Subject transpires as the essential nature of the object, so that they coalesce and are one and the same. But in its early stages consciousness does not recognize itself as the result of the natural process, and regards its object as external and other. Hence it thinks in finite categories. Only after a long and arduous development conducting it through successive stages of increasing self-awareness does it come to see that the object is its own self and itself nothing other than the object come to consciousness of itself. It is then 'at home with itself in its other', and only then is its thought infinite. At this point the soul (the self-conscious subject), the world (that which brings itself to consciousness as subject), and God (the absolute, infinite subject-object -- the thought which thinks itself) are all revealed as different ways in which the infinite expresses itself. But so to comprehend the infinite is far in advance of the old type of metaphysic, which is still stuck fast at the level of the understanding.

Therefore the older metaphysicians adhered to finite categories like 'existence' and raised the question whether God exists. The category is attached as a predicate, as it were, externally, to the subject; but as a finite predicate it is 'unworthy' of an infinite subject. Existence strictly applies only to finite things. If you ask whether God exists, or ascribe existence to him in the same sense as to a table, you imply that God is a finite object -- and so not God. Similarly, the predicate 'simple', as applied to the soul, 'finite' and 'infinite' as applied to the world, 'free' and 'determined' as applied to the will, are all finite categories borrowed from common discourse and used without criticism like labels attached to the subjects under investigation. They are conjoined with them externally, whereas, Hegel maintains, the subjects ought of their own free (dialectical) motion to specify, or determine, themselves, to develop the characteristics out of their own essential nature -- for they are infinite, self-specifying, concrete ideas. He does not explain here how this is possible, because the logic itself pursues this course of self-specification -- the self-differentiation of the Concept. His immediate point is that topics like those of the traditional metaphysics, the soul, the world, and God, are concrete universals, which when adequately conceived must specify themselves and develop their attributes from their own essence. They cannot be treated as abstract ideas, nor can the attributes be attached to them externally as accidental predicates.

Further, the old metaphysics adheres tenaciously to one side of an opposition to the exclusion of the other, asserting in so doing what Hegel calls a half-truth. Thus it maintains that God is the sum-total of all positive predicates, or of all possible perfections -- excluding negativity. The soul, it avers, is simple, not complex, free not determined. The world is either finite or infinite, either completely determined causally or wholly undetermined. Again, God is separated, as infinite, and held over against finite beings, and is thus limited by the world and himself transformed into a finite being. The soul is conceived as 'a thing' (ein Seelending) with a seat in and a spatial relation to the body, which implies that it is some sort of physical entity. But these one-sided and mutually exclusive predicates are too abstract and too poor to do justice to the subjects to which they are applied. Thus the traditional metaphysics is classified as Dogmatism -- the uncritical asseveration of one contrary to the exclusion of the other; so that, as is typical of finite thinking, the one-sided concept turns into its opposite: the infinite God becomes by implication finite, the immaterial, simple soul becomes by implication material and complex, and so on; and the doctrine belies its own purport.

Hegel directs these criticisms to the traditional branches of the old metaphysics: Ontology, Rational Psychology, Cosmology and Rational Theology. In effect, he is here agreeing with Kant that they are pseudo-scientific -- that they apply the categories of the understanding illegitimately to the infinite objects of reason. But, as Kant has it, the ideas of reason are illegitimate and illusory because they result from the attempt to bring things-in-themselves under the categories. Hegel, on the other hand, maintains that the thing in itself (die Sache selbst) is the proper object of reason -- is in fact reason itself -- and is the appropriate subject matter of metaphysics. But as it is an infinite object it certainly cannot be grasped under finite categories, and when

52

the attempt is made so to conceive it contradictions (antinomies) are inevitably generated.

In Section 33, speaking of the old-fashioned Ontology, Hegel touches on the question, 'What can be meant by attributing truth to a concept, as opposed to its application to a subject?' Again, all he says here is that the Concept is a whole of differing characteristics, as is each of its determinations, because it is concrete and not abstract. His point is that truth as commonly understood pertains to propositions, the question being whether the predicate belongs to the subject, assuming there is no contradiction between them. This is a merely contingent matter of correct correspondence with fact. Even so, it should be necessary to inquire whether the concept (the predicate) itself does not contain an inner contradiction. How this might be he does not explain at this point, but we have already observed examples of abstract concepts which developed inner contradictions when pressed.

If an abstract predicate is applied to an isolated particular, it will not be possible to answer the question whether the proposition so formed is true, unless investigation is first made into the nature of the particular as well as into the connotation of the predicate. This, in both cases, requires exploration and development of a systematic context. Appeal must be made to a body of accumulated knowledge in order to understand the terms in the proposition and to explain their connexion (or, as the case may be, its impossibility). Apart from such exploration and development, we should simply be juggling with words, and the terms 'truth' and 'falsity' would have no intelligible bearing on the conjunction of the terms in the proposition. The systematic background of knowledge is what Hegel calls the Concept. It is the whole which gives meaning to any and all of its specifications (Bestimmungen), each of which, again, is a concept (a provisional version of the whole) and so itself a systematic self-differentiated unity. This is the concrete universal which determines all its own instances and holds them within itself. The 'truth' of any concept depends on whether it can be fitted, or developed, into such a system and upon its status within it, or whether on the contrary its abstraction from the system generates internal contradiction.

If objection is made to this view of truth on the ground that all we need do to test the truth of a proposition (e.g., 'The rose is red') is to observe and see whether it corresponds to the fact, appeal is being made to an empirical criterion. Criticism of this position is deferred to the next chapter (Sections 37-39), on Empiricism; but we shall find that, properly understood, it gives the same result.

In Section 34 he deals with Rational Psychology, or Pneumatology, which was concerned with the metaphysical nature of the soul, conceiving it as 'a thing'. Such a notion, as we have said, Hegel regards (to say the least) as inept. It seeks immortality, he says, in that sphere

53

where composition, time, qualitative change and quantitative increase or diminution hold sway.[3] The futility of this quest on behalf of an allegedly 'simple' entity is so obvious that Hegel leaves the statement without further comment as self-evidently absurd.

In the appended note he says that 'nowadays little is said in Philosophy about the soul, but more commonly Spirit (Geist)' is spoken of; and then he adds, somewhat cryptically, that the soul is distinct from spirit (or mind), being the middle term between body and mind, and the link between them. 'The mind, qua soul, is submerged in corporeity, and the soul is what animates the body.' For an explanation of this passage we must turn to the Geistesphilosophie where the idea here expressed is developed in detail.[4] The soul is there shown to be the awakening, as it were, in sentience, of the organism to its relations with its environment. As body the organism is subject to, and registers the effects of the whole of nature: of climate, of seasonal and diurnal change, and of geographical conditions. It is 'servile to all the skyey influences'; and these are felt in subconscious and pre-conscious sentience characterizing both sleep and waking. This totality of diverse yet undiscriminated feeling, the inner aspect of the body (what Merleau-Ponty calls 'the lived body'), Hegel identifies as the soul. Its contents are variously brought to consciousness through the discrimination of its internal differences and the distinction of object from the mind as subject. This is effected by the activity of attention, which segregates the elements of sentience one from another, projecting some as objective and assimilating others as subjective. So nature is brought to consciousness through sentience, and the soul mediates between the bodily organism and the mind (or spirit) as the link between the two. Thus 'Spirit comes to be as the truth of Nature.'[5]

Remarking on the ineptitude of imagining the soul as a thing, as if it could be sensibly pictured, and the unsuitability of the epithets 'simple' and 'compound' as applied to it, Hegel nevertheless commends Rational Psychology as superior to the empirical form of the science in its effort to comprehend spirit through thought as opposed to merely describing introspected experiences. He concludes the note with the remark that spirit is activity in the sense (adopted from Aristotle) in which the Mediaevals said that God was 'absolute actuosity'. It is ἐνέργεια, or as Hegel later says of the Idea, 'absolute restlessness'; and as such it must express or utter itself and cannot therefore be treated as a processless ens, separated from the outward processes of changing life and activity. The determination of this self-expression (Äusserung) by the inwardness of spirit must seriously compromise its alleged 'simplicity' in the meaning usually ascribed to that term. It will be 'simple', if at all, in some quite different sense.

The next section (Section 35) turns to Cosmology as dealt with in dogmatic metaphysics and lists a number of contrasting attributes which were applied as mutually exclusive to the world as a whole. The questions here raised (Hegel says in the Zusatz) are undoubtedly of importance, but the old metaphysics never succeeded in giving satisfactory answers to them. In particular it treated them only on the level of the understanding, imagining that the opposing terms of an antithesis could subsist each in isolation and in independence of the other. Consequently this Cosmology alleged that Nature was wholly subject to necessity and Mind (Geist) entirely free, a distinction which is not without foundation but which misconceives both freedom and necessity. True freedom, says Hegel, is self-determination, and so at the same time necessity. This unification of opposites is only later explained more fully, and we may therefore defer discussion of it.

Again, at the end of the note, he acknowledges a certain justification for treating evil as rigidly opposed to good, but warns us against misunderstanding those who maintain that evil is ony relative. They do not mean that it is merely subjective, that 'thinking makes it so' and that in the Absolute there is no distinction between good and evil. This is, perhaps, a cryptic allusion to his own critics and those of Schelling. But he does not enlarge upon this statement or explain what he means. 'The error is', he says, 'that one takes evil as a firm positive, whereas it is the negative, which has no existence (Bestehen) in itself, but which wants to be (something) for itself and is indeed only the absolute illusion of negativity in itself.'

What does this mean?[6] He leaves us guessing; but it is clear that he does not wish to deny absolutely the reality of evil as opposed to good. He does wish to draw attention to the fact that we can judge something to be evil only by reference to some standard of goodness. All evil is relative in this sense and belongs to a scale of degrees. Compare Socrates' remarks in the Phaedo about the relativity of pain and pleasure, when his shackles are removed. In spite of the impression which the quoted passage might give, Hegel is not asserting that evil is an illusion. 'The apparent and relative nature (of the opposition between good and evil) ought not to be taken', he says, 'as if evil comes to be something only through our way of looking at it.' It is the appearance of opposition to good resulting from and created by negativity -- that is, finitude, limitation and defect. All evil is incident upon finitude. It is the consequence of the finite nature of its cause or agency. Neverthless, that cause or agency must have a positive content, and in its positive nature it is so far good. Thus evil has no being, no Bestehen, in itself, but is parasitic on goodness -- the positive character of the agency which produces it; and qua evil it is shortcoming, the result of the finiteness and limitation of that agency, the negativity which restricts and confines its capacity. This limitation, therefore, generates an appearance or illusion (Schein) which distorts the positive nature of the act and presents the evil as something positive in itself.

To take an example from modern history, the consummate evil perpetrated by Hitler was possible only because he was able to engender a powerful sense of community and national solidarity in the German people, and because they had a strong capacity for organization and discipline, as well as an energetic determination to concert their efforts towards national revival and power after their defeat in the first World War. These characteristics in themselves and in their positive bearing were virtues. But because of Hitler's limitations and those of his followers, his talents and their energies were apallingly distorted and misdirected, producing a monstrous evil which blinds us to the potential and positive good on which that evil was dependent and parasitic.[7] It is the positive aspect that truly belongs to reality (which, as was explained earlier, corresponds to its idea); but it is the negation and limitation that occasions the evil which bulks large in our perception of it and assumes the appearance of reality. Its reality in the whole dialectical process to which it is integral is something quite different, as will transpire only when it is aufgehoben at a later stage in which the evil is overcome and transcended.

Rational, or Natural Theology, the fourth branch of the traditional metaphysics, is given similar treatment. Remaining on the level of the understanding, it conceives God and his attributes merely imaginatively in finite terms, and then becomes entangled in contradictions because of the demand that they should be infinite. The result is a vacillation between separation and identification of God and the world, producing either Pantheism or a dualistic Deism, both of which reduce deity to a finite level, while resorting to vague and confused notions in the attempt to conceive God's attributes. These are strictly quantitative concepts made indeterminate by the profession that they are to be taken in sensu eminentiori, but issuing only in a list of meaningless names in which all reality is lost.

Alternatively, God is represented as the sum of all possible perfections, or positive predicates, exluding all negation (that is, all imperfection). So he is reduced to an empty abstraction, with the poorest instead of the richest content. The concrete content which, Hegel says, the mind rightly seeks is one which contains in itself its own determinations (which involve negation). This means, not that it contradicts itself, or cancels itself out, but that it specifies and differentiates itself on its own principle of organization, which distinguishes within it the differentiae that negate one another. It contains the negative within itself. We shall return to this concrete self-differentiation later, when we come to discuss the logical categories, in particular that of 'being-for-self'.

The traditional proofs of the existence of God suffer from defects related to those above mentioned. In criticizing them Hegel is in substantial agreement with Kant. They use the logic of the understanding, which presupposes finite objects in external relation, abstract concepts and rigid separation of distincta. Such logic, as Kant also declared, is incapable of dealing with the infinite, and it falls into logomachy in the attempt. The form of the proofs is syllogistic, beginning from a premiss or postulate that is taken as true and accepted as known. Then a conclusion is drawn from this, so that the postulate ranks as a ground on which the conclusion depends and from which it is derivative. Meanwhile, the original premiss is simply accepted as given and its truth is not investigated. But if the conclusion is that God exists, God and his existence are thus made to depend on something else, something prior to and independent of God; yet still something unsubstantiated and merely accepted without reason. By such a proof we could not establish the existence of an infinite God, but at best of something finite, and some fallacy must be involved. God's existence, if God is adequately conceived, cannot depend upon anything other than himself. There can be no extraneous ground for his existence, for God is the universal ground of everything that exists.

Accordingly, the traditional proofs are bound to reveal themselves to the formal logician (the logician at the level of the understanding) as invalid. They commit the fallacies of ignoratio elenchi, or of quaternio terminorum, or of non sequitur. To prove the existence of something finite in place of God is to commit the first of these fallacies, and that is a fault Kant attributes to all the traditional proofs. He also contends that the Ontological Argument involves non sequitur, and the Cosmological quaternio terminorum.

It does not, however, follow that speculative reason sees no value in these proofs of God's existence, nor that belief in God in incapable of sound rational support. The process from finite premisses to infinite conclusion is, in one aspect, the process of our intellectual and moral advance from finite experience to the knowledge of God -- to absolute knowing; and, in another aspect, it is the process of self-development of the finite (e.g., Nature) in which the infinite is immanent (and so also the self-development of the infinite immanent in it), as the concrete self-specification of the Absolute, which is the supreme result of the process, and which gathers up into itself (aufhebt) the entire process -- 'als der die Vermittlung in sich aufgehoben Enthaltende'[8] -- and so is at the same time both process and end.

NOTES: Book I, Part II, Chapter 2

1.   Enzyclopädie, Sections 26-36.

2.   Wallace translates: '...suppressed and transformed..'

3.   Cf. Descartes, Discourse on Method, Pt. V: '...it is not sufficient that it should be lodged in the human body like a pilot in his ship... but

it is necessary that it should also be joined and united more closely to the body..'

4.   Enz., Sections 388-411.

5.   Cf. ibid., Section 388. See also my essay on 'Hegel's theory of Feeling', New Essays in Hegel's Philosophy, ed. Warren E. Steinkraus (New York, 1971).

6.   Cf. pp. 297-302 below.

7.   Cf. my Aquinas Lecture, The Problem of Evil, Marquette University Press (Milwaukee, Wis., 1977).

8.   'as that which contains the mediation sublated in itself.'

Chapter 3

Second Attitude to Objectivity

Empiricism[1]

The craving of the mind for a concrete content, to which Hegel referred above, is the main-spring (he asserts) of Empiricism. The abstract theories of the understanding can never get from their universal principles to particulars and to determinate actualities. On the other hand, from their generalities anything can be proved indiscriminately. To ensure against such speculative extravagance Empiricism insists on facts, on experience, on the solid and presently perceptible reality. The reference here is not only to the philosophy of the British Empiricists (of Locke, Berkeley and Hume) but also to the scientific empiricism of Newton, whose watchword was 'Hypotheses non fingo'. Neither the philosophers nor the scientists, however, were wholly faithful to their professed principles, for Empiricism elevates the particulars of sense into laws and general notions, and, although it admits no meaning for these save their empirical reference and content, yet universal terms such as 'force', 'matter' and the like, are used abstractly and appeal is made inadvertently and tacitly, without question or criticism, to metaphysical concepts simply taken on trust. This is as true of Newton and the scientists as it is of the philosophers, and although Hegel does not here mention that fact, he does so in no uncertain fashion in the Naturphilosophie.[2]

First, he commends Empiricism for seeking to ground itself firmly in the actual, existent, perceptible world, and for its refusal to set truth in an unattainable beyond in comparison to which the present actuality is despised. 'The external world', he says, 'is the truth implicitly, for the truth is actual and must exist.' In this statement there is far more than merely a commendation of empirical attitudes. The truth, for Hegel, is ultimately spirit; but that is no wraith or phantasm. The truth must be real and existent, concrete and self-maintaining. So it must display itself as a material world. But the spatio-temporal world, so far as it is only material, does not know itself as the truth. It is so only implicitly (an sich): as Wallace translates the sentence, it is the truth 'if it could but know it'. To become truth in its own right it must develop out of the torpor of its material nature to life, mind and self-consciousness and must know itself as spirit. Thus it brings to light its own true immanent essence, which is self-knowledge, in science as the knowledge of Nature and in philosophy as the knowledge that Nature is implicitly mind. This knowledge is thus the truth of Nature and is what Nature becomes through the process of its own dialectical development.

The fault of Empiricism is to omit and to overlook this condition of verification and to take the immediately presented 'fact' as the final truth. But the presented fact breaks down under scrutiny. Either it is a mere surface appearance indicating something further which lies behind; or it is a collection of 'secondary qualities' supplied by the mind and veiling the actual reality, which proves to be inaccessible. On the one hand, what is immediately presented never exhausts 'the fact', which turns out to possess an inexhaustible number of empirical characteristics; besides which, its sensible presentations are constantly changing and fluctuating. To discover the truth, then, we must pile 'fact' on 'fact' in never ending series which never attain the goal. On the other hand, the immediate is only a secondary representation of something more substantial hidden behind it. Experience, therefore, must be analysed and reduced to its ultimate and bare particulars; the characters of the presented object must be peeled off like the skins of an onion, and the reality with which the truth is identified is never reached, even by the standards of Empiricism itself. It has to confess that that standard lies beyond its reach, and then the infinite and supersensible, initially altogether denied, have in some sense to be reacknowledged, though they are banished to an unattainable and incomprehensible beyond. So again we find that, caught as it is in the trammels of finite thinking, the persistence of Empiricism in its demands for purely empirical grounds leads to the same conclusion as its opposite Rationalism.

Fixing its faith in immediate sense-perception, Empiricism is inevitably confined to the finite and the understanding is its natural element. Its acclaimed method is analysis; but the analyst imagines that the dissected parts remain unaffected by their separation from the whole and from one another, and that the disintegrated fragments can explain the totality, overlooking the fact that what has to be understood is their original unity and cohesion. But what held them together is no one of the disjecta membra, and the concrete reality from which the analysis began is lost to sight.

In common with the old metaphysics Empiricism has first this restriction to the finite: the former reduced its assumed infinites to finites by abstraction, the latter admits nothing in evidence but he finite deliverances of sense. Secondly, both begin from a presupposedly fixed given: in the first case it was the finite conception borrowed from common sense of God, the soul and the world; in the second case it is the external congeries of sensible objects. Accordingly, because Empiricism cannot admit (at least in the first instance) the infinite and supersensible, it tends to materialism, and because finites can never be self-determining, it tends likewise to determinism. Furthermore, as singular facts are observed only in juxtaposition and succession, one beside, or after, another, no necessary connexions between them are to be found. Universality and necessity are thus reduced to a subjective habit of thought, to merely contingent association, with the consequence that religious beliefs, moral precepts and legal prescriptions all become subjective and all objective knowledge is undermined.

In these three paragraphs and their Zusätze Hegel compresses a wealth of commentary, which brilliantly sums up the characteristic development of British Empiricism. Hobbes represents the tendency to materialism; but this (like all one-sided concepts) turns into its opposite in the course of the progress from Locke to Berkeley and Hume. Locke began by insisting that the basic elements of all knowledge were 'simple ideas of sensation and reflection', alleging that the first were causally produced by the effects upon our senses of external bodies, the second being the product of subjective introspection. Simple ideas our minds associated together to form complex, whose general arrangement made up the body of our knowledge. When he came to consider in what the truth or falsity of our ideas consisted, Locke wavered between 'agreement of ideas' and 'agreement between ideas and their archetypes'. Complex ideas of substances, he said, were true if the simple ideas contained in them were put together as they actually go together in nature, but he provided no means of discovering this. Complex ideas of modes could not fail to be true so far as their archetypes were of the mind's own making. The criteria of truth were thus, in the one case, inaccessible, and, in the other, subjective. The ideas of secondary qualities, being mind-dependent, Locke declared to be resemblances of nothing in the external objects and altogether unlike the 'powers' in the bodies that produced them; and although those of primaries were pronounced to be copies of the qualities in the bodies they represented, no means was provided of validating this claim. Both types of qualities were said to inhere in substances, our general idea of which was altogether indefinite. It was the idea of 'something -- we know not what', and the real internal constitution of bodies, alleged to be the source of their 'powers' to affect us, was pronounced to be altogether inaccessible to and beyond our knowledge. So are the qualities 'peeled off' the perceived objects 'like the skins of an onion' to reveal nothing but an unknown substance with an unknowable internal constitution.

Berkeley, in consequence, banished the external world altogether from our purview and identified all bodies with ideas in the mind. For their truth he appealed to a transcendent infinite -- the mind of God; but that, along with our own minds (spiritual substances), remained as inaccessible, Hume was presently to show, as was Locke's material substance. Matter Berkeley dismissed as an abstract idea, and as all ideas are now seen to be particular, the existence of the abstract is denied. But the particulars are mere sense impressions which appear in bare succession, and under the scalpel of Hume's analysis universality and necessity cannot be found among them. They are reduced to constant conjunction and customary expectation, while morality becomes subjective sentiment and religion dubious belief.

This brief section on Empiricism in the Encyclopaedia is also astonishingly prophetic, for what Hegel says here applies as aptly to contemporary, 20th Century Empiricism as to that of the 17th and 18th centuries. That perhaps should not greatly surprise us, for Empiricism, wherever it raises its head displays the same physiognomy. Its main characteristics, as apparent today as they were to Hegel, are positivism, the demand that sense-perception be taken as the sole measure of meaning and truth, radical pluralism, analysis without synthesis, and a strong tendency to materialism. The proscription of metaphysics explicit in Hume[3] was renewed by the Logical Positivists of the Vienna Circle. Their enunciation of the Verification Principle, that no statement has factual significance unless it can be verified by direct sensuous observation, reaffirmed, as the source and basis of our knowledge of the world, the immediacy of sense. Physicalism, the reduction of all factual discourse to material object language and eventually to statements of physical science, was their ideal, a materialism which persists ever more openly and undisguisedly today in the philosophies of J.J.C. Smart, D.M. Armstrong, George Pitcher and the like. Analysis is the very name currently adopted by Empiricist philosophy, a natural consequence of its origins in the Logical Atomism of Bertrand Russell, reiterated in the Tractatus Logico-Philosophicus of Wittgenstein, and, despite more recent disclaimers, surreptitiously presupposed in analytic philosophy right up to the present day. The doctrine reflects the radical pluralism maintained by Russell in Our Knowledge of the External World and is echoed by A.J. Ayer in The Problem of Knowledge.[4] It is, moreover, a metaphysical doctrine, as later analysts have come to recognize,[5] bearing out Hegel's allegation that the empiricists' renunciation of metaphysics is belied by their own doctrine.

Contemporary Empiricism, both in its logic and in its metaphysics (latent or overt) analyses everything down to bare particulars, represented in protocol sentences by primitive terms, the replacements for the variables a, b, c, in the language of symbolic logic. But the universal is lost. If ever admitted it is only as an abstract notion, more usually a class, or a set of particulars, or a general term, a mere name for such a class or set referring indifferently to any of its members. Most empiricists are at heart nominalists, even when they profess otherwise. Closely akin to this analysing, atomizing tendency is the current zeal in both science and philosophy of science for 'reductionism'. Thus Empiricism now, as in the past,

Hat die Teile in ihrer Hand,
Fehlt leider nur das geistige Band.[6]

The missing bond is the principle of wholeness which Empiricism cannot admit. It recognizes only collections and fortuitous ones at that, for it can discover no necessary connexions between sensible particulars, the sole source of its knowledge. It finds at most constant conjunctions which can never justify universal judgements, for no universal conclusions follow validly from particular premisses. In its logic, therefore, necessity is reduced to tautology and all deduction is purely analytic. But empirical science seeks and requires universal laws which are more than statements of merely contingent conjunctions and are not tautologies devoid of factual content. They must be both necessary and synthetic and can be stated only as synthetic judgements a priori, which strict Empiricism excludes.

It was Kant who first drew attention to this truth, and to Kant's philosophy Hegel turns in the next section; but he still alligns Kant with the Empiricists as an example of the second attitude to objectivity, because Kant, he avers, never succeeded in emancipating himself fully from the strictures of the understanding. Kant insists to the end that the only acceptable content of 'objective' knowledge can be empirical, sensuously given material, and that metaphysics as a constitutive science is not possible. Thus he persists in confining knowledge to 'experience', the sphere of the finite; and for him, as for Berkeley and Hume, it remains incurably subjective, despite his search for, and in large measure his success in finding, criteria of objectivity.

The Critical Philosophy[7]

Hegel recognized very clearly that the philosophy of Kant represented the watershed between the earlier 'dogmatisms' of Rationalism and Empiricism and the speculative construction of his own system.[8] He commends Kant for his advance on the former, but criticizes him for stopping short at what is at best a half-way station. There can be no doubt of the paramount importance of the Critical Philosophy as the turning point in the development of modern thought; and one is inclined to feel that Hegel failed to give Kant sufficient credit for his stupendous discoveries that 'objects conform to concepts'[9] and that without the spontaneous synthetic activity of 'our faculty of cognition (Erkenntnisvermögen)' no experience of objects is possible. But Hegel did not really underestimate this achievement, and he praises Kant unstintingly in the Greater Logic for what amounts to precisely this advance. Yet he was also aware of the cramping and restrictive effects of Kant's subjectivism, which Fichte had pressed to an extreme, and which Hegel was, above all, anxious to counteract. He is, therefore, unsparing in his criticism of those features of Kant's philosophy which he believed to be regressive. And just because Kant was so influential in Hegel's day, and because he himself owed so much to Kant, Hegel felt acutely the need to point out and to overcome Kant's shortcomings. It is presumably for this reason that Professor Charles Taylor has formed the impression that Hegel is always eager, as he puts it, 'to take a swipe at Kant'. It would, however, be wrong and unfair to conclude that Hegel's criticism is either vindictive or gratuitous, whether of Kant or of Fichte,[10] and was not directed to issues essential to the development of his own position.

Hegel begins by applauding Kant for his refusal to go along with Hume and to abandon universality and necessity, and for insisting that

63

these are as essential to experience as the sensuously apprehended particulars. He applauds him likewise for his discovery of the immanence of concepts in all experience, and in particular for recognizing the self-conscious ego as the source of conceptual synthesis. He commends further Kant's critique of the older dogmatic metaphysics in its attempt to comprehend the infinite under finite categories of the understanding. He credits Kant also with an awareness, if only a dim one, of the structure of the Idea at every level of thinking and being, so that in the Critique of Judgement he all but recognizes the actuality of the rational.

Kant was right to question the presuppositions of the old metaphysics (for free, philosophical, thought does not proceed on unexamined assumptions), and to make the categories of the understanding the central object of his investigation. He made the mistake, however, of thinking that one could investigate the principles of thought prior to using them, as if one could learn to swim without venturing into the water. Thinking and its categories, Hegel tells us, are at once both object and the activity which examines it. They must criticize themselves. Thinking is a self-critical, self-developing dialectic, not the imposition from without of critical standards upon knowledge, but the self-examination of consciousness, in which the principles of criticism are already immanent (innewohnend) 11.

Another fault in Kant's procedure is that he makes the question primary whether or not our experience, even as organized under the categories, is subjective. In contrast with the common notion of objectivity, he rightly identified it with universality and necessity and not with what is presented to the senses. The reproach against Kant of confusion of language in this regard is therefore unjust. But Kant went further and asserted that objective (scientific) knowledge, being dependent on our thought, was for that reason only subjective as opposed to things in themselves.

In effect, Kant's advance was to realize that the distinction between subjective and objective is one made within experience, according to the nature of its content and not with reference to its externality or internality to consciousness. It is subjective if the content is fortuitous and contingent, fleeting and arbitrarily changeable, idiosyncratic and capricious. It is objective if firm and constant, universal and necessary. The notion of an external reality beyond the content of consciousness, however, proves meaningless. An unknowable thing in itself is a mere abstraction -- a caput mortuum,12 Hegel derisively calls it -- and is no less a thought and a content of consciousness than anything else. So, for Kant, it becomes a noumenon, a product of νοῦς, of the mind. What he calls objective knowledge, meanwhile, is only of phenomena, of things as they appear to us, and so in the end is only subjective. Likewise the ideas of reason are downgraded by Kant to mere illusions, as Hegel says, Hirngespinste, factitious products resulting from the attempt to apply the categories to things in themselves. At the other end of the scale, the reputed effects on our senses of things in themselves, the manifold of sensation, is itself the most subjective level of all experience. In consequence, Kant's theory is a thorough-going subjective idealism, and this is Hegel's main objection to it.

Objective idealism, on the other hand, what Hegel himself advocates, insists on the reality and self-externalization (Aussersichsein) of the Idea, as Nature and finite Spirit. It is thus at once realistic, objective (both in Kant's and in the ordinarily accepted sense) and also idealistic, in that the ultimate and essential reality for it is spirit.

Another major objection that Hegel raises against Kant is that he fails to deduce the categories from the transcendental unity of apperception in which he finds their origin. He simply takes them over from the classification of judgements in the traditional formal logic, which, as he puts it, finds them 'empirically given'. It is Fichte, Hegel points out, to whom we owe the insight that the categories must be deducible as the necessary outcome of the self-identity of the knowing subject.

Hegel's appreciation of Kant's major advance in epistemology is apparent from the Zusatz to Section 42. Sensation and perception present us with a manifold, a diversity in which nothing has sense or identifiable character except by reference to something else, by reference away from itself ('now' to 'before' and 'after', 'red' to 'yellow' and 'blue'). The ego, on the other hand, is the point of self-identity to which all this diversity is to be related if it is to be apprehended in experience. It is the crucible in which the plurality of sense is fused into a unity. This, says Hegel, is the essential nature of knowledge. It is the endeavour to appropriate the diverse materials of the world, to subdue them and make them our own, by understanding them as a single system. The reality of the world, he says, must be pulverized and fused (Zerquetscht) -- that is, idealized.

Of this idealization we shall have more to say later. For the present we may observe that it corresponds to what Kant calls synthesis. But Hegel here asserts that it is not, as Kant maintains, merely the subjective activity of our finite consciousness. 'This identity is much more the Absolute, the truth itself. It is as if the grace of the Absolute is to allow the individual things to indulge themselves, and this itself drives them back to the absolute unity.' Into these two obscure and bewildering sentences a wealth of meaning is compressed. Hegel is not denying but rather endorsing Kant's argument that consciousness, by relating every item and nuance of its content to the 'I think', synthesizes and unites its experience into a single systematic whole. But the point for Hegel is that the ego is the epitomization of the world, the immanent universal which, through Nature, has brought itself to consciousness and is realizing itself as the awareness of the whole (die absolute Einheit). This drive to unified self-awareness is what constitutes the spontaneous activity of the faculty of cognition in its impulse to synthesize its sensuous data. It is because the world is a unity of diverse individual things ranged in gradations of wholeness that each individual is what it is. Each thing is determined by its relations to and interaction with others and with the whole, and this is eminently true of individual minds. In virtue of this very interdependence of individual beings, the whole is one, and the principle of unity expresses and specifies itself in each and all of them; and through each of them exerts a nisus to more complete self-sufficiency. Thus, by the grace of the Absolute, individual things are permitted to express themselves, and by so doing to express likewise, and to realize more fully, the universal principle which is ultimately the Absolute itself.

The individuations, or specifications, of the universal principle are the phases of its self-development, and our minds with their consciousness constitute one such phase. These individuations, moreover, are indispensable to the whole and to its self-realization, which must therefore allow each individual to 'enjoy' and assert itself. But in the course of the dialectical development, in which every individual is immersed, it is led back to the absolute totality as the transcendent unity in which all live and move and have their being. Our thinking, our awareness of the world, as it is derived from our sentient reaction to it through the relation of the manifold of sense to the unifying activity of the self-conscious subject, our entire conscious personality, is the expression of the whole immanent in us and impelling each one of us to fuller unification and wholeness. It proceeds through the community of selves and the expansion of self-consciousness, to an atonement with the whole which is transcendent as well as immanent. This conception provides the key both to the value of the individual and to its self-transcendence in relating itself to, finding its reality in, union with the Absolute -- what religion calls atonement with God.

Kant's transcendantal ego, therefore, is just one phase of the dialectical development, which, in the account he gives of it, is taken in isolation from the whole series, and so out of context. What he tells us about its cognitive synthesis in the transcendental deduction is true and of major importance; it is, in fact, an epoch making advance upon his predecessors. But it has to be seen at its proper dialectical level and in its distinctive relation both to the external world, which is the truth only implicitly, and to the Absolute whole, which is the truth in and for itself.

Hegel criticises, further, Kant's allegation that the categories are empty of content, apart from what comes from sense-perception. Certainly they are not given in sense. The substantive unity of an object, which cements together its various sensible qualities is not perceived, nor is the necessary connexion between cause and effect.

These are concepts, but not, Hegel insists, for that reason either empty or merely subjective. The categories have a content of their own, though not a sensibly intuitable one, and that, Hegel avers, is to their advantage rather than the reverse. They are, like the Idea of which they are differentiations, abstract only in the sense that they are the ideal structure of which Nature and concrete Spirit form the embodiment; not in the sense that they provide a pure form for which the filling must be supplied from without.

More accurately, the categories are the real or essential content of the sensuous manifold, and they contain their particulars within them as the aufgehobene phases from which they have developed. For it is equally true that the categories and the idea they constitute develop out of nature through the activity of finite minds, and this circularity of the dialectic is due to the nature of the whole. What is implicit (an sich) in the external world becomes explicit (für sich) in consciousness and explicates itself in categorical forms. As the mind becomes aware of that truth, it sees Nature as the self-expression (or self-externalization) of the Idea. The development of the abstract concept in thought, as we shall see demonstrated in the Logic, explicates from itself the objective world.

In the Dialectic of Pure Reason,[13] Kant demonstrates that the attempt to apply the categories of the understanding to things in themselves leads to contradiction. Hegel agrees, for the thing in itself is the unconditioned, which is the Absolute, and the categories of the understanding are finite categories by which the Absolute cannot be determined. The Absolute cannot be presented to sense-perception (Wahrnehmung), and is not a phenomenon. But the finite categories of the understanding apply only to phenomena. Kant, however, treats the thing in itself in abstraction from determination of every kind; and so it becomes a completely empty notion. One wonders, Hegel asks, why it should be so persistently alleged that we cannot know what the thing is in itself, for nothing is easier than to recognize it as an empty abstraction.

It is reason, the faculty of the unconditioned or infinite, that discovers the conditioned and merely phenomenal status of sense-experience. But, Hegel points out, the unconditioned or infinite is in fact nothing other than what is equal to itself (Sich-selbst-Gleiche), precisely what the original self-identity of the ego is. This, in Hegel's dialectic, turns out to be the Concept; and when we see this as the unconditioned, we see also that the presentations of sense are, by comparison, mere appearances. It is to Kant's credit that he drew attention to this distinction and to the finiteness of the understanding and its categories. His error lies in his refusal to permit progress beyond this negative result, and in regarding the object of reason as an abstract unconditioned whose identity excludes all difference. It then becomes just another finite, what lies beyond the empirical finite, a

67

mere 'ought to be' which is not. The infinite is not merely transcendent; it holds the finite absorbed (aufgehoben) in itself.

Kant, of course, is not wholly consistent in his exclusion of difference from the unconditioned. He maintains, for instance, that the unity of apperception is an analytic unity, 'I = I', but also that we become aware of it only through our apprehension of the unity of our diversified experience. 'Only in so far, therefore, as I can unite a manifold of given representations in one consciousness, is it possible for me to represent to myself the identity of the consciousness in these representations.'[14] The three ideas of reason, the soul, the world and God, exclude difference so far as they are purely noumenal and may not be brought under the categories. But their content, ultimately, (even for Kant) culminates in the Ideal of Pure Reason, which contains all possible conditions and is 'the supreme and complete material condition of the possibility of all that exists'.[15] Nevertheless, this ideal is never realized in experience and remains only a regulative idea, what ought to be but never is.

According to Kant it is in metaphysics that the attempt is made to apply the categories to the unconditioned, first to the soul, then to the world, and lastly to God. In the first case, the metaphysical argument that the soul is simple, a self-identical substance separate from and opposed to matter, is a series of paralogisms in which the term soul (or self) is used in different senses in different premises, because the predicates can apply only to the self as a phenomenon, intuited in inner sense, and not to the thing in itself, which the metaphysic professes to determine. Hegel approves of the criticism that the predicates are inappropriate to the soul; but this is not, he says, because they overstep their legitimate limits, but because the soul is a living, active being, just as complex as it is self-identically simple. In fact, its simplicity is just its indivisible wholeness, but that is constituted solely by the cohesion and inseparability of its diverse traits, aspects and activities. Kant's objections are valid, but his reasons are the wrong ones.

When Rational Cosmology applies the categories to the world as a whole it falls into inevitable antinomies. This Kant tells us, is because the categories apply only to phenomena and not to things in themselves. Hegel says that what the antinomies prove is that the body of cosmical fact, descriptions of which fall into contradiction, is only appearance, and that every finite actuality contains in itself opposing characteristics and can be rightly cognized only as a unity of opposite determinations. This is true not only in the four cases given by Kant, but at all levels of reality and in all concepts. But Kant attributes the contradiction to reason and regards it as a mark of reason's failure to comprehend its supposed object, drawing a merely negative conclusion and missing the true signficance of the advance he has made on the older metaphysic, which always tried to keep opposing predicates separate and to apply each to the exclusion of the other, a separation in which neither had any validity.[16]

Hegel's treatment in Sections 50 and 51 of Kant's criticism of Rational Theology is somewhat general, although, and perhaps because, he returns to it frequently elsewhere.[17] There is, moreover, no need either for him or for us to repeat what was said in discussion of the older metaphysic about the proofs of God's existence. The two moments, whose unification is sought by the understanding as the 'ideal of reason', are pure abstract identity (here called concept) and equally abstract 'being', thought of as mere determinateness. Meanwhile God is conceived as the sum of all realities, which is understood as excluding all determination (what the understanding sees as sheer limitation) and so as the 'unconditioned'. If one proceeds from abstract being to abstract thought, the proof is the Cosmological or the Teleological, moving from the world taken, in the first case, as a collection of contingent things, or, in the second case, as a purposive arrangement of such things, to God thought of as a rational mind which is Being, stripped of its individuality and contingency and become universal and in itself necessary: and this God is regarded, further, as acting and determining himself in accordance with all rational purposes.

This process Hegel represents as that of thought, from the particular to the universal, the legitimacy of which Kant, following Hume's lead, denies. But such denial, Hegel says, is nothing other than a prohibition against thinking. As man is essentially a thinking being, the tendency characteristic of his mind is to rise from the empirical appearances of the world to God, its universal and necessary rationale, and that, he says, is what the proofs of God's existence actually represent. Their formal inadequacy is the result of the finite syllogistic type of argument offered by the understanding. But when we realize that dialectical thinking transforms its starting point as it proceeds, and that its conclusion sublates its own mediation, gathering up into itself the process by which it has been achieved, a conception of God is attained which is no longer abstract, but is the concrete whole in its eternal activity of generating itself out of, or specifying itself into, its own finite moments, which are then (and only then) seen as such, and as, in themselves, no better than appearances.[18]

Finally Hegel protests that mere existence is the poorest of predicates (Kant, himself said it was not a predicate at all) and to prove that it attaches to God is virtually to say nothing about him at all to the point. Finite things exist in space and time, but God does not; rather it is the spatio-temporal phenomena that exist in him. We neither can nor should wish to prove that God exists as a phenomenon, in the way finite things exist.

Here, as in the Greater Logic,[19] Hegel is scathing in his comments on Kant's use of the example of the idea of a hundred dollars as an analogy to the idea of God in the Ontological Proof. There is no analogy between a finite, imaginal notion such as the former and the infinite Idea. The first, to be real requires specific relationships to other finites (my fortune and my purse, for instance, as well as countless other relevant circumstantial conditions); but the totality of this network of finite conditions is grounded in an unique and integrated system, transcendent beyond as well as immanent in all of them. It is to this we refer when we speak of God, and it is this which is concretely real (and must be so conceived) in the sense described above, namely, that it develops out of and sublates within it all finite moments.[20]

The essential point is that God is the Truth, which is the whole; and that, we have said, is a result, which enfolds and encompasses the entire process through which it has been engendered, and in which it has disposed itself as its own self-differentiation. God is Absolute Spirit, in and for himself, the realized Idea or concrete universal, holding all its particulars within itself. This is the essence and the very being of everything that is, in which and through which all things are and are conceived. To speak of its non-existence is therefore wildly nonsensical (the underlying truth of the Ontological proof); but to speak of God's existence is equally inadequate to the fulness of his reality. The Absolute is immanent in all things, and every finite entity and concept develops through its dialectic into the totality of Absolute Spirit (the truth underlying the Cosmological and the Teleological proofs); but the leap from the finite to the infinite is illegitimate, unless this process is grasped in its true form and traced through its continuously growing elaboration, and unless the final outcome is rightly conceived as sublating the entire process.

In Section 50 we are reminded that the world does not consist merely of contingent existents (as is presupposed in the Cosmological proof), and that to conceive it so, and then to use the conception as the premiss for a proof of the existence of God, is far from appropriate. The world has to be seen as an organic whole, as Hegel states it to be in his Naturphilosophie; it includes living and purposive beings in an environment to which they are organically related. It is thus intrinsically teleological -- not in the childish sense that natural beings are designed to serve human purposes, but as tending in its processes to realize the whole which is immanent in the parts. From Nature so conceived, as Hegel shows in detail in the Naturphilosophie and the Philosophie des Geistes (though here in the Logic he is only obscurely allusive), mind, consciousness and self-consciousness emerge, and we rise to the sphere of Spirit, which is the proper starting-point (so far as thought requires a starting-point) from which to approach the concept of God, who is essentially spirit, essentially the awareness of his own infinity and all-inclusiveness.

It is on such grounds that Hegel raises objection to the common misinterpretation of Spinozism as Pantheism, or even as Atheism.

70

These misinterpretations, he tells us, spring from the incapacity of the understanding to imagine that a philosopher could deny the reality of the finite world, which Spinoza does, in effect, by making it derivative from the unity of Thought and Extension (material existence). This unity is, for him, Substance or God, through which all finite things are conceived. Common sense finds it easier, Hegel says, to deny the existence of God, and then fathers this denial on Spinoza, who, on the contrary, declares that everything is God and that God alone exists in the full sense of that word.

Kant, because he failed to recognize the validity of anything beyond the categories of the understanding, reduces reason merely to the assertion of abstract identity. He leaves it no better than a regulative function in knowledge. For him it is a canon and not an organon of truth. It has no valid constitutive or constructive function. Hegel is about to show that reason, by resolving and sublating the contradictions of the reflective understanding, does in fact reveal itself as the constitutive and self-constituted truth -- the absolute Idea, which is the eternally self-specified and ever self-specifying concept. This is the substantive theme of the whole of the Logic.

Practical Reason, conceived as the self-determining rational will, reaffirms the automony which for Theoretical Reason had been abrogated. But, alas, it is left contentless. It is alleged to determine an objective law, but this law is only to will the good, and provides no answer to the question what the good is. The rule that the will should not contradict itself does no more than repeat the principle of abstract identity and consistency, and the net result is only to set the deter- minacy of empirical nature (and the natural self) in irreconcilable opposition to the free self-determination of the rational will. Never- theless, Hegel rates highly Kant's restoration of the notion of an objective moral law as against the current eudaemonism, which he says opened the door to every whim and caprice suggested by inclination.

In the Third Critique Kant comes nearest to recognizing the true character of the Idea, as the universal determined and determining in itself -- i.e., as concrete. Here too the identity of subject and object in purpose is foreshadowed, an identity displayed in art and in organic nature. But in the end Kant draws back from the acknowledgement that teleological judgement can encompass the truth; and it remains merely a regulative idea finally and unrelentingly subjective.

In Section 60 Hegel sums up his criticism of Kant with the famous objection to the Critical Philosophy that it in effect contradicts itself when it assigns to reason the sole function of limiting the understanding. It declares that objective knowledge is confined to phenomena and fails to see that knowledge of the limit can only be acquired from a viewpoint which is already beyond the limit. Things without consciousness, Hegel points out, are limited but are not aware

71

of the fact; only we are aware of it. A limit can be cognized only by a consciousness from a point of vantage beyond the limit. The negation imposed by limitation generates a contradiction with the limiting other, and both moments of the opposition must be comprehended by the subject of consciousness. Consequently that subject cannot be restricted only to one of them. At the level of feeling the contradiction is registered as pain -- the privilege, Hegel says, of living things. At the level of awareness it is negativity, the motive force of self-transcendence and the finger-post pointing to the true infinite.

The Kantian philosophy is plagued by dualisms: analytic and synthetic judgements, a priori and a posteriori knowledge, intuition and conception, understanding and reason, the elements of which it holds apart while declaring them to be inseparable. It vacillates between the extremes of the antitheses, indicating that neither is viable by itself, yet refusing to allow either to overstep the demarcation between them. Kant retains and preserves intact the main metaphysical tenets of Empiricism, while he tries desperately to clamp on to it the freedom of self-determining rationality, which he affirms in common with Rationalism. But the latter is bereft of content and the two refuse to unite in his thought.

Hegel ends his discussion of the Critical Philosophy with a note on Fichte's advance on Kant. Fichte saw the need for a genuine deduction of the categories and essayed to provide one, beginning from the self-identity of the self-conscious ego, which, though alleged to be free, spontaneous, self-determining activity, is not genuinely so, because it is held to need the stimulus of an external and unaccountable shock or impulse (Anstoss) against which to react in order to become aware of itself as limited by a non-ego. This Anstoss, Hegel perspicaciously remarks, replaces the Kantian Ding an sich. The activity of the ego thus excited is a continual striving to overcome the antithesis to the non-ego and to free itself from the Anstoss, but is a striving which never succeeds. If it could succeed it would destroy itself, for its whole being is nothing other than its activity; hence the subjection of its opposite would be the extinction of itself. Fichte's conclusion, therefore, is none other than Kant's; that knowledge is restricted to the finite and is for ever transcended by the infinite; and the content of experience, which the activity of the ego generates in its efforts to overcome its opposition to the non-ego, is simply the common content of experience with the persistent stigma of mere appearance.

NOTES: Book I, Part II, Chapter 3

1. Enz., Sections 37-39.

2. Cf. Enz., Section 266, footnote, and Section 270.

3. Cf. the concluding passage of An Enquiry into Human Understanding.

4. Penguin Books, Harmondsworth, 1956; cf. p. 29: 'It is a logical truism that if two states of affairs are distinct, a statement that refers to only one of them does not entail anything about the other.' Compare this with Hume, Treatise, Bk. I, Pt. I, Sect. vii, loc. cit.

5. Cf. J.O. Urmson, Philosophical Analysis (Oxford, 1958), p. 53, and G.J. Warnock, English Philosophy since 1900 (Oxford, 1958), p. 41f.; L. Wittgenstein, Philosophical Investigations, Blackwell (Oxford, 1958).

6. 'Has the parts in its hand but lacks, alas, only the spiritual bond.' The quotation is from Goethe's Faust.

7. Sections 40-60.

8. Cf. the footnote to p. 59 (in Suhrkamp) in the Introduction to Wissenschaft der Logik; Miller's translation, p. 61.

9. Kritik der reinen Vernunft, B xvii.

10. Cf. Differenz des Fichte'schen und Schelling'schen Systems der Philosophie (commonly referred to as Differenzschrift). Hegel's criticism of Fichte is less fair in Glauben und Wissen. Both these works have been translated by Walter Cerf and H.S. Harris (State University of New York Press 1977).

11. Cf. Phänomenologie, Preface.

12. In fact, the thing in itself, the death's head in Kant's epistemology, is the decayed relic of Locke's idea of substance.

13. Cf. Enz., Sections 44 et seq.

14. Kritik der reinen Vernunft, B 133.

15. Op. cit., A 576, B 604.

16. Hegel raises further objections to Kant's demonstrations in the Antinomies of the opposite theses, on the ground mainly of petitio principii. But this criticism is purely formal and adds little to the main points concerning the abstractions of the old metaphysics and the relation between the understanding and reason.

17. Cf. W.L., Erste Teil, Istes Buch, Kap. I An., 1, and Vorlesungen über Religionsphilosophie, 1831.

18.   Cf. Vorlesungen über Religionsphilophie, 1831; and my Atheism &
Theism, Ch. IV.

19.   Cf. loc. cit.

20.   Cf. my papers, 'Mr. Ryle and the Ontological Argument', Mind
XLV N.S., 1936, and 'The Categorical Universal' in Critical Essays on
the Philosophy of R.G. Collingwood, ed. Michael Krausz (Oxford, 1972).

Chapter 4

Third Attitude to Objectivity

Immediate Knowledge[1]

Kant had said that he 'found it necessary to annul reason in order to make room for faith'. But he recognized that reason had some role to play in knowledge, though he denied the objective validity of its ideas. Scientific knowledge he limited to the understanding; and this, Jacobi thought, was the ultimate terminus of the capability of thought, which could never go beyond phenomena or grasp the ultimate truth. Only faith or intuition could do that. For Kant, faith was not knowledge, because it went beyond the understanding and reason, and gave credence to objects (freedom, immortality and God) which they could not comprehend. But Jacobi acclaimed faith as the highest form of cognition and gave it the place that Kant had reserved for reason. So what Jacobi calls 'concepts' are the Kantian categories, restricted to knowledge of the finite. Any attempt to grasp by their means the infinite and unconditioned converts it to a finite object and perverts the truth.

Jacobi, according to Hegel, had in mind the successes of the natural and mathematical sciences when he spoke of knowledge. This is the only proper sphere of the understanding and its categories, and they give us nothing but mediate knowledge -- explanation of one thing in terms of another. They can never reach the infinite nor bridge the gap between it and the finite. But the real truth is of God, and this can be reached only by the immediate intuition of fatih. If reason is what men live by, and reason is the knowledge of the truth, then reason must be immediate knowledge identical with faith. But strictly what Jacobi recognizes as knowledge is only science, and faith is not discursive knowledge at all.

For treating the categories, in their own right and according to their content, as what they essentially are -- finite, Hegel approves Jacobi. Kant had limited them to the finite merely because of their subjectivity, whereas Jacobi sees their finitude in their subject-matter. On the other hand, Hegel complains, Jacobi and his followers use terms such as 'knowledge', 'faith', 'intuition', 'thought', arbitrarily and in uncritical ways guided at best by empirical psychology. They qualify intuition as intellectual while opposing it to thought, and yet assign to it objects which cannot but be objects of thought; for example, Eternity, God, and the transcendental ego. Further, they claim certainty for intuition which stamps it undeniably as knowledge, from which, however, they seek to distinguish it. At the same time Jacobi includes the animal faith we place in sense perception with the faith that comprehends the ultimate truth, confusing sense-certainty with concrete intellectual assurance. The most important confusions to

75

which Hegel draws attention, however, and those which are the most dangerous, are, first, that between personal conviction, on the one hand, faith in and intuition of an immediate revelation to the individual, and, on the other, faith in a systematic doctrine taught and backed by the authority of an organized Church (Section 63). Secondly, there is the difference between the immediacy of all awareness and the immediacy consisting in lack of derivation and discursive process.

A developed religion, Christianity especially, is a doctrine worked out through a long tradition with a complex history of reflection and criticism stretching back for centuries. It has a definite structure resting on a profound philosophical base. Faith in the teachings of a church or organized religion of this sort is not just individual caprice but is based in part on the authority of those best qualified to know, and in part on systematic thinking about ultimate issues. In contrast, the blind conviction of persons which is sometimes claimed to be 'divine guidance' is vague and indefinite, unsystematic and unsupported by grounds, imperfectly articulated and unreliable. It may as easily be unrecognized (and even immoral) wish-fulfilment prompted by repressed and unconscious desires, or even sheer stupidity and ignorance, as anything genuinely true and holy. Yet Jacobi is disposed (if somewhat vaguely) to approve indiscriminately of such uncritical belief. In fact, the word 'faith' is so vaguely used that its advocates tend to include under it everything frequently attributed to common sense, inspiration, the heart's inner conviction, innate truths, and whatever else capricious temperament is prompted to suggest.

Moreover, immediate intuition so-called, the blind hunches which many claim as inspired, can embrace all sorts of beliefs, and every religion can appeal to them equally for support, the most primitive and barbarous, as well as the most sophisticated and humane. Thus the deliverances of such 'intuition' may well be, if the term is taken generally to cover all such claims, quite incompatible one with another; and if intuition is taken as the supreme source of truth, no criterion is left by which to decide between conflicting claims.

But if by 'faith' no more is meant than firm conviction in the existence of God, or belief in the reality of what we imagine about the infinite and eternal, there need be no real conflict between philosophy and intuition, for the chief aim of philosophy is to demonstrate the unity, as truth, of thought and being, and to grasp the nature of Absolute Spirit as self-mediating and as concretely holding within itself (aufhebend) its own mediation. We may remind ourselves that Fichte and Schelling identified speculative philosophy with intellectual intuition.

This intuition takes two forms: the cogito ergo sum of Descartes, and the Ontological Proof of the existence of God. Neither of these is really a transition from premisses to conclusion. Descartes himself,

76

and also Spinoza on his behalf,[2] denies that cogito ergo sum is a syllogism. If it were, the major premiss would have to be derived from the conclusion, for 'illud omne quod cogitat est, sive existit' is known only as a consequence of 'cogito ergo sum' and is not the precondition of our conviction of the latter.

The Ontological argument similarly cannot properly be stated syllogistically, because 'Whatever is infinite exists necessarily', the ostensible major premiss, is equally the conclusion. Spinoza's first proof in the Short Treatise concerning God, Man and Human Wellbeing makes this apparent:

> Everything that we clearly and distinctly understand as belonging to the nature of a thing we can absolutely assert of it with truth. But that existence belongs to the nature of God we can clearly and distinctly understand. Ergo...[3]

Thus the awareness of my own existence and of that of the Absolute is intuitive, but it is also discursive, for each of these cognitions is an affirmation of a nexus between moments,[4] between being and thought at the very least, and in the case of God it is a nexus between the universal and the particularization necessarily involved in its infinite activity -- that activity without which it is not concretely universal.

So Hegel declares (as he undertakes to demonstrate in the second part of the Logic -- the Doctrine of Essence) that all objects of thought, and in fact all things, are at once both mediate and immediate. What is mediated is the result of process. It is reached, or brought into being, by the mediation of something else, whether the process be causal or organic natural process, or a discursus in thought. But the result sublates the mediation. In it the mediation is contained yet cancelled, aufgehoben (in Wallace's translation, it 'vanishes'), and the outcome is accordingly immediate. This interdependence of immediacy and mediation is evident in the most diverse subjects:

(1) In thought, the moments into which every concrete concept differentiates itself display themselves as rudiments, or premisses, the origins from which the concept is derived and by which it is mediated. But, strictly speaking, they are abstracta which cannot exist (or genuinely be thought) in isolation. In mutual independence they are strictly nothing, and if they are so regarded they contradict themselves and are unstable, reverting into their opposites. In abstraction each is a falsification and a negation of the whole of which they are moments. They are definite and can be maintained, either each in its own self-identity, or together in mutual contrast, only within the whole concrete concept. Only there are they really intelligible. So the concrete concept is the immediate whole, in which the moments are 'intuitively' cognized, although it is also mediated by them. They are its self-differentiation, which is indispensable to its concrete nature. This will

become clearer and will be more fully established in the first triad of the Logic, and is adumbrated here, in Section 70, only provisionally as always in the Introduction.

What Hegel wishes to stress is that all experience is at once immediate -- at least so far as it is immediately present to consciousness -- and at the same time mediate or discursive -- insofar as it as always diversified. There are no 'simple natures' such as Descartes, and also Aristotle, postulated. Whatever is conceivable or perceptible is complex and articulated and is grasped as the interplay of distinct though inseparable elements. This is true even of percepts that are vague and confused, for to be perceived at all the object must be to some extent variegated and must contrast with a background. In this interplay of elements we have mediation though the whole is apprehended immediately without ratiocination. The entire course of the Logic demonstrates this point and reiterates regularly the alternation of mediacy and immediacy.

(2) In nature, every developing thing includes and incorporates in its developed form all the phases of its generation. Hegel refers here to the generation of the human organism, and contemporary biology gives us an account of ontogenesis that offers us better evidence than was available to him of the truth that he is trying to drive home. The adult organism is mediated by the process of its development from the germplasm. Yet everything which that process involves, from the genetic code in the chromosomes (derived differentially from the parents), by way of segmentation of cells, specialization of tissues, and differentation of organs, right up to the final phase, is immediately present in the full-grown animal, aufgehoben, embodied in and intrinsic to its being; or, as we say, is inherent in it. The mature organism is an immediate, existent whole, which has sublated the mediation of its embryogenesis.

(3) The third example, which Hegel elaborates in Section 66, is that of expertise. The skilled scientist or technician has 'at his finger tips' and can produce 'from the top of his head', without hesitation or deliberation, the results of long training and practice. He can produce them immediately, either verbally or practically, without having to repeat the processes by which he acquired his knowledge and his skill. Yet this process is both necessary to and sublated in his performance, which would be impossible without it.

Practical skills are further cases in point. When acquired they can be activated immediately, but without learning and practice they cannot be performed at all. In learning the process is sublated in the product. As Hegel says, the acquired knowledge in practical activity is present immediately in the very limbs of the practitioner. Consider the skill of an athlete, a tennis player, or a pianist. It is something acquired by long and arduous practice, and so is mediated. But once it has been learned it can be brought to bear as a whole in an infinite variety of unprecedented situations, immediately, without hesitation, reflection or deliberation. According to Aristotle, all virtue is of this character -- a habit acquired by practice and performed immediately as required on the appropriate occasions. Hegel's example, 'that I am in Berlin' is somewhat cryptic, but it no less apt. I know where I am at any moment immediately and without consideration; but only because I am tacitly aware of how I got here, and my awareness is mediated by my acquired knowledge of the town or terrain, my familiarity with my surroundings and their orientation. My consciousness of my whereabouts is a mediated immediacy in which a mass of diverse information is aufgehoben.

We have, in Section 67, a number of penetrating comments on the alleged presence of innate ideas in the mind, on 'sound common sense' and 'natural reason', as all really instances of immediate awareness of implicitly mediating connexions. Plato's doctrine of reminiscence Hegel interprets as a figurative representation of the fact that we grasp the universal immediately from our experience of the particulars, in which it is implicit and by which our 'reminiscence' is mediated. Aristotle's doctrine of ἐπαγωγή is to the same effect: that repeated experience of the particulars enables us to grasp intuitively the universal which they exemplify. The same truth is vaguely half understood in the empiricist theory of induction -- only half understood, because the universality is there denied and debased to a mere frequency of conjunction.

These penetrating insights seem to have been altogether overlooked by Gotthard Günther[5] in his criticism of Hegel for reintroducing immediacy as characteristic of the third attitude to objectivity. Günther alleges that once we have passed to the second attitude, in which the object has become subject-object, we cannot recover the externality attributed to the object in the first attitude. When we come to see objectivity as dependent on universality of thought (and not just on the 'publicity' of the external observable), he maintains, we see it as 'absolutely mediated'. What Hegel makes clear, however, is that the apparent ('publicly observable') immediacy of the perceived object is itself tacitly mediated; that perception itself is a sort of concealed thinking, and that this same 'immediacy' of observation reasserts itself, completely assimilating mediacy, wherever skill or expertise is acquired. For perception itself is a kind of skill (Gilbert Ryle calls it an achievement) which, as contemporary psychologists agree, has to be learned;[6] and every form of knowledge is expertise. Hegel, therefore, is not mistaken. The third phase of knowledge, later explicated fully in the Doctrine of the Concept, is at once both mediate and immediate, but its immediacy is no longer naive but has its mediation aufgehoben within it, and it is foreshadowed in the syntheses of every triad in the dialectic.

79

Günther's conflation of the third attitude to objectivity with the third subdivision of the Logic is, as already mentioned, suspect; for Hegel, under the former heading is dealing with intuitionism, not the Concept; and the defects and disadvantages of that theory are precisely due to its oversight of the ambiguity in immediacy illustrated above. First, it makes truth dependent on presence to consciousness, instead of upon content. Yet anything and everything that we experience is immediately present to consciousness, and subjective conviction by itself is neither evidence for nor guarantee of truth. Even the consensus gentium often adduced as evidence of the truth of religion is very precarious evidence. It would seem as if fifty thousand nations, like the fifty million Frenchmen of the popular song, could hardly be wrong; but the consensus is proof only of their holding the same opinion, and scarcely that, as we shall presently see; it is no proof of its truth. The presumption is that the agreement is based on sound reasons, and that most people, being reasonable, will not reach similar conclusions merely by accident. But that implies mediation, and the apparent immediacy of common opinion must be properly mediated (supported by good evidence) to be reliable. In fact, however, it is frequently the case that the appearance of agreement is only superficial. The ubiquity of religious belief covers a multitude of different creeds, and what some hold sacred others will revile as idolatrous and atheistic. But all may have immediate conviction of the truth of their own doctrines. Hence the second disadvantage of the philosophy of immediate intuition is that it opens the door to every superstition and gives any belief the pretext for claiming the stamp of truth.

Finally, so far as religion is concerned, the theory authorizes only the poorest of dogmata, with the least possible content, namely that God exists. It does not reveal what God is. Intuition tells us that something or other is true, but it does not tell us why. It makes nothing explicit or intelligible, but gives assurance without explanation, which is therefore a bogus assurance, because what really convinces conclusively is systematic determination and explanation of the obscure. The claim of faith to exaltation above the senses and sentiments as well as above finite ratiocination certainly has some foundation, but it is warranted only if the mind has reached it by following its natural course -- that of idealizing or universalizing its perceptual and finite experience -- and that again requires mediation, is in fact its very process. The identity of being and idea is the real object of intuition, but that in itself involves mutual mediation of the two moments, and the genuine intuition of the identity is only reached through a whole system of intermediate antitheses and syntheses, as the course of the Logic demonstrates.

In short, interpreting immediacy as it does, the philosophy of Jacobi reduces immediate knowledge to an abstraction and makes it the precise opposite of what is claimed for it; that is, the concrete truth. Moreover, abstraction itself implies mediation, for what is abstract has been separated from the whole to which it rightly belongs, and what it leaves out is also implicit in it. It is, therefore, doubly mediated. The truly immediate is always and only the self-mediated, that the mediation of which is its own self-differentiation, held in complete and final unity in its own immediate self-knowledge. This, as we shall see, is the Absolute Idea.

Meanwhile, a philosophy like Jacobi's, licensing as in effect it does, every sort of unsupported subjective conviction, and giving the stamp of truth to what can well be contradictory opinions, is liable to produce as a reaction and antidote the advocacy of Scepticism. But common scepticism is a sorry remedy, for it makes assumptions itself which it does not recognize and in the end is self-refuting. As Spinoza says, the consistent sceptic must remain silent. Methodical scepticism, like that of Descartes in the First Meditation, seeks a presupposition-less beginning for philosophy. That is a legitimate aim, but is to be otherwise achieved, as we shall discover in the following chapter. As Hegel puts it here (Section 78), it can be reached only through the purifying of thought, a sort of catharsis of all its prior mediation in experience, which is nevertheless a sublation or Aufhebung of mediation, revealing absolute immediacy as total abstraction.

In spite of itself, this philosophy of immediate intuition is a reactionary doctrine, returning, as it does, to the 'either-or' alternatives of the abstracting understanding. We are forced to choose between mediate knowledge (science), which is said to be rational in one sense, and intuition or immediate knowledge, which claims rationality in another sense, or none at all; and no possible reconciliation between the two is ever contemplated. It is even more reactionary than the 'dogmatism' of the Rationalists; for they sought to make intuition a means and a stepping stone to full systematic knowledge.[7] Descartes and his followers believed that pure rational thought could lay hold on the infinite objects of metaphysics, the soul and God. But Jacobi denies its capacity to go beyond the finite.

NOTES: Book I, Part II, Chapter 4

1.   Sections 61-78.

2.   Cf. The Philosophical Works of Descartes, Reply to Objections II, Haldane and Ross, Vol. 2, p. 38. Spinoza, Principia Philosophiae Cartesianae, I, Prolegomenon.

3.   Cf. my Salvation from Despair (The Hague, 1973), pp. 40-41.

4.   Cf. H.H. Joachim, Logical Studies, II (Oxford, 1949), and Descartes's Rules for the Direction of the Mind (London, 1957), p. 46.

5.   Cf. Op. cit.

6.   Cf. G. Ryle, The Concept of Mind (London, 1949), pp. 222ff., and M.D. Vernon, The Psychology of Perception (Harmondsworth, 1968), Chs. I and II.

7.   Cf. Descartes, Rules for the Direction of the Mind, passim.

BOOK II

THE SCIENCE OF LOGIC

INTRODUCTION

INTRODUCTION

WITH WHAT MUST THE SCIENCE BEGIN?[1]

In the Introduction to the Encyclopaedia (Section 1) Hegel remarks that, as the thinking treatment of the subject inherently requires that it display the necessity of its content, it cannot begin with any dogmatic assertion or presupposition. With what, then, can the science begin? In the Greater Logic the question is discussed at some length, and what he says there is to some extent a continuation of the above discussion of immediacy, and in some sense is complementary to it. For the beginning must either be something mediate or something immediate, and it is easy to show that it can be neither.

The first principle of a philosophy might be considered the appropriate starting point, but that would not be, to use the Aristotelian phrase, 'first to us', but rather 'first in nature'; for it professes to be the origin of things, and does not specify how we are to begin our inquiry into their nature. Whether the original substance is water, the One, Nous, the Monad, or whatever, or whether knowledge originates in perception, self-consciousness, or idea, is of prime importance for the subject matter, as providing its ground. But it leaves the starting point of the inquiry undecided. For obviously, to decide what the first principle is, we must first inquire, and our inquiry must begin somewhere. Presumably, as we begin in ignorance, we cannot immediately light on the first principle (unless by accident). It is therefore rather the conclusion than the point of departure of our voyage of exploration.

The question is side-stepped by those who assert a principle dogmatically, or begin 'like a shot from a pistol' from their own subjective revelation and immediate intuition, for they exempt themselves from any method or logic. As soon as it is realized, however, that the way in which knowledge is acquired has a bearing upon its truth, it becomes evident that the method or form of inquiry is inseparable from the principle (of being), or its content, and what is first in the one should equally be first in the other. The question then is whether the beginning of logic should be a mediated statement of the principle, or an unmediated postulate.

Now we have already seen that there is nothing, as Hegel declares, in heaven or earth, in Nature or Spirit, which does not contain mediation and is not also immediate. The treatment of the opposition of mediacy and immediacy as well as of their inseparability is, moreover, part of the subject matter of the science and cannot be scientifically explained prior to its systematic development. Nevertheless, we must make a beginning and how is this to be determined?

85

We are reminded that logic is 'pure' or 'absolute' knowing, which was found to be the ultimate phase, or 'truth', of the progressively developing forms of consciousness in the Phenomenology. Hence the Logic is mediated by the whole dialectic of self-revealing spirit (erscheinender Geist), and presupposes the demonstration in the Phenomenology of the necessity of its standpoint. What the Phenomenology demonstrates is how the mind, through the necessary development of its awareness of itself and its object, through the diverse forms and phases of consciousness, attains the standpoint from which subject and object are one, where thinking becomes its own object, and 'is at home with itself in its other'. This is philosophical consciousness, self-differentiating, systematic thinking, at once real and ideal, the self-knowing, self-specifying Concept, or science (Wissenschaft), which is Logic.

Now the object, as originally set over against the subject of consciousness, is the manifold of particulars in which the Concept is immanent; and the universal (as Kant had shown) is the subject (the 'I think', or unity of apperception) itself. The latter as concrete universal is mediated by the former, but in the self-consciousness of their unity the mediation is aufgehoben and the determinate content vanishes in the pure identity of the real with the ideal. This pure identity is wholly immediate, purely abstract, indeterminate being, at once by its very designation pure object, and also due to its sheer generality pure subject -- at once real and ideal, and so typically what absolute, or pure, knowing is.

This pure being is simple immediacy, but it is also mediated (a) by contrast with and reference to what is mediated, and (b) by the prior development expounded in phenomenology. But in it the mediation is sublated and merely implicit, to be re-elicited as a scale of logical categories.

Another way of explaining this beginning is to point out that what has been developed from the immediate (sensuous) forms of conscious-ness is self-determined, self-reflective system (or knowledge), aware of itself as the conjoint truth of subject and object. This system is self-contained and complete in its own nature. Its starting point, therefore, cannot be anything extraneous or accepted from an alien source. It must therefore be the Concept itself in its most abstract form. It must be abstract because its concrete determinations have not yet been developed out of it, and because when they are so developed they will presuppose the process of development. That is as yet only implicit, and can begin only from what does not presuppose it, from what has not yet differentiated itself, from what is therefore completely indefinite, unspecified and abstractly universal. The only concept which answers to these requirements is pure, immediate, indeterminate being.

Hegel says that it must be an <u>absolute</u> beginning, for it is the beginning of absolute knowing, or thought thinking itself; and pure thought <u>is</u> pure being (as <u>cogito ergo sum</u> gives evidence), and pure being is a pure thought, as we shall presently see. About it more will be said when the beginning has in fact been made. Here all we are concerned with is why we begin with it.

If this identification of pure being as the natural and necessary beginning of the science is not convincing, we can but consider the possible alternatives. Reinhold had maintained that whatever we begin with can be only hypothetical and must be established by further reflection and inquiry. This, says Hegel, rests on sound insight, for progress in philosophy is indeed a kind of retrogression, or delving back into the grounds of whatever content we begin from. We seek to penetrate to the original, fundamental reality and truth which is the ground of all else. This final result of the process is then revealed as that upon which the beginning rests, or what it had all along presupposed. So we shall eventually find that the ground of being is in truth Absolute Spirit, which, as immanent in all reality, is actually prior to being, and is the principle on which all existence depends. Hence the important truth about science is not that it begins from pure immediacy but that it is a circular movement of self-substantiation, in which the first shall be last and the last first.

The ultimate ground, therefore, although it is (as Aristotle says) 'first in nature', is not 'first to us'. We cannot begin with it, because such a beginning would be unintelligible to us, and until we had developed it in thought it would be unwarranted. It is, Hegel insists, a <u>result</u>, and what it results from is what it is mediated by. We cannot begin from the mediate just because it demands examination of what it presupposes and so proves to be a false start. Nothing therefore will serve us as an absolute beginning except pure simple indeterminate immediacy, or being.

At the same time we must not imagine that as we proceed from this beginning and develop its implications we leave it behind and abandon it. Every step forward is but a determination of that from which we begin. So there is also a sense in which the starting point is the ground and foundation of all that follows from it, though it is only implicit in its initial form. Pure being is implicitly (<u>an sich</u>) the Idea.

Moreover, this starting point, if it is in a sense only provisional , is not arbitrary; nor is it provisional in being something with which we might dispense. It is dictated by the nature of the subject matter itself, which is absolute self-knowing. It must begin from an abstract undifferentiated self-identity, because any determination is already beyond the starting point. Hegel says that although there is a sense in which pure being is just as much absolutely mediated (by the immanent

Idea), we must take it in its one-sided aspect as pure immediacy in the first instance, because it is as a beginning that we so take it.

But could we not dispense with being and simply begin -- by analysing the very notion of a beginning? This suggestion might commend itself to those who are dubious about pure being,[2] and even more so about its identification (soon to be made) with nothing. But the beginning is where the subject matter (die Sache) is not yet -- is not yet anything -- though, also, it is not wholly non-entity, for it is beginning. In other words, it both is, and as yet is not. The beginning is, therefore, precisely that coincidence of being and not-being which was held in suspicion. And if the device of starting with an analysis of the notion of a beginning was intended to avoid the proposal to begin with pure being, it fails, because it offers us just that -- a being which is as yet indeterminate.

We cannot begin from a concrete object because that, if concrete, will contain internal differentiations and will be the result of their interrelation. It presupposes an internal process or discursus, a mediation which involves simpler moments and so a prior beginning. There can be no multiplicity in that from which we begin, because what is multiple implies a first and then another (or others) and so bespeaks an earlier beginning. What is multiple is mediated by its internal diversity; it has to be construed in terms of its parts, and they in terms of one another. We should, therefore, have to begin from them, and which ever we choose would have to be mediated by its relation to others, and so would not be a genuine beginning. We can begin neither from the parts as such nor from the whole. Our beginning can only be from something simple and undifferentiated if it is to be immediate. In fact, it can be nothing other than pure abstract immediacy.

If one becomes impatient with this whole discussion and demands that a start be made forthwith by attacking the subject-matter itself, the question at once arises what precisely the subject matter is. It is in large measure the object of philosophy to answer this question, but the answer is not to be found at the outset, but only after some considerable investigation, and that cannot be undertaken without having made a beginning. Yet, of course, whatever the beginning is, it must be with the subject itself; and if, as is the case in logic, the subject-matter is the Concept, the beginning must be made with pure being, for that is the subject matter itself -- it is the immediate abstract concept, and whatever the subject-matter may involve besides is what has to be developed out of this abstract concept in the course of the systematic pursuit of the science, which begins from this concept of immediate being.

What then must we say of the ego, which Fichte and Schelling make their point of departure -- the pure self-identity of the self-conscious subject? But so long as this is empty of content, does it in

88

any way differ from mere being? Cogito is initially equated only with sum. The ego initially simply is. What more can we say of it at the beginning? Cogitatio, you may object, is surely something definite -- but what, to begin with? Simply immediate awareness, sheer immediacy, indefinite being. Hegel does not make this point precisely so, but it is implicit in his statement of the imagined objector's case. What he does say is more important, that properly speaking the self-conscious ego is a consciousness of an infinitely manifold world, the most concrete of all things; and so to abstract the self-conscious subject from the content of its consciousness, in order to make it the starting-point of philosophical speculation, requires a highly sophisticated act of thought which is far from being immediate. Its object is the transcendental ego, the product of mature philosophical reflection, and one which is frequently confused with the empirical ego, a complex concrete idea of the self, which is uncritically accepted or postulated by naive consciousness. This notion (whether one of the transcendental subject, or of the empirical, or of a confused mixture of the two) is anything but unmediated, and is far from being a genuine beginning. The common notion is based on all kinds of presuppositions; the transcendental ego, on the other hand, is quite unknown to common consciousness; and the conflation of the two is the worst possible muddle, creating disastrous confusion and misunderstanding.

If for the identity of the self-conscious subject intellectual intuition[3] is substituted, or if they are identified, again we have a highly developed concept. Intellectual intuition is supposed to apprehend the infinite and eternal, the final product and not the beginning of investigation. If it is claimed that this is present ab initio in principle, that may well be true, but it is not anything from which we can begin. We cannot begin from what is in principle, for the principle has first to be elicited. In the beginning, moreover, the content of intellectual intuition can only be undiscriminated -- pure, indeterminate being.

Finally, it may be claimed that the only legitimate beginning is God. But with this suggestion we have already dealt. True, indeed, God is present from the beginning, but only as pure being.[4] Whatever else the idea of God connotes has to be developed in the course of the science. We cannot begin from God in the full panoply of his infinite glory. Even Spinoza's definition of God, as an infinite substance with an infinity of attributes is empty of content (i.e., is mere being) until he has developed by stages what is involved in the concepts of substance and of attribute (to say nothing of modes), and it is only in the final Part of the Ethics that the full meaning, the true glory and blessedness of the infinite being is established.

We might ask whether Hegel might not better have begun his science of logic with mere nothing, instead of being. We shall presently see that, had he done so, it would really have made no difference, and we shall also see why he did not. For apart from Being there can be no

Nothing. we cannot, therefore, substitute anything else for pure being as a legitimate beginning of the science, and after a preliminary word about its sub-divisions, Hegel embarks upon die Sache selbst.

General Division of the Logic

The Logic is 'the whole' come to consciousness as Concept, or principle of structure. As such it is concrete and self-differentiating. The divisions of the science are therefore intrinsic to its subject matter and develop themselves in the course of its unfolding. What is said of them beforehand is, like everything else in the introduction, only provisional, and is offered as a preliminary guide to the reader, although it constitutes a departure from the method of self-development proper to the science, in which it is justified and becomes intelligible in the course of its exposition.

Logic proceeds from the realization of the inseparability and unity of subject and object in consciousness. These now rank as moments of the Concept in which the opposition between them is aufgehoben. The objective moment is Being, the immediate content of knowledge; the subjective is thought in its conceptual phase. But there is, as we have seen, an intermediate moment, represented in the main by the understanding, in which reflection upon the immediate content reveals an inner essence in terms of which the external appearance of immediate being is explained. This is attributed to the objective content of knowledge, while it is unquestionably a product of thought. The inner essence does not appear sensibly, nor even in imagination, but is a conceptual essence, revealing the different moments of the concept as correlative to each other. Speculative thought combines being and essence, and, in a manner typical of the dialectic, recapitulates the antithesis of the earlier phases at a higher level, revealing the concept as both subjective and objective, and the Idea as the concrete unity of the two, as it is intelligent living beings who are, both in being and in concept, their own object.

The main divisions of the Logic are, therefore:

Part I the Doctrine of Being;
Part II the Doctrine of Essence, and
Part III the Doctrine of the Concept proper.

NOTES: Book II, Introduction

1.   W.L., Pt. I, Bk. I

2.   Professor Gilbert Ryle is reputed to have complained that he could not imagine what one could possibly mean by the phrase.

3.   Another allusion to Schelling, as is also the mention, in Enz., Section 86 of 'absolute indifference', Schelling's definition of the Absolute.

4.   Cf. Aquinas' identification of God with Being. God's essence, he says, is his being. Cf. Summa Theologica, I, Q3, 3 and 4.

PART I
THE DOCTRINE OF BEING

PART I

THE DOCTRINE OF BEING

Chapter 1

Quality

Logic now begins in systematic form and we see the dialectic, about which Hegel has hitherto spoken only ab extra, in actual operation. At the same time, in the course of its movement, everything which has been provisionally asserted in the Introduction is scientifically established. We are to begin with Being, and this is both the general term covering the whole of the first division of the Logic and also the first category. Attending for the moment to the general term as naming one main moment of the Concept as a whole, we find that it resolves itself into three principal categories, which are then subdivided, or more correctly differentiate themselves into others more specific. The principal categories of Being are Quality, Quantity and Measure, suggested, no doubt, by Kant's 'mathematical' categories, but treated quite differently in Hegel's dialectic. Hegel reverses the order of the first two, for what are very natural and obvious reasons. They are the categories of perceptual thinking, but also the principles of the actual being of its objects. They are the determining principles of things and are nevertheless the concepts without which perception is blind. Let us now consider them in detail.

Being, Nothing and Becoming

Being

Logic is the thinking study of thinking which is equally the thinking study of things, of the objects of thought, of what is actual. So it must from the very beginning have as its subject matter both thought and reality in one. Further, its starting point must be presupposition-less in the sense we have discussed, and must be the presupposition of any other possible thought or reality -- of everything that follows. It is that which is prior to all determination, all mediation.[1] So we begin with pure, unmediated (immediate), unspecified, indeterminate being. (1) This is an object of pure thought -- or rather it is a pure thought. It cannot be an object of perception, or sensation, or imagination, yet it is presupposed by any object of any of these. (2) It is the most general form of all reality; whatever it may be, prior to any other qualification, it must be. (3) It is thus both thought and reality at once, and both in their purest and most general form. It is prior to any distinction of form from content because it is both. Its form is its content and its content is its form. Thus (4) it is pure abstraction and sheer immediacy.

Being, as being, is all inclusive; it has no external limits and is thus not distinguishable from anything outside it. As mere being it has no internal differences or distinctions, and thus no content. It is therefore completely empty -- as Hegel says, 'it is in fact nothing and not more nor less than nothing.'[2]

Nothing

Why then did we not begin with nothing? If nothing is strictly nothing, it is not an object of thought, or is the object of no thought -- and so is no beginning. Likewise it is no reality. Yet, so far as Nothing is made an object of thought it is, it is then the same as Being. It is no reality, yet if taken as a starting point it must be thought, and so involves the being of the thinking -- of the Cartesian cogito. it is therefore again indistinguishable from being. Sartre, we may note in passing, identifies consciousness with 'le neant', which for Descartes indubitably is.

Accordingly, Being and Nothing are identical.

In the Greater Logic Hegel raises the question whether 'Not being' is to be preferred to 'Nothing'. He says that the suggestion is welcome because it states verbally the very identity of opposites which he is maintaining. Not-being is at once not and also being. The objection to the term, if any, is that it implies a relation between a being and its negation, which suggests determination as yet absent at this early stage. Similarly, the opposition of nothing to something is an opposition of determinates which belongs to a subsequent phase of the dialectic.

In this first synthesis, however, the identification is straight-forward and simple, with nothing complex or abstruse about it. It consists simply in the lack of content of either term. Both are all inclusive, neither excludes the other as an external contrary, for they coincide. Being embraces everything, yet the very word 'everything' implies multiplicity and distinction which are absent from being, so that, in effect, it really excludes 'everything'; and that equates it with nothing. On the other hand, there can be nothing outside being to contrast with it; and if there were anything outside nothing, it would, by contrast with it, convert it into something, and so would violate its pure nothingness. Here we are not dealing with contrasts; yet the two concepts are opposites, for being excludes nothing and nothing precludes being. Hegel says of these opposites (in Enz., Section 87 Zus.) 'Der Unterschied dieser beiden ist somit nur ein gemeinter'. The difference between them is only intentional, for difference implies determination, and the identity of being and nothing is precisely their common lack of determination. Yet each, as we have seen, negates the other, and each, as we think it, reverts into its opposite. They are at once identical and opposite and identical in their opposition. Each is immediately its opposite.[3]

Their unity is thus a perpetual oscillation, a perpetual timeless activity or discursus, which requires the self-identity of each, their mutual opposition and their mutual identity, all at once. It is the dialectical movement per se, in a word, Becoming. It is not, however, a movement in space and time, albeit motion in space and time is a manifestation of this dialectical becoming. 'It is the principle of all change, all movement, all activity in the actual world' (Enz., Section 81 Zus.). It is all at once eternally active (the Aristotelian ἐνέργεια). So Hegel uses the past tense in describing it. 'The truth', he says, 'is neither Being nor Nothing, but that Being has gone over into (not that it goes over into) Nothing, and Nothing into Being.' The transition is already fait accompli in the truth of their mutual identity. Yet it is an identity dependent upon, and not exclusive or destructive of, their opposition, which is preserved in it aufgehoben. Hence it is no static, blank self-identity, but an eternal restlessness or oscillation -- ein Übergegangensein -- Becoming.

The preservation of the difference in the identity is of paramount importance. If it is neglected, the identity is simply a reversion to the original thesis, whereas the whole point and significance of the negation is that it produces a new and positive result. Hegel draws attention to the unsuitability of the form of expression 'Being and Nothing are one and the same' because it stresses the identity at the expense of the difference. Thus he says the subject-predicate form of proposition is inappropriate for the expression of speculative truths.[4]

Becoming

Neither Being nor Nothing, therefore, is self-subsistent or stable on its own. Each is an abstraction, and the truth of both is Becoming. Each, by itself, is a mere ens rationis, ein Gedankending, and vanishes in identity with its other into the more concrete concept of becoming. The real beginning is thus Becoming. It is, as Hegel says, the first concrete thought, the first genuine category (Gedankenbestimmung).[5] It is likewise the principle of all dialectic, and this first triad is the paradigm case for all others.[6]

Once the character of the identification of opposites in this first triad is properly understood, we have the key to the whole of the dialectic, although subsequent phases become (as we shall presently make plain) more complex and the process is consequently modified. It is not, however, modified in any way that is not already implicit and germinal in this first triad. In the first place the opposites reveal themselves as moments, and not self-subsistent separable parts in a fuller and more concrete whole. They are interdependent and inter-changing, and can maintain themselves only in perpetual interchange. Secondly, their difference is maintained in their identity. The negation of either does not abolish it utterly, but produces a positive result in which that which has been negated is nevertheless preserved. The unity of the opposites is a discursus and at the same time a whole in which both the identity and the difference is affirmed. It is the truth of what each in isolation is at best a premonition. And it is universal to the moments, which constitute its self-differentiation and its very being (Bestehen). The element of identity and immediacy is emphasized in the first moment; the element of difference and mediation (negativity) in the second, and the synthesis is the differentiated unity, the particularized universal in its systematic concrescence, in which immediacy is restored and the mediation aufgehoben. The whole is immanent in its moments, for except as moments in the whole they have no reality or truth, and it is this immanence that impels each of the abstracta, or partial forms, to pass over into and demand supplementation by its opposite. This is the principle of advance in virtue of which dialectic is the indwelling nisus of all finites, of all movement, all life and all activity in the actual world.

But such adequate comprehension of the dialectical movement and of the function of negativity is difficult to come by and calls for speculative maturity. The identity of being and nothing in becoming is more than the understanding can stomach; so it either pronounces it unthinkable or treats it as a joke. But while on the one hand it is difficult (Hegel says the most difficult task that thought sets itself) to conceive the opposition of two completely indeterminate abstractions, whose identity is constituted by this very indeterminateness, the difficulty is really no more than that occasioned by the urge to visualize what cannot be an object of imagination; and, on the other hand, nothing is easier to conceive once Hegel's exposition is mastered. In fact, there are plenty of examples of the unity of being and nothing in becoming. We have already examined one in the notion of a beginning, which is not yet anything and is nevertheless necessarily something in order to afford a beginning. Plato was particularly fond of giving examples of the coincidence in becoming of being and nothing: whatever is in process of change, he points out, both is and is not what it is becoming; and all relative terms indicate what has this character of at once being and not being what they are said to be. Simmias is tall in comparison with Socrates but short in comparison with Phaedo. He both is and is not tall.[7]

The criticism of Trendelenburg that Hegel has surreptitiously introduced the concept of time with that of becoming is mistaken, and again derives from the habit of trying to visualize logical categories pictorially. Time presupposes becoming; becoming does not presuppose time. Time does not become, and in pure time there is neither change nor movement, for it is change that generates time and not vice versa. The relations between events of before and after cannot change and time is but the measure of change. As a measure or metric, it is a sort of static calibration, which is applied to change to measure its rate.[8] But all this presupposes more advanced and complex categories than mere becoming, which is itself presupposed even in change, as we shall presently discover. McTaggart, therefore, is right to point out that Hegel's category of becoming is not intended to include change, which is a later category, and Stace is wrong to disagree.[9] But Hegel is not at fault, as McTaggart implies, in using the name of a concrete fact for a logical category. 'Becoming' is the name of a concept, which Hegel calls the first concrete concept because it is the first union of opposite abstracta. No 'fact' is implied or named; though, of course, as already noted, every fact involving change is an instance of becoming.

Many common criticisms of Hegel's first triad in the Logic, and the ridicule to which it is subjected, spring from an oversight of the difference between indeterminacy and determinacy. The refusal to identify being and nothing derives from the obvious impossibility of assimilating the being and the non-being of determinate objects. If this tree exists its non-existence is excluded and vice versa. Determinate existents exclude what they are not and cannot at the same time both be and not be. True enough, but they are determinate existents and we shall come to them in due course. But here we are dealing with the wholly indeterminate, purely abstract being and nothing, and to attribute to them the mutual exclusiveness of determinate entities is not only a category mistake but is also to persist in the effort, typical of the understanding, to hold apart at all costs things which go together.

Hegel tells us that each category is a provisional definition of the Absolute; that is, it is the Concept (or the whole, or the concept of the whole) at a specific level of development. He illustrates this from the history of philosophy and from different philosophical systems. That the Absolute is pure Being was the teaching of Parmenides, and for him Being excluded all diversity, all change and any beginning or cessation. 'That which is is; and that which is not is not.' There is and can be no Nothing. Other Greek thinkers, like Anaximenes, identifying the Void with air, maintained that all things were air. In effect they identify the Absolute as Nothing -- or Void (empty space). Hegel points out that the Buddhists define God as Nothing, and consider man as uniting himself with God by self-annihilation. Aristotle, in effect, identifies God with Being when he defines Metaphysics as the science of Being qua Being and at the same time says that it is Theology; and the Mediaevals, asserting that in God being and essence are identical, are virtually doing the same -- though, as we shall see, the identity of being and essence is truly the Concept. Becoming is the Absolute for Heraclitus, who declared that all things flow (πάντα ρεῖ) and that being no more is than not-being. Equally notable in this connexion is his remark: 'what is at variance agrees with itself, as an attunement of opposite tensions'. On the critical and polemical character of Heraclitus' sayings Hegel comments that philosophical refutation is nothing more than the exhibition of the dialectical movement displaying the principle of the negated doctrine as a moment in a higher synthesis, in which it is cancelled yet still preserved in a more concrete form of

97

the Idea. So the Being affirmed by Parmenides and the not-being which he denied are united 'as the attunement of opposite tensions' by Heraclitus in Becoming.

Commenting on the aphorism, ex nihilo nihil fit, Hegel remarks that it is either an empty tautology 'nothing is nothing', or it is a denial of becoming, which is the perpetual transition of nothing into being and vice versa. In that case it is false and (he says) was countered in Christian metaphysics by the doctrine of God's creation ex nihilo of the world, an imaginative expression of the conception of becoming, which, we shall see presently, is the equilibrium of coming to be and passing away.

The level of Being is the level of immediacy. It is unmediated as a beginning and it is immediately nothing, its opposite. And the same is true of Nothing. Hence both being and nothing are immediately in becoming, and becoming is likewise immediate. It is not mediated through being and nothing, it is immediately both, as they are both immediately becoming. But the immediacy of becoming has sublated their opposition and so is mediated immediacy. Also, in the case of each opposite, so far as it is what it is by negation of the opposite, it is mediated in its immediacy. Becoming, as the truth of the opposite moments, is their Übergegangensein each in the other, and that Übergegangensein is what constitutes becoming.

The movement of the dialectic at the level of being, in consequence, is transition (Übergehen), not mediation in the proper sense. The categories of being do not mediate one another, they become one another; each goes over into its opposite unreflectively. Each is implicitly (an sich) what it becomes, but this implication is not yet explicit -- or, as Hegel expresses it, not yet posited (gesetzt).

Becoming remains the nature of the dialectical movement throughout its course, but it develops as it proceeds, and at subsequent levels it is a different kind of becoming. At the level of Essence it is no longer mere becoming, it is also reflection-into-self. There the identity in difference is more explicit and the complementarity of the opposites is 'posited'. At the level of the Concept the movement is explicitly development, at once transition and reflection. Here the unity in and through difference is overt and fully set out so that each moment is the whole concept from one point of view or in one special capacity -- each is at once the whole and only one moment in the whole. The movement is thus the unfolding, the explicit development (Entwicklung), of the whole through each of its specific forms and phases. The self-reflection characteristic of Essence along with the transition from one opposite to its other typical of Being are both aufgehoben in development proper, so we get a higher immediacy sublating the mediation through which it is actualized. Yet there is a sense in which development is the character of the whole dialectical movement, for it is the movement of the Concept, and the whole of the Logic is the movement of the Concept, differentiating itself into the categories of Being and Essence and sublating them in its own self-explication.

The Unfolding of Being

As Being is all-pervasive, mere being implies and holds within itself, an sich, everything that can and will eventually develop out of it. This is why and the sense in which, it is a provisional definition of the Absolute. Its becoming is its unfolding of its implicit content. At the beginning it is pure unspecified vagueness, but it has in it in germ all possible differentiation. So its becoming is its 'descent into its own depths'.[10] We can see this only after the first triad has been completed. The nothing which opposes pure being is nothing but itself and is equally undifferentiated; but becoming the Übergegangensein of being into nothing and nothing into being, as identity of opposites, is the principle of differentiation, the operation of negativity upon immediate being.

The Moments of Becoming

The transition from Becoming to Being-determinate (Dasein) in the Encyclopaedia is difficult and obscure. In Section 89 we are told that Being and Nothing are vanishing moments in Becoming, and as they vanish so Becoming itself vanishes, but not into pure nothing (its original moment) but into a nothing which includes being, and equally a being which includes nothing ('ein Sein, welches das Nichts in sich schliesst'). This is a new result, determinate being. The transition here seems abrupt and arbitrary, even though it is more fully explained in the Zusatz. But if we take it along with what is written in the Greater Logic about the moments of Becoming, what Hegel means is more clearly understandable. There he tells us that the inseparability of Being and Nothing in Becoming makes itself evident in the concepts coming-to-be and passing-away (Entstehen und Vergehen). Here they are clearly moments and make no pretence at separate self-subsistence, for coming-to-be neither is nor is not, yet it is both, and passing-away is the annihilation of what is. Moreover, each is what it is by reference to and in contrast with the other. Process, or becoming, involves a coming into being of what, by the same process, passes away, and only what has come to be passes away. Further, the contrast of the opposites here is a contra-position implying a determinate something which comes to be and passes away.

Coming-to-be and passing-away are thus interdependent and in equilibrium. The equilibrium, Hegel says,[11] is becoming itself, but in it becoming congeals (geht zusammen) into a stable unity. We are put in mind of what physicists call a dynamic equilibrium, or open system, in which matter and energy are in constant flux but which remains stable

in form. Examples would be, a vortex, or a wave, or a candle flame.
At the biological level the living organism is such a system, and here
the stable unity is a determinate being marked off from its surroundings
by definite bounds which set it in relation to other things. This is
determinate being (Dasein), which comes to be and passes away in the
flux of becoming, as in contemporary physics we are told elementary
particles come to be and pass away in the flux of radiant energy.[12]

M. André Léonard, in his commentary on Hegel's Logic, suggests
that, as being and nothing disappear in the mutual transition from each
to its opposite, becoming consumes itself and should disappear likewise,
as Hegel explains in Section 89 of the Encyclopaedia. But the
movement of becoming is, as it were, in both directions at once, from
nothing to being and from being to nothing. This is the double
movement of coming to be and passing away. It therefore stablizes in
equilibrium at a point of mutual oppositon between being and nothing as
being determinate.[13] So stated, this will not do, for it hardly gives us
the desired transition from becoming to Dasein, which is by no means a
mid-point between being and nothing, but, as Hegel tells us and as M.
Léonard notes, is a being which includes nothing in itself and a nothing
which includes being. Nevertheless, M. Léonard is so far right that
becoming is the movement in two contrary directions at once, and it is
just such motion, in the physical realm that stablize in dynamic
equilibrium, as for instance, in a standing wave created by the contrary
motions of waves reflected back upon themselves. And such stabilized
becoming is, I believe, what Hegel had in mind as a determinate being
which has become.[14]

Dr. Bernhard Lakebrink, in his Kommentar zu Hegels Logik[15]
(p. 113), gives an account of Werden which likewise falls somewhat
short of what Hegel intends. Lakebrink rightly notes that the unity of
becoming is not static identity or relation to self; but he says that if we
set aside the moment of restlessness and difference and regard
becoming simply in its aspect of unity and inertia (Ruhe), it reveals its
peaceful self-containedness (Friedenschluss) in this one-sided result as
Dasein -- determinate being. He admits that determinate being still
retains an element of restlessness, but explains this as the potentiality
of change. But this is not quite right. Unity and difference are wholly
united in becoming and its equilibrium is thoroughly dynamic, so that
the determinate being which emerges is a defined configuration in the
flux, at once fluid and stable, like the picture on a television screen.
Its restlessness is not merely the potentiality of change within it but is
the perpetual process in which alteration is always incipient.

Being Determinate[16]

In the Encyclopaedia, at the beginning of the Zusatz to Section
88, Hegel says that even becoming, 'taken on its own ground' (as
Wallace translates 'an und fur sich'), 'is an extremely poor term'; and

100

that its fuller manifestations are to be found in life and mind. It seems then that he is alluding to just such forms of stability in flux as we have suggested above. They would in some sense answer to his statement in the Zusatz to Section 89 that 'being identical with negation is what we call Dasein, the meaning of which shows in the first instance that it has become.' Clearly Hegel wishes to insist that Dasein is not a static entity, nor a fixed object of thought. It is in becoming, and that, he says, is perpetual restlessness. What comes to be in this fashion is a being which includes (in sich schliesst) or involves negation; it is a this-not-that, a determinate being. So the 'truth' of both being and nothing is established through dialectical becoming: they are united in their difference and opposition as a stable entity (or rather, as will presently appear, quality[17]) which both is, and is not what is other. It is an A which is A and not B, as B is B and not A. So Plato in the Sophist concludes that 'that which is not' is the Other. Both are, and each is not the other. So each both is and is not -- and that is what we found Becoming to be, an übergegangensein; and as a stable entity in the flux, its Other is precisely that into which it goes over. Each such stable being is what it is in not being its other. It is defined by what it excludes and by what excludes it -- omnis determinatio est negatio, and also vice versa. Hegel's first emphasis, however, is simply on the determinateness of a being which is not anything else -- as it were, a figure distinguished from a ground.

Being determinate is qualitied being. The mere being with which we began was completely indeterminate and so without quality, except that (as Hegel puts it) its very indeterminateness constitutes its quality. Even so, it is only a proleptic qualitativeness, for it has this quality only in contrast to determinate being.[18] The being of the determinate, moreover, is its quality. Its quality is what it is -- its what. Unqualitied being, as we have seen, is nothing. So Being and Quality now are one and the same, and it becomes evident that what we have been, and henceforth are, dealing with are the sub-categories of Quality.

Objection might be raised at this point, perhaps by Thomists (and others) that an important distinction has been overlooked between what something is (its essence) and that it is (its existence). But any such objection would make another category mistake. At this early stage the distinction between being and essence is still merely implicit. Later we shall see how. What we are concerned with here is the determination of being, and the being of the determination is the being of the quality. The distinction between essence and existence requires reflection, which will come later. Here we are still at the level of immediacy, where being is immediately what it is. Indeterminate being proved inadequate to its own purport, because, through its sheer emptiness, it was identical with Nothing, and so could become more concrete only by uniting with its opposite to generate differences in a flux of becoming, converting itself to a being which includes negation.

101

It has been impelled by its own inherent dialectic to differentiate itself. The differentiations are what Hegel terms Bestimmungen, characteristics or qualities, and they necessarily involve mutual distinction -- that is, negation. Only through such distinctions are the qualities definite (bestimmt), and only in virtue of distinction from what it is not is any quality precisely what it is -- or, for that matter, anything at all.

It is quite extraordinary how reluctant philosophers commonly are to acknowledge this obvious and unavoidable fact. If they do not deny it loudly and indignantly, they frequently simply ignore it or assume that it is not so. Quality they tend to believe is, as it were, dyed in the wool, and is as it is remaining unchangeably constant whatever anything else may or may not be. But this belief is palpably false and is supported only by the prejudice of the understanding in favour of separating and holding as self-dependent distincta that are mutually inseparable. Every quality has its intrinsic character only by contrast with and distinction from others, as may be illustrated by any we care to choose: colours are what they are because of their position in the colour series, and that is fixed by nothing but their mutual relations, in other words, by their mutual contrast and distinction. This is so obvious as to be almost tautological. Phenomenally colours are, besides, unstable, made so by changing contrasts and illumination; but that, important as it is for any theory of perception, is not the main point at issue here (though it has relevance to what follows). Even were they not so unstable, they would still be mutually relative and mutually interdependent for their very quality. Regarded physically, they are interdependent in exactly the same way. The series of wave-lengths corresponding to the different hues is a series the parts of which, like those of every series, depend for their identity on position in the series, or on their mutual relation. We mean nothing else by calling it a series. Likewise in physics the series is relative to the velocity of the frame of reference in which it is measured, shifting the colours in the spectrum as it changes. But this is not an additional piece of evidence, it merely reinforces the truth of what we are maintaining.

What is true of colours is equally true of sounds, which are similarly and obviously dependent on a graded scale of differences for their individual tones. Other types of qualities may be more complicated and less regular in their divergences, but are equally dependent for the precise character of each quality on contrast and relation to others. Remove these and not merely do qualities become unperceivable, they become indefinable, indistinguishable, indeterminate -- they revert to mere being which is the same as nothing.

The example Hegel offers is that of a piece of land (Enz., Section 92 Zus.) which is meadow insofar as it is neither pond nor woodland, and the more closely we look into this example the more apt it appears. A piece of ground is a meadow in virtue of what grows on it, and that depends on climate and the condition and content of the soil. If any of

102

these change the quality of the area changes with it. Excess of moisture converts it into a bog, other changes of conditions may convert it into a thicket or a wood. It is any one of these simply by not being any of the others, and it is none of the others because of its intrinsic quality. The quality depends on the relations and the relations on the qualitative differences. It is their negativity that defines them and makes their positive characters definite.

A caveat is issued here against confusion of qualitative difference with quantitative limit. The latter we shall deal with anon. The definition which the negation of qualitative being effects to make it determinate is not a quantitative limitation but a qualitative distinction. Quantity, we shall find, at least in the first instance, is indifferent to quality; and we must avoid the error of thinking of contrasted qualities as necessarily set beside one another in space (though, of course, they may be). It is their qualitative difference that defines them mutually. In the Greater Logic Hegel points out that, although Dasein literally means being in a certain place, the spatial image does not belong to this stage of the dialectic.[19]

The Finite

The determinate character which is, is reality in the sense of positive being. The negation which determines it is its opposite, not as unreal but as another determinate. Both negation and opposition, however, are categories of essence, and reference to them here is merely proleptic. Here the mutual determination of determinate beings is immediate, it is not posited in them. The determinate being is something (or better somewhat) as opposed to some other, and so is being for another (Sein für Anderes). But as somewhat, as intrinsically qualitative, it is being in itself (Ansichsein). But taken alone and in isolation it is merely abstract, its definiteness is wholly dependent on its limitation (Grenze, Schranke), which, making it what it is, is one with it. In short, it is its definitive limit, and it is far from being indifferent to its other. This identity of determination with limit is more obvious and easier to illustrate in the case of quantity, as we shall notice in its proper place, but it is no less, in fact even more, true of quality. Thus determinate being is essentially finite, and because its definition is always and only reference beyond itself to its other, with which it must identify in order to be itself, it is essentially alterable -- literally 'otherable', or as G.R. Mure has it, 'othering'.[20]

This identity of Something and Other is the dialectical transformation, through Becoming, of the identity of Being and Nothing. The dialectical movement throughout, besides being the identification and sublation of opposites, is also their transformation into higher forms or phases in which their implicit nature (or the totality immanent in them) is more truly and adequately expressed. Just as Becoming is the truth of Being and Non-being, so Dasein, as the unity of the One and the

103

Other, is the truth of the first triad as a whole, which will shortly be sublated into Being-for-self.

There are here several points to dwell upon. Something and Other are opposed but none the less identical. First, as observed above, through the limit which each determines for the other, each is defined and made what it is. Each is thus at once identical with, in being different from, its other. But further, each is equally other to the other and it is indifferent which is taken as this and which as that. They are each something and both other. In these respects they are the same, yet they have these mutual relations only because they are different. Hegel draws attention with approval to the Latin usage, aliud, aliud, in which the same term is used for 'the one' as for 'the other', and is nevertheless a term indicating that each differs from and is other than the other. Identity in and through difference is thus doubly established.

Secondly, Hegel draws attention to the ambiguity of the word 'reality'. We use it to denote mere Dasein, just being there and then, but also we use it to mean being as and what it should be 'according to its concept'. The first sense corresponds roughly to 'existence', but must not be confused with it, for 'existence' is a higher category of reflection with more sophisticated connotation as yet not reached. Still less must it be confused with 'actuality', a far richer and more significant category much nearer to the second sense of the word 'reality'. This second sense is that in which we speak of 'a real friend', 'a real vocation', or 'a real person', meaning genuine and good. Hegel frequently recurs to this usage and to similar examples, and he explains them as examples of correspondence between the Dasein of the object to which reference is made and its concept. Such correspondence is not what Kant called conformity of object to concept (which establishes objectivity) although it is akin to it, and develops from the Kantian usage. The concept for Hegel is not simply the concept of a friend, or of a vocation, or of a person. Strictly there is only one Concept, which is universal, and of which all specific examples are moments or differentiations. The Concept is in truth the whole, and a whole which is no mere aggregate, nor anything analogous to a spatial pattern or a mechanical system. It is the whole specified (and specifying itself) in the dialectical discursus. What a 'real friend', a 'real vocation' or a 'real person' would be can only be fully appreciated when we have traversed the entire system, not only the Logic but also the philosophies of Nature and Spirit. They would be what the Absolute Idea and Absolute Spirit in its full efflorescence and reality require. Thus the 'real' man, or the 'real' vocation, is identical with the 'ideal' man, or the 'ideal' vocation. And we shall find later that 'ideal' also has more than one sense, although only when real and ideal coincide is the truly concrete universal realized.

Some students have taken this talk of correspondence between a thing and its concept to indicate that Hegel espoused a correspondence theory of truth. But any such interpretation is mere stupidity. The correspondence is the teleological conformity of the thing with that which it has in it to become, its destiny or 'potential'. It is, in short, what it is when it fulfils its concept or ideal. There is not the slightest suggestion of a correspondence such as that between a picture and a landscape, or between a blueprint and building (except so far as the former has purposive intent). In Hegel's sense of the words one could never speak of a blueprint as the concept of the building -- though there might be sense in speaking of a painting as expressing the concept of what is represented. The popular (as well as the Empiricist) use of 'concept' implies something abstract and diaphanous, as opposed to the 'concreteness' of the actual thing (its Dasein), whereas Hegel's usage is precisely the opposite. For him, the concept is concrete, and Dasein, by comparison, abstract, and the only sort of correspondence between them is that between the germinal and the mature.

Thirdly, the significance of the limit is, as we should expect, two-fold. It defines the intrinsic character -- Being-in-self (Ansichsein) -- of each moment, and it also refers it away to its other so that it is Being-for-another (Sein-für-Anderes). The inseparability of these two aspects from limitation, and their enunciation in the dictum attributed to Spinoza:[21] 'omnis determinatio est negatio', is plainly apparent. Being-in-itself has its external reference only implicitly. It is for another in the sense also that it is only from outside itself and beyond its own limits that it has the quality it exhibits. Not being 'for itself', Dasein has its quality only implicitly in itself. When these relations are (at a later stage) translated into those involved in consciousness it becomes clear that Being-in-itself and Being-for-another constitute the status of the unconscious object. What I am for another, I am rarely, if ever, for myself, but that is just what I am liable to be in myself. Hence the poet's cri du coeur

O wad some pow'r the giftie gi' us
To see ourselves as others see us.[22]

Alteration

The determination of the finite by its limit and its other means that it is as much outside itself as intrinsic to itself. But here again we must beware of spatial metaphors with quantitative overtones. Perhaps we should rather say that it is as much equal to itself (sich selbst gleich) as also different from itself (an sich das Andere seiner selbst), and so alterable. 'Change', says Hegel, 'exhibits the inner contradiciton which infects Dasein from its inception (von Haus aus) and which drives it out beyond itself.'[22] Change or alteration (Veranderung, the literal translation of which is Mure's term 'othering') is not here primarily

105

change of place, or size, or shape, but qualitative change, what Aristotle calls ἀλλοίωσις as opposed to αὐξησις and φορά.

Charles Taylor maintains that this transition from limitation and finitude to alteration or change is a confusion.[24] The confusion, he maintains, is first in the notion of negation, between contrast and annihilation or suppression; and hence, secondly, in the conception of limitation, as 'contrastive frontier' and as interactive influence or causal pressure. Determinate being is limited because it contrasts with its other, but also because the other exerts a causal influence upon it against which it has to maintain itself in its own quality. For example, something is red, not only in contrast to other colours, but also so far as it does not fade, or tarnish, or become infused with other colours. A field is not a bog so long as its drainage is sufficient, and not a wood so long as its soil conditions and culture prevent the growth of trees. The other is perpetually pressing causally upon determinate being and threatening it with extinction. Now taken in the sense of causal persistence or susceptibility to external influence, quality is changeable; but taken as defined by contrastive limitation, it is not. Hegel, Taylor alleges, slips from one sense to the other, and in so doing and by confusing the two senses he effects a transition to which he has no logical right, although (Taylor allows) it is strongly suggestive of the ontological position that Hegel wishes to maintain.

The culprit here, however, is not Hegel but Taylor. First he makes an unwarranted distinction in the meanings of negation. For Hegel, negation is at once contrast, contradiciton and supplementation, but in none of these aspects is it annihilation. It is, if you like Aufhebung (cancellation), but not total abolition, and always with the implication of preservation and transformation of what has been cancelled. Secondly, causal impingement introduces a category of Essence which is quite inappropriate to Being and for the introduction of which the text gives not the least warrant. And finally, Hegel makes no separation between logical requirement and ontological fact; so there can be no question here of an ontological suggestion which has no logical foundation. Any ontological condition must, for Hegel, be rooted in a logical connexion.

Hegel's transition from Limit to Alteration has a different explanation from that which Taylor seeks to give. Something, to be whatever it is, must be relative to something else, must be qualitatively what it is by virtue of, or for, another. If we abstract from or seek to eliminate, the contrast the quality evaporates and is destroyed. In itself (sich selbst gleich), therefore, taken abstractly, it is not itself, and it maintains itself only in reference to its other, only in and through what it is not. It is thus always in contradiction with itself, always a conflict between Ansichsein and Sein-für-Anderes; hence it is always a becoming, an oscillation between opposites, a dynamic equilibrium. Thus it is implicitly (an sich) alteration. Moreover, as dynamic

106

equilibrium it is always liable to break down. As finite it maintains itself only precariously as against what it is not and so is liable to alteration.

If one appreciates the dynamic equilibrial character of Dasein consequent upon its being in becoming (see p. 99f above), one must realize that the two aspects to which Taylor points, and which he accuses Hegel of illegitimately confusing, are necessary and inseparable aspects of finite being. No confusion of thought is involved, therefore, in the transition from Something-and-Other to Alteration, and no surreptitious slither from logic into ontology.

Let us for a moment look backwards and consider the dialectic in reverse. Alteration, or change, involves contrast and otherness. Without difference change is inconceivable. It is always, as Aristotle insisted, a process between opposites, and by that he meant that it moved from A to not-A, or in Hegelian language, from One to the Other, from something to something else. But this process or becoming is the discursus which Determinate Being (or Dasein) essentially is. Just as Becoming is the perpetual oscillation of Being and Nothing (das durchaus Rastlose),[25] so the perpetual oscillation of the One and the Other is Dasein. Its becoming is change. In the Greater Logic Hegel says, 'Somewhat as becoming is a transition the moments of which are themselves somethings and which is therefore alteration -- a becoming already become concrete.'[26] Here he has explained that Dasein is the negation of the negation of mere being (i.e., of Nothing) and is thus ein Daseiendes, an existent. It is so, however, only by reference and in contrast to an other which is also existent, but determined as negative of the first somewhat. Accordingly Dasein is an sich Becoming (loc. cit.). It is intrinsically a transition, and therefore intrinsically alterability.

Taylor concludes that in consequence of the failure of Hegel's argument at this point, on which the entire subsequent movement of the dialectic depends, the Logic as a whole fails of its purpose -- namely, to demonstrate 'the ascending movement which takes us from finite consciousness to the vision of things issuing from the Idea.'[27] Whether or not this is a sound and sufficient statement of the purpose of the Logic, Taylor's criticism falls away, because his objection to the argument of the chapter on Dasein is ill founded and mistaken. The causal influences to which he appeals are manifestations of the becoming of Dasein, of its alteration and change, but the logical category of cause and effect is not simple alteration, it is its ground or essence; and here we have moved to an altogether higher phase of the dialectic, which is not reached until after we have encountered Being-for-self and subsequently the categories of Quantity and Measure, until, in fact, we have reached the level of reflection.

107

The False Infinite[28]

Being determinate is virtually synonymous with being finite. The determination is constituted by the limit and the determinate quality is a constant implicit reference beyond it to the Other. The reference is only implicit in Being-in-itself, which is always Being-for-another and not for itself. As Hegel explains in the Greater Logic, the reference is for us as reflecting philosophers; we see that being determinate is and can only be what it is by comparison and in contrast with what it is not. This comparison is not 'posited' in the somewhat which is the determinate being.[29] It is only implicit. It is posited only in later phases of the dialectic at the levels of Essence and the Concept, where being is not simply in itself, or for another, but also for itself.

Nevertheless, the reference always is to another, and the other is also a lmited somewhat referring beyond itself to yet another, and that to another, and so on ad infinitum. But the infinite so generated is never truly infinite; it is always and forever still finite. It never comes to an end, yet wherever it bides there is always a limit beyond which it refers, and what it refers to is always a beyond. It is endlessly finite.

It is in this form of infinity with which the Absolute is identified when it is defined as Dasein -- and Dasein, like all other categories is a provisional definition of the Absolute. If the understanding ever contemplates the Absolute at all, this is the definition of it that it offers. The Absolute (or whole of reality) is thus conceived as everything that is -- the aggregate of all existing finites, or the succession of all events, past, present and future. It is the infinite, in its efforts to comprehend which the understanding inevitably falls into antinomies, like those so brilliantly expounded first by Zeno and later by Kant, and the understanding of which Spinoza so clearly evinces in his 'letter on the infinite', Epistle XII. This is the notion of Reality put forward by Quine and Wittgenstein and at least by implication in Russell's conception of the world.[30]

Moreover, this perpetual reference to an external other is the same as the incessant process of alteration on which some philosophers have insisted as fundamental to the nature of things, philosophers, for instance, like Heraclitus among the Ancients and Bergson and Whitehead in our own times. The process is ceaseless and has no ultimate goal. Wherever it reaches its product is still (in Whitehead's terminology) 'an actual entity' -- Dasein, a finite being.[31] It is thus infinite because endless, but it never attains anything beyond the finite. Hegel, therefore, calls this endless progression the false or the bad infinite. It is the vicious infinite regress which ranks in logic with vicious circular reference as the mark of fallacy. It involves a contradiction between finite and infinite which demands resolution, and such resolution is immediately forthcoming in Being-for-self.

Reflection, at the level of the understanding, Hegel remarks, holds endless progression to be something very elevated and elevating, whereas, in fact, it is only very tedious. Our minds cannot comprehend it, indeed only for that reason. The true infinite, as we shall see, is not this interminable alternation from this, to that, and to another, from here to there and from now to then, each term immediately taking the place of its predecessor; for every that is also a this, every there is also a here, and every then is also a now. The beyond remains always beyond, however far we proceed. The progression ought to be infinite, but never is; the end ought to be attained, but never is; the finite ought to be transcended, but never is. In fact, the rigid opposition maintained by the understanding between finite and infinite converts the latter, the beyond (Jenseits), into another finite, though one that is never reached. This way of thinking, especially in ethics, is characteristic of Kant and Fichte, for whom what ought to be is never attainable except through (or because it involves) an infinite progression. The true infinite, which the understanding fails to grasp, is that which is 'at home with itself (bei sich selbst) in its other', and comes to itself through and in unity with its other. This is Being-for-self.

McTaggart cannot understand this character of the false infinite (see his Commentary, Section 30, pp. 29ff.). He fails to recognize its contradictory nature and seems to regard the criticism of Kant and Fichte as a gratuitous intrusion at this point -- a simple failure of comprehension. As little can he understand Hegel's insight into the nature of an ideal 'ought to be' as that absolute whole immanent and potential in the finite which the dialectic generates. Nor has he any clear conception of the true infinite as Hegel presents it. On the other hand, Bernhard Lakebrink gives an admirable exegesis of Enz., Section 96, in his Kommentar zu Hegels Logik and of the transition from the false to the true infinite, of their mutual relation, and of the immanence in the finite of the true infinite. (Vide pp. 124-133).

Being-for-self[32]

Being determinate, we have seen, is ipso facto alterable; but change or alteration is properly change only if both terms, that from which and that into which change occurs, are held together as the phases of a single process, and as the qualities (attributes) of a single being (substance). The terms in brackets are proleptic, for they apply to a higher dialectical stage, but even there they signify a developed form of what we have before us here at the level of Being. The necessity for unification of the distincts in alteration and change was recognized by Kant, who insisted that if the first phase was totally obliterated as the second phase arose, there would, strictly speaking, be no change but only substitution. For then there would be nothing undergoing the change, no continuous substratum persisting throughout. The two contrasting moments must be held together in one continuous differentiated process, and the process, to be cognizable or designated

109

as one of change, must be a unity, a whole of differences, or a schema. As Kant has it, 'only the permanent is changed'.[33] But Kant, in the Analogies of Experience, from which the quotation comes, is dealing with categories treated by Hegel under Essence. Here in the sphere of the immediate, what we have reached is a mediated immediate, a whole in which the mediation, or differentiation, is sublated. It is a whole of distinct though inseparable moments held together in explicit relation. 'Relation', however, can be used here only in anticipation, for it is a category of reflection. But what is explicit for reflection is implicit in Being, though it is not posited.

Whereas determinate being is being for another and has its identity in its contrasting relation to its other, the whole which embraces both and identifies each in its total context is not what it is by reference to anything beyond it, but has its determinate character solely in its own self-differentiation. It is, therefore, for itself. Its other, or specific differentiation, is within itself and, in fact, is itself. While determinate being in its inevitable reference to another is the essential form of the finite, and its abiding self-insufficiency, referring always away from itself to another, and that again referring away to yet another, generates (as we have just noticed) the false infinite, which never is infinite (but is endlessly finite); Being-for-self, on the other hand, having its determination in its own self-differentiation, is self-complete and whole and is thus the true infinite beyond which there is nothing.

Fürsichsein is the primary definition of the Concept as such. It is whole, and in principle there is nothing outside it to which it is relatable. It is, therefore, one. It is not, however, one among many, although, as we have already said and shall presently elaborate more at length, it is one of many. Its multiplicity is its intrinsic self-differentiation.

To say that Being-for-self is the primary definition of the Concept is, however, only relatively or provisionally true. With emphasis on the word 'primary' it is strictly correct, but it is by no means the final definition. It is the One of Parmenides, which is Being, but is now developed into Being-for-self, and so has gone beyond what Parmenides offered. It is more properly the One of Plotinus, from which all finites emanate. Essentially it is whole, or ordered, self-differentiated unity. This is the true infinite, self-contained, self-sufficient and self-complete. But to describe it in this way is again, as is unavoidable, to anticipate; for this description belongs eminently to the Absolute Idea. We must, however, constantly bear in mind that every category is a provisional definition of the Absolute, and that Being-for-self, at the level of the immediate, is analogous in its relation to the earlier categories of Quality (Dasein, Something and Other, which are its moments) to that of the Idea in its relation to the categories of the Concept.

110

In the othering of Dasein, Somewhat becomes an Other which is equally both somewhat and other. The two moments are thus just the same. In uniting with its other, therefore, Hegel says, it unites only with itself. But the self thus in unity with its other is self-differentiated. It is for itself in relation to its other. The other which is the negation of the one, and the one which is the other of the other, are now united as belonging together in one and the same whole; and so the negation is negated and, as Hegel has it, Being is reinstated at a higher level. It is reinstated as a whole or system of elements (which are in fact the prior categories in mutual self-constituting commerce). The finite whose being and quality were defined by negation, that is, by what it excluded, is now supplemented by what it omitted and that by which it was negated. The negation is thus negated by their mutual supplementation in the whole, where the negation of each gives it a distinct and definite place.

What is special about Being-for-self is that it is the final and consummating category of qualitative Being, in the sphere of the immediate, the unreflective -- what corresponds to perception in human cognition -- the simply presented. It is of course, relatively speaking, mediated, because it involves as one of its moments the intrinsic differentiation and mutual inter-relation of determinate beings. Its other moment is their unity or wholeness. But, as so far considered, it is only a category of Quality, and its differentiated integrity and intrinsic discursiveness are not yet in full measure explicitly formulated (in Hegel's terminology, posited, gesetzt). It is one and whole and self-determined, but it is not reflectively explicated in its detailed self-specification (as it is to be in later phases of the Logic).

The self for which, in Being-for-self, the qualitative being is, is one, but it is identically the same as that which is for it. It is für sich -- for itself -- and the self which is for it (its intrinsic differentiations) is as much itself as the self for which it is. Accordingly, in Hegel's words, 'it is related in its other only to itself.'[34]

This being for itself of its other, this grasp of the relation between self and other, as for one and for itself, is the essence of ideality. Relations between inanimate objects pertain, and each is defined in and by relation to others, but the relations are not for the terms, only implicit in them and for another. Thus the reflection of an object in a mirror is not reflection for the mirror but only in it. It is for me, the spectator, for whom it is a reflection. Only so can I become aware of it, or of anything else. In the history of philosophy, the theory of perception has constantly fallen foul of the fallacy of mistaking Ansichsein for Fürsichsein. the 'idea' of an 'external' thing is depicted as an image or a representation of its object. But no image or representation reflects or represents the relation between itself and its archetype -- the relation of imaging or representing. The idealizing of

111

the object, however, is precisely the awareness by the subject of the relation between the idea and the object, as well, at the same time and by the same token, as the awareness of the object. It is the relation between subject and object translated from simple being-in-itself (or being implicit) to being for itself. It is the whole relational structure differentiating itself into its moments for itself. Fürsichsein is thus the principle of consciousness and ideality, and Hegel says of it (Enz., Section 96 Zus.) that its most apposite example is the 'I' and that it must in general be conceived as ideality. The relation of such ideality to reality, he says, is that of Fürsichsein to Ansichsein (or Dasein). It is not something merely parallel, or alongside of the real, not a reflection, or an image, not a volatilized 'essence' or an epiphenomenon. It is 'the truth of' the real, the becoming aware of what it is in itself, its being for itself.

In the Naturphilosophie (Enz., Section 269.) Hegel identifies the centripetal moment of gravitation with Fürsichsein, and he says (in the Zusatz to Section 268) that the solar system is the first manifestation in the heavens of the system of reason in reality; for in it the totality determines the motions of the members, governing them from a single centre. It is this unification through the dominance over the parts of the ordering principle of the whole which is Being-for-self. The unified structure of the solar system is reflected in the formation, motion and dispositon of the earth (Enz., Section 339), the unfolding, he says, of an underlying idea: the earth's position in the solar system and relation to other bodies, the inclination of its axis to its orbit, the solar, lunar and cometary relations and movements of the other bodies in the system, and so forth, are the explication of that single system. All this, in its bearing upon the earth, constitutes the 'geological organism', which again burgeons forth into myriad forms and species of living things, through each of which, once more, the entire system is epitomized in the living organism; and, as we learn from the opening sections of the Geistesphilosophie, all this is innerly concentrated (erinnert) as sentience in the soul and is subsequently brought to consciousness, presented to a self-conscious ego. Consciousness is thus the explication of what is implicit in the organism as the epitome of the natural world. It is the totality emerging as ideal. Hence it is the developed form in idea of Being-for-self, which is not truly for itself except as ideal.

Both the explication and the awareness of an objective world, as Kant and Fichte demonstrated, are the self-specification of the self-conscious unity of the ego, which is for itself ('I') and for whom its other, the object, is its explicated content. Being-for-self is not just the reflection of an object but the awareness of the relation between subject and object, and yet further the awareness that they are identical as one self-consciousness. This is what the self-conscious whole is, the whole come to consciousness of itself. And this is being for self.

112

Kierkegaard castigates Hegel and his Logic for divorcing pure thought (which Kierkegaard also calls 'abstract thought') from existence, particularly the existence of the thinker,[35] so that it becomes an unimaginable thinking without a subject. But Kierkegaard is astonishingly obtuse about the Hegelian dialectic. It is true that without thinking there could be no dialectic in the full and highest sense, but thinking and dialectic are no more nor less than the explication or idealizing of what in thought is aufgehoben from lower nature and from the organism's life in which the thinking takes place. So it necessarily requires an existent subject. The logic as a whole is this explication of what at all lower levels of being and reflection is only implicit. It is, therefore, the self-explication of the ego (which, we shall later discover, is indeed the Concept) -- that deduction of the categories which, Hegel complains, Kant omitted, although he recognized their source as the unity of apperception and left it to Fichte to trace its self-specification.

The experience of self as barely immediate, however, as Heidegger understood, is just Dasein, which implies das Andere and the consequent feeling of Geworfenheit. When made explicit this again reveals the self at first in conflict with another, which is equally a self, and later reconciled with its other in mutual respect.[36] The other and the self eventually prove to be the same, especially as the objective world of spirit develops into society with which the individual is identified. The self is then at home with itself in its other, and is eminently for itself.

Being-for-self, accordingly, is the primary emergence of the dominant holism which propels the dialectic. It is the whole, sustaining and comprehending itself in its differences, sublating and uniting its diverse moments. This holism prevails at all levels, but only comes to itself in its true nature in the consciousness of the ego, in Concept and Idea.

In the Greater Logic,[37] Hegel asserts that 'every philosophy is essentially Idealism, or at least has idealism as its principle', and this, it seems in several ways. First, every philosophical first principle (e.g., even the water taken as such by Thales) is an idea. It is the universal, water, not the actual liquid itself, so far as it constitutes the universal essence of different and changeable finite things. Also the finite forms themselves are reduced to mere appearances of the universal, which is their essence and so are idealized. Much more so is this the case with Concept, Idea and Spirit, taken as first principles. Secondly, the finite so-called 'concrete' reals are all sublated in consciousness, in concept and idea, and only as so sublated can they become objects of philosophical reflection. Thus the truly concrete, or whole, turns out to be the ideal -- it is only grasped as a whole in idea -- while its finite moments (its specific differentiations, its content) as moments, are no less ideal. Even Realism, accordingly, is a type of idealism, because the reality

113

which it affirms is a conceived or thought reality, a reality defined and conceptualized by philosophical thinking, as is the antithesis it postulates between the real and the ideal. And any philosophy which hypostasizes finite existence as such as the ultimate truth, or as absolute, Hegel says, is not worthy of the name.

On the other hand, the subjective idealism which reduces everything to the content of finite consciousness still preserves that content as finite, as the self-differentiation of the apperceptive unity, and as sensuously given, in the form of intuition and representation. So nothing affirmed by realism is lost; but equally nothing is gained, for the content does not disappear when it is so idealized, nor has the opposition of subject and object been abolished. In short, Hegel remarks, the opposition of idealistic to realistic philosophy is ultimately unmeaning.

The point of all this is that philosophy of any sort can emerge only on the level of self-awareness and self-reflection, the level at which an organism has become conscious and brings to self-awareness the natural world with which it is in contact and in organic relationship. Here the thinker has become conscious of him or herself as subject confronted by an object, which, on reflection, is found to be the subject's own self-development. In other words, the subject is now aware of itself as the object sublated in and as Being-for-self. Philosophy is this turning back upon itself, the reflection upon the experience of the world and the discovery of itself as the world brought to consciousness as subject. So whether it be called 'realism' or 'idealism' it is inevitably the idealization of the external world -- its Fürsichsein.

In Being-for-self all the prior categories of qualitative Being are aufgehoben and held in explicit relation within itself as a whole. In Dasein, the one and the other, each taken in itself is what it is only by virtue of the implicit bearing upon it of the other; but this relation grasped as an explicit whole is One. Again we must remind ourselves that explication is a matter of degree and that here 'relation' is proleptic. Yet again, each of the opposed moments, being inseparable from the other, is implicitly the whole. Here this fact is barely adumbrated, but it will become much more insistent as we proceed, and will be fully apparent in the Concept.

In the Greater Logic, Hegel expands the dialectic presented in the Encyclopaedia considerably, subdividing the categories and interpolating subordinate links between them. I have not thought it necessary to refer to all of these in detail, for in many cases all that he does is to explain more fully various aspects and stages in the exposition of each main category. McTaggart follows these step by step, but for the most part (and despite occasional flashes of insight) he seems to understand the nature of the dialectic so inadequately and to grasp so little of Hegel's meaning that it is hardly fruitful to discuss his Commentary at

114

length. Where Hegel juxtaposes <u>Dasein</u> and <u>Fürsichsein</u>,[38] pointing out that the first is a moment in the second, McTaggart thinks he is mistaken. McTaggart persists in thinking of Being-for-self as if it were a finite, although he recognizes that it is not limited by a determinate being other than itself. For him, the infinite is always and only what for Hegel is the spurious infinite. It does not seem to occur to McTaggart that Being-for-self, as explicit determination, is and must be determinate (having <u>Dasein</u> sublated within it), although it is self-determined, not determined by another. Nor can he see that the 'other' of Being-for-self is its own internal differentiation, which is <u>itself</u>. Consequently his exposition and criticism of the subordinate categories is hopelessly confused, and so likewise is his account of the One and the Many which follows.

The One and the Many -- Attraction and Repulsion [39]

As whole, being for self is simply one -- not one among many, but one differentiating itself into and as many internal moments. These moments are mutually adapted and interdependent, so whichever of them is singled out develops into a being for itself. Moreover, what is the same fact looked at (so to speak) from the other side, each moment is distinct from every other and must be so in order that together they may constitute the unity of the system. Hence being for self has two aspects, (1) its unity, and (2) its multiplicity. The first expresses itself as attraction, the second as repulsion. We must remember that both aspects are of the same whole; the unity is the unity of the differences and the differences are the specific content of the unified whole.

G. R. Mure remarks that the One, which is Being-for-self is the all-inclusive infinite and so 'cannot lose itself in self-othering'.[40] Its other, therefore, can only be its other aspect, as many. As negative relation to itself, Hegel says, the One repels itself, it projects itself as its other, but the other is only itself, thus it is opposed to itself. We have to try to make sense of all this.

Being-for-self is a differentiated whole, a one; and the many are (in Aristotle's phrase) for the sake of the whole. Thus in being for itself it is 'being for one'.[41] Its two aspects, its unity and its multiplicity, are both the same whole and are nevertheless contrasted opposites. It is a one which is also many and a many which is one. Let us turn briefly to the treatment of these categories in the Greater Logic.

The One and the Many in <u>der Wissenschaft der Logik</u>

(1) Hegel makes the point that Being-for-self assumes immediacy, but an immediacy which is the sublation of mediacy, one that contains its differentiation within itself as moments.

115

(2) As immediate it is One, with all its moments collapsed within it; but these moments, in their distinction and opposition, their mutual determination, which has now become self-determination, and negation of negation, are all posited (gesetzt) ideally within the one (subject), and at the same time distinguished (as it were, extruded) from it as an external other (an objective world). To this objectified manifold the one (subject) is related as other, yet its other is simply itself. It thus stands opposed to the many, but this opposition is at the same time the unity of itself with its own self-determining (or self-specifying) self -- 'the unity of the one with itself as distinguished from itself'.[42]

The one is itself. It is not related to an other external to itself because it has negated or sublated all the categories of determinate being. So Hegel says that it is unalterable. This is what Mure refers to when he says that there is nothing outside Fürsichsein as the One for it to exclude, or to be opposed to. It is undetermined from without, but it is determined from within -- it determines itself.[43]

But Hegel makes a very complex and obscure transition from the One to the Void, by drawing a distinction within the One between abstract self-relation as empty, or sublating all difference, and its concrete affirmative being. He calls the former the Void, by contrast to the latter which, qua One, reverts to determinate being, and so converts the Void likewise to a determinate exclusive somewhat. Thus the One becomes related to itself as the Void. Yet both in being for self are moments of the one whole -- its self-differentiation. Hegel says they emerge from this whole as determinate beings.

It is difficult to understand and interpret all this. If one grasps Being-for-self as a differentiated whole which is nevertheless integrated and undissectable, one calls it (as Leibniz does) a simple unity. Hegel uses this phrase also. The simplicity then tends to be conceived as blank or empty. But it is the simplicity of Being-for-self; why should it be extruded as an exterior surrounding void?

The differentiations are mutually determining and the qualitative being of each is entirely dependent upon the other(s). They are, therefore, inseparable, and, in the whole which they together constitute, they are indissolubly one. They are absorbed or sublated in the unity, and so in that aspect, Hegel maintains, they vanish. The whole presents itself in this way as a simple unity or monad, as it is for Leibniz, who claims that the monads are 'simple' substances despite their admitted intrinsic differentiation (their 'perceptions'). The sense in which they are 'simple' is that they are indivisible, their internal differences being what constitutes the single wholeness of each. As in this sense one, Being-for-self is an abstract unity (like Kant's original unity of apperception, the ego of which Being-for-self is the typical form, and which Kant tells us is, in the first instance, an analytic unity, I = I).

116

If one thinks in terms of consciousness all seems to fall into place. The pure ego is empty and abstract, yet essentially related, as conscious ego, to its content -- the unified world of objects. But the One and the Void here tend to be regarded by Hegel's reader as they are conceived in the history of philosophy, as the content and structure of the object of consciousness; and the puzzle is how the two aspects of experience come to be externalized in this way. Perhaps we may be able to help ourselves by direct reference to the history (which undoubtedly is in Hegel's mind throughout this section) by going back to Parmenides and the relation to him of the Greek pluralists.

The One which is Being is the All or infinite totality, and there is nothing extraneous to it. But as so conceived it is a blank unity excluding all difference -- a mere void. This is pure Being and mere Nothing over again. Once difference is admitted (as it was by Heraclitus and Empedocles, and must be as Being differentiates itself through Becoming and Being-determinate), the differentiations are its content and constitute that which is. These differentiations then come to be seen each as a being, uncreated, unchanging and indestructible, each internally uniform like the Parmenidean One; and they are also its differentiations, so they subsist within the emptiness of its pure being. Thus the distinction between the real and the not-real (or other), Being and non-being, can be presented as a distinction between being and the void. This tends to be imagined either as the One floating, as it were, in the Void, or more frequently as many ones (differentiations) within the otherwise empty inclusiveness of the original One. In Empedocles' theory we find the notion of a One which sublates all differences as a uniform whole, and alternately, differentiates itself indefinitely into separate elements, each of which has the characteristics of the Parmenidean One. There is a persistent tendency to separate and contrast and set over against one another the unity of being -- what Hegel calls its simple self-relation -- and its concrete fulness and diversity. The Atomists present these as atoms in contrast and opposition to the Void, each atom having all the characteristics of Parmenides' One.

Hegel points out that the One, or ones, and the Void together constitute a single differentiated totality -- together they are moments of Being-for-self; that is, as its simple self-related immediacy and as its differentiated moments. The latter correspond to the fulness of infinite being as opposed to its emptiness or negation.

Again, the moments of a whole are distinguishable, and if projected as separable, each a determinate being, what separates them can only be a void, because what they exclude is always another determinate, and between determinates there is nothing. Thus the void itself becomes a determinate something.

117

These considerations are not wholly convincing, but they seem to indicate the direction in which Hegel's thought moves in the Greater Logic.

As one and void are determinate beings they are so far alike. As being-for-self relates only to itself in its othering, what it relates to is another being-for-self, but only qua determinate being. As in principle all its relations are internal, its relation to itself as an other being-for-self is only external and abstract. It is the relation between the many ones (or atoms) and expresses itself as repulsion. This is yet another obscure transition, which Hegel says is not really a transition, but merely self-repulsion. Yet again, the repulsion is both internal and external: internal so far as the differentiations are distinct, and external so far as the unity of the one is distinguished from its multiplicity. The category of repulsion is the concept of the dissipation into mutually repellant distincta of the self-differentiating unity. But each, when fully comprehended as what it really is, involves all the rest and is implicity being-for-self (whole).

Furthermore, every such multiplicity is a single whole, or one. The parts must cohere to make one multiplicity; so they are mutually attractive. Put otherwise, the very relation of mutual repulsion, or distinction, because it is dependent on mutual supplementation, is a connective relation and so, by the same token, attraction.

To sum up, in the guise of abstract unity, the merely contentless one opposes the full concrete differentiation, as an empty void. The differentiations are the many, related one to another as determinate beings. Yet each is in principle the whole which is being-for-self, each one and whole, each self-contained. And as each is related to other as determinate being, together they are a repeated reduplication of the one, each negatively related to the other. Thus the relation is external and is repulsion by each of every other which has in principle no limit; each perpetually reverting to its opposite thus generates an indefinite multiplicity of ones in purely external relation. The monads in Leibniz are windowless -- and they constitute a sheer multitude -- a mere aggregation.[44] This purely external relation of each to each is indifferent to and irrespective of their qualitative nature, which is intrinsically determined; and their mere multiplicity is a quantitative determination that can vary independently of quality.

We have thus reached the complete self-determination of Being under the concept of quality: what it is in and for itself. Although in this last section the terms 'one' and 'many' have been introduced, we must not forget that we have still been dealing with the category of quality, and therefore they are not to be given a quantitative signifi- cance as yet. They are strictly quantitative terms, and quantity is, in more ways than one, implicit in quality. Here, moreover, we are on the brink of the transition to quantity, at the point where the one category

118

goes over into the other. Being-for-self, however, is the self-differentiated whole of Quality. It is one, but it is not a unit, not one among many. Its oneness is qualitative and so is its inner diversity. It is qualitative ideality, in which identity and difference (again proleptically used at this stage, for they are categories of Essence) are implicitly unified and distinguished. The multiplicity of 'ones', corresponding to the multiplicity of the Leibnizian monads, is not properly quantitative. The monads are distinguished from one another, as are their internal perceptions, not simply numerically, but as degrees in a scale of clarity. And this is equally true of Hegel's 'ones', though not yet evident at this stage of the dialectic. It becomes fully apparent finally only in the Absolute Idea.

But when all diversity is sublated and absorbed, cancelled out in the immediate unity of the One, quality, which has hitherto been identical with being, is taken for granted and becomes indifferent. All that then comes to be considered is determinateness as such, in antithesis from quality, and we shift from what Locke called 'secondary' qualities to 'primary'; that is, to the quantitative and measurable. This is being more or less: Quantity to which quality is irrelevant so that it may remain unchanged while quantity varies.

Charles Taylor finds the transition from Fürsichsein to Quantity strained, and accuses Hegel of trying to have his cake as well as eat it, when he denies that the sublation of differences (mediacy) in Being-for-self is a return to the intederminateness of pure Being.[45] The passage is indeed a difficult one, but the criticism seems to ignore the principle laid down by Hegel from the beginning that negation is never barely negative and always has a positive significance. Being-for-self is mediated immediacy, not sheer immediacy, and the opposition to mediacy is now explicit, whereas at the beginning it was merely implicit. The unity of being, therefore, opposes its diversity and the One opposes the Many. Once we transfer attention from their qualitative significance to the merely external relation between them we have Quantity on our hands, indifferent to quality, and the transition is made quite naturally and without any strain.

Qualitied being, even as Being-for-self, is still relatively indeterminate. To be determinate, quality, we found, had to be circumscribed within a limit and opposed to another. But this limitation remained vague. Just how and where is the frontier between the one and the other to be drawn? That it should be definite is essential to the determination of quality; yet it has not been distinctly specified. It can be so specified only in terms of quantity, which is thus implicit in the concept of quality; and yet, until it is made explicit, that concept remains inadequate to it own pretentions and claims. Thus it goes over into its opposite, quantitative being which is indifferent to quality.

119

The Movement of the Dialectic

The Logic grows like a fugue or a set of variations in music. A theme is announced and then repeated with growing contrapuntal complication and more complex harmonies, constantly augmenting in depth and involution. The theme of the Logic is, in a sense, the first triad: Being, Nothing and Becoming. on the next level this is repeated as Something, Other and Being-for-self, with intermediate transitions simliarly presentable. In Fürsichsein all the categories of qualitative being are sublated, and this immediately opposes itself to its negation -- Being indifferent to quality, mere quantitative existence. Again, under Quantity, we find the categories of Quality repeating themselves in a new form. Pure being becomes quantity in general; determinate being becomes Quantum or magnitude -- determinate quantity; and Being-for-self becomes Degree.

NOTES: Book II, Part I, Chapter 1

1.   Cf. Enz., Section 86 Zus.

2.   W.L., I, p. 83; Miller, p. 82.

3.   Cf. W.L., I, pp. 82-83; Miller, pp. 82-83.

4.   W.L., I, p. 93; Miller, p. 90.

5.   Cf. Enz., Section 88 Zus.

6.   Cf. W.L., I, p. 86; Miller p. 85: 'Since this unity of being and nothing as the primary truth now once and for all lies at the base and forms the element of all that follows, all further logical determinations, besides becoming itself,... are examples of this unity.'

7.   Cf. Phaedo 102b-d, and Republic V, 476e ad fin.

8.   Cf. my 'Time and Change' in Mind, Vol. LXVI N.S., No. 262, 1957.

9.   Cf. McTaggart, Commentary on Hegel's Logic, Section 18, p. 18, and W.T. Stace, The Philosophy of Hegel, Pt. II, Section 183n.

10.   Cf. Phen., Preface.

11.   Cf. W.L., I, p. 113; Miller, p. 106.

12.   Cf. E. Schrödinger, 'Our Conception of Matter' in What is Life? and Other Essays (New York, 1956), p. 177.

13.   Cf.   Commentaire Litteral de la Logique de Hegel (Paris and Louvain, 1974), pp. 55-58. M. Leónard illustrates his interpretation with a series of diagrams as follows:

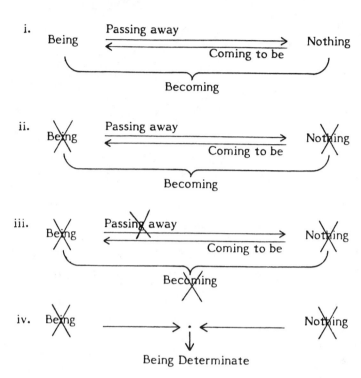

14.   Cf. Enz., Section 89 Zus.

15.   Freiburg/München, 1979.

16.   Enz. Sections 89-91.

17.   We are not dealing here with things or with substances. Determinate being is not that kind of entity. These are categories which emerge only later under Essence.

18.   Cf. W.L., I, p. 82; Miller, p. 81.

19.   Cf. W.L., I, p. 116: '...Dasein, etymologisch genommen: Sein in einem gewissen Orte; aber die Raumvorstellung gehört nicht hierher.' (Miller, p. 110)

20.   Cf. A Study of Hegel's Logic, p. 48.

121

21.　I have never been able to discover that Spinoza himself stated this principle precisely in these words. The nearest he comes to it is in Epistle L: 'figura non aliud quam determinatio, et determinatio negatio est...' and in Ethics I, Prop viii, S.I: 'Cum finitum esse revera sit ex parte negatio...'

22.　Robert Burns, 'To a Louse'.

23.　Enz., Section 92 Zus.

24.　Cf. Hegel (Cambridge University Press, 1975), pp. 236 ff.

25.　Cf. Enz., Section 89 Zus.

26.　W.L., I, p. 124; Miller, p. 116.

27.　Cf. Taylor, op. cit., p. 346 et seq.

28.　Enz., Sections 93-95.

29.　Cf. W.L., I, pp. 130-131; Miller, pp. 121-122.

30.　Cf. W.V.O. Quine, From a Logical Point of View (Harvard University Press, 1953), Ch. I; L. Wittgenstein, Tractatus, 1.2, 1.21; Bertrand Russell, Our Knowledge of the External World, passim.

31.　As a comment on Whitehead this must be qualified by his doctrine of God in His Primordial and Consequent Natures -- a doctine which brings Whitehead into remarkable agreement with Hegel, whom he had not read. Cf. my Nature, Mind and Modern Science (London, 1954), pp. 436-438.

32.　Enz., Section 96.

33.　Cf. Kritik der reinen Vernunft, B. 231.

34.　W.L., I, p. 177: '..es bezieht sich in seinem Anderen nur auf sich.' Miller, p. 159.

35.　Cf. Concluding Unscientific Postscript, Trans. D.F. Swenson (Princeton, 1971), pp. 268ff.

36.　Cf. Phen. B, IV, A.

37.　Pt. I, Bk I, Ch. IIC, Remark 2. W.L., I, pp. 172-73; Miller, pp. 154-56.

38. <u>W.L.</u>, I, p. 176; Miller, p. 158f.

39. <u>Enz.</u> Sections 97-98.

40. Cf. <u>Study of Hegel's Logic</u>, p. 55.

41. Cf. <u>W.L.</u>, I, p. 176; Miller, p. 159.

42. '..dessen <u>Einheit mit sich, so als unterschieden von sich,</u> ist <u>zur</u> Beziehung <u>herabgesetzt und als</u> negative <u>Einheit Negation seiner selbst</u> <u>als eines</u> Anderen <u>aus sich, dem Eins.</u>' <u>W.L.</u>, I, p. 183; Miller, p. 164.

43. This self-determination, we shall presently notice, is mistaken by Taylor for indeterminateness.

44. This is, of course, only half the truth about the Leibnizian monads, for they are internally differentiated, as we have already noted, and in pre-established harmony, which re-establishes internal relations.

45. Cf. <u>Hegel</u>, pp. 244ff.

123

Chapter 2

Quantity

Kant gives quantity precedence over quality but that is because he maintains that the categories are applicable only to sensuously intuited experience the *a priori* forms of which are space and time. Space and time, therefore, take precedence over that which fills them, and space and time are quantitative schemata (as Hegel is presently to assert). Quality for Kant is a function of intensive quantity the minimal terminus of which is nothing, and the degree of which is a degree of reality. So Kant, by implication, admits that quality and being are one and the same. But being is intuitable only under the forms of space and time and thus is, for him, primarily quantitative. This reflects the predelection which Kant shared with Locke for primary qualities as the foundation of objectivity.

But Hegel was aware (no doubt benefiting from Kant's analyses) that space and time are far from being primary in experience, but that they are quantitative schemata which sublate a presupposed differentiation of qualitative content. It is being which is spread out in space and endures through time, and being must be some-what. Quality, therefore, precedes quantity which emerges only as the sublated result of transition from differentiated quality demanding precise determination.

Magnitude (Quantity)[1]

Magnitude, Hegel maintains, is not the same, not equivalent to or synonymous with, quantity, because it denotes determinate and not pure quantity. Mathematicians define magnitude as what may be increased or diminished, but this definition is circular because the terms 'increase' and 'diminution' involve the definiendum. Quantity is that of which the alterability (in contrast to Dasein) is indifferent to quality. Increase and diminution make no difference to the qualitative identity of that which becomes more or less (be it a house, or the colour red, or whatever else; it remains a house, or red, or whatever it may be, whether smaller or larger, more or less intense, etc.).

Being, conceived as quantity, Hegel tells us, is equivalent to the conception of being as matter.[2] He does not mention Aristotle in this connexion (as he so frequently does elsewhere), though he might well have drawn attention to the Aristotelian doctrine of prime matter. For Aristotle, this is pure potentiality of becoming informed (or qualitied). It is being indifferent to quality (or form) yet capable of assuming such form. In itself, if it is specified at all, it is simply more or less. Similarly, in Anaximenes' theory, the matter of all things is air, but its quantity in a given space is what determines its qualitative differences. In itself it is simply more compact or more thinly dissipated.

Materialism in general, which treats being as pure matter, reduces quality to variations of quantity and motion. Quantity is thus in a significant sense the opposite of quality. It opposes quality as Nothing opposes Being. It is Being posited as Nothing -- that is, without quality.

Pure Quantity

Quantity is pure being of which the determinate qualitative character is no longer regarded. Changes in being which make no difference to quality are changes of quantity.

The three kinds of change distinguished by Aristotle were ἀλλοίωσις, αὔξησις and φορά, of which only the first is change of quality. What distinguishes the second, αὔξησις, from the first is that it does not involve ἀλλοίωσις. Hegel points out that increase and diminution, the terms in which mathematicians define magnitude, mean nothing other than change in quantity (αὔξησις). The essential point is that it is a change which (with reservations later to be explained) leaves quality unchanged. Φορά, change of place, or movement, is in one aspect really a form of quantitative change because it can be specified only in terms of distance from a given point (or of quantity of space), but prima facie it makes no difference either to the quantity or the quality of the body moved. But for Hegel space and motion are not logical categories, but are phases in the dialectic of Nature, of the manifestation of the Idea in the form of externality (or other-being).

Quantity is the proper sphere of mathematics, which is usually esteemed as exact science par excellence. That it is exact science Hegel is far from denying, but he protests against the assumption that mathematics is the only form of exact science. It is the exact science of quantity and of external relationships, but of nothing else. Its methods are not really applicable to the fields of morals, politics, or religion, and we might today, in spite of much prejudice to the contrary, add many others. Hegel contends that there can be exact science in these other fields as well, although it is not mathematical but dialectical. Even in the natural sciences exactitude is not always proportional to mathematization, which is appropriate in mechanics and kinematics, but less so in biology, and even less in psychology.

Despite all our modern advances in quantified science this remains true to this day. We can account for nearly all biological processes in physico-chemical terms, largely amenable to mathematical procedures, and the contribution of mathematics to biology and medicine is stupendous; but what physico-chemical and mathematical principles have not yet been able to cope with is the holistic or teleonomic character of life, its tendency to maintain and reassert organic wholeness autonomously, to restrain or decrease entropy in the organic system. Of course, there is no reason to suppose that physics,

125

chemistry and mathematics may not in time prove equal to the problems of teleonomy, for quantum physics itself is at least incipiently teleonomic, and its major exponents have declared that its principles become properly intelligible only if understood as applying to the total energy system under scrutiny. But that means that physics itself is dialectical, and the same may be true even of mathematics in its higher reaches (as we shall find Hegel hinting at a later stage). The point, however, is that exactitude in science is not confined to techniques of calculation, which are restricted in their scope, as we shall presently see, to abstract particulars in external relation. Morals, politics and religion, where our main concern is with values, belong to a region quite beyond the reach of mere calculation, and some have thought, therefore, that no precise scientific treatment can be applied to them. It is this belief that Hegel seeks to combat. Not only does he hold that these levels of human activity are as rational as any other; he maintains that they are the most fully and intensely rational of all, in fact the paradigm of rationality and the truth of all other forms. Dialectical treatment of them is then as precise and exact a science as any at the mathematical level, and even more so.

Discreteness and Continuousness[4]

The repulsion of itself by the One of Fürsichsein left us with an indefinite multiplicity of ones in purely external relation. When quality is aufgehoben these appear as bare particulars. Each is what every other is and they form a mere aggregate or Menge -- a set divisible into sets which are themselves aggregable. This is the Wittgensteinian universe of 'objects' which combine into atomic facts each wholly indifferent to the character of every other. Their intrinsic natures make no difference to one another, so that each may be what it will irrespective of the rest. In this respect they are all exactly alike, and together they form a collection of externally related particulars.

Yet, as we found with Fürsichsein, the external relation remains a link which binds the collection into one aggregate and is in effect attraction, the other aspect (or moment) of Being-for-self. When we abstract from quality, these two aspects issue as the two moments of quantity: discreteness and continuity. They are not two kinds of quantity, for every quantity is both. Every magnitude (Grösse) is a multiplicity of discrete units and also a continuum or extent. Continuous quantity is just as much discrete, because it is a whole of many distincts; discrete quantity is just as much continuous, because it is equally a whole of that same many, a unity or set.[5] Thus a continuous spatial extent is measurable in spatial units, and a crowd of people is a single concourse.

What is condensed in the Encyclopaedia into two paragraphs (with their Zusätze) is much more fully elaborated in der Wissenschaft der Logik. There Hegel remarks that pure quantity has no limit, neither is

126

it as yet quantum, nor even when it becomes quantum is it confined by the limit. In other words, it remains quantity beyond any limit set. Quality is determinate only within definite qualitative limits, but (at least prima facie) it is unaffected by change in quantity. On the other hand, whatever quantitative limit is set, there is a potentiality of more beyond it which is uniform with what remains inside the limit. Quantity consists, indeed, of this limitlessness, for it is the sublation of Being-for-self, which has its differentiations within itself and so is absolutely continuous (or 'simple'). Quantity is, for the same reason, 'the real possibility of the One', which accounts for its discreteness in its very continuity.

Consequently we tend to imagine continuity in the form of composition, but such imagination is obtuse (begrifflos). As Spinoza writes,[6] it is very easy to imagine space as divisible, and we commonly do, but when it is conceived as an attribute of Substance, which is very difficult, it is infinite, one and indivisible.

Space, time, matter and the self are all examples of pure quantity, each in its special way. Space is essential self-externality. Like time, it is a continuous going beyond itself, or self-producing, without change of quality. Space is uninterrupted self-externality -- a perennial other-being which is nevertheless the same. Time is the continuous generation of moments, or 'nows' (the units of time), all equally 'now', yet each immediately annihilated. As space is continuous self-expansion, so time is continuous self-destruction (Sicherzeugen des Nichtseins). Matter is in external existence what quantity is as pure concept. It is, so to speak, the externalization, or spatio-temporaliza-tion (if that verbal barbarism may be forgiven) of the Concept qua quantity. This is remarkably well exemplified in modern physics by the identification of curvature in space-time with the energy field and of energy with matter and the quantitative expression of all these in a mathematical formula. Space, time, matter and quantity are thus seen as dialectically continuous, and in their mutual diversity, nevertheless identical. The self, considered in terms of quantity, is the one indivisible (as the old metaphysics insisted, 'simple') individual subject, actualizing itself continuously in a ceaseless multiplicity of 'states' of consciousness.

In the second Anmerkung, Hegel gives an extended criticism of Kant's second antinomy[7] into the detail of which we need not go. The main point is that continuity and discreteness are both equally necessary moments in the concept of quantity, and the antithesis (as well as reconciliation of the opposition) is inherent in the concept itself (as a specific instance of the Concept proper, or the absolute whole). The antinomy which breaks out in the analysis of any concrete application of the category, therefore, is only to be expected, and its resolution is not, as Kant implies, that the inevitable contradiction indicates an inherent fault or deficiency in our subjective thinking -- a limitation of reason in its effort to think things in themselves under the categories -- but that the two moments of the concept are inseparable and the the logomachy is the result only of the effort of the understanding to hold them incommunicado.

The same opposition of moments in space and time leads to the paradoxes of Zeno, whose dialectic Hegel admires in preference to Kant's. But he hands the palm to Aristotle for his solution of the paradoxes, and for his recognition that infinite divisibility is implicitly potential (an sich) in continuity.

As a concrete unity, quantity involves both moments of continuity and discreteness, each implying the other. It is therefore posited as a whole, both as continuous and as discrete -- as continuous magnitude and as discrete magnitude. But each is as much the other. Continuous magnitude is continuous discreteness and discrete magnitude is discrete continuity. We shall see these aspects expressing themselves more fully in number.

Discrete quantity, having the One for its principle, implies a limit in the continuity of the One which proliferates ones (or units) within it. Yet each discrete quantity is indifferent to its limit and is repeated beyond it. It is one with its limit, yet is continuous with, and at the same time distinct from, what lies beyond the limit; and that, being also discrete quantity, resolves itself into further 'ones' continuous with the first. Such discrete quantity is determinate quantity, or Quantum, defined by a limit and distinguished from other quanta similarly defined. The indifference of quanta to limit and to one another makes them all exactly alike. They are each indifferently one, and so are all equal. The continuity of discretes is thus a colligation of equal units (or ones) prefiguring the two moments of Number.[8]

The Quantum (Determinate quantity)

Quantum is limited, or determinate, quantity, and (like Dasein) is exclusive of and defined by other quanta. In pure quantity continuity and discreteness are moments both implicit in the concept of quantity and each implicit in the other. In the quantum, Hegel says,[9] the distinction is posited (gesetzt). The imposition of limit upon quantity breaks up the continuum into a multiplicity of quanta, or determinate magnitudes, a continuity of many distincts, each of which is a unity internally continuous, yet indefinitely divisible. The complete determination of quantity in this way issues as Number.

We may note in passing how quantity as a continuous whole automatically differentiates itself into quanta each of which is a continuous whole. The totality, while continuous, is ipso facto discrete, and each quantum is likewise a whole which is a continuous magnitude and is in the same way discrete. The whole specifies itself into wholes which replicate it, as well as one another. This is the peculiar nature of the Concept, exemplifying itself here in Quantity in an exemplary manner, despite the fact that quantity, as Hegel frequently emphasises, is a singularly abstract version of the Concept, one to which he is often moved to apply the epithet begrifflos. That term, however, we must never forget, is always relative, because, as der Begriff is eminently the whole, and is immanent in each and all of its particular specific forms, nothing is ever utterly begrifflos.

Number[10]

In Quantity, the one and the many, which emerged from Being-for-self, are sublated. Essentially the one is the whole, containing all its differentiations in suspension, and thus indifferent to, or rather unaffected by, any confining limit. But it proliferates into many ones, each indifferent to every other, and each having the characteristics of the whole, just as the atoms of Democritus each have the characteristics of the Being (or One) of Parmenides. This, we have noticed, is just what occurs under Quantity, sublating Fürsichsein. It proliferates into quanta, each with the characteristics of the whole and each indifferent to and indistinguishable from every other, except by its position in a series. The quanta are bare particulars in external relation. Taken in sets or collections, each set, in its aspect of discreteness, constitutes a sum (Anzahl)[11] and at the same time, in its continuous aspect, is a unity (Einheit), which taken together are the moments of a number. The quanta thus aggregated are each unities (or units) and the mutual relation of their unities is equality. Every number is a sum, or annumeration, of equal units, and is also a unity or specific number; and as the units are all mutually indifferent and are externally related, calculation consists simply in counting (Zählen).

The number is the determinate quantum and is accordingly limited. Its amount (Vielheit) is identical with its limit, which is thus its magnitude posited as a single unity. The limit, moreover, gives the number its identity, circumscribes its units as discrete elements within it, and distinguishes it from all other numbers -- it is self-relating, inclusive and other-exclusive. The limit of determinate being determines its quality in such a way that it negates what lies outside and beyond the limit, while within the quality is positively affirmed. But in quantitative determination the limit merely bounds a collection of similar units indifferent to it and mutually indistinguishable. The limit is simply the last one to make up the amount. Yet it is not altogether indifferent to the rest, for they all make up the amount and constitute its number. If that is, for example, ten, the tenth unit is the limit, though any one might be the tenth as well as any other. And units beyond the limit are no different, except in so far as together they make up a different sum. Consequently the sum does not contrast with what limits it and encompasses its multiplicity, but is itself the determinate quantum which constitutes the number -- ten, twenty, a

129

hundred, or whatever. The number is at once the discrete quantity, continuous as one quantum, and the limit which determines it.

The unity of this determinate quantum is, however, exclusive of others, and its limit, or amount, distinguishes it from other numbers. But the distinction is not qualitative, only quantitative, and the relation is external, not internal, so far as the component units are concerned. This mutual externality of quantities is pervasive. The sum is the amount of the unity which is the number, and is in itself a collection of mutually external unities. The internal contradiction of unity and sum Hegel calls 'the quality of quantum', a characteristic which develops further as we proceed.

Because number is a sheerly external colligation of units and has no inner coherence, all calculation is simply counting, or, more strictly counting (collecting) together.[12] Consequently, Hegel points out, numeration is purely analytic, and he criticizes Kant for giving 7 + 5 = 12 as an example of a priori synthetic judgement. Unlike some contemporary critics who do likewise, however, Hegel sees that the example is inept while the general epistemological insight is sound.[13]

The forms or methods of calculation are thus all varieties of counting, or the annumeration of units. There are strictly only three, each having a positive and a negative process.

(1) The first is addition, with its negative, subtraction; and it consists in the annumeration of numbers not necessarily equal and contingently presented. The numbers added each represent the moment of Einheit, and the sum that of Anzahl: thus, in 7 + 5 = 12, 7 and 5 are the unities of which the sum is 12. In 12 - 5 = 7, the unities are again 5 and 7 into which the sum 12 is broken down by a process that is merely the negative of addition.

(2) Multiplication is addition of equal unities, and here we count together unities each of which is a sum. Thus in 3 x 4 = 12, four is a unit (Einheit) taken three times, three being the annumeration. But it matters not whether we take three as sum and four as unity, or four as sum and three as unit, for 4 x 3 = 3 x 4. The product is a sum of sums of which the multiplier indicates the discrete aspect and the number multiplied the continuous units. It is found by adding or counting, originally discovered by counting on one's fingers or on an abacus, and later reached immediately through the memorization of multiplication tables. Division is the same process in reverse. To find how many of a certain number taken as a unit (Einheit) are contained in another, we divide by it, and the quotient gives us the sum (Anzahl). If we seek to divide a number into a given number of equal parts, and to discover their magnitude, the divisor becomes Anzahl and the quotient Einheit.

(3) In addition the unities are unequal both to one another and to the sum; in multiplication the unities are equal to one another but not necessarily to the sum. When unit and sum are the same, we have a square and its negative the square root. Here the two moments of number are equalized and their opposition counteracted. The square is the complete self-relation of the number squared.

Raising a number to higher powers is a merely formal continuation of the process of involution. The even powers simply repeat the squaring ($2^4 = 2^2 \times 2^2$) and the odd powers reintroduce inequality from which the next even leads back to self-relation. For this reason equations in higher powers can be solved by reducing them to quadratics.

That calculation in all these forms is nothing but enumeration and addition is born out in our own day by the working of calculating machines and computers; and the principles fundamental to contemporary mathematical logic (which is used in the latter) are those which underly these basic methods of calculation, namely, the associative, distributive and commutative laws of algebra. But Hegel is very clear in his mind that calculation is not genuine thinking. These forms are not 'an immanent development of the Concept', for the Concept is the concrete universal which specifies itself into mutually dependent, mutually determining, internally related particulars, and thereby governs their natures and the relations between them. These methods of calculation, however, are only possible with particulars mutually indifferent and externally related, collected together loosely in sets, whose mutual relations are similarly external. They may be internal in the sense that some sets can contain others and that they may intersect, but they are not mutually determining in the organic way required by the Concept. Nevertheless, they are derived from the Concept in its form of Being-for-self, which provides the principle of self-related unity (Einheit), and as one whole (das Eins) figures as the exclusive unit merely external to others like itself. For this reason, calculation is founded not on the principle of unity in and through difference, but on that of equality and inequality, the rigid distinction and separation of distincta typical of the understanding. It is, at best, a by-product of the Concept's dialectic, but is not (as Hegel puts it) 'an immanent development' of it. To cast philosophical speculation (of which logic should be an essential part) into the moulds of these algorithms is to turn it into something merely formal, and so to distort its subject matter. And Hegel remarks that to make calculation the foundation of educational method is to stretch the mind on a rack and to turn it into a machine.[14] But where, as in mathematics, the subject matter can be treated as self-external colligations of bare particulars, calculation is appropriate.

The external relation of mutual indifference between quantitative units seems to have been altogether missed by McTaggart, possibly because he ignores Hegel's clear definition of quantity as what may be augmented or diminshed without affecting quality. So he alleges that units of quantity are each 'a simple and unique quality', which is obviously not the case and for which there is no vestige of warrant in the text.[15] Yet he admits (failing to notice the inconsistency) that each unit is the 'one' (i.e., the whole) of Being-for-itself. In this confusion, he contemplates the possibility, which, he says, Hegel overlooks, that there might be a finite number of simple qualities and so of quantitative units. We have already seen, however, that the very concept of quantity, as such, implies an indefinite multitude, or extent. This, McTaggart alleges, pertains only to 'the purely abstract conception of quantity, which can be applied to anything that can be thought of at all', whereas Hegel's categories, he avers, refer only to 'what is existent.' Just what this means is obscure, but of Hegel's logic it is palpably false. Existence is a category emergent at a much later stage than either quantity or quantum, and 'application' (or embodiment) of any category belongs not to logic but to nature. McTaggart presumably has in mind certain ideas peculiar to his own metaphysics, which is by no means identical with Hegel's philosophical position.[16]

Degree[17]

Quantum specifies itself further into extensive and intensive magnitude[18] (or degree). The first is the delimitation of the determinate multiplicity (of quanta), and the second is quantum für sich, indifferent to its limit in the sense that it has its intensity (its identity) in itself; yet also determined by what is outside itself -- i.e., by its position in a series of intensive magnitudes or degrees. It thus points beyond itself and generates (like Dasein under Quality) an interminable succession of degrees, the quantitative infinite.

In the Encyclopaedia the exposition of extensive and intensive magnitude is very condensed. In the Greater Logic it is very involved. First we are warned against confusing extensive magnitude with continuous magnitude. The former is the antithesis of intensive, not of discrete magnitude. Extensive magnitude is determinate as number, in which the extensive aspect is reflected in Anzahl or sum, whereas continuous magnitude is quantity extending itself indefinitely without respect to limit. Even when thought of as limited, the discreteness is not posited numerically in continuous magnitude. It is not considered as a unity with precise quantitative value. It is not yet number. We must not, however, forget that continuity and discreteness are ubiquitous aspects of quantity; the continuous is just as much discrete and the discrete continuous. So determinate quantity, qua number, is both sum and unity, a multiplicity of units continuous as one annumeration. Further, in determinate quantity (Quantum) and especially in Number, the determinateness rests in its limit (Grenze), which is united and identified with the sum as extensive magnitude and so marks off the unity as a specific number (of units or ones).

This determinateness is dependent primarily on the numerosity (Vielheit) of the units which make up the sum constituted by their mutual external relationship, and so is internal to the unity of the quantum and independent of what lies beyond its limit. But, being simply a continuous multiplicity of equal and indistinguishable units, the summation is not the full determinateness of the quantum, but only one moment in it. It is only a multitude or set (Menge). But in the number as a unity this multiplicity is sublated and vanishes into an intensity expressed numerically as a grade or degree. This again is the limit of the extensive sum expressed as a simple determinate quantity. It is the nth degree of whatever quantity is being considered. It is, Hegel says, magnitude (Mehrheit) rather than a many (Mehreres, Menge), a unique grade, not just a sum or aggregation. Numerically expressed, Degree is the complete determinateness of Number, posited in its Being-for-self.

Thus expressed, the quantity is related to other quantities as something to another, and they determine one another as a continuous scale. Each grade (or degree) as self-related quantitative determination is indifferent to the others, yet it is what it is only through its position in the series, and thus through its relation to what is beyond it. So distinguished and related, each gradation has, as it were, a quality of its own.[19]

As Degree, continuous and discrete magnitude are united in the limit. While it is self-related and the multiplicity is outside of it (as other grades), yet it has the numerical sum within itself. For example, 20 is the sum of twenty units and contains them, but as so doing it is the 20th. degree of magnitude, which is the simple expression of the continuity of this amount. Intensive magnitude is, therefore, doubly determined: (1) as its own annumerative quantum, and (2) as simple determination against other degrees which it excludes. Extensive and intensive quantity are thus, once again, simply aspects of all magnitude, for evey quantum is both, and each goes over into the other: the multiplicity of the former is concentrated together in the latter; and in the latter, gradations are distinguished one from another forming an extended succession of degrees, each having sublated in itself the annumeration which gives it its determinate quantity.

The reciprocal transition and mutual identification of extensive and intensive magnitude is evident in the number series itself. Each number is a sum, and so an extensive magnitude, but it is also the nth number, and as such it is a degree or intensive magnitude. Ten is the sum of ten units (or two fives, or one plus two plus three plus four), and it is also the tenth integer. Even more obviously is this the case with a series of fractions. One is, so far as indefinitely divisible, an extensive magnitude, and so is each division made in it, each fraction; but they

133

are denominated one third, one fourth, one fifth, and so on, as intensive quanta.

Number as we presented it earlier, as annumeration, was mere addition of units (equal quanta); but in its fully developed concept number is Degree, the union of extensive and intensive magnitude. It is only with Degree that we get the explicit notion of gradation or scale, in which each step is a sum of units and at the same time a precise number, or degree, or position on the scale. The grade is at one and the same time a total (Anzahl) -- the sum so far accumulated -- and a limit. Plato, in his later (mostly unwritten) philosophy, insisted that each number had its own ideal character distinct from every other number. Each was a distinct Form. Yet, though each is reached by colligation of ones, or units, the continuous series which results is not a succession of units or ones, but of degrees or specific numbers. Hence, as Frege declared, each number is a determinate object and has a proper name.[20]

In physical phenomena we see the same two-sided quantitative character. Mass or weight expressed in pounds or kilograms is an extensive quantity, but as pressure per unit area it is intensive quantity. Temperature expressed in terms of the expansion of a column of mercury is an extensive quantity, but as a degree of heat it is intensive. Tones and colours are at once extensive, as lengths and amplitudes of waves, and intensive, as perceptible qualities.

What is especially noticeable here is that with degree quality returns to quantity. Not only is each intensity distinguished qualitatively from every other as a mere quantum (for example, in the ordinal numbers), but physically the series of intensities is a qualitative as well as a quantitative series. This coalescence of quantity and quality realizes itself fully in Measure, the final category of Being, and the transition point between Quantity and Measure is Degree.

This important point McTaggart dismisses, wrongly and for insufficient reason.[21] Nevertheless he raises the question whether intensive quantum is not a higher phase of the dialectic than extensive, rather than a co-ordinate aspect of all magnitude, and he believes, on the strength of the Encyclopaedia Logic as well as certain passages in the Greater Logic, that this is the case, in spite of the titles of Hegel's subdivisions. It is, however, pretty clear that extensive and intensive magnitude are two opposed moments the reconciliation of which comes in Degree, and throughout the dialectic there is always some element of progression, even between thesis and antithesis, which continues into the synthesis.

In the Encyclopaedia (Section 103 Zus.), having just insisted that extensive and intensive quantity are complementary, Hegel immediately protests against the reduction of the second to the first, especially by physicists. His complaint at first seems rather captious, for surely every intensive magnitude, for instance intensity of light, is concomitant with an extensive magnitude, e.g., the number of photons impinging on the illuminated surface. The usual excuse of the physicists of his day, that it is more convenient to treat intensive quantities as extensive quantities, Hegel rejects; for, he says, intensive quantites are as easily and as properly expressed in numbers as extensive. But many modern scientists and philosophers would protest that the intensive denominations simply are measurements of extensive quantities: temperature just is the number of calories per unit volume, pressure just is the number of pounds or kilograms per unit area. Hegel's point, however, seems to be that empirical scientists profess to rest their theories on observation, and observation is perception, which again is sensory. Now sense qualities can only be quantified in terms of intensities of one sort or another, and these intensities cannot be reduced to extensities. Where we do entertain the idea of an extended sensation (e.g., a coloured surface or an extended tactual sensation) we are constrained to explain its possibility rather by relating it to intensive magnitudes than vice versa. If the neurophysiologist tells us that the intensity of sensation corresponds to the number of neuronal discharges involved, it makes no difference, because the firing of neurons, if it can be observed at all, can be detected only through the sense-perceiving of the pointer readings of instruments recording electrical transmissions, and this is in the medium of sensed qualities. The number of neuronal discharges is never immediately felt. But the intensity of feelings, whether of warmth, or pain, or pressure, and that of sensations, of colour, or sound, or scent, cannot be summed. Each may be more or less, but they cannot be collected together and added up to give a sum (or Anzahl). They are not extensive magnitudes and their numerical expression can only be that of degree. The numerical expression is extensive only in the sense in which it applies to ordinal numbers, which involve counting up yet are each unique.

Now, if science depends on observation, the correlation of the intensive perceptual qualities and extensive quantities will depend entirely on theory and inference. As Berkeley argued, primary qualities can be perceived only through and by means of secondary. Therefore, Hegel points out, the reduction of intensive to extensive magnitudes commits one to a metaphysical theory (in fact to materialism) which holds that all the cognized qualitative content of experience is nothing but matter and motion, the movement and arrangement of material particles. As Hobbes maintained: 'Neither in us are they anything else, but diverse motions; for motion produceth nothing but motion.'[22] Such a doctrine, Hegel contends, is a product of the abstract understanding 'just as much in conflict with unsophisticated perception as with genuine concrete thinking.'[23]

Degree is the concept of quantum für sich. The limit is at once the whole quantity (magnitude) and is determined by other magnitudes outside it. The limit is both the determinate magnitude and the exclusion of all others, so each magnitude posits the next and the interminable quantitative series results. The principle of progression fixes the limit of each gradation and ipso facto presses on to the next beyond, for it is the next beyond which determines the limit. Thus the progression is a continuous becoming, marked by determinate steps, like the rungs of Jacob's ladder. It displays itself par excellence in the number series, an indefinite progression constituting quantitatively the false infinite, every step in which is a finite number.

Endless progression and regression are implicit in the very concept of quantum. Its continuity is self-generating and boundless, and its discreteness is necessarily self-repetitive. As with Dasein, the progression professes to be infinite, but it never reaches beyond the finite. Because each determining and defining other is equally quantum, it is always finite and always demands transition beyond itself to another finite, so that progression is an unceasing oscillation from quantum to limit, which is perpetually reasserted. Accordingly no real progress to the infinite is ever made. However large the quantum reached it is still infinitely distant from the infinite, and so no real approximation to it. And as the continuity of quantum expresses itself equally in endless extensity and in endless diminution, the progression is interminable either way, though neither the infinitesimal nor the infinite is ever attainable. This inability to reach its bourne Hegel describes as eine Ohnmacht des Negativen -- a weakness of the negative -- in that what it abolishes by its own cancelling immediately reasserts itself. The true reason for this is that the essential difference between quantum and the infinite is not quantitative but qualitative. The essential quality of quantum is to be self-external, and thus by extending itself, however interminably, it always remains quantum, that is, finite. The infinite is the negation of quantum altogether, and that is strictly quality, as opposed to and not as a repetition of, quantity. It is, however, not pure immediate quality as we had it before, but quality mediated by quantity, quality quantitatively determined.

The false infinite that occurred under Dasein was qualitative, and now we have it re-established under Quantity. The difference between the two is important and must be made clear.[25] Dasein is a determinately qualitative finite being determined by what it excludes; but that is another determinate quality. As we noted when we were discussing Dasein, the antithesis is not between spatial or quantitative externalities but only between qualities. The 'othering' is therefore only implicit in determinate quality, but it is so in whatever quality you happen to select. It is, then, a continual and limitless Veranderung, but only, as Hegel says, an sich. The externality is not posited an ihm, that is, as it were, inevitably tacked on to the finite quality, as it is to the quantum.

Quantum is unit and sum and can be neither without the other. Unit is a unit only in a <u>Menge</u>; sum is its <u>Anzahl</u>, which is a summation of units. Quantum is thus essentially and perpetually outside of itself in its very nature as quantum. Number, as such, flows out of itself: it is always n + 1, the successor of some predecessor, which is equally a successor. Even zero is n + 1 (-1 + 1) and so has its predecessor. Likewise, space and time as quantities are, in Hegel's term, <u>sicherzeugende</u>. They are self-producing and self-produced. Only by being beyond itself is any space a spatial extent, or any time interval a duration; and the same must be true of any of their parts. Thus is the self-externality of quantum <u>an ihm gesetzt</u>.

Quantum is a standing self-contradiction. As we have seen, its identity and particular magnitude is inside itself, yet is set by its limit and defined by its other as lying outside of itself. Moreover, its other is not a qualitative other, but is an extension of itself beyond its own limit, and is still indifferently the same all over again, the limit notwithstanding. The quantitative infinite is the expression of this contradiction, not its solution, and it differs from the qualitative infinite, despite features which they obviously have in common, because its othering is set out, posited, <u>gesetzt</u>, in its very nature. It is its own self-expansion, not merely implicitly (though it is that as well), but actually, so to say, beside itself.

In the <u>Encyclopaedia</u> Hegel puts his criticism of Kant and Fichte for their inability to get beyond the false infinite in his exposition of the qualitative progression.[26] There too he comments on the error and futility of regarding such endlessly finite iteration as something sublime, rather than merely tedious. In the Greater Logic this remark comes with the discussion of the quantitative infinite, where he quotes Kant more at length and commends him here more for his inadvertent recognition and demonstration of the fruitlessness, as well as the impossibility, of trying to encompass the quantitative infinite than chides him for his reverence of it. Hegel shows, however, that Kant still gives too much deference to this endless endeavour to attain the unattainable, and that he succumbs in the end to the false infinite, whether in the spatio-temporal cosmos or in the self-identical <u>ego</u>, whose self-fulfilment (for both Kant and Fichte) lies ever beyond the limit of achievement in an ought to be which never is.

Kant's famous statement: 'Two things fill the mind with ever new and increasing wonder and awe, the more often and persistently reflection dwells upon them, the starry heaven above me and the moral law within me.'[27] expresses his deference to this twin infinity, and Hegel's criticism is not mere captiousness. That the aim of Kant's and Fichte's thought is sound he recognizes and concedes; it is the solution of the problem of reconciling the finite and the infinite. But Hegel sees that this does not and cannot lie in the conception of the infinite as endless self-externalization of the finite, and he quotes von Haller's poem in apt illustration:

Ich häufe ungeheure Zahlen
Gebirge Millionen auf,
Ich setze Zeit auf Zeit
Und welt auf welt zu Hauf,
Und wenn ich von der grauzen Höh
Mit Schwindel wieder nach dir seh:
Ist alle Macht der Zahl,
Vermehrt zu tausandmal,
Noch nicht ein Teil von dir
Ich zieh sie ab, und du liegst ganz vor mir.[28]

The real solution is in the concept of infinity as wholeness, as negative self-relation, the identity of self and other in the absolute transparency of self-knowledge. It is to bring this out that Hegel criticizes Kant and to show, rightly, that Kant stops half way along a path which leads in the right direction.

The infinitude sought by Kant and Fichte as what ought to be is a qualitative perfection unattainable by quantitative augmentation however long lasting. So likewise the mathematical infinite, Hegel argues, is a qualitative whole or <u>Fürsichsein</u>, which has 'returned into itself from its other' ('<u>aus seinem Anderssein in sich zurückgekehrt</u>').[29] The true infinite, he says lies at its foundation. This mathematical infinite also cannot be reached by mere quantitative accretion (or by mere counting) and must be otherwise conceived. The quantitative ratio is Hegel's resolution of the false infinite of quantity; it relates quantum to its other to produce a self-contained stability foreshadowing Measure, in which quality and quantity unite.

Ratio[30]

The contradiction of Quantum is that its internal determination rests in a limit which in its very nature posits an external other, on which the precise magnitude of the quantum is as much dependent as it is on what precedes the limit. The limit is, as it were, opposed both to the quanta it includes and to those it excludes, and only by this opposition is the specific quantum determined. Thus is the quantitative endless progression generated, which only repeats and perpetuates the contradiction. To resolve it the externality of the other must somehow be internalized to produce a true infinity. In numerical ratio this is achieved, for in it one quantum is related to its other to produce a third (the exponent) which is not merely immediate but is mediated by the inter-relation of the first two. It depends upon them, as they do upon each other. If one of them is altered, either one of the others must change, but the exponent remains constant so long as the related quanta maintain the same proportion, and an infinite number of pairs can be substituted to this end:

$$\frac{1}{2} = \frac{2}{4} = \frac{3}{6} = \ldots, \text{ and } \frac{4}{2} = \frac{6}{3} = \ldots = 2.$$

The ratio thus constitutes a whole in which each element depends upon and determines the others. The related numbers are but moments which are absorbed and vanish into the exponent. In the fraction the denominator is unit and the numerator is sum, and they are so related as to produce a quantum which is mediated by them and has an incipient qualitative character peculiar to it.

Numbers conceived as the exponent of two such related quantities are called 'rational numbers'. Each is a whole in itself, Fürsichsein, and each has a specific character or quality, as we remarked earlier, such as prompted Plato to rank the numbers each as a unique form or 'mathematical'. In such a rational number the negative relation to other is made internal to itself, and that it comprehends an infinity in its own self-determination is revealed by the infinite number of related pairs which have an identical exponent, as well as by the infinite decimal expansion of so called 'irrational' numbers and incommensurables (like π or $22/7$). In effect these quantites are definite and unique. In them the infinite regress is contained as a whole, so that in Hegel's view it would be more appropriate to call them rational, as the true expression of an infinite self-determined whole, to which the decimal expansion is the continuous approximation represented by the false infinite. Hegel here refers to and endorses Spinoza's distinction between what he calls the infinite of the imagination and the infinite of conception, or infinitum actu, illustrated by the space between two unequal eccentric circles inscribed one within the other.[31] There is an infinite number of distances between the two circumferences but they are all contained within and encompassed by the two circles.

The persistence of the identical exponent of infinitely variable numbers identically related is also paralleled in Spinoza's account of the unchanging individuality of a body constituted by the continually varying amounts of motion and rest which maintain a constant proportion. This relationship Spinoza uses to explain how an infinite mode of Extension (facies totius universi) can remain whole and unchanged though constituted by endless and infinitely varying changes.[32] Spinoza's conception of individuality, maintaining itself in perpetually changing self-manifestation, is precisely Hegel's conception of the concrete universal, and Spinoza's infinite modes or 'eternal things' are examples of Hegel's true infinite, specifying itself in an inexhaustible variety of finite particulars.

In the Greater Logic Hegel develops the category of Ratio through the subordinate triad of direct, inverse and exponential ratio, the interest of which is more technical than philosophical. His aim throughout is to emphasize the steady reemergence of quality in the quantitative determinations. This is especially so in the case of ratio, which has strong links with the mathematical notion of function and with the ramifying implications of the Greek word λόγος used so pregnantly by Aristotle in his doctrine of the Mean in the <u>Nicomachean Ethics</u>, <u>De Anima</u>, and elsewhere. What the mean determines is essentially a qualitative character, be it sensation or virtue. It is somewhat surprising that Hegel makes no reference here to this use by Aristotle of λόγος as ratio, or mean, the determining principle of what is right and just and virtuous.

In degree and ratio, quality begins to reestablish itself in quantitative form. This, as we have observed, while it is a return to quality is not to immediate quality, unmediated by quantity. It is a quality which depends upon and is identifiable with quantitative determination. Such qualitative quantity, or quantified quality, is Measure, the union of the opposites which the prior process of the dialetic has developed. This is the truth prefigured by the Pythagorean declaration that all things are numbers, and by the modern scientists' insistence that qualities be reduced to quantities. They are <u>not</u> to be so reduced, but the truth of the matter is that the reality is both at once, a quantified quality expressed as measure. Hegel's earlier protests against the reduction of quality to quantity and of intensive quantity to extensive quantity are protests against onesidedness and abstraction, from which we now ascend to a more concrete concept of Being. In the <u>Zusatz</u> to Section 106 in the <u>Encyclopaedia</u>, we are told that every mathematical treatment of the objective world in fact aims always at measure rather than at mere quantity, as is indicated by our description of our operations as measurement, and of quantities as 'measures'. So the difference of tone in vibrating strings is correlated with the measurement of lengths, and the properties[33] (qualities) of chemical compounds with the proportions of the substances in combination. The merely quantitative aspect of things is of interest only as it affects their qualitative nature.[34]

NOTES: Book II, Part I, Chapter 2

1. <u>W.L.</u>, I, pp. 209-227; Miller, pp. 185-199; <u>Enz.</u>, Section 99.

2. <u>Enz.</u>, Section 99 <u>Zus.</u>

3. <u>Enz.</u>, Section 99; <u>W.L.</u>, I, pp. 211-227; Miller, pp. 187-199.

4. <u>Enz.</u>, Section 100; <u>W.L.</u>, I, pp. 211ff; Miller, pp. 199ff.

5. Cf. <u>Enz.</u>, Section 100.

6. Cf. Ethics I, xv, S.

7. W.L., I, p. 216ff.; Miller, p. 190ff.

8. See below.

9. Enz., Section 101 Zus.

10. Enz., Section 102; W.L. I, pp. 231-249; Miller, pp. 202-217.

11. Wallace translates this term 'annumeration'.

12. Cf. W.L., I, p. 235; Miller, p. 205f: 'Die Zahl ist um ihres Prinzips, des Eins, willen ein äusserlich Zusammengefasstes überhaupt, eine schlechthin analytische Figur, die keinen inneren Zusammenhang enthält. Weil sie so nur ein äusserlich Erzeugtes ist, ist alles Rechnen das Hervorbringen von Zahlen, ein Zählen oder bestimmter: Zusammenzählen.

13. Cf. W.L., I, p. 240; Miller, p. 209, and compare Hans Reichenbach, The Rise of Scientific Philosophy (University of California Press, 1951), pp. 40ff; A.J. Ayer, Language, Truth and Logic (London, 1964), pp. 77-78.

14. Cf. W.L., I, p. 249; Miller, p. 216f.

15. Cf. Commentary, pp. 49-50.

16. Cf. McTaggart, The Nature of Existence (Cambridge, 1921, 1968), Bk. I, Ch. II.

17. Enz., Sections 103-104; W.L., I, pp. 250-260; Miller, pp. 217-226.

18. Cf. W.L., I, p. 231; Miller, p. 202.

19. Cf. W.L., I, p. 253; Miller, p. 220.

20. CF. G. Frege, Grundlagen der Arithmetik, Section 38. Frege, however, is not altogether clear or consistent on this point.

21. Cf. Commentary, Section 57, p. 53.

22. Leviathan, Ch. xlvi.

23. Enz., loc. cit., Cf. p. 61 above, and Enz. Section 38, Zus.

24. Enz. Section 104; W.L., I, p. 260ff., Miller, p. 225ff.

25. Cf. W.L., I, p. 261; Miller, p. 226.

26. Enz., Section 93, Zus.

27. Kritik der praktischen Vernunft, Beschluss, 161.

28. Albrecht von Haller, 'Unvollkommenen Gedicht über die Ewigkeit', from Versuch schweizerische Gedichte, Bern 1732.
> 'I heap up monstrous numbers, range upon range of millions,
> I set aeon upon aeon and world heaped upon world,
> And when from the appalling height I look dizzily towards thee,
> All the might of number, multiplied a thousand times
> Is not a fraction of thee.
> I sweep them all away, and thou liest wholly before me.'

(Wallace, in his note, quotes a later version).

29. W.L., I, p. 287; Miller, p. 246.

30. Enz., Section 105. W.L., I, pp. 372-386; Miller, pp. 314-325.

31. Cf. Spinoza, Epistle XII.

32. Cf. Spinoza, Epistle XXXII and Ethics, II, Lemma VII, S.

33. The conception of a thing and its properties does not properly belong to this stage of the dialectic. It belongs to Essence. But it is precisely Essence that is here foreshadowed and which emerges from Measure. The thing and its properties develops (by stages) out of quantified quality, as will appear below.

34. On the whole of this and the previous sections McTaggart's interpretation (Cf. Commentary, Sections 61-70, pp. 58-70.) is so obviously wrong and inadequate in almost every point, that detailed refutation becomes supererogatory. His proposed reconstruction of the last triad (Ratio) is ingenious but quite invalid, because it reintroduces quality gratuitously from without to establish, in effect, an abstract universal, and does not generate it from quantity itself as is Hegel's clear intention.

Chapter 3

Measure

Quality is in immediate unity with being as its immediate
determination. When it is sublated in quantity the determination is no
longer internal, but, as is the case with the quantum, it lies in an
external other. The equality of quanta is an external equality,
indifferent to the quality (whatever it may be) of the quantified beings
which are equated. But each as thus described is abstract, the first, as
was observed earlier, because the determination of quality is not fully
definite until it is precisely defined by measurement, and the second
because the unity of the quantum depends ultimately on its qualitative
distinctness. What constitutes one (das Eins), as Frege came to realize,
depends upon the concept of which the one is an instance. Abstract
quality and abstract quantity, therefore, unite in the concept of
Measure. Like other categories, Measure is a provisional definition of
the Absolute. God has been conceived as the measure of all things, or
as prescribing and fixing all measures. In the Book of Job, He is
represented as asking rhetorically, 'who laid the measures of the
foundations of the earth'; and the Psalmist declares that 'He hath set
bounds to the earth and to the sea.'

The section on Measure is extraordinarily difficult and involved in
the Greater Logic, whereas its counterpart in the Encyclopaedia is
much abbreviated and relatively straightforward. On this topic the
Greater Logic is so obscure as to be, for the most part, hardly
intelligible, and while it contains some astonishingly prescient scientific
comments, it also indulges in what, to us in the twentieth century, must
appear ill-informed and perverse polemic against sound scientific
insights. Hegel inveighs against Berzelius' shrewd anticipation of the
atomic theory and inspired gropings towards the identification of
chemical bonds with electrical attractions, yet he sees the possibility
and even the necessity of a chemical series such as, at a later date,
Mendeljeff discovered.[1] Similarly, though he rejects the notion of a
natural standard of measurement,[2] which, in our day has been
established by Eddington, Hegel points to the need for a scientific
theory that will deduce the laws of motion from the fundamental nature
of space and time, as well as unite space and time in a single manifold,[3]
a theory that at the beginning of the twentieth century was produced by
Einstein and Minkowski.

What makes this section so unintelligible to modern readers is
probably its veiled allusions to science now altogether obsolete and
forgotten, which was, however, in the early nineteenth century, the
latest development. And Hegel's scientific insights were very mixed;
sometimes quite perverse and even in implicit conflict with his own
philosophical convictions, and sometimes wonderfully perspicacious and
prophetic. His rejecton of atomic interpretations of chemical

143

phenomena goes counter to his own conception of the correlation of the quantitative and qualitative aspects of things, yet he is unfailingly aware of the holism governing physico-chemical entities and the essential relationships between them that this necessitates.

Perhaps this complexity and obscurity is the reason for McTaggart's complete failure to understand, and his utter rejection of, all the categories of Measure as wholly invalid.[4] And his exposition of them only confounds the apparent confusion. We have already noted that he misconceives the significance of Ratio, without which it is impossible to grasp that of Measure. The correlation of quality with quantity (even as foreshadowed in Pythagorean philosophy) seems quite incomprehensible to McTaggart, and his notion that the ones of the quantum are doubly qualitied units is wide of the mark. He says that each has one quality in common with the others to which it is conjoined in the quantum, and another peculiar to itself. This is virtual nonsense and far removed from what Hegel has argued. Hegel's doctrine is that the units are bare particulars, indifferent to quality and to each other, mutually in external relation. The nature of their aggregation and annumeration follows from these facts, and it is only when quanta in integral relation (or ratio -- Verhältnis) constitute definite quantitative configurations that they reassume an element of quality. This then develops into Measure as the quantified quality of determinate being. For whatever has quantity must have some quality (the fact presupposed but suppressed in pure mathematics) and the precise determination of that quality turns out in the end to be quantitative, in the form of a measure or 'logos', a mathematical function.

In the Encyclopaedia the complicated and detailed dialectic of the Greater Logic is condensed and curtailed to one tenth of its length. In fact, what appears there is scarcely more than a summary of the second chapter of the three into which, in the Greater Logic, this category is divided: the one on Real Measure, with brief references taken from the other two. Perhaps because of this the dialectical progression in the Encyclopaedia is clearer, and it is made more understandable by the Zusätze. I shall therefore use the shorter version as the basis of my comments, selecting from the longer only what seems to fit in with or naturally to extend it.

A large part of the long introduction to Measure in the Greater Logic is digression. Some of it appears in summary form along with material from the Chapter on 'Specific Quantity' (Ch. I)[5] in the Zusatz to Section 107 of the Encyclopaedia. It contains some rather unexpected examples from the history of philosophy and comparative religion, which at first look inappropriate, but which serve to show that Measure in the Doctrine of Being is really an inchoate disclosure of the relation between universal and particular, which emerges explicitly only in the Doctrine of the Concept. Hegel criticizes as Pantheism Spinoza's use of the concept of Mode[6] as the particularization of Attribute and

144

Substance, as well as the Hindu representation of Vishnu and Siva as particularizations of Brahma. His objection is that, while the necessity of differentiation is recognized, the differences are then lost in a universal which obliterates them. It is not at first obvious how this is relevant to measure, until one realizes that there the quantitative aspect corresponds to differentiation (or particularization) and the qualitative to unity (or the universal), and Hegel's point is that the concrete universal is both in one, is a self-differentiating whole in which neither aspect may be suppressed. Such a whole is what Measure as the culminating category of Being prefigures.

The Greater Logic then continues, subdividing Measure into sub-categories as follows:

(1) Specific Quantity, subdivided yet again into (a) Specific quantum, (b) Specifying measure and (c) Being-for-self in measure. The second of these subdivisions is again resolved into Rule, Specific quantity (or measure) and Relation of both sides as qualities;

(2) Real Measure, with (a) Relation of self-subsistent measures, further divided into Combination of two measures, Series of measure relations, and Elective affinity, (b) Nodal line of measure relations, and (c) the measureless;

(3) The Becoming of Essence: (a) Absolute indifference, (b) Indifference as inverse relation of factors, and (c) transition to Essence.

The precise relationship of the subdivisions in this complicated list one to another, and even what some of them mean, is difficult to divine. Some of them recur at different levels without obvious regularity, and the scientific phenomena to which they are supposed to apply are obscure. I shall make no serious attempt to sort all this out and shall simply do what I can to follow the sequence of the Encyclopaedia.

In Ratio we found a qualitative character emerging within quantity itself, and now we discover that the very quality of being is determined as a ratio or quantitative proportion. As Measure is Being in its complete self-development, sublating all the prior categories, it is Being as a whole, and in it the major moments which have already been traversed are recapitulated. Pure Being corresponds to immediate measure, where a quantum is associated (angebunden) with a determinate quality. This quality and the associated quantity are taken in their immediacy and give the impression at first of being mutually independent. They are, however, not so, in fact they are closely connected. In this phase of the category we speak, for instance, of 'a measure of corn', or in money matters of a 'pound' or 'a talent'. These look like mere quantities but they are not, for they have definite and inescapable qualitative associations. The 'measure' of corn is not one

145

applicable to cloth or metal, and the 'pound' is no simple weight, it is a specific value attached to the weight because of the quality of the metal (e.g., silver) used as currency. The reference is to a definite quantity of a specific qualitative grade of material. So everything that exists is perceived as a somewhat of a certain magnitude; as the Greeks maintained, 'Everything there is has its measure', and believed that whatever exceeded its due measure would be overtaken by Nemesis, a redressing diminution or destruction. So Heraclitus declares, 'The sun will not overstep his measures; if he does the Erinyes, the handmaids of Justice, will find him out',[7] for, as he also tells us, 'This world...is...an ever-living fire, with measures of it kindling, and measures going out.'[8] Anaximander, before him, had spoken of things coming to be out of the ἄπειρον and going back into it again by 'making reparation and satisfaction to one another for their injustice,'[9] by which he appears to mean reparation and satisfaction for exceeding due measure. Similar references to 'measure' are to be found in Diogenes of Apollonia who closely followed both Anaximenes and Anaxagoras.[10]

At this stage each aspect asserts itself in relative, or apparent, independence of the other, so that increase or decrease of quantity seems to leave the quality unchanged, and differences of quality seem to make no difference to magnitude. Two measures of corn are still corn, two pounds are still silver (or whatever the metal used as legal tender); and (as Hegel points out in Section 107 Zus.) in inorganic nature a rock may weigh a ton whether it be sandstone or granite. But this independence is superficial and for the most part deceptive. A slab of marble used to face a building has a very different quality from the geological stratum of rock from which it was hewn, and different again from the same marble ground to powder or degraded to chalk. But this sort of interdependence is far less significant than another, that is more integral to the chemical nature of the subtances -- the proportions in which their components are combined, and the degree of temperature or humidity that determines their physical state.

Further, size and proportion are inherent determinants of the character of natural phenomena. Hegel views the solar system as a pure manifestation of proportion between quanta of mass, motion and distance -- or, more strictly, of space to time, in motion. He calls it free motion -- a conception foreshadowing the relativistic theory of gravitational movement as the tracing out by a body of a geodesic in space-time. In organic nature, species of plants and animals are characterized by specific sizes and proportions, and the quantitative relations between the organs of a living body have important organic determinants and consequences.

But such examples anticipate and illustrate a more advanced stage in the dialectic of Measure than the merely immediate. Its first phase is a matter of simple quantitative comparison of qualitied entities (Etwas). It is simple measurement in terms of a standard unit

(<u>Massstab</u>). We must note, however, that this is not pure and simple quantitative comparison (not mere counting up), for the standard has, or is given, a qualitative significance. A foot, or an ell, for instance, is chosen as a standard with distinct reference to its practical convenience and its natural relationship to the human body. As was mentioned above, there is a certain appropriateness of the measuring unit to the measured stuff. So eighteenth century French scientists sought a measure of length which was a definite fraction of the earth's diameter in a bid to find a natural standard. This, Hegel declares, is futile and foolish, for all standards, however chosen, are arbitrary in relation to the measured quantities to which they are applied. With respect to the examples given he is right; but today the physicist, following Eddington, will claim that there is indeed a natural standard of length, namely, the radius of curvature of space. This one can hardly expect Hegel to have foreseen, but it gives special force to the idea that the unit carries in it a qualitative value, when we remember that curvature of space is intimately connected with field and with matter and with the motion of bodies.

The relation of quantity to quality at the level at which they seem independently variable is sometimes problematic.[11] When, for instance, does the loss of hair amount to baldness? How many grains of corn are needed to constitute a heap? Such questions, Hegel says, are not idle because they direct attention to the interdependence of the moments of measure. The real folly is to insist on the sheer quantitative aspect to the neglect of the qualitative.

Just what Hegel means by 'specific quantum' is puzzling. one would expect it to be a quantity determining a specific quality, as a temperature of $0^{\circ}C$ determines the state of water to solidity, and sometimes Hegel appears to be using it thus. But he also speaks of it as if he meant by it the unit or standard of measurement (<u>Massstab</u>). In the first sense it constitutes a rule according to which quality varies, but not in the second; yet Hegel actually identifies <u>Massstab</u> with <u>Regel</u> in one context.[12] Again, 'specifying measure' is something rather different and more complicated, being (apparently) a relation such as that between the specific heat of different bodies immersed in a common medium.[13] Yet specific heat is also an example of quality-determining quantum, though a less complex inter-relation than the previous example. Moreover, the notion of specific measure seems also to be applied to concomitant variations of, for example, space and time in motion, particularly in the law of falling bodies and of gravitation.

What Hegel appears to be doing here is ranging these examples in an hierarchical scale, with each presupposing and developing out of its predecessor. First simple measurement, which is a comparison of some qualitied quantum with a standard (<u>Massstab</u>) considered and used as a rule for quantifying; then a quantity correlated with a special quality or state, which serves as a rule ambiguously, in part as a critical point on

147

a measuring scale and in part as an indicator of qualitative change; next there is the ratio of one quantified quality to another which defines and regulates yet a third quantified quality, such as specific gravity or specific heat; following on this come the correlation between spatial and temporal quantities which determine the degree (velocity) and acceleration of motion, and finally the proportions of qualitied substances which in combination determine the specific character of chemical compounds. This scale of forms does not cover nor explain all the nuances of Hegel's exposition, or clarify all his obscure mathematical and scientific allusions, nor is it obvious just how each step arises from the previous one, but it might serve as a guiding thread to a reader attempting to disentangle the complexities of the dialectic in this section.

Specific measure, which seems somehow to span what Hegel calls by that name as well as much that he treats under 'Real Measure', corresponds to <u>Dasein,</u> for here distinct correlations determine distinct qualitative states, and each is other to the rest. Yet these distinct quantified qualities or qualitied quantities are again brought into combinations determined in specific quantitative proportions to characterize a further level of differentiated entities with characteristic qualities in determinate amounts.

The Infinite of Measure

The progression of quantitative change is continuous and, as we saw, is in some cases apparently indifferently related to quality, as in the changes of temperature which fall between the freezing and the boiling points of a liquid. But these critical points are nodal, and they are not necessarily isolated, for the series may be extended -- steam may become superheated and eventually is converted into plasma. There are however analogous series which continue indefinitely. The number series is the paradigm case, being compactly continuous while each number has its own specific relations to selected others (as multiple, factor, square, cube, and the like); so each has a distinct qualitative value which appears only at nodal points in the continuum. The tonal scale in another example. The rates of vibration increase or decrease continuously, but harmonics occur only at nodal points on the scale and certain intervals are critical. Chemical combination between elements with mutual affinity also occur at critical proportions of mixture, so one finds certain metalic oxides occurring in series, as do also certain carbon compounds. Such are the examples that Hegel gives, but had he known what more recent science has disclosed, he could have quoted even more convincing examples: the various kinds of electro-magnetic waves, for instance, which at specific frequencies change their nature from gamma-rays to X-rays, ultra-violet to chromatic, infra-red to Herzian (to say nothing of other forms of radiant energy); and yet more spectacular are the states of the atom with quantum jumps of electrons from one shell to another.

148

What results is an infinite series (at least in principle) of nodal points at which quality changes abruptly within a quantitative continuum of gradual increase (or decrease). It is a persistent oscillation from quantity to quality, the quantity varying between nodal points without affecting the quality, and the quality being sharply transformed at the critical junctures of correlation. In the infinite series, the specifying measure is perpetually being exceeded and the constituted quality is constantly dissipated, hence the sequence is measureless. As a whole it has no determining measure, and the excess by which any particular qualitative state is destroyed is, with reference to it, indeterminate and so measureless. It has violated the rule of correlation and is no longer a specific measure. This indeterminate measurelessness, however, resolves itself into a new specifying ratio determining a new qualitative phase, only to be exceeded again and once more to dissipate into measurelessness. The false infinite has overtaken us once again, this time as a ceaseless oscillation between quantity and quality which, as Hegel puts it, sublate one another repeatedly in measure and its dissipation.

All this is admirably explained and expounded by Bernhard Lakebrink in his Kommentar (pp. 169-182). He stresses particularly the far reaching consequences of the contrast between the continuous progression of quantity with the sudden and discontinuous changes of quality concomitant with critical (or nodal) points. As he points out, for example, in the evolutionary scale, the hominids approach homo sapiens continuously in various quantitative respects, but, as he puts it,

> not only humanity, but every terminus of development, indeed from the physico-chemical to the moral, is above all else a qualitative occurrence, where the gradualness of mere quantitative approximation to a persistent goal leads finally to something wholly different, the qualitative leap, namely, a measure which is 'absolutely dissevered' from its prior qualitative determinatenesses and now stands before us as something incalculably new. (p. 175)

McTaggart also observes the contrast between the continuous quantitative process and the discontinuous qualitative succession, but without the perspicacious comprehension displayed by Lakebrink.

Considering the continuum of quantitative progression in itself, we see that it has no specific measure and is a limitless persistent substrate from which the qualitative determinations emerge in correlation with appropriate quantitative ratios. In the dialectical progression of measure, the original moments, quality and quantity, appeared on both sides of the opposition and generated concomitances of measured quality with measured quality, and specific quantity with specific quantity, so that the determinate qualitative beings which emerged were entities, things, Etwas. 'Entities', 'things', are not legitimate

149

terms at this stage, but are appropriate only to categories of Essence. Here, however, Essence is beginning to show itself in the opposition of quantity and quality and their mutual determinations, as substrate and qualified manifestations. Thus the substrate has the aspect of permanent existent matter taking different and changeable forms according to the quantitative disposition of its elementary constituents.

The measureless, as the false infinite of measure, becomes in this way transformed into the true infinite of self-determined measure. The infinite regress is not really possible, because the relation between quantity and quality in measure is a precise ratio re-established in each variation of quality, so that every nodal form shows quality and quantity mutually determining and equivalent. In each node the quality is determined by the quantity and is what it is through that determination, and conversely, the quantity is defined by its quality. Neither can be what it is without the other, and each in and through its other is identical with itself. To take an elementary example, liquid heated beyond its boiling point ceases to be liquid and becomes, qua liquid, quantitatively and qualitatively immeasurable. But its new quantitative expansion is correlated with a new qualitative state as a gas. The succession can proceed indefinitely as a false infinite only if the qualitative identity of the liquid is overlooked. Scrutinized more closely, the various physical states are seen as manifestations of the same substance -- water, or whatever the original liquid might have been -- which has its own specific measure as a proportionate combination, or ratio, of elementary constituents. It is H_2O, or some other specific combination, the formula or measure for which persists intact throughout its various changes of state. This measure does not change but remains the inner or latent substantial basis which determines both the qualitative states and the nodal points in the quantitative scale at which they appear.

The persistent substrate is not rightly thought of as a merely indifferent quantitative progression, but is a perennial principle of correlation constantly and repeatedly reestablished in a succession of graded self-manifestations which it generates as an hierarchical sequence of qualitative forms. The measureless has thus transpired as the self-determined, which is not measured by any external standard but is itself the universal standard, or measure, of all its manifestations. It is in this sense that Measure is (or was) a provisional definition of the Absolute. We may now put the statement into the past tense because Measure is being left behind. It is ceasing to be an adequate definition, and is becoming something more potent and significant than mere measure. It has turned into the inner essence which explains the outward appearance, and so we proceed to the concept of Essence.

NOTES: Book II, Part I, Chapter 3

1. <u>W.L.</u>, I, pp. 426-435; Miller, pp. 359-366.

2. Ibid., p. 395; Miller, p. 334.

3. Ibid., pp. 405-07; Miller, pp. 342-43.

4. Cf. <u>Commentary</u>, Ch. IV, Section 75, p. 72.

5. <u>W.L.</u>, I, pp. 394ff; Miller, pp. 333ff.

6. Hegel interprets the term as meaning literally 'manner' -- of particularization. I have argued in Ch. IV of <u>Salvation from Despair</u> that this criticism is a misintrepetation of Spinoza.

7. Fr. 29 (Bywater's numbering).

8. Fr. 20; cf. Fr. 23.

9. Cf. J. Burnet, <u>Early Greek Philosophy</u> (London, 1963), p. 52.

10. Cf. Burnet, op. cit., p. 357.

11. Cf. <u>Enz.</u>, Section 108 <u>Zus.</u>

12. Cf. <u>W.L.</u>, I, p. 399; Miller, p. 337: '<u>Die Regel oder der Massstab</u>...'

13. Cf. <u>W.L.</u>, I, p. 401; Miller, p. 338, <u>Anmerkung.</u>

151

PART II

THE DOCTRINE OF ESSENCE

PART II

THE DOCTRINE OF ESSENCE

Chapter 1

Essence as a Division of the Logic

Let us recall at this point that logic, as philosophical thinking, is an activity which has required a long and complex process of generation. It presupposes not only the philosophical science of Phenomenology, but, like that also, all the empirical and mathematical sciences and all the intellectual activity putting to use what Hegel calls 'unconscious logic' -- morality, politics and religion, and prior to them, perceptual experience and common sense. Logic is reflection upon all of these, eliciting from them the categories embodied in the thought they express. At the same time it presupposes, is a product of and a reflection upon, the history of philosophy, which, developing as it were, in a different dimension, has come to recognize these categories in their dialectical relationship as its own logical form. One might represent these two aspects of dialectical evolution quasi-diagrammatically as vertical (historical) and horizontal (phenomenological) processes converging upon what Hegel calls <u>Wissenschaft</u> proper (Absolute Knowing).

In logic, the Doctrine of Being is the self-generation of the thought determinations implicit in the range of perceptual or intuitive awareness and common sense, roughly designated immediate experience. But more sophisticated thought reflects upon this and strives to understand it, taking the form of empirical science. This is the reflective phase of thought characteristic of the understanding, and its logic is more especially the Doctrine of Essence -- 'more especially' because, of course, the other divisions of the Logic are not irrelevant to it, for the understanding is already at work in common sense, involving the categories of Being, and the union of both Being and Essence is what the Doctrine of the Concept develops. But the logic of the understanding specifically is, like the understanding itself, a reflective turning back upon the sphere of Being, developing the special categories of empirical science. This logic is, however, two-fold. The understanding, being reflective, devises a logic of its own -- formal logic -- which expresses and formalizes its own type of thinking. Then philosophical logic again reflects upon this, at the same time as it traces the development of the categories of science; for formal logic is in fact one of the special sciences and exercises the same kind of reflective thinking.

Now, perceptual experience and scientific reflection upon it are both phases in the develpment of our consciousness of the world of nature, and they involve mental processes sublating the natural processes, physiological and physico-chemical. On their epistemological side these processes are the coming to consciousness of the natural processes and the making explicit in consciousness of their essential principles of being. They constitute, by the same token, phases in the activity of mind, as it becomes aware of itself and reflects upon its experience. This constitutes the first, the horizontal, dimension of the dialectical process in nature and experience. The movement of the Logic through the categories of Essence is thus (just as it was in the transition through the categories of Being) at once subjective and objective. Its categories, like those of the sciences on which it reflects, are at once categories of thought and principles of existence.

Let us take an example at random. We perceive water flowing over the land after rain and washing out gullies through the soil. We interpret this scientifically in terms of cause and effect. This is both a category of thought, a thought-form by which we think the objects of experience (as Kant might have expressed it) and equally a principle of relationship between events in the world -- the flow of the water and the erosion of the soil.

Understanding, however, does not stop at interpreting the perceptual experience of nature. On its own level it is self-reflective and becomes philosophical. So it calls in question its own categories, and asks how far they are merely subjective, or to what extent they are applicable to the real. Do we apprehend things as they really are, or do we experience only phenomena? In interpreting experience science applies universal concepts -- it universalizes particular experiences -- producing the categories of the understanding. But then the understanding separates the universal from the particulars and, taking the latter as real, questions the reality of the former. Such reflection, with the questions that it raises, and the answers that it proposes, are typical of the philosophical theories of Empiricism and the Critical Philosophy of Kant. This represents the second dimension (the historical or vertical dimension) of the dialectic. The reflections and questions of this type of philosophy may be summed up in the general question of the relation between appearance and reality, which is itself only the subjectivized version of an older antithesis traditional especially in Mediaeval philosophy, that between essence and existence.

Philosophical logic, besides giving an account of all this, also mounts a critique of it. It reflects upon it (in its turn) as a phase in the development of the Idea (the Truth), but it does so from a philosophical, or speculative viewpoint, from the point of vantage of the Concept, because philosophical logic is speculative thinking; it is the Concept itself in active operation.[1] So it criticizes, while it also traces the dialectical emergence of, the relevant categories. We shall find therefore, as we go through the Doctrine of Essence, that Hegel, as he develops the categories dialectically, criticizes the use made of them

154

by the understanding, giving in effect a double interpretation of each, one as a significant phase in the progress of thought, and the other as an inadequate and misused idea falling short of the concrete requirements of the Concept.[2]

The Dialectic of Essence

The Doctrine of Essence is the middle section of the Logic, the doctrine par excellence of mediation. Here the general nature of the dialectic displays itself more evidently than it did under Being, with an accompanying increase in complexity. As always, the dialectic is both sublative, absorbing and carrying forward what has been superseded, and proleptic, anticipating and foreshadowing what is still to come. Essence accordingly recapitulates and makes explicit at a higher level what has already been traversed under Being but was there only implicit; and at the same time the Concept an und für sich is prefigured in it -- the Fürsichsein of interdependent and interlaced moments within a whole.

As the categories of Being each in turn broke down through their inadequacy to the whole which was unwittingly implied in their attempt at self-maintenance, they passed over each into the next. The later was substituted for the earlier, which, even if held as it were in suspension in the new category, was nevertheless superseded and left behind. In Essence the correlations merely implicit in Being are now set out (gesetzt) and made explicit, and the interdependent concepts are retained and held together as related pairs. Where under Being the movement of the dialectic is transition, under Essence it is introreflection.

At the end of the Zusatz to Section 111 in the Encyclopaedia, Hegel writes:

> In the sphere of Being the relationship is only implicit; in Essence on the contrary it is posited. This is in general the difference between the forms of Being and Essence. In Being everything is immediate, in Essence, on the other hand, everything is relative.

But this relativity is repeatedly sublated and mediation tends continuously to return to a new mediated immediacy.

The relative and dependent character of each category of Being was apparent only to the reflective scrutiny of the philosopher, not to the naive consciousness employing the category. But the scientist is aware of the relativity and makes it explicit. Consequently the categories of Essence repeat those of Being, and the Doctrine of Essence does over again what was done in the preceding division of the Logic, setting out in extenso what was previously only für uns but in

155

immediate awareness itself was merely <u>an sich</u>. What in Being was implicit interdependence in Essence becomes explicit inter-relation.

Immediate intuition is inadequate; it fails to express its own concept. It is only apparently immediate, for to maintain itself its object has to go over into its other, by implicit reference to which alone is it what it purports to be. What forces it over into its other is the totality which they together constitute and which is immanent in them both. So what the original, apparently immediate, presentation really is, is not really immediate but is mediated by an other. This mediation became apparent to us, as philosophers, reflecting upon presented being, but for the unsophisticated consciousness it results merely in the transition and alteration through which what is lacking in the immediate makes its immanent presence effective. In reflection this mediation is explicated, and under Essence is posited and set out -- as it were, diagrammed. Essence is the Concept in diagrammatic form, not yet wholly explicit in and for itself, but evidently differentiated in mutually related moments.

We have already had to use terms characteristic of Essence to explain the implications of Measure, and now again, in introducing Essence itself, we have said that Being was only <u>apparently</u> immediate, though <u>really</u> mediated by a reference beyond, or behind, what was immediately presented. What it really is is not what it appears to be; what it is <u>essentially</u> differs from what it seems on the surface. What Being implicitly was (<u>ist gewesen</u>), Essence (<u>Wesen</u>) now makes explicit. Hegel remarks that once again language reflects our intuition of the truth.

The inquiring mind seeks to penetrate the immediacy of Being and to discover what lies behind the outward appearance or show (<u>Schein</u>); i.e., what shows itself as immediate object. This has already been foreshadowed in the dialectic of Being, where we found the meaning, or quality, or inner being of a determinate something always in something else -- always referred away from itself. As we have said, this transition into something else is powered by the immanence in Being of the whole, or Absolute -- the Concept -- which is 'sensed' or 'intuited' as lying behind, or within, what is outwardly apparent, constituting its essence. The essence is in truth the Concept, or the Idea, the Absolute immanent in Being. It is the 'underlying reality'. Essence, therefore, explicates Being, and mediates the immediate, while it adumbrates and prefigures the Concept in which the mediation is finally sublated.

In the doctrine of Being each category disclosed a reference away to an other. The dialectic moved from one to the other, from this to that, from something to something else, in order to discover its 'what'. Now the reference is from outer to inner, from appearance to reality, from outer shell to an inner hidden truth. Being now appears as the outer shell or show -- a mask behind which the true essence resides.

But, on the other hand, the essence is the true being, the real or actual, and immediate presentation is only appearance, the inessential, a mere show, or even an illusion. At the same time the pure essence, taken apart from its showing, is an abstraction -- a mere self-identity, or abstract inner -- which can actualize itself only as manifested in its outward show. It can be actual only as appearance or phenomenon.

Accordingly, in Essence there is an inherent contradiction, a diremption into two mutually opposed and even repugnant abstractions, which are nevertheless mutually dependent, and each of which in turn claims precedence over the other. Hence all its categories are dual. In Essence being has been split into correlative aspects. It is the relational phase both of being and of thinking.

Hegel tells us that the doctrine of Essence is the most difficult part of the logic, and his treatment of it in the Greater Logic certainly makes it so. The reason he gives is that it contains the categories of metaphysics as well as of all the sciences. By 'metaphysics' he means here the old pre-Kantian metaphysics which remains within the bounds of the understanding. But we must constantly bear in mind that it is a critique of these categories as well as a philosophical development of them, the underlying basis of which is the immanent, or 'presupposed' Concept. As a result each category can be taken in either of two senses, either abstractly or concretely. Further, the dialectic is complicated by the fact that it is the dialectic of reflection, and Essence is a double reflection, first upon Being, and secondly of the Concept. Not only are the categories each duplex in consequence, but each member of every pair has the double aspect of outward show and inner truth. The understanding stubbornly holds them apart as if they were mutually independent, yet gives each of them a significance which makes their mutual dependence inescapable. As abstractly separated each is only appearance, but as concretely inter-related they are the rational real -- the foreshadowed concept.

The key conception is system, structured wholeness, which underlies the entire treatment of the categories of Essence (indeed, it underlies the whole of the Logic, but here it is becoming ever more evident and important). It is as yet still held in the background as what the external appearances hide, while they nevertheless express. The articulated system is truly the essence, but in its explicit form it is the Concept. In Essence it is tacitly presupposed, at most only adumbrated; it is represented in abstract and provisional forms, which emerge as identity, ground, law, content, force, whole, substance and actuality, each with its outwardly apparent counterpart. These inadequate forms are categories of the understanding, which, seen as what they truly are -- phases in the evolution of the Concept -- are legitimate and necessary thought-determinations. But regarded as ultimate and final, they are stunted abstractions misrepresenting the full-blown truth.[3]

It should now be clear in what sense Essence is a definition of the Absolute. It is 'the truth of' Being, and that is what the Absolute is -- its essence. God, as supreme being, is translated into German as das höchste Wesen. The sense of this phrase, Hegel points out, implies that God is one (though the greatest) of a number of beings, for Wesen is commonly used of finite beings and is more generally applied to humans and to specialized collectives. This conception of God is typical of Deism, which pictures God as separate from the world, as external Creator and reigning Lord. It is the product of the understanding and, for all its importance as a step in the development of religion, is far inferior to the true Christian conception which it fails to comprehend. The analogy here with essence lies in the dualism which this conception of deity involves.[4]

General View of Essence

In the Greater Logic Hegel begins by setting out the sphere of Essence as a triadic series of degrees of reflection. Being with all its determinations is aufgehoben, but now seen to be, not the truth, but mere outward show, in which on reflection we find no truth. 'The truth of Being is Essence', or what is essential to it. Merely immediate being is thus, first der Schein, show, illusion, in Berkeley's words, 'a false imaginary glare'. But, secondly, this is recognized as the outward appearance, die Erscheinung, of the truth: its phenomenal being, proceeding from a ground which is its essence. Finally, it ranks as manifestation, die Offenbarung, the actual revelation of the essence concretely embodied in being, or Actuality.

This scale of degrees of appearance is important and illuminating, but the sub-categories elaborated in the Greater Logic become complicated and obscure, and seem to a large extent to overlap, so that the later triads are virtually subdivisions of the earlier ones repeated in more detailed form. In the Encyclopaedia all this is much condensed and becomes more easily comprehensible. The section on Show is reduced to an introductory discussion of the nature of Essence generally. Then what here figures as the first triad in fact covers the whole field, and the later subdivisions are more detailed developments of the first three categories: Identity, Difference and Ground. These compose the theme song, or Leitmotif of the doctrine of Essence, on which the subsequent triads are variations and elaborations. We have thus a parallel, on a higher level, of what occurred under Being, where the first triad, Being, Nothing and Becoming, set the tone for the entire dialectical movement, and reappeared transformed in every subsequent triad. The process now continues in the guise of reflection, which takes the forms of reflection-into-self (Identity) and reflection-into-other (Difference), synthesized in Ground as self-reflected-into-other or self-differentiated totality.

In the Greater Logic the first division of Essence is Intro-reflection (Reflexion in ihm selbst), which is sub-divided into Show (Schein), Essentialities or Determinations of Reflection, and Ground. Identity and Difference appear as sub-categories of the second sub-division and their mutual opposition is synthesized as Contradiction.[5] This movement is quite clear and seems legitimate, for contradiction is the conjunction of A and not-A, identity and difference. But in the Encyclopaedia this arrangement is altered. The first division is Essence as Ground of Existence and is subdivided into Pure Determinations of Reflection, Existence and Thing. Identity and Difference are the first two pure determinations and the resolution of their opposition is Ground, while Contrariety is the synthesis of Positive and Negative, which are subsumed under Difference. This process seems justified and intelligible, nor is it really a divergence from that of the Greater Logic, because there Contradiction is immediately resolved as Ground.[6]

The exposition of the earlier sub-categories of Reflection-into-self in the Greater Logic is difficult and often obscure. McTaggart represents it as a texture of errors and makes of it largely nonsense;[7] but little would be gained discussing his mistakes in detail, for he misunderstands and misinterprets Hegel's entire project, treating it more as Realphilosophie than as Logic and failing to notice that what is going on throughout the dialectic is the self-specification of the Concept into a series of graded categories. Lakebrink's treatment of this section is much better, though still rather obscure (as is Hegel's own), for, unlike McTaggart, Lakebrink is fully aware of what Hegel is trying to do, and he is properly appreciative of the movement of the dialectic.[8] His shortcoming is his failure to explain Hegel's phraseology, which he simply repeats. For instance, Hegel tells us that the movement of Essence is 'from nothing to nothing' and that it then negates the two nothings in a return to itself in the emergence of Essence. But just what does this mean? Lakebrink does not tell us. The two 'nothings' are the abstract aspects distinguished by reflection, each of which by itself is the negation of immediate being, and as such is a mere shadow. Yet each is correlative to (and 'shows' in) the other, each reflecting into each to reveal an inner essence issuing in outer disclosure or self-expression. Lakebrink understands this well enough, but he does not make it as plain to his reader as he might.

NOTES: Book II, Part II, Chapter 1

1.   Cf. G.R. Mure, A Study of Hegel's Logic, Ch. V Section 5.1, p. 88.

2.   McTaggart fails to appreciate this distinction and repeatedly takes Hegel to be advocating what in fact he is criticizing, although at the same time he is demonstrating how the inadequacy necessarily arises in the dialectical development.

159

3.   Of this McTaggart shows not the slightest awarenes and in consequence his exegesis of Hegel's argument is for the most part merely fantastic (especially of the categories under 'Essentialities or Determinations of Reflection'), and his criticism is often ludicrous.

4.   Cf. Enz., Section 112 Zus.

5.   W.L., II, pp. 17-80; Miller, pp. 393-443.

6.   Cf. Enz. Sections 119-120; W.L., II, pp. 64-79; Miller, pp. 431-443.

7.   Cf. Commentary, pp. 95-102.

8.   Cf. Kommentar, pp. 183ff and 197ff.

Chapter 2

Essence as Ground of Existence[1]

Identity[2]

Identity, says Hegel, is self-relation, not as immediate but as reflection. It is reflection-into-self, or self-identity. As immediate it would be simply being, but as reflected being, or being reflected into itself, it is the total structure of Being with all its moments sublated, grasped as the identity or self-sameness of which they are all simply moments. It is the identical essence of Being, of which the moments are the diverse expression (or outward show); but in Being, taken as identity, the diverse moments are suppressed, or absorbed, and we envisage an identity pure and simple.

Hegel distinguishes between true identity and abstract identity,[3] the second being the mere formal identity as conceived by the understanding. True identity is the identity which includes difference, whereas abstract identity is held to be wholly exclusive of all difference, either by leaving out 'the multiple features of the concrete' (i.e., analytic identity), or by blurring all diversity into one. It is this abstract identity which philosophy of the understanding commonly claims to be the basis of exactitude and precision, but in truth, by ignoring the diversity of the concrete, it becomes the nadir of vagueness and confusion. The true identity is the identity of the whole, of the system or Concept, which is an identity of differences. In its immediate phase it is mere being; but now it is mediated as essence and is an identity issuing in diversity. As Hegel puts it, if we make it the predicate of a proposition with the Absolute as subject, we say: 'The Absolute is identical with itself', that is, the whole is one and self-identical. Now this is vague so long as it is not made clear which sense of identity is intended, abstract or concrete. If it is concrete, the dialectic at once proceeds and the identity of the whole emerges as the ground, and that again transpires as the Concept. In short, the ground both of identity and of diversity is the systematic totality of the concept -- the structure of the ordered whole, or the system articulating itself as a dialectical scale. If it is taken in the abstract sense, the whole or Absolute becomes a blank unity (what Hegel and most of his followers allege of Spinoza's Substance), a block universe (what Bergson and most Process philosophers allege of the Hegelian Absolute), or 'the night in which all cows are black' (the reproach which Hegel himself voices against Schelling). The faults so often found by critics in Hegel's doctrine are frequently only the consequences of their own misinterpretation of his thought in terms of the abstract identity of the understanding, so that they accuse him of defects which he himself recognized and rejected as the direct results of such abstract interpretation.

As envisaged by the understanding, identity is devoid of all diversity. It is sheer self-coincidence, a relation with only one term. It is accordingly immediately in contradiction with itself. A relation, to be a relation, must have at least two terms, so a relation with only one is a self-contradiction, like the Buddhist's attempt to imagine the sound of one hand clapping. A diadic relation requires distinction between the two terms and that implies difference. But here we are supposed to exclude all difference, which, if we did, would destroy all relation.

A is A. But then the first A must be distinguished from the second; and if it is, the second is not the first. They cannot be the same and yet the proposition identifies them. If they were the same, identical without distinction, the proposition could not be formulated. So it contradicts itself, and the traditional statement of the Law of Identity violates the Law of Non-contradiction.

'No,' you will object, 'the two As are merely two tokens symbolizing one entity. The proposition affirms that what A signifies is what A signifies.' Now either this proposition enunciates nothing by its repetition, or it becomes significant by making a distinction between the two significations which it then seeks to overrule. In short, it affirms an identity in difference. But identity is not supposed to tolerate any difference, and here it fails to exclude it, or, so far as it does exclude it, it vanishes altogether. A sheer tautology makes no assertion, or, as Hegel says, is merely silly.

Again you may object. The identity affirmed is distinct from the difference. What the two As signify is one object. They may (in fact must) be different, but that to which they refer is one and the same. They differ in sense but are identical in reference. This, however, is itself an identity in difference; for what is it to which the As refer but something which in two distinct contexts asserts its self-sameness? Whatever A refers to is the same on every (different) occasion that A refers to it. The differences are different appearances of one thing, or different times at which it occurs, or is noticed, or different aspects which it presents. Its identity is always disclosed in or through differences. And the original objection is disingenuous, because when the formal logician asserts that A is A, what A represents is said to be a proper name, and is supposed to be the same token at each occurrence. It is actually A that is being identified with A. Yet if they were indistinguishable there could be but one occurrence and the statement could not be made. Tiglathpileser is, no doubt, Tiglathpileser, but unless in saying this we were making some distinction, for instance, between the name inscribed on a tablet and that mentioned in Kings II, xv, 29, or between either or both of these and the name of a certain King of Assyria, or between the proper name and the person to whom it belongs, we could be making no significant assertion.

162

In other words, bare identity is equivalent to pure being, which is the same as nothing. If it excludes all diversity it has no content; if it abjures all external differences it has no intrinsic character, no identity; and if it disowns all internal diversity it becomes blank non-identity. One single point without the rest of space ceases to be a spatial determination of any kind and cannot be identified. It is an identifiable point (it has identity) only as a position distinct from and related to other identifiable positions. Tiglathpileser has identity only in relation to other kings, of Assyria and of other countries, to his subjects and all other people, to his historical period (which is identifiable only in relation to other historical periods); and only as the man with such and such personal characteristics, appearance, disposition and stature, as presenting himself at different times and in different places (all similarly identifiable) can Tiglathpileser be identified.

To identify, then, is always at the same time to distinguish. To identify onself is either to make a distinction within oneself (between that in oneself that one acknowledges as one's own and that which one disowns), or to assert a distinction between oneself and others. Self-identification is the grasp of two or more aspects, features, traits or sentiments, both, or all, of which are mine and so define my personality as one. It is also to distinguish my character as expressed in all of these from that of anybody else. The 'I think' which accompanies all my experiences is identifiable only as common to the variety of objects which diversify my consciousness, and as the centre of all possible syntheses of and in this diversity. Self-identity is, therefore, always a distinction of self (in one respect) from self (in another), and a unification of different contents within the self. This may be stated otherwise, as it is by Hegel, as the identification of the self with its other, which it recognizes to be only itself distinguished from itself. The ultimate self is Absolute Spirit, whose identity is nothing but the unity of all the distinctions that fall within it. It is thus at home with itself in its other.

Much of the above has already been encountered under Dasein, where it was made clear that omnis determinatio est negatio. But here it is being made more explicit by reflection. Negation is being explicated as difference and determination as identity, as we are now seeing that all identity is at the same time differentiation.

Difference[4]

Hegel points out that abstract identity immediately resolves itself into diversity.[5] A world of self-identical entities is ipso facto a multiple world of different entities, and to be self-identical is to differ from everything else. Or again, from another angle, abstract identity, by excluding difference, is different from difference and so goes over into its other. It is simply one moment of difference itself. Difference is, again, different from identity and together they constitute difference which is thus both itself and one of its own moments. Thus they become indifferently other and so virtually the same. The whole constituted by the difference of identity from difference can be regarded either as Difference, which is the whole as well as one of the moments, or as Identity, which is likewise the whole (in which both are indifferently the same) and one of the moments.[6]

This seemingly complex and slightly suspect argument is really quite sound and simple. To be identical with self is obviously to be different from other things, and to be different is necessarily to be identical with self. Without identity, difference is impossible, and equally vice versa. If identity is blurred, difference disappears, and if all differences are dissolved we are back in the darkness of the night in which all cows are black. Omnis negatio est determinatio. But identical particulars which differ from one another are, in their particular self-sameness, as well as in their mutual difference, all equivalent one to another. The self-identical differents are thus indifferently alike and differ, if at all, only numerically. But to differ only numerically is to have no mutual difference, and so difference collapses once more into identity. It will presently become apparent that there can really be no such concept as purely numerical difference.

Abstract difference, as maintained by the understanding, is alleged to be absolute difference, which leaves the terms wholly unaffected, so that there is said to be 'no relation between them' (a truly senseless description). Difference thus becomes different 'in and for itself',[7] not difference from an other outside itself. So Hegel distinguishes the 'difference of reflection' from the 'other-being of Dasein'. As he puts it, the difference of A from not-A is the simple (bare) negative, 'not'.[8] This is pure, absolute negation, the logical operation pure and simple. The difference is thus diversity in which the diverse moments are wholly diverse and indifferent to one another and to their internal determination. The otherness of Dasein was not so indifferent, for its determination was its otherness or distinction from its other. But the reflective understanding elevates this difference into a separation which tolerates no affinity with any other, an absolute diversity. Relations thus (so far as one can contemplate them at all) become wholly external and their terms degenerate into bare particulars without internal determination, which are mutually simply diverse.

Such a conception, common as it is in all forms of Empiricism, is really quite unthinkable. Different items cannot be known to be different unless they are compared and related. Difference is and can be but a relation, and the terms cannot possibly be so different as not to be related at all. Moreover, if they are different, it must be in some respect or other which is common to both of them. They must belong to a single complex whole, which is grasped all together as one, and within which distinctions are made. Kant was quite clear on this point when he insisted that elements completely isolated from one another are unrelatable even as different. If each representation in consciousness fell away and were annihilated as the next appeared, no such thing as cognition could ever arise.[9]

Furthermore, comparison can be made only in terms of the intrinsic determinations of the things compared. Where we find the same characteristics we say that the things are alike, and when we find different characteristics we judge them unlike. These then are the subcategories of Identity and Difference. Similarity and dissimilarity, however, must have a common basis. Only what belongs to a common domain can sensibly be compared. We may, for instance, compare the earth with Mars as planets and find them alike in some respects and unlike in others. But it would make no sense to say that the earth was unlike larceny, or that Mars differs from schizophrenia.[10]

The significance of Leibniz' principle that no two things can be indiscernible rests for Hegel on the internality of all relations and distinctions.[11] If everything 'is what it is and not another thing', and if each is indifferent to its relation to every other, you cannot strictly say that 'everything is different'. Each is what it is and that is all. Its difference from other things can be asserted only on the basis of comparison, which again concludes from the inner natures of things compared to their likeness and unlikeness. A square differs from a circle because it is bounded by straight lines at right angles, which is its own intrinsic character, and because the circle has a circumference equidistant at all points from its centre. Hence the difference is determinate and intrinsic, and only in this sense is it true that no two things are indiscernible and that indiscernibles are identical. Sheer numerical difference would be a difference without distinction, which is self-contradictory and impossible. Even abstract points in empty mathematical space are distinguishable by their positions and the relations between them of distance and direction, and identical repetitions must at least differ in the times of their occurrence.

Likeness is the element of identity in the different. Only the disparate can be alike. And Unlikeness is the difference between what are fundamentally the same (as we saw above). It is the bearing upon one another, the relation (Beziehung) of the kindred. They are thus mutually dependent -- no likeness without unlikeness, and no disparity without kinship. They reflect into one another.

Identity in contrast to that from which it differs is Positive as opposed to Negative. These, like the last pair of correlatives, are also mutually dependent. Each is what it is only in contrast with the other, and in their mutual antithesis we have Opposition. The negative is the other of the positive; they exclude each other and in their mutual exclusion they are opposed. As competitors for the same place in the system they are mutually in conflict and contradict one another; but as

165

mutually defining they are interdependent, and as mutually complementary (in the system) they are compatible and at one.

Positive and negative posit, or make explicit, the contrast of Dasein as the one to the other, and are also the reflective phase of that contrast, so that each as implying the other is the whole contrast in itself, each is implicitly a Being-for-self, a definite something. The whole, therefore, is immanent in both sides of the correlation, and the negative, in excluding the positive (as also the positive in its repulsion of the negative) implicitly excludes (or negates) itself in negating its other. Thus the opposition becomes explicit contradiction.[12] It is, once more, the internality of the relation that brings this about. Because in the integrity of the whole each element is constituted by the universal principle of organization, and so by its inter-relations with every other, each reflects and implicitly contains all the rest, so that their mutual negativity is at the same time self-exclusion. Consequently any attempt either in thought or in fact to hold the finite part in isolation and to make it independent of the rest (or concomitantly to displace it from its systematic context) gives rise to conflict and contradiction.

It is laid down in formal logic that of two opposed predicates only one can be truly affirmed of any given subject, and that there is no third possibility. This is the Law of Excluded Middle. Hegel says that the Law of Contradiction conflicts with the Law of Identity and that the Law of Excluded Middle, which is intended by the understanding to guard against contradiction, is itself the source of contradiction. This may look thoroughly perverse, but so long as we think in terms of system, or the cohesion of diverse elements, we can see it to be entirely sound; and, if we fail to think in these terms, we suffer from 'the typical thoughtlessness of abstraction which puts two contradictory principles next to each other without even comparing them.'[13]

We saw above that 'A is A', in abstraction from 'A is distinct from A', contradicts itself. Now we must acknowledge that it also contradicts 'A is not non-A'. Hegel says that the first maxim (Identity) states that A must be related to nothing but itself, whereas the second (Non-contradiction) states that it must be opposed to something else -- i.e., related to another. If we take the copula literally, the first says that A is nothing but itself, the second that it is something else, namely, an opposite to not-A. But surely, one might protest, these two assertions are mutually consistent. If A and non-A are related elements in a system they are indeed compatible; but if, as the logic of the understanding alleges, A is nothing but A, and non-A is absolutely different from and unrelated to A, then to equate A with not-non-A is to contradict these assumptions. In 'A is A' the second A is not the first (and if it were no proposition would be enunciable); so it should really be written "A is A'", but the abstract understanding contends that there is no difference, and then $\underline{A}'$ is non-$\underline{A}$ and "$\underline{A}$ is $\underline{A}'''$ contradicts itself. And if $\underline{A}$ is $\underline{A}'$, '$\underline{A}$ is not non-$\underline{A}$ (=$\underline{A}'$)' is false.

To begin at the other end '$\underline{A}$ is not non-$\underline{A}'$ is convertible as 'Non-$\underline{A}$ is not $\underline{A}'$, and these two propositions are equivalent. This means that, so far as their mutual opposition is concerned, $\underline{A}$ and non-$\underline{A}$ are equivalent. So far as each is other to the other there is no significant distinction between them and $\underline{A}$ is as much non-$\underline{A}$ as it is $\underline{A}$. But in that case both the Law of Non-contradiction and the Law of Excluded Middle are violated. The contradiction involved in the Law of Excluded Middle is simply that involved in the Law of Identity compounded with that of the Law of Opposition (as Hegel calls it). If bare identity is no more self-consistent than bare difference, it is false that $\underline{A}$ is exclusively either $\underline{B}$ or not-$\underline{B}$.

Hegel is here insisting on the significance of negation and the inanity of bare negation. To say that $\underline{A}$ is not $\underline{X}$ is to say that it is something else. Its A-ness depends on and is constituted by what it excludes and is not, but only if that is something positive and complementary to it in a larger whole. If not to be non-$\underline{A}$ is a bare negative, if it has no positive significance, then it is not $\overline{A}$. On the other hand, what are complementary in a larger whole are not mutually exclusive so far as they are mutually constitutive, and the 'either-or' of the understanding does not apply to them.

It is quite wrong and misguided to conclude from all this, as many do among Hegel's defenders as well as among his opponents, that he denied the validity of the laws of thought. He insists that contradiction is ubiquitous both in thought and in reality, but he could not do so if it were not really contradiction and were not recognized as such. He also declares that it is the principle of all movement and activity, which it would not be unless it were an irritant, that is, if it were tolerable. Indeed it is contradiction to maintain at once that $\underline{A}$ is $\underline{A}$ and that it is not-$\underline{A}$, and it is impossible for anything to be, or to have, two different qualities in the same place at the same time and in the same respect. And when conflicts occur either in thought or in fact the immanent urge is to resolve them and to restore harmony. None of this could be maintained if the laws of thought did not hold. But they do hold, and contradictions do occur, and there is a universal nisus towards the resolution of conflicts, because and only because the real is rational, because it is a system of inter-related and inter-determining moments, of which the truth is the whole. It is only in this system that things, or terms, or particulars of any kind can be identified; and their identity involves the principle of organization which relates them intrinsically to others. Contradiction arises when we seek to deny this, overtly or by implication, and to maintain the identity of partial forms in isolation from the system; or, what amounts to the same thing, when we transpose them while assuming that it makes no difference either to them or to the context so disrupted. This abstraction from context is constantly practised by the understanding in the name of precision and alledgedly in accordance with the laws of thought. But it is abstraction that violates these laws and produces the contradiction. This is Hegel's message. His criticism is directed, not at the laws themselves, but at the misinterpretation and misuse of them. It is abstract identity and abstract difference that he castigates, not the concrete identity in and through difference which is the hall-mark of system.

But at the same time, the dialectic must account for the occurrence of the abstractions, and demonstrate their generation in the process of reflection. So we find in the Logic a double process of exposition, tracing the dialectical emergence of the abstract concepts, and also demonstrating their failure to do justice to the system they are supposed to characterize and the contradictions into which they fall in their vaunted championship of the self-consistent.

True identity and difference are, then, the interdependent moments of everything precisely distinguishable through contraposition in an articulated system. In such a schema differences are not just juxtaposed and mutually indifferent atoms. On the contrary, the parts of the whole fit into one another and are mutually adapted; so they negate one another definitively and significantly. They relate to each other as systematic opposites. Every concrete whole is thus systematically differentiated, and every concrete, whether whole or part, holds within itself contrary aspects. Each implies what it is not and invokes what it essentially opposes.

The source of the opposition is the discrepancy between what something is <u>immediately</u> and what it is <u>essentially</u>.[14] Essentially it is the whole to which it belongs, that is, it is the expression of the principle of order which actualizes itself as a whole through the particular differentiations. Thus it has a nisus to develop what is implicit (an sich) in it. The whole immanent in it is its potentiality of becoming. The example Hegel gives (loc. cit.) is the tendency of an acid to react with a base. Here the principle of the whole is the chemical affinity expressing the universal electro-magnetic tendency of matter towards equilibrium, which, as it embodies itself in an acid compound, contains the potentiality of reacting with a base to become a salt. The chemical affinity signalizes a finitude or particularity, which implies opposition to that which it lacks and with which it combines when conditions are appropriate. Contradiction, Hegel says, is the very moving principle of the world.

Positive and Negative, which are supposed to be mutually exclusive and each self-sustaining, are nevertheless wholly dependent each upon the other. So, says Hegel, they are both explicit contradiction, and each in abolishing the other abrogates itself (positive <u>negates</u> the negative and negative <u>affirms</u> a contra-positive -- each in negating the other on which it depends for its own significance negates itself).

168

Accordingly, he says, 'they fall to the ground' (Sie gehen hiermit zu Grunde). By this play on words he means to emphasize the truth which has been implicit all along and has been steadily emerging in the course of the dialectic of identity and difference, that the ground or basis of all opposition and negation is the structured whole or system, within which alone precise distinctions and identifications can be made and contrariety arises. This is the true ground of identity and difference.

The whole of this section of the Logic is really an exposition of the nature and dialectical function of negation. Negation is the principle of differentiation which distinguishes identity from difference and establishes both. It equally is the principle of structure and systematic inter-relation, which is the substantive underlying basis of identity and difference. So it is the root of organization, which equally sustains it. Distincts are themselves identical, and are so by being mutually different. Hence they negate one another. As mutually positive and negative they are opposed, but as mutually dependent and inter-determinant, they are mutually supplementary and thus compatible contraries. At the same time, treated as substitutes one for another (in the system) they are contradictories; and each, so far as it negates the other, while, because for its own identity it depends on and is determined by the other, contradicts itself. This self-contradiction, however, is resolved in their systematic relation, or the ground, which is the system of which they are integral moments.

The common distinctions between contrariety and opposition ignore this dialectic and are based on the abstract notions of identity and difference, which inspire the doctrine of the square of opposition in traditional formal logic. Critics of Hegel who allege that he confuses opposition and contrariety and both of these with contradiction have utterly missed the point that systematic structure is the underlying basis of all three. The concrete inter-determination of moments in a whole makes them (according to the viewpoint taken) contraries, opposites and contradictories, as dialectical phases, of which the truth and outcome is the Ground in which they are all rooted.

Once this is understood everything that Hegel says about identity and difference, positive and negative, falls into place.

> The Positive is that which is distinguished (jenes verschiedene) as what is to be for itself and at the same time not indifferent to its relation to its other. The Negative is just as independently to be for itself, the negative relation to self, yet at the same time to have this, its relation to itself, its positive, sheerly negative, only in its other. (Enz., Section 120).

In the ordered system each element is for itself what its relation to its other makes it. That other is the negative, whose self-sufficiency is just as much located in its other, the positive. Each, in short, is as much what it is because of its other, which is immanent in it, and which it implicitly is. Each is at once both itself and implicitly the other. 'Hence both are the posited [explicit] contradiction, both implicitly the same' (ibid.) -- as well as opposed. Hegel continues:

> The essential difference, as difference in and for itself, is only its own difference from itself, thus it contains the identical; thus to the whole difference (as it is in and for itself [i.e., as it is in reality]) the identity as well as itself belong. (ibid.)

The whole system, in other words, consists of its essential differentiations, and is at one with itself in its differences. This is its identity, which is as much contained in (and constituted by) its differences as they are in it; and is at the same time the basis (or ground) of the identity of each of its parts. The system is the ground both of the identity and of the difference.

Ground[15]

'Ground is the unity of Identity and Difference' (Enz., Section 121). A whole or system is just such unity. It is one and its unity is constituted by the intermesh of the differences which make it up, as a jigsaw puzzle is made up and united into a whole by the fitting together of its interlocking pieces. Further, 'Ground is essence posited as a totality' (ibid.). It is essence because it is the explanatory ground. The principle of structure explains the differences and disposition of the details. It is this principle of structure which binds them together into a single whole; and when it is set out in its explicit pattern, it is the ground of all that it contains.

But qua essence it is totality reflected into itself, and therefore its dual aspect comes to the fore as ground expressing itself in a consequent. Fundamentally the content of both is the same, but they reflect into one another and one is represented as essential, the other as inessential; or they are represented as the essential and its external expression, or result. The ground is the sufficient reason, and that which it supports or explains is its outcome or result. So we have two terms corresponding to explicans and explicandum.

Again all this is both 'subjective' and 'objective' (keeping in mind that these terms are as yet proleptic). We have not yet reached the category of actuality, but in ground actuality is implicit, and it is difficult to avoid the terminology appropriate to later sub-categories in explaining those of ground. Hegel is hard put to find names for his categories which will distinguish them satisfactorily. But this proleptic tendency is inherent in the nature of the dialectic and is especially characteristic of Essence. For every phase is a reflection of Being on

170

to and into itself, and each category reflects every other and in every other, so that it appears again and again in different forms. 'Subjectively' ground is sufficient reason, but the sufficient reason of things is always something that is, and later it transpires as objective cause.

Yet again, ground may be conceived concretely or abstractly. If we stress the identity of the unity of identity and difference, to the neglect of its diversity, we conceive ground abstractly. One extreme shows itself in the tendency to understand essence as self-same in both ground and consequent (explanans and explanandum); the other is the insistence on repeating the content once as immediate and again as mediated. Both abstractions can be seen in an explanation such as is popularly given of lightning that it is a discharge of static electricity from the clouds to the earth. But what is it that discharges? We say simply, electricity. The content in both cases is the same, for the discharge is simply the lightning; and the explanation that it occurs because of an electrical charge does no more than state as mediated what was first simply apprehended immediately.

The opposite abstraction is to insist on difference without regard to identity, which results in the exploration of grounds of all kinds for every proposition or event, grounds both for it and against it, and to elaborate these ad lib. in abstraction from the actual determining circumstances and the laws that govern them, or the principles relevant to the matter in hand. Thus in legal and moral concerns, all sides and every aspect of each case can be examined and pursued by all sorts of casuistry. Thieving, it may be argued, is indeed violation of the right of property; but also the needs of the thief must be taken into consideration and the superior capacity of the rich to provide for lost possessions, etc., etc. This is what we usually call sophistry; and Hegel points out that historically the Sophists came into prominence when traditional customs and religion were in decline and a ground had to be sought and an explanation (or 'rationalization') given for every demand and activity.

The complete and scientific explanation, of whatever explanandum, is the Concept -- the true Ground. But the finite sciences think in terms not of the concrete self-differentiating universal, but of an abstract universal, which embraces a number of externally related particulars identified only by an alleged similarity. The manner of explanation is then to forumulate a law under which a number of like cases are subsumed, and the law is then given as the sufficient reason of whatever can be deduced from it or brought under it.

True explanation, or proof, in dialectical logic, is nothing more nor less than the tracing out of the development of the Concept (or whole) itself -- its self-specification.[16] It is the process of self-

171

explication of the system of the real, and explanation is seeing, or finding, the proper place of each phase and item in the light of the whole and its principle of order. This is in truth (as we shall see later) teleological explanation,[17] not merely explanation in terms of efficient causation, which at this stage is the basic relation under which sufficient reason is being conceived. Strictly, causation is a category still to be deduced, but ground is conceived largely, though vaguely, and in varying degrees, as causal explanation. In the Zusatz to Section 121 in the Encyclopaedia, Hegel draws attention to the contrast between final and efficient causation in a comment on Leibniz, who elevated the principle of sufficient reason to a status co-ordinate with that of identity, but who made it clear that one may not remain at the level of efficient causation but must come to see it ultimately as an appearance of final causation.

In the Greater Logic, Hegel sets out in some detail the succcessive degrees of concretion through which the concept of ground develops. First it is simply an essential basis which takes various external forms. So he begins with what he calls Absolute Ground, and specifies this as form and essence, which becomes form and matter (in the Aristotelian sense), and thence form and content. The last pair reverses the order of the previous pair. In form and matter form is the more specific, matter being merely the unspecified potentiality of becoming informed. In form and content, form is the more general and external, whereas content is specific and determinate. In the Encyclopaedia these double sub-categories appear elsewhere; but their place in the dialectical series is in any case ambiguous because, in effect, all categories of Essence have this dual aspect of inner and outer, content and form, essential and inessential.

Hegel proceeds in the Greater Logic to a second triad, which he subdivides into Formal Ground, Real Ground and Complete Ground. Formal Ground is simply the enunciation of a law or principle as explanans, which, when examined turns out to be no more than a summary statement of the explanandum -- a merely formal and tautological explanation. For example, the law of gravity is given as sufficient reason of the revolution of the planets around the sun. But when we seek to discover what gravity really is, all the scientist can tell us is that it is the force of attraction which causes the planets to move as they do around a gravitational centre. The motion of the bodies is attributed to a force (or to two forces, gravitation and inertia), but when we ask what the forces are, we can describe them only in terms of the motion of the bodies. Hegel points out similarly that to explain the shape of a crystal in terms of the disposition of its molecules, is simply to invoke the same form over again, for the disposition of the molecules is the disposition of the parts of the crystal. The extreme case is Molière's satire on such explanation; the reason why opium causes sleep is that it has a virtus dormitiva. Moreover, the formal ground is so general that it will explain many

172

diverse facts and phenomena other than the explanandum for which it was originally invoked. Gravity is the universal law of motion for all bodies in the universe, however they move, and not only of the planets in our solar system. What is really required is a ground of the different kinds of motion, which will differentiate one from another.

Once again, we must not forget that ground can be taken abstractly as well as concretely, and that Hegel is both criticizing the abstract interpretation, and 'deducing' the legitimate concept. The law of gravity is a universal law, and concretely developed it is the principle which specifies itself as different kinds of motion according to the relevant circumstances, spatio-temporal or whatever, in which the bodies concerned are disposed. But if scientific explanation is no more than it is said to be by contemporary pundits, who describe a scientific system as a formal deductive system and explanation as formal deduction from higher laws to subordinate laws and thence to observable consequences, what we have is precisely what Hegel regards as Formal Ground, especially when laws are said to be merely statements of constant conjunction of particular facts. Explanation then can be nothing but tautological restatement, either of the law or of the description of the phenomena to be explained. For formal deduction is held to be purely analytic, and inductive generalization no more than the reiteration of what is constantly observed.[18]

The next stage makes the ground determinate or real. To remedy the defect of formal ground the generality of the explanans is specified into individual events. It is the impact of one billiard ball upon another that causes the second to move, or the collapse of the pillars under Samson's thrust that brings down the Philistine temple. But now the question arises, which among all the numerous conditions involved are the essential ones constituting the real ground? We select from among them those we consider to be necessary conditions; but then we find that they are not sufficient -- and what we seek is the sufficient reason.

At this stage, because the grounds proliferate into a multiplicity of conditions, it is arbitrary which we select, and so, Hegel says, we may give all sorts of grounds for any phenomenon or event, and we can find 'good grounds' for whatever we please, either for it or against it. Grounds in this sense are contingent (as with the billiard ball, which could be set in motion equally well by other causes), and as many can be found for the opposite action as for the one to be explained. But this is only when we fail to identify the true grounds, or the system within which the event occurs -- when we fail to see the ground in the concept of whatever it is we seek to explain.

Finally we discover that no reason is sufficient short of all the conditioning circumstances, and that in the end involves everything in the world. John Stuart Mill came to the conclusion that the only really

173

adequate causal account we can give is that 'the cause...philosophically speaking, is the sum total of the conditions positive and negative taken together; the whole of the contingencies of every description, which being realized, the consequent invariably follows.'[19] But, as the consequent, 'philosophically speaking', is equally complex and comprehensive, it should follow that the state of the universe at one instant is the cause of the state of the universe at the next. This is, indeed, complete ground, but it is altogether futile for it explains nothing and fails to identify either ground or consequent in any precise way. In complete ground, formal and real ground are united.

Ground has now broken down into <u>conditions.</u> It is, in effect, the unconditional whole which conditions all finite things. Its moments are necessary condition and sufficient condition, which unite as necessary-and-sufficient condition, and this gives rise to <u>Existence.</u>

<u>Existence</u>[20]

Here we have a return from mediacy to immediacy. The existent emerges from the conditions as the consequent from the ground, but it appears as an immediate given <u>fact,</u> in which the conditions are sublated.[21]

In the Greater Logic, existence is brought under the general heading of Appearance, but that again is sub-divided, and the second triad of sub-categories is also called 'appearance', the third triad being Essential Relation. In the <u>Encyclopaedia,</u> the concertina is (as it were) compressed: from Ground and Consequent it moves immediately to Existence, under which we have Thing and its Properties, and Matter and Form. Then we move to Appearance, or Phenomenal Being.

Existence arises out of ground, or conditions. It sublates them all and presents itself once more as immediate being, but now a being the immediacy of which is mediated by the sublated ground. As a category of Essence it is again reflected into self and into other. What exists presents itself immediately as a fact, but it also exists in inseparable relation to everything else that exists. Every existent depends on every other for its existence. So we have a world of existents reciprocally interdependent, each of which is a <u>Thing.</u> This is the category of 'thinghood' usually called by contemporary philosophers the 'material object' category.

<u>The Thing and its Properties</u>[22]

The thing, as reflected into self, is a somewhat 'in itself', as opposed to its reflection-into-other, its relations to and reactions with other things, which are described as its properties. What we are dealing with here is what John Locke called 'substances', of which the complex ideas are made up of the ideas of simple qualities that 'go constantly

174

together'. The qualities are primary if the thing cannot exist without them, secondary if merely the effects produced in us or in other things. These latter are the manifestation of the thing to others -- its being-for-other, or reflection-into-other. They are its properties and they inhere in 'the real internal constitution' of the thing (which is their ground or substance -- the latter category, which we shall reach anon, being the dialectical development of the former. But in itself this 'real internal constitution' is unknown and unknowable.

In the history of thought, this unknowable internal constitution (which is the actual reality of the thing) becomes, in Kant's hands, the unknowable <u>Ding an sich</u>. The 'in itself', the real internal constitution, is supposed to be the essential nature of the thing, what it really is as opposed to how it appears to us; but, as we have no way of reaching it except as it appears, its real internal constitution is hidden from us and our postulation of it is a sheer abstraction. It becomes an empty substratum,[23] 'something we know not what'.

Hegel, however, gives the phrase 'in itself' a different (though related) significance, to which he draws attention in the <u>Zusatz</u> to Section 124 of the <u>Encyclopaedia</u>, and one which he much prefers to Kant's. To stick with the mere 'in itself' of an object, he says, is to think of it, not in its truth, but in an inadequate abstract form. What it is 'in itself' is what it has in it to become, what it is potentially. What it is in itself is the germinal form of everything that will (or can) emerge from it. The infant is <u>an sich</u> the adult -- in itself, or potentially. The seed is implicitly, in itself, the plant. This is, of course, inaccessible to our perception. It does not appear on the surface, but it is not in principle unknowable, because what is implicit develops in thought as in existence. In fact, what develops in thought and becomes explicit, is the thing as it is brought to consciousness, and is its concept or its truth.

Under Being, something and its qualities were inseparable, and without qualities something ceased to be anything. Under Essence, the thing reflected into itself (as substratum) is distinguished from its properties, its reflection into other, and is said to <u>have</u> them rather than to <u>be</u> them. This carries with it a suggestion of independence which will presently develop further. Meanwhile, we think of properties as individually contingent to the thing's essential being, so that it continues to be whether it has this or that property, though of course it cannot exist without any at all. Yet in truth its properties are but the manifestation of its inner nature in relation to other things, and are simply the other aspect of its concrete unity -- the diversity which in itself it unites.

175

Matter and Form[24]

At the next stage the properties which a thing has themselves assume the status of existence and are reifed. We are still dealing, at a further developed stage, with ground and consequent. First we take the thing in itself as ground of its properties (or, in Lockean terms, its secondary properties), then we consider the properties as explananda and seek the ground for its possession of them by the thing. The explanans is then conceived as a material something, a fluid or 'essence'. Scientists of Hegel's day postulated fluids such as 'caloric' and ' the electrical fluid' to explain the properties of things. Phlogiston had not long gone out of fashion. And still today, a better scientific thinking reduces properties to constituents: chemical elements, their atoms and their physical states. The generalized concept of these underlying substrates is matter, as such, which takes varying forms expressed as things and their properties.

Hegel deprecates the practice of reifying properties (as many contemporary philosophers inveigh against the hypostatization of qualities as universals). He says that both intelligence and experience go counter to the idea that all inquiry ends with the dissection of things into their components in the search for colorific or odorific matters and the like. Chemical analysis is well enough justified, but to seek for 'caloric' or 'electrical fluid' is to be deluded by 'figments of the understanding'.[25] Still less can organic life be regarded as made up of mere conglomerations of constituents, as if these were indifferent to their systematic unification, for it is only in organic union that any of them are what they are and function as they do. This category of thinghood, therefore, is of limited validity and must be superseded.

The thing has thus become dual, as matter and form;[26] yet each is the whole in one aspect. Matter is reflection-into-self as well as into-other and so is form. It is only as constituting a whole that matter has its specific form, and the form is only what it is as uniting the material components according to a specific principle of structure. The distinction between matter and form, as Aristotle well knew, is a relative one. What in one connexion is form in another is matter. The form of the statue is contrasted with the marble, as its matter; but the marble itself is one form of calcium carbonate, of which the matter is calcium and carbon. So we can proceed down the scale, and every stage is but a manifestation in some form of a more recondite matter. Each correlative, at every level, makes up the whole of the thing, which, to be itself, requires both.

Lakebrink remarks that form in this context has nothing to do with the Platonic eidos,[27] which is a transcendent, eternally subsistent, archetypal reality in which the sensible object participates. What he calls dialectical form, on the other hand, is a determination of reflection, of difference; it is the negativity which constitutes essence, an element in its reflective movement, and the sublation of all the prior categories of Essence. Virtually everything that Lakebrink says of form as it occurs at this stage of the dialectic is correct. Nevertheless, it is not right to say that it has nothing to do with the Platonic Idea. That, in Hegel's logic is the absolute Idea, which is eternal, complete, and everything that Plato affirmed of Idea as such. But it must not be forgotten that Hegel's absolute Idea is essentially active, infinite restlessness, unceasingly self-differentiating; and that it differentiates itself through the dialectical movement into all the categories which constitute the system of the Logic. Essence is the Idea an sich. The Idea is immanent in all things as their essence, and it specifies itself, at the stage we have reached, as the category of matter and form. This category is indeed exemplified in the history of philosophy both in Plato and in Aristotle. Plato's struggle to explicate the relation between the Forms and the sensible world does produce something very like the reflective relationship here categorized by Hegel as form and matter -- to this the Timaeus gives evidence. The category develops in Aristotle's thought dialectically and is (as Lakebrink says of Hegel's category) 'processual'. Aristotle uses the category as one of explanation in the natural sciences, and it is the logic of such explanation that Hegel sets out in the Doctrine of Essence. Nor must it be forgotten that Plato also speaks of dialectic, and that the account he gives of it was Hegel's inspiration. Plato, further, as he develops his doctrine of ideas, especially in the Sophist, rather more than suggests that they form a dialectical scale, which culminates (if we bear in mind the passage in Republic, VI, 509b) in the Idea of the Good[28] (Hegel's absolute Idea). It would therefore be misleading to say that Hegel had no thought in his mind of the use made by Plato and Aristotle of the category of matter and form when he introduced it into the Doctrine of Essence, although he does not explicitly mention either of these philosophers here. Nor is it correct to say that the Hegelian conception of form 'has nothing to do with' the Platonic and the Aristotelian. In fact, Lakebrink himself goes on to give an outline of Hegel's development of the category to the point at which it becomes absolute form or Method, sublating all matter[29] (though Lakebrink does not remind us that sublation is preservation as well as cancellation), and issues in precisely what Aristotle (followed by the Mediaevals and later Leibniz) called 'actus purus'. So there are close connexions between Hegel's category and the thought of all these thinkers. Lakebrink warns us not to confuse Hegel's concept of form with contemporary notions to be found also in Phenomenology and Existentialism. But these too are (unwittingly) presentations of a phase in the dialectic of the Logos, which Hegel had anticipated.

Existence, in the course of its development in Essence, finally collapses in self-contradiction. The category of thinghood to which the understanding pays so much deference, and which so predominates in empirical science, seems at first to be real, solid and publicly observable; but at once it degenerates into an unknowable thing-in-itself with an unobservable 'real internal constitution' displaying to observation only sensible qualities, which themselves are contingent, variable, and at best only appearances of the underlying inaccessible substrate. They are, therefore, attributed to hypothetical 'matters', which claim thinghood of an indefinite sort but are no more than theoretical entities again eluding observation. These coalesce to become matter in general, completely indefinite and unspecified apart from form. As Berkeley argued, it is altogether unobservable and, in and by itself, inconceivable and self-contradictory ('repugnant'). Its identifiable specification emerges solely in its form; yet apart from matter the form alone is nothing actual and is the precise opposite of the formless matter it is taken to inform. Meanwhile the form dictates the interpenetration of the presumed 'matters' determining the properties of the thing, and these properties constitute its form in a manner contradictory of their alleged material nature (i.e., impenetrability).

The understanding resorts to images (Vorstellungen) to overcome these difficulties, of which the 'matters' are themselves an example. A theory current in Hegel's day postulated 'pores' in the matters admitting the injection of other matters. Once more these are unobservable and represent only the negative relation of each matter to every other. But this negation is itself a contradiction of the solidity it is invented to maintain. The being is honeycombed with nothingness which it must again repudiate if it is to maintain its compact integrity.[30]

Accordingly, the existence of the thing cannot be accepted as a reality, yet it has being, or rather, it is what Being has become in the process through Essence, or is the way in which it appears. The essential element was first the thing in itself with its real internal constitution; but this revealed itself only in its properties. These then became the essential aspect as the matter (or matters) of which the thing was composed, and its manifestation was its form. We then found that matter and form were relative and that both are manifestations of something deeper-lying. They are phenomena, in the Kantian sense of the word. the appearances of a hidden reality, but without the subjectivist implications of the Kantian doctrine.

NOTES: Book II, Part II, Chapter 2

1. Enz., Sections 115-125.

2. Enz., Section 115; W.L., II, pp. 38-46; Miller, pp. 411-416.

3. Enz., Section 115.

4. Enz., Section 116; W.L., II, pp. 46-55; Miller, pp. 417-424.

5. W.L., II, p. 47f; Miller, p. 418.

6.   Cf. W.L., II, ibid. As Lakebrink points out, each shows (scheint) in the other, as is always the case in the reflectiveness of Essence.

7.   Cf. W.L., II, p. 46; Miller, p. 417.

8.   Ibid.

9.   Cf. Kritik der reinen Vernunft A 97: 'Wenn eine jede einzelne Vorstellung der anderen ganz fremd, gleichsam isoliert, und von dieser getrennt wäre, so würde niemals so etwas als Erkenntnis ist, entspringen, welche ein Ganzes verglichener und verknüpfter Vorstellungen ist.

10.   In Virginibus Puerisque, Robert Louis Stevenson remarks that 'stillicide is not a crime', the comparison being in respect of the sound and spelling of the word and its suffix. Apart from this likeness the difference is without interest or meaning.

11.   Cf. Enz., Section 117.

12.   Cf. W.L., II, pp. 64ff., Miller, pp. 431ff.; and Lakebrink, Kommentar, Section 120, pp. 232ff.

13.   Enz., Section 119.

14.   Cf. Enz., Section 119, Zusatz 2: 'Die Endlichkeit der Dinge besteht dann darin, dass ihr unmittelbares Dasein dem nicht entspricht was sie an sich sind.

15.   Enz., Section 121; W.L., II, pp. 80-123; Miller, pp. 444-478.

16.   Cf. Enz., Section 121, Zus.: 'A content determined in and for itself and for that reason self-active, the Concept will hereafter provide us...'

17.   Cf. ibid., and Plato, Phaedo, 97d-98b.

18.   Cf. R.B. Braithwaite, Scientific Explanation and my criticism in Hypothesis and Perception, Chs. II and III.

19.   A System of Logic, Book III, Ch. V, Section 3.

20.   Enz., Section 123; W.L., II, pp. 125-164; Miller, pp. 481-498.

21.   McTaggart, commenting on the exposition in the Greater Logic, objects to Hegel's use of 'immediate', except as figuratively meant, or in a qualified sense (cf. Commentary, Ch. VI, pp. 129-130). He contends that immediacy increases as we proceed upward in the dialectical process only in the sense that the relation between the two correlates of essence becomes progressively closer. This reveals complete failure

to understand Hegel's doctrine of immediacy (as discussed above in Bk. I., Pt. II, Ch.   VII) and his conception of mediated immediacy -- immediacy sublating as moments within itself the phases through which it has been mediated.

22.   Enz., Section 125; W.L., II, pp. 129-147; Miller, pp. 484-498.

23.   Cf. Enz., Section 124.

24.   Enz., Sections 126-130.

25.   Cf. Enz., Section 126 Zus.

26.   Cf. Enz., Sections 127-128.

27.   Kommentar, p. 272f.

28.   Cf. my Nature, Mind and Modern Science (London, 1954), pp. 95-7.

29.   Cf. below, Bk. II, Pt. III, Ch. 4, pp. 295ff.

30.   Cf. W.L., II, pp. 144-147; Miller, pp. 496-498.

Chapter 3

Appearance[1]

The Phenomenal World

The key to Appearance is given in the transition from matter and form to form and content. Hitherto essence has been expressed as the showing of an essential being in an external display or reflection. In matter and form, matter was the subsistent element and form its outward, contingent, inessential, showing forth. Yet everything definite about the thing is in its form, and its matter is wholly indeterminate by contrast. The essence, which should have been the subsistent real, is now seen to be in the form, which was the outward show, and essence is now embodied in material form. Form and matter have coalesced, and when we modify the correlation, as Aristotle does, so that proximate matter is an already informed substratum, we approach Hegel's category of Content and Form, where the content is both subsistent and determinate, and the form is the way in which it appears or is expressed. But it is the content itself in its determination which appears, so both form and content are on a par and are both Appearance.[2]

'Essence', says Hegel, 'must appear'. Schein has become Erscheinung, and essence is not now behind or within the appearance but on its face. It exists as phenomenal being. Nevertheless, this existence is not self-subsistent but is the way in which the essence appears or has its existence, the ground of which is in another. The other, however, is another phenomenon, so we are presented with a world of phenomena, interdependent and in mutual relation, which are appearances of a real whole that is not itself phenomenal, but of which the phenomenal world is at once the appearance and the essence.

Hegel makes no reference here to Spinoza, only to Kant and Fichte, whom he criticizes for their subjective idealism. But Spinoza is no subjective idealist and he has set out the position very well in his doctrine that the Attributes of Substance, which express its essence, are (among an infinity of others) Thought and Extension, the modes of which constitute our existent world, the world of appearance. These modes are not unreal (as Spinoza is frequently accused of alleging) but are the ways in which Substance (or God) expresses its (or His) essence. Hegel in the Zusatz to Section 131 of the Encyclopaedia says much the same thing in different words:

When we speak of Appearance, we associate with it the idea (Vorstellung) of an indefinite manifold of existing things, the being of which is merely mediation and which to that extent do not rest upon themselves but have their validity only as moments. At the same time it is implied that essence does

181

not remain behind or beyond the appearance, but rather is, as it were, the infinite Grace releasing its own showing in immediacy and granting it the joy of existence. The appearance thus posited does not stand on its own feet and has its being, not in itself, but in another. God as Essence, as he is likewise Grace, in that he lends existence to the moments of His showing (Scheinen) in himself [cf. Spinoza's Attributes], to create a world, reveals himself at the same time as the power over it and the righteousness displaying the content of this existing world as mere appearance, so far as it wills to exist for itself.

God is the essence revealing himself, through the creation of the world, that is, through his Attributes of Thought and Extension, as appearance, the modes of those Attributes. For Spinoza, the Attributes are God's powers, and the modes are the ways in which they manifest themselves in existence.

Hegel commends Kant for establishing the distinction between appearances and the real. However, Kant makes the former merely subjective and the latter unknowable; and the unphilosophical also tend to treat appearances as something less substantial than immediately presented things. The mistake in both cases is that appearance is really a higher category than being. It is the truth of being -- what reflection reveals, namely, the specific inter-related content of immediate being set out and made explicit. But, as appearance, it is still far from adequate to reality (or the Absolute) and so will shortly develop further to Actuality. The common sense preference for the real is thus in part justified, as impatience with subjective idealism; and Kant's failure (as well as Fichte's) is not the recognition of the objective character of phenomena, but the allegation that what makes them phenomenal is their being merely our representations or ideas (Vorstellungen). They are objective as opposed to our imaginings (as the vulgar also agree), but they are phenomenal in that they are only partial manifestations of a totality in which they inhere, which expresses itself in them, but which, in their immediacy they do not fully reveal.

Hegel himself puts both aspects of the matter in perspective. Vorstellungen, for him are mere appearances in contrast to der Begriff; and they are also subjective, whereas der Begriff, which is also our thought (Gedanke), is not merely subjective. But then again Vorstellung is a phase in the dialectical development of Gedanke and so is also not merely subjective. The proper conception of these moments is that they are moments in a scale which, as a whole, is real. Qua moments they are only phenomena, merely appearance, but not therefore pure illusions or sheer errors, because they are essential moments of the reality which appears in them. Our consciousness, while it has the status of appearance (for nothing appears except to a conscious subject) is the developed outcome of the natural world sublated in our organism.

182

It is thus not merely appearance, but the appearance in consciousness of the truth about the world.

Content and Form[3]

The world of phenomena is the form in which the real (content) appears, and the phenomena are mutually related in various ways. How they are related, and consequently how they appear, is governed by the content in the form of a law. The law does not appear, except in the pattern of the relationships; it is, as it were, an underlying essence or ground. Yet the ground, as content, is also phenomenal and appears as a world of phenomena in relation, mediating one another's existence in infinitum. So now the form is the reflection-into-self of the phenomenal. It is the unstable, changeable appearance, a merely external form displaying the governing law of its appearances equally well in all its changes. Thus the form is two-fold, or ambiguous. The content is not formless but is the medium in which the form appears and it has the form in itself, although the form in which it appears is indifferent existence that is constantly changing.

For instance, the content (or subject-matter) of a book, however ill-organized, is not without form, yet the form in which it is published does not affect it and may be various in a number of ways -- as instalments in a journal, as a paperback, or as a leather-bound presentation volume. Content and form (at least at first sight) are irrelevant to each other. Nevertheless, a well produced book will have an external form (e.g., the dust jacket and cover design) appropriate to its content. The form, as we have noted above, is both immanent in the content and is its external appearance or outward manifestation. As phenomenal, each tends to become the other; there is an oscillation from one to the other. Form, as the law governing appearance (e.g., the law of falling bodies, that they accelerate 16 feet per sec.[2]) is simply the content of the phenomenon (what the falling body does) and the phenomenal content is just the form in which the law is actualized (whether in the vertical fall of a stone, or in the parabolic path of a missile, or the elliptical orbit of a satellite).[4] Content and form thus become interchangeable; each is simply the reversion of one into the other, and the immanent whole can as well -- or better -- be called content as can the overt phenomenal series in the form of which it (the whole or content) is displayed.

Hegel illustrates this ambiguity from the relation in a work of art of form to content. The form, he says, is as essential as the content, and without it the epic, or tragedy, or statue, would not be the work of art that it is. Yet it is the content which the form shows forth, and the form that moulds the content. Each is appearance, the content is what appears and the form is how it appears. Hence they are interchangeable, for the plot of the tragedy is the form in which it works itself out and is equally the tragic content, but the tragedy is the form in which the content (the story) is presented. The epic form of the Iliad is the expression of the epic significance of the wrath of Achilles and that content is what gives the poem its epic form and stature.

Correlation

(1) Whole and Part. This essential identity of opposites now presents itself as Correlation, where two terms are mutually correlative so that the very meaning and being of each depends upon the other. The first phase of such correlation is Whole and Parts. Here the content is the whole and the form the parts in which it expresses itself. Yet again, the content is the parts and the whole or structure in which they are assembled is the form -- the pattern of arrangement or organization. Form and content, as we have seen, are interchangeable and each is the revulsion of one into the other.

Hegel clearly has in mind the sort of whole which determines its parts by its over-all structural principle, so that what manifests itself in the parts is that principle. They are the forms in which it appears; and the whole as such is nothing more and nothing less than the parts in their mutual interdependence and interdetermination. This is the true nature of whole and part.[5] But commonly the whole is represented (vorgestellt) by the understanding as an aggregate of separable entities. In this form it contradicts itself (its idea) because, divided into segments, it ceases to be a whole, and undivided it ceases to have parts. There are, of course, aggregates in which the items are separable, but as such they are not genuine wholes, and when separate items are brought together to form a whole, they lose their separable character and are transformed as parts of the whole into interdependent moments.

One can regard the whole as the true existent and the parts as adjectival to it; or one can take the parts as the existents and the whole as a mere appearance: for example, a lake is a whole made up of water drops, or a mountain a whole made up of rocks and grains of sand. On the other hand, as represented in some Empiricist theories, a state is held to be nothing but a collection of citizens, and its acts nothing but the acts of certain of its officials. In the first type of example the whole is taken as primary and the parts merely putative; in the second the whole is considered to be a mere appearance or a conventional way of referring to the parts, which are held to be the only reality. Oddly enough, the more mechanical kind of whole is treated as a true whole, which it is not, and the genuine whole (the state) is short-sightedly regarded as a mere aggregate.

Correlation is the linkage of the two aspects of Essence, reflection-into-self and reflection-into-other. The first is the aspect of unity (or identity) and the second of multiplicity (or difference). We have seen this exemplified all along, in identity and difference themselves, in ground and existence, in thing and its properties, in matter and form and in form and content. But thus far the interdependence has only been implicit and now it becomes explicit as correlation, in which the unity is explicitly correlative to its diversity in whole and parts. This interchangeable correlativity develops further when the whole is seen as a primary principle or force expressing itself in innumerable phenomenal occurrences. Whole and parts is a mechanical correlation -- the whole is the mere togetherness of the parts, yet if and so far as it is divided it ceased to be a whole; and if the parts are amalgamated they cease to be parts. Further, the alternation of whole and part is what is entailed in the reputed infinite divisibility of space and time; for the whole is dissected into parts and then each part is treated as a whole and dissipated once again, and so on ad infinitum. This, as we know, is a false infinite, but Hegel says that if it is regarded as the aspect of the negative of the relation to self, it is Force, in which the whole is implicit and, sublating the implicit being of the whole, utters or expresses (äussert) itself in inexhaustible multiplicity.[6] The transition is somewhat obscure, although the analogy between the two correlations (whole and part, and force and expression) is not difficult to grasp. If we think of force and expression in terms of the earlier conception of material properties, it becomes more easily comprehensible. The electrical 'fluid' (for instance) as a whole displays itself as the series of electrical phenomena, which are its parts; and equally if we conceive it as a force, the phenomena constitute its expression.

There may well be latent here the doctrine that the true whole, the Concept, or the Idea, immanent in Nature, expresses itself as energy or force, in which that whole is indeed implicit, but only implicit, and with limitations presently to be noticed. Here we are concerned with the logical categories and not with natural forms, the treatment of which belongs to Naturphilosophie. The category, whole and part, is an adumbration of the Concept (or the Absolute) and its self-differentiation, and this resolves itself into the power or force which issues in the inexhaustible variety of phenomenal forms and events.

(2) Force and expression[7] are to be identified more intrinsically than whole and part. The force is nothing but its expressions or manifestations, and they are nothing but what expresses itself in them. The expression of the force is the force itself in operation, and is itself the force. For example, energy is what manifests itself in every discharge, and in every discharge is conserved. Moreover, the discharge does not dissipate the force, but merely translates it into a new form. Energy is transformed from one kind of manifestation into another: potential into kinetic, kinetic into heat energy, heat into mechanical energy, and so on. Force and its expression are, therefore, (1) identical opposites or correlates, and (2) interchangeable.

Hegel objects to the widespread view that the nature of the force is unknowable, as only its expression can be observed, because the entire inner nature of the force is precisely its utterance or observed consequences. It was for this reason that it was remarked earlier that explanation in terms of forces was tautological. But the more genuine knowledge of the force is in the law of its exertion, the universal principle ordering the phenomena observed and constructing them into a whole.

This whole, however, is none the less only provisional. It is not the whole, even though the Absolute is immanent in it. For it is at best a finite whole. First, the alternation of force and exertion is a false infinite never taking us beyond the finite expression, secondly, any one kind of force requires elicitation by another, which is similarly limited, and a new indefinite regress is generated, which never debouches finally upon any ultimate, original force. If the various kinds of forces could be reduced to one fundamental force, Hegel says, it would not remedy the situation, because that would only be an abstraction and would be as inscrutable as any finite subsidiary force. Here then there is some justification for saying that force in itself is unknowable -- as the expression of the implicit awareness of its irremediably finite nature. It is not self-determining, and to become so it must develop further, through intervening stages, into purpose and self-conscious self-direction. In contrast to these, force works blindly, and both its excitation and its discharge are contingent.

'The stars', she whispers, 'blindly run.'[8]

Once more the urge is for teleological explanation, an urge we shall find recurring until we reach the Idea itself.

It is not surprising, therefore, that the conception of God as Divine Force and the explanation of all natural phenomena as the manifestation of Divine Power fall short of what reason demands. First of all, force as a finite category is inadequate to God, so we find the Church denouncing as heretical the view that the events of nature are the expression of specific forces rather than the direct acts of God. In the second place, if one declares, as the Enlightenment did, that the forces of nature are no less God's creation, one sets God outside nature, as an 'infinite' beyond the finite, which results in a virtual agnosticism with regard to the Divine, restricting itself merely to the confession that there is a God. On the other hand to resort to blind faith in God's Providence is to explain nothing and to withdraw into obscurantism, which abjures the scientific understanding that is indispensable to full philosophical and true religious insight. Christianity, Hegel points out, enjoins the love and the knowledge of God in spirit and in truth, not the bigotry of dogmatic and arrogant fanaticism.

186

(3) <u>Inner and Outer</u>[9]. Force and its expression, seen as identical opposites resolve themselves into inner and outer aspects of one and the same phenomenon. This category of Inner and Outer is the sublation of all the previous categories of appearance. Inner corresponds to ground, outer to existence, and their identity is the content which appears in the exertion of force. This content is the same in both aspects, nothing appears which is not contained in the essence and everything so contained is manifest in the appearance. Inner is the aspect of reflection-into-self, outer is reflection-into-other. Each taken in abstraction is utterly opposed to the other (identity to difference), but as they are moments of a single form, each posited in abstraction is immediately the other. If essence is held to be the mere inner of the thing, it is an abstraction which is external to its concrete content. Thus the so-called inner heart of Nature is said to be impenetrable by the finite mind. The real internal constitution of the thing is unknowable; and so it is external to and excluded from its actual content, which then appears only as the external shell. The poet Goethe protests that Nature is far from being so grudging, for the core and the shell are not separable, and what appears outwardly is the very inner essence itself.[10]

As we go up the dialectical scale and our object becomes progressively more concrete, inner and outer reveal themselves as inseparable and indispensable aspects of one identical content. At the more abstract levels they oppose each other and revert one into the other. Where the concept is merely implicit, what presents itself is mere Being, an outer mechanical facade. When essence is degraded to a subjective idea (a mere inner), it remains external to that to which it is held to be essential. On the other hand, at the more concrete levels of human personality and society, it is obvious that (for instance) a person's inner disposition is revealed only in outer conduct, and what is not so expressed cannot be credited to the agent but remains irrelevant to his or her effective character. Accordingly, Hegel is led to expostulate against 'psychological' historiography, which instead of accepting the deeds of world-historical figures in their obvious significance, burrows beneath the surface to find ulterior motives as pretexts for besmirching and denigrating their achievements.

What is <u>merely</u> implicit or potential in a child is external to him in the form of the authority and knowledge of his elders, and through education (drawing out) has to become internal to himself. Then, in the adult, what is internal (knowledge and experience) expresses itself outwardly immediately in action. The imposition upon the criminal of punishment by an external authority is really the return of his own true conscience upon himself.[11] At the very end of the logic, in the absolute Idea, as the final outcome of the dialectic, we shall find that inner content and outer form are one and the same. They coalesce in the dialectical process itself, the absolute Method, the subject-matter of which is its very self. But at the level we have reached the reversion

187

of abstract inwardness into abstract outwardness and of the latter again into the former reveals their mere illusoriness (als Schein gesetzte Schein des Wesens), essence posited as a mere show, and also the actual concrete content in which they are immediately identical each with the other. This concrete identity is Actuality.

NOTES: Book II, Part II, Chapter 3

1. Enz., Sections 131-141.

2. Cf. G.R. Mure, A Study of Hegel's Logic, Ch VII.

3. Enz., Sections 133-134.

4. The relations of substance and causality are here inchoate and are developing throughout the succeeding categories, but they come to maturity, or actuality, only in the next chapter.

5. Cf., once again, Spinoza, Ep. XXXII.

6. Cf. Enz., Section 136.

7. Enz., Section 136.

8. Tennyson, In Memoriam.

9. Enz., Sections 137-141.

10. See Wallace's note in Hegel's Logic, (Oxford, 1975), p. 327.

11. This doctrine of society and the state depends on the conception of the individual as a social product -- which he inevitably is -- so that wilful defiance of accepted standards is, in effect, rebellion against one's own better judgement and moral sense. The aspects of inner and outer and their relation to each other are here obvious, inner conscience being expressed in outer legality. In this theory, reforming opposition to an accepted code is seen as no less the product of the social order which has established the code and in which the seeds of the reform are already latent. The overt opposition is then the utterance (Äusserung) or externalization of the inner implication of the traditional code. Crime has to be distinguished from legitimate opposition by the degree of coherence of the will involved, the claim of the reformer being that his reform makes the system more consistent with itself, whereas the act of the criminal is in conflict with his own ultimate best interest. But the full discussion of these matters belongs elsewhere.

Chapter 4

Actuality[1]

The Rational Real

The content of both the inner and the outer is the same, and they are each (taken apart) empty abstractions, which, going over one into the other, sublate themselves in their identity. The abstractions are a mere showing (Schein) of the essence, and the concrete content which is externalized by its immanent force once more digests its own mediation, which vanishes in the identity of the opposite abstractions and is now superseded in what emerges as actuality.[2] This is the next major category; it is the immediate whole which has sublated and contains (as it were, in suspension) its mediation through reflection-into-self and into-other. Actuality is the unity of essence and existence, an antithesis which has been before us in successive forms throughout the scale of the categories of reflection. The unity has become immediate so that its utterance is its essence and is essential only as actual or real.

What must again be stressed is the immanent presence of the whole in all the categories of Essence. The whole is the ground of all identity and difference. It is the whole which issues in existence and appears as the phenomenal world. The whole is both content and form. It resolves itself into parts and expresses itself as force. It distinguishes within itself an inner essence which is revealed in outer show, both of which are identical in actuality. Once again, actuality recapitulates the earlier categories, and the correlatives we have been examining will now reappear in new forms (possibility and necessity, substance and attribute, cause and effect, and reciprocity). But also it anticipates, because the actual is the real which is the rational, the coherent whole which is the self-differentiating Concept. It is Being-for-self as essence in existence, and that is proleptically Concept. All that is as yet lacking is explicit self-consciousness. The various correlatives of the previous categories have now proved to be only two aspects of the same actuality, which is itself essential being manifesting itself, not in another, or as appearance only, but as its own concrete self, essence and existence in one.

In the history of philosophy we have already encountered this identity as the Ens realissimum, the essence of which involves its existence -- God, who is identical with Being and whose essence is to exist, the infinite and perfect, than which no greater can be conceived. The Greater Logic, where the dialectic is more extended and more detailed than in the Encyclopaedia, makes this identification of actuality with the Absolute explicit in the first division there set out of this section. In some sense, it is nothing new, for every category from the very first has been a provisional definition of the Absolute, and now

189

we have it as actual and real. But likewise every category is a thought-determination and is a conception typical of a certain level of thinking; and this category has appeared in every philosophy in the west since Aristotle, whether as οὐσία or God, or Substance, or the Absolute. Even in classical Empiricism it is found in Berkeley's doctrine that actuality (as opposed to imagination and illusion) is the mind of God. In Leibniz it is the Monad of monads reflecting the whole universe with absolute clearness and distinctness. In Kant we find it first as the thing in itself, which later is transformed as noumenon and consummated as the Ideal of Reason. And here again we shall find Hegel both criticizing earlier theories and claiming to show how they prefigure his own conception of the Absolute as self-differentiating Spirit.[3]

The Absolute as actuality is not yet the true Absolute 'in and for itself', that is, aware of itself as actually existent Spirit encompassing both being and essence in one complete self-consciousness. That is the Idea. But Actuality is the Idea in principle. It is the rational, structured whole manifesting itself as fundamentally real. On this level, actuality is the Absolute posited, or set out, as a complete structure actually existing. Now, of course, such a structural whole is only fully explicit as structure and as whole for a consciousness. As mere Dasein, simply being there, the interlaced structure of its differentiations is only implicit. One may say, therefore, that Actuality is the Absolute for us, but not yet for itself. It is the whole absorbing into itself all differences -- das mit sich identisch geworden Verhältnis -- reflecting itself in its own externalization, which is its own self-manifestation, not the reflection of an other.[4]

Mere Being is pure immediacy which cannot maintain itself and passes over at once into its opposite. Existence is what proceeds from a ground and from conditions; it is a reflection of and into something else. But Actuality is self-determined, coherent, totality, manifesting itself as it essentially is in its outward self-expression. It is the unity of essence and existence as the concretely real, no longer just appearance, but self-manifestation (Offenbarung).

In Hegel's view, this stage of the dialectic is represented in Spinoza's conception of Substance, which is an absolute whole, its essence expressed (or uttered) in diverse Attributes, and its existence appearing as evanescent finite modes -- but, according to Hegel's interpretation, lacking any principle of self-differentiation to make this internal diversity explicable. In consequence, the Spinozan Substance alone is real, and its modes (and consequently its Attributes also) are simply overridden as appearance and engulfed within its indivisible and seamless unity.[5] The Absolute of Schelling, in Hegel's opinion, was tainted with the same fault. It is the indifference-point at which all difference is submerged.

But if Actuality falls short of the Idea, it is by no means incompatible with or exclusive of it. 'Mere ideas' are no doubt abstractions, and are no more what Hegel refers to when he speaks of Idea than what Plato meant by Form. 'Mere ideas' may justly be contrasted with actuality, but Idea, as the Truth, is actual and must exist; hence actuality as the truth is the rational-real, 'the absolutely active as well as actual.'[6] And this is an equally good description of the Idea. The actual is real precisely as rational, as truth or idea, and only what is rational is actual.

The common interpretation of Plato and Aristotle, which places them in mutual opposition, is thus a misconception of both. The 'Idea' in Plato is no abstraction or fantasy, but is the truth of what in common perception is a transient appearance; and Aristotle is not at loggerheads with Plato for discounting the observable fact, but for failing sufficiently to insist that what is ideal is real not only in principle (δύναμις) but also in actuality (ἐνέργεια).

The understanding separates idea from actuality so as to make both abstract. Then the first is simply 'what is in our heads' and may or may not correspond to the actual. It may be simply empty intention, such as Hell is paved with, or a mere theory which as such may seem sound enough but 'does not work in practice'. Correspondingly, actuality is then taken to be what is casually met with in common perceptual experience, unexamined and only superficially observed. This antithesis of shallow abstracta serves the purposes of everyday life more or less, but it will not bear close philosophical scrutiny. What looks good in theory but does not correspond to actuality even the understanding will confess to be false, and what passes in theory but does not work out in practice is clearly bad theory that has overlooked something essential. The idea which is adequate to its object is a clear conception of what the object actually is, and the actual fact is not just what appears on the surface but that of which, by full and thorough investigation, we have formed a concrete and systematically coherent idea.

Categories of Modality

This concrete concept of actuality is specified as the three so-called categories of modality (as we find them in Kant's Postulates of Empirical Thought). In the Greater Logic this triad is the second division of the main category, given, as is so often Hegel's practice, the same title, 'Actuality'. But in the Encyclopaedia he proceeds, after the general introduction of the category in Section 142, immediately to the sub-categories of modality. This produces a truncated triad for the whole section, as it leaves only two minor triads under the heading of Actuality.

Kant makes the categories of modality subjective by asserting that they refer simply to the relation of the object (without in the least affecting its concept) to the capacity of cognition (Erkenntnisvermögen). And this, as we shall presently see, is the abstract attitude towards them. But Kant recognized these categories, like the rest, as categories of objective knowledge -- objective, that is, as opposed to subjective fancy and delusion. Objectivity in this sense is precisely actuality, for objective knowledge is actual knowledge, knowledge of the actual; fantasies about the world, however apparently factual in content, not being knowledge at all. That the modal categories are aspects of the actual rather than of our subjective attitude to objects should be clear from the circumstance that actuality is the name normally given to one of them. The other two, possibility and necessity, are ways, or degrees, in which the actual is determined (bestimmt).

The complex dialectic of the Greater Logic gives us (a) Contingency, or Formal Actuality, Possibility and Necessity; (b) Relative Necessity, or Real Actuality, Possibility and Necessity; and (c) Absolute Necessity. The points being made seem to be (1) that actuality, possibility and necessity are always interdependent aspects of one actuality -- one systematic world, and (2) that they can be viewed in three ways which form a scale of degrees of concretion: as formal, as real, and as absolute. Each is a view of the absolutely actual, which is the key to interpretation of them all; for, as ever in the dialectic, it is what emerges at the end that explains and is the truth of what has gone before.

Possibility

The aspect of identity and reflection-into-self of actuality is possibility. Formally it is simply non-self-contradiction. In his discussion of the Ontological Argument, Leibniz maintains that the concept of God (what Hegel equates with the Absolute) must be shown to be possible before it can be proved to be actual.[7] That is, it must be shown that the idea of God as the most perfect being does not involve a contradiction. This demand is an application of the principle that only what is possible can be actual, or, as Hegel puts it, 'the actual is possible'. This formal notion of the possible as what does not contradict itself is what modern philosophers call 'logical possibility'. Brand Blanshard, in Reason and Belief, declares that the world is rational because it does not contradict itself.[8] Nothing actual is self-contradictory, nor does it contradict anything else that is actual. In short, to be actual is to be possible, to be self-consistent, not to cntradict itself.

The possible, as the formally consistent and non-contradictory, ranks for the understanding as the essence, or concept, of what may or may not be actual. Thus Kant, in his discussion of the Ontological

Argument, asserts (against Leibniz) that what is merely possible cannot be proved a priori to be actual, but must be shown to be somehow related to experience if we are to claim actuality for it. The idea of a possible hundred dollars is, in essence, the same as the idea of an actual hundred dollars -- but essence does not involve existence. Possibility is thus essence to actuality as existence. Consistency is a necessary condition of actuality, though (on this showing) it is not sufficient. Hegel, however, is in process of showing that this dichotomy of the actual into essence and existence is the product of abstraction, resting upon a more concrete conception both of possibility and of actuality.

The logically possible, however, is an extremely thin and rather futile conception. Everything, as Hegel points out, is logically possible so long as one abstracts from all conditions of actuality. Mere terminological, or linguistic, contradiction is not relevant here, for we are speaking of fact -- actuality -- not just words. Liguistic consistency depends on the definition of terms. If 'a ship' is defined as what sails on water, 'a ship of the desert' is an impossibility; but a modification of the definition will make it possible. (We need not here confine ourselves to camels). If the term 'motor-car' is restricted to vehicles that run on land, an amphibious vehicle (a so-called 'duck') is not a motor-car; but it is not therefore impossible, nor would it be absurd to call it an amphibious motor-car. Analytic self-identity is common to all things, and it is otiose to require it as a condition of possible existence. A square circle is impossible, but this is not just a matter of nomenclature, for it is rooted in the nature of space.[9] On the other hand, a hippogryph is logically possible only if we abstract from physiology. Physiologically a horse with the torso of a man in place of its neck and with a human head is altogether impossible and is actually self-contradictory.

Hegel goes further and declares that just as anything and everything, as self-identical, is possible, so everything real contains implicit contradiction. By the same token, therefore, everything should be impossible. This, we have already seen, must be true of every concrete reality as a coherent whole, for that is an identity of unity and difference, each being the condition and medium of the other. But unity and diversity are opposites and cannot be identified without apparent contradiction. Hence, as every actuality involves an identity of opposites, nothing is possible. This sceptical argument is, however, the fruit of abstraction. It was well known to the ancient Sophists, and as Hegel points out Scepticism (and Sophism) are negative products of the same dialectic that generates the truth.

The truth of the matter is that differences mutually adapted in a system can be, and universally are, united, and opposites in appropriate contexts may well be identical. What determines whether they are mutually compatible or not is the principle of order governing the system. It is the structure of the system that decides possibility and impossibility, the actual whole. What conflicts with that, what goes against the principle of organization, is impossible, and what fits in and is compatible with that principle is possible. In the last resort, then, nothing is possible except what is actual, and possibility derives its sense from actuality rather than vice versa. As Hegel contends, actuality, being more concrete, is really the wider term.[10]

Contingency

To say this here, however, is to anticipate, for we should commonly hold that not everything that is possible is actual. What is actual just happens to be the case, and there are many other conceivable things and events which could occur, ostensibly without violating the laws of nature. Actuality is here taken as the outer, immediately presented, fact, in abstract opposition to the merely formal possibility which posed as its inner essence; and as such the actual becomes itself unessential and merely possible. This way of representing actuality and possibility conflates the two by making the actual contingent -- that is, merely possible. It could have been otherwise and its occurrence is a matter of chance.

Pure chance is indeterminate possibility, once again the logically possible without regard to conditions. The calculus of probability is based on the assumption that pure chance governs the alternatives. It derives from the ratio of positive cases to the total number of possibilities. But that number must be finite, and so must be limited by some condition. However, within this limit no determinants are assumed and the probability is calculated simply upon the ratio of the alternative possibilities to each other. Nevertheless, what limits possibilities is always the relevant factual conditions, so we are led from formal possibility to a real possibility and to a more concrete conception of the probable.

The probability of an event, more adequately conceived, depends upon the extent to which the ascertainable conditions are favourable to its occurrence, when we do not know what all the circumstances are, or whether all that are present are sufficient. In actuality all the circumstances present must produce some result, but the probability of one rather than another is calculable from the ratio of the number of factors known to be favourable to the total number of factors relevant.

What is contingent depends upon the conditions requisite to its occurrence. If they are present the outcome is possible, and this is real possibility. But again it is contingent only if and because the conditions are contingent on the same terms, and so we have an indefinite regress of conditions, each of which issues in something other than itself which it conditions. The conditions contain the germ of the outcome and are 'used up' in its issuance. In the outcome the essence of the actuality (instant in the conditions) is aufgehoben in its existence. So (says

194

Hegel) is the process of the actual in general constituted.[11] But as the outcome is nothing other than the actualization of the potentiality contained in the conditions, they, in producing it, Hegel asserts, only unite with themselves. The complete circle of conditions is the necessary and sufficient determination of the fact. If all the necessary conditions are present the fact is not only possible but necessarily actual. Thus the contingently actual may be defined as the hypothetically necessary.

Hegel, however, asserts that contingency is an actual feature of reality, and not just a subjective matter due (as Spinoza had maintained) to the deficiency of our knowledge. To pretend that everything is fixed as it must be and could not have been otherwise is a mistake. All the same, this contingency is a feature which is aufgehoben in the actual event, and is something which the quest for knowledge seeks to overcome. It is but one aspect of actuality and must not be confused with true actuality in its concreteness. Hegel's view on this matter seems to be ambivalent, for while he insists on the really contingent character of certain happenings, both in nature and in human action, he also claims that, in its fullness, actuality abrogates this contingency. While the contingent is to be acknowledged and given its due weight, therefore, to give it excessive importance and to view it with wonder and admiration is misguided.

The examples Hegel gives, in Enz. Section 145 Zus., are, first, the profusion of natural forms which proliferate beyond what is required for systematic interrelation. There is nothing wonderful or admirable, he declares, about these, for they multiply at random and tend only to obscure the essential moments of the Idea embodied in them. They are to be seriously considered only so far as those moments are disclosed in them. Such proliferation, however, does occur randomly and it is ridiculous to imagine that its products could be construed a priori. To attempt to deduce them in detail from first principles is pretentious pedantry and would be a waste of time. The aim of science and philosophy is to discover the necessity that lies beneath the surface of contingency, as perhaps we may say, contemporary meteorologists have discovered regularities governing the changes in the weather. But more important, in Hegel's opinion, is the teleological nature of organic activity, of which he has more to say at a later stage. When, in the footnote to Section 250 of the Encyclopaedia, in the Naturphilosophie, he rejects Herr Klug's satirical demand that Hegel should deduce the existence of his pen, Hegel says that there are more important matters for philosophy to consider. But if Herr Klug's pen is really a contingent matter, no such deduction should be possible, irrespective of its importance. It is not altogether clear from Hegel's argument whether the 'inner harmony and regularity of nature'[12] is supposed to encompass the contingent aspect, so that the indeterminacy is only a surface appearance, or if the profligacy of nature is really random, yet by some law of great numbers reducible to a general orderliness which serves an

195

ultimate organic purpose, as modern biologists believe the excessive profusion of gametes serves vicariously the ends of survival and evolution.

The second example of contingency which Hegel discusses is free will. This, as commonly understood, is the indeterminate ability to do whatever one chooses. Such indeterminacy is usually considered indispensable for free action, and Hegel agrees that the very meaning of will implies untrammelled option. But this is only a necessary, not a sufficient, condition of freedom, which much more indispensably requires resolute self-determination. The decision must be mine and no other's and the conditions of action must be of my own creation. Freedom is not just caprice, or the capacity for arbitrary choice; it is purposeful (zweckmässig) decision in which free choice has been sublated. The decision made, no further choice is open; it has been cancelled though still preserved in the resolution made. Arbitrary choice is the abstract notion of freedom. The concrete conception, as we shall presently see, coincides with the concrete conception of necessity.

The kernel of Hegel's position seems to be that there is an actual element of chance in the nature of things, but that it is always founded on a determinate structure and is subordinated to a rational purpose.

A.N. Whitehead, who had not read Hegel, makes a similar distinction between abstract, or pure, possibility and real possibility, though he treats the former with greater respect (whether deservedly or not) than Hegel does.[13] Whitehead does not understand by pure potentiality merely formal self-identity. What he calls 'pure potentialities of definiteness' are, for him, 'eternal objects', available for prehension by actual entities from the 'primordial nature of God', and also passed from actual entities (in what he calls their 'superjective phase') to their successors as data. Real possibility is what is offered in this latter way by the actual entities (or 'occasions') of the immediate past (that is, the totality of causal conditions provided by the immediately passing state of the universe). These passing actual entities are all prehended by the present occasion in a process of 'concrescence' or integration, which is its own spontaneous act of creativity, powered by a 'lure for feeling' constituting its 'mental pole' and involving the first type of prehension of eternal objects. The 'physical pole' is the sum-total of prehensions of other actual occasions from the past. Real potentiality, here, seems to be complete conditioning, and how it is to be distinguished from necessity is not easy to see. Pure potentiality is apparently an indeterminate possibility made definite by the spontaneous activity of the mental pole of the prehending subject. This is a kind of embryonic consciousness in some ways reminiscent of Empfindung in Hegel's account of the soul in the Geistesphilosophie, which for him is the rudiment of mind, from which self-conscious spirit develops. But this emerges in Hegel's system only at the end of the dialectic of Nature, whereas Whitehead makes it integral to every atomic actual entity in physical existence, and his theory of the process of development up to conscious mind is obscure. It comes about through increasing complexity of nexūs and historic routes of actual entities, in a way which Whitehead never works out in detail or explains with any clarity. Nevertheless, there may well be more affinity between the two thinkers than appears from a superficial reading; for the mental pole of an actual entity, in Whitehead's theory, is its prehension of eternal objects, the source of which is God's Primordial Nature, where all eternal objects are ordered. This is not very far removed from Hegel's 'mind of God prior to the creation of Nature and finite spirit' with which he identifies the absolute Idea. The mental pole of the actual entity would then constitute the immanence in Nature of the Idea.

Whitehead and his followers reject absolute determinism both in nature and in mind, but the immanence of the Primordial Nature of God and the transcendence of his Consequent Nature suggest a holism not dissimilar to Hegel's. And Hegel's view of necessity is to be understood, quite otherwise than as often assumed by superficial and hostile critics, in terms of his holism. In Whitehead's theory the spontaneity of the mental pole in its activity integrating the prehensions of the actual entity, saves real potentiality from rigid necessity, but how the concrescence of individual occasions and their nexūs are related to the Consequent Nature of God is something that Whitehead never fully or explicitly works out.

Conceptions of God and of the absolute Idea, however, take us far beyond the stage we are discussing here. Real possibility is no more than the availability of relevant conditions, and, as Hegel goes on to say, 'If all conditions are present, the fact must become actual ... Developed actuality ... is necessity.'[14]

The resolution of the opposition between contingency and necessity lies properly in the sequel and is probably the same for Whitehead (if one can penetrate his obscurities) as for Hegel. The immanence of the whole (in Whitehead the Primordial Nature of God) is what both explains and integrates the profusion of the contingent, and the contingent is the self-proliferation of the concrete universal in its finite differentiations. Hegel asserts that in all finitude there is contingency, and as finitude is a necessary moment in the self-specification of the infinite, contingency is a necessary element in the real. It is the moment of difference which is as essential to the whole as the moment of identity.

Again, as an incident of finitude the contingent is yet another manifestation of the false infinite, the endless sich-erzeugende proliferation of finite upon finite. In another aspect it is randomness, whether of movement, of occurrence, or of procreation. But

197

randomness is always and inevitably relative to order. Motion is random only if something ordered is moved (particles, waves, things, or what have you), and randomness itself is but a dissipation of ordered segments.[15] Random events are events themselves having coherent structure, which are determined (as we have seen) by law-governed conditions. Further, random occurrences resolve themselves into ordered systems, from the bell-curve of statistics to the physical effects of thermodynamics and quantum mechanics. These examples are not Hegel's, but he does say that the interest of science is to penetrate to the principles of order and necessity underlying the chaotic confusion of contingency, which is precisely what the physics of our own day persistently seeks to do.

The finite and the random, chance occurrence, or contingent action is intrinsically what it is, in its own nature, only as the specific manifestation of the principles of structure which are themselves the specifications of the Concept -- or the ordering principle of the whole. The order which it determines is no mere spatial pattern, nor even simply a causal structure extended in time, nor yet an organic series of organic symbioses. All these are degrees of its realization and all are necessary phases in its self-specification. But its own over-all structure is no less than the entire dialectical scale, within which there are necessarily finite, and so contingent, moments, but these are all aufgehoben and sublated in the final totality.

This pervasive holism governs the contingent and elicits from it trends to and processes of order, which due to this very holism are teleological. This is the cunning of reason of which more is to be said anon. This is the divine Providence of religious faith and the free determinism which the next section is about to expound.

Necessity

Once again, the category has an abstract as well as a concrete interpretation; and here also three phases are distinguished: formal, relative and true (or absolute) necessity. Of the first Hegel says little except that it is the identity of possibility and actuality, a definition he gives in the Greater Logic and acknowledges in the Encyclopaedia as correct but merely superficial. If we take formal possibility as our clue, we may say that formal necessity is logical necessity, but this meant something much more concrete and significant to Hegel than it does to contemporary formal logicians. Today, logical necessity is simply tautology and is rigidly distinguished from factual, or causal, necessity. This syntactical tautology is, perhaps, the example par excellence of formal, abstract, necessity, for it is no more than abstract self-identity, which is the hall-mark likewise of logical possibility; and, if one takes actuality as the guarantee of self-consistency on the ground that nothing self-contradictory can exist, then the identity of formal possibility and formal actuality does give an apt definition of formal necessity.

In this Hegel has little or no interest. Necessity for him is what the Concept prescribes. It is the dialectical necessity of self-specification of the universal, which impels the abstract to supplement itself and remedy its shortcomings in union with its opposite. He gives us, therefore, a fuller account of relative and of absolute necessity.

Relative necessity is still not fully concrete and may be classified as abstract necessity. It is no more than what is fully conditioned, or hypothetically actual. The necessity is dependent on the conditioning; what is necessitated is not self-determined, for what determines it lies outside. As so conditioned it is no better than the contingent, for it has no control over its conditions, nor is their outcome under their control. The necessity is therefore 'blind'. The mediation is not internalized by the necessary fact and made its own so that it determines itself and is its own product.

Hegel says that necessity is a very difficult conception, because it is really the Concept, only with its moments still conceived as actualities, transient and dissipated. Necessity is the unity of possibility and actuality, as was said above; it is hypothetical actuality, i.e., what is, on stipulated conditions, necessary. But this definition, we have been warned, gives only a superficial and relatively unintelligible impression of something very complex. Hegel distinguishes three factors: (1) the conditions, (2) the fact or outcome (die Sache), and (3) the activity which converts the conditions into the fact.

(1) The conditions are in the first instance scattered, contingent, and apparently indifferent to one another as well as to the fact. They are merely posited as conditions relative to the presupposed outcome (the fact). But they become, from its point of view, the complete circle of determinants, which are translated into the characteristics of the fact, or thing conditioned. They are potentially the fact, but only if and as related together in a certain way.

(2) The fact is first presupposed as a possible self-subsistent in relation to which conditions can be identified. It then, so to speak, consumes the conditions in order to emerge into external existence, in which its content and detailed characteristics (corresponding to the conditions) are realized.

(3) The activity is the process or agency which brings the fact into existence by converting the conditions into actuality. It is (or can be) an independent self-subsistent being, a man or his character (his will), yet the possibility of its action is resident only in the conditions and their relation to the result.

These three moments of necessity are really an elaboration of what we earlier encountered as real possibility. They set out in order and appropriate relation the necessary and sufficient conditions of the fact. As examples we may take (1) a volcano (a natural object) or (2) a house (an artefact). The conditions for the existence of the first are existent rock strata, gaseous contents of the earth's crust, or core, certain degrees of temperature and pressure, molten lava, and the like. Of the second they would be available stones or bricks, timber, sand and cement, a suitable site, and so on. All these exist in apparent independence, and only as related to the presupposed outcome do they rank as conditions. As so related they are then, as it were, absorbed into the fact. The subterranean heat melts the lava and expands the gases to create pressures which explode and throw up substances to form the cone of the volcano, the characteristics of which are determined by the conditioning factors. Alternatively, cement is laid as a foundation, and stone and woodwork are constructed together to form the walls and doorways and windows of the house, along with other features, the properties and structure of the whole building being dependent upon these materials. The activity which brings all this about is, in the first example, the working of the internal geological forces of the earth's core and crust; in the second, the agency of the architect and the builder, none of which could produce the result without the pre-existing available conditions. All of them are contingently actual, in all of them taken together the outcome is potential, and the combination of these actualities and potentialities in a single unity is the necessity of the fact -- the present actuality of necessary and sufficient conditions.

As long as these factors are conceived as mutually external and independent existences, so long is the necessity only external, blind, and limited. This is the abstract conception and it is conceived as efficient causation -- the category which develops from it in the next phase of the dialectic of Actuality. It is, in short, causal necessity.

True necessity, on the other hand, is the complete coherent system, which sublates the totality of conditions. It is the totality, and the principle of structure which it embodies determines the nature of the conditions, their mutual relations and their outcome. It is the determination of the parts or moments by the whole, which is self-determining, and as such it is properly unconditioned. It is as it is, simply because it is so. This kind of necessity is teleological. Its end and outcome is known beforehand and is what guides the process of its realization throughout its course. It is the true conception of free action, namely, what is dependent only upon itself and not upon another. In the last resort, this is fully possible only for a self-conscious mind, but it is already immanent in organic wholes, which themselves create and regulate the conditions of their own self-maintenance by their own activity. In such cases the conditions, the outcome and the activity are all one and the same, so that the activity is free. Thus true necessity and true freedom are identical, but it is only in the Concept that their identity becomes clearly and transparently visible.

In the Zusatz to Section 147, Hegel embarks upon a long discussion of fatalism and the conception in various religions of fate, destiny and divine Providence. But the discussion is not long enough, and the conclusion is not supported by sufficient argument to be convincing. Hegel himself says that, for fuller discussion we must refer to the philosophies of History and Religion, neither of which are our immediate concern. We shall, however, return to these issues in Part III; here he argues that the ancient acquiescence in Destiny is not so much resignation to the inevitable as recognition of the fitness of things as they are, which eliminates the pain and distress produced by wishing for an unattainable 'ought to be'. It is the setting at nought of finite personal desires in acceptance of the universal justice of things. The Christian doctrine of ultimate salvation and consolation for the tribulations of this life in an after-life is an imaginative representation of the insight that the whole is the truth and God is the infinite subjectivity in which all finite subjectivity finds ultimate fulfilment, a fulfilment in which our personal individuality is preserved and trans-figured. God's freedom is not incompatible with necessity, for it is the governance by the whole of its own constituents. His will is not, like ours, a choice between alternatives, capricious and arbitrary, nor is it subject to frustration by circumstances, but is the infinite, eternal and immutable design irresistibly accomplished through its own self-determined dispensation. This same self-determining capacity is imparted to men (created in God's image) through their own self-consciousness, by which they become masters of their own fate, so that what happens to them is as much the result of their own attitudes and characters as of blind circumstance --

> The fault, dear Brutus, is not in our stars
> But in ourselves ...[16]

The more conscious we are of our own freedom, the less are we at odds with our fortune and our lot.

The true whole in the inter-related compactness of its elements is the ground of necessity. But this whole is fully realized only in the consciousness of itself as whole, in and through its own self-specification in the dialectic. As such it is subjectivity. In the Zusatz Hegel traces three phases, or degrees of this self-consciousness: (1) consciousness of the finite self and of its subjective aims and wishes, as confronted by the actual: imposed necessity -- what ought to be in contrast with what is; (2) awareness of the whole as determined and of one's own desires as limited and futile except so far as they are restricted to one's own responsibility -- the Stoic conception of ataraxia or resignation; (3) the realization that conforming one's desires to the

201

wholeness of being is the actualization of the totality that is being realized through one's own awareness as atonement with the infinite -- consolation. This last is what Spinoza called 'Blessedness', what supervenes upon the knowledge and love of God, or Substance, or Nature -- the absolutely infinite being in which everything has its existence and through which alone anything can be conceived. But for Hegel this does not go far enough. God is to be conceived not as substance but as subject. He is Absolute Spirit, in the true knowledge of whom human persons find their ultimate satisfaction and salvation, as necessary moments in the divine totality.

The foundation of this reasoning is the Concept, the self-realizing whole which is the truth, and which fulfils itself by way of man's intellect and will in Absolute Spirit. Man brings to consciousness, in theory and practice, what is implicit in lower nature, and fulfils his own humanity in the knowledge of himself and his world, and in a self-transcendence that unites him with the infinite. The universal design expressing itself in the universal dialectic resolves the opposition between necessity and freedom, between destiny and finite self-assertion, between human fortune and human redemption.

Absolute Correlation[17]

Necessity specifies itself as substance, cause and reciprocity. These are the special categories of necessary connexion which prove a stumbling block to the empiricist, in particular to Hume, the most consistent empiricist philosopher of the understanding. The empiricist sees actuality as a congeries or succession of atomic particulars (in Hume's terminology, 'perceptions', 'impressions' and 'ideas') among which no necessary connexion is ever apparent, possibility is degraded to abstract self-identity, and probability to frequency of conjunction. What is missing is the systematic structure of an ordered whole, and the consequent determination of its elements and the regulation of their inter-relations by the organizing principle. This now reveals itself in the dialectic in the form of a substance determining its accidents, which succeed one another in time as cause and effect and finally cohere in mutual reciprocal determination. Again, it was Kant who reinstated necessary connexion, virtually on the empiricist's home ground, by showing that without it no coherent knowledge of objects would be possible -- that is to say, without systematic structure, no scientific thinking is feasible. Hegel's thesis is that reality in Nature, as the Idea in the form of other-being, displays the same characters of necessary connexion as are requisite for scientific knowledge.

Substance

Ground expressed itself in its consequence as the existent, and that, as the form taken by an underlying matter, was appearance, which now through the united correlates, form and content, whole and part, inner and outer, has become actuality. This actual or real is now seen as the substance of all things and appearances, which are related to it as its accidents. It is the power or force that expresses itself in its accidental (contingent) manifestations. This correlation develops further into necessity of the second level, the causal relation. The necessary connexion between cause and effect, which Hume failed to discover among impressions of sensation, is now revealed as the structure of the system which is the substance underlying the accidents into which it differentiates itself. Their relation to it and to one another is a necessary relation, expressible as the correlation of concomitants constantly conjoined according to causal laws; and that finally reveals itself as reciprocal interaction. Thus, in the categories of absolute correlation, all the prior categories of Essence are summed up and recapitulated.

Kant, in his exposition of the Principles of the Understanding, made it clear that substance is that permanent matrix (or substratum) without which no change is conceivable. It is the counterpart of time itself, which does not change, but in which all changes occur. Whatever changes, he declared, is permanent.[18] The changes in the permanent are the forms in which it appears or manifests itself. They are the 'accidental' forms which it successively takes. In each of them it manifests its active power, so that they are necessarily related in this process (what Hegel calls Formtätigkeit). The relation is first that of force expressing itself, or of inner to outer: substance to its accidents or determinations (Bestimmungen), which, Kant has told us, are all that change affects, so that we may say paradoxically, 'only the permanent changes.'[19]

The necessary connexion then is first between substance and its changing determinations (necessary, because the two are identical). But these changes are successive self-manifestations of substance, and their relation to one another is therefore that of successive events in time. The necessary connexion is thus transferred from that between substance and its accidents, to that of the changes in the accidents to one another. They issue as a succession of causes and effects, in which the causal efficacy is at once that of the substance exercised upon its determinations and that of the prior 'state' or self-manifestation of substance upon its successor. In reality substance is the system or ordered whole, which, to be ordered and to be whole, must both be self-complete and be differentiated. It can be completely differentiated, however, only by running off its specifications, or 'spelling out' its determinations. This running off or spelling out is, for Hegel, essentially the dialectical process; but on the level of the understanding (on which Kant takes it) it appears merely as the sequence of events successively related as cause and effect. The true causal series is dialectical development, but that that is so can only be clearly recognized when viewed from the level of the Concept.

203

We are often reminded that there are two main types of metaphysics, substance metaphysics and process metaphysics. The first identifies the real with the permanent, the second with what changes. Plato and Aristotle are said to be representatives of substance metaphysics, and, among moderns, Descartes, Spinoza and Leibniz. Heraclitus is an obvious example of the second kind of metaphysics, and among contemporaries, Bergson and Whitehead are process metaphysicians. Those who profess to renounce metaphysics altogether will reject any such placement for themselves, but the implications of their explicit doctrines usually tend one way or the other. It should be clear from the above that each type is merely emphasizing one side of an antithesis both sides of which are equally essential, each of which implies the other, and neither of which can stand alone. Substance philosophers tend to play down the changing as appearance (which indeed it is, but no less significant on that account), while process philosophers disregard, or reject altogether, any conception of an underlying substratum, forgetting that something must persist through change, and that process without some matrix is inconceivable.[20] This is but one more example of what Hegel means when he says that every category is, and has been given as, a definition of the Absolute. Certainly, the real has been defined as substance, and those who declare that it is ultimately in process are defining it as causal sequence.

Hegel here defends Spinoza, once again, against his detractors, while repeating his own (by now well-known) criticism,[21] that the differentiation of Substance finds, in Spinoza's system, no immanent principle.

Cause and Effect

Substance, as cause, is the primary reality (Ursache), which, as it continually specifies itself, passes over into effect. The effect is dependent upon it; yet, inasmuch as nothing is a cause without producing an effect, cause is equally dependent (ein Gezetztsein). Moreover, whatever is in the effect is derived from the cause, and everything in the cause passes over into the effect.[22] Their content is the same although they are differently determined as to form. The wetness caused by the rain is the same water which falls as raindrops. The flesh and bones sustained by eating are the same proteins, fats, salts, etc., as were consumed as food; only they have been transformed. The change is brought about by the form-activity of the substance -- the identical content which expresses itself through the changes. The necessity of the connexion is the necessary self-specification of the identical substance, but as it occurs in time it is effected through the series of events and issues as the transformation of the identical content from the prior event to its successor. The active principle which determines the change and the course of the transformation is the organizing principle of the whole (which is the substance), but this is, as it were, channelled, and its essential activity is exerted, through the prior event as cause in its self-issuance into the consequent effect. The effect is the self-utterance of the cause; it is the way the cause, as cause, realizes itself. It therefore causes itself and is causa sui. More accurately, it is the identical content, which expresses itself as both cause and effect, that is causa sui, and that content is in fact ultimately the substance. Spinoza is right, therefore, to maintain that Substance is causa sui; and it is only when conceived as finite that cause and effect are kept apart. Even then, every cause is also an effect and every effect a cause, so that the substantial content liquefies and runs away into an infinite series. This false infinite of cause and effect is, however, aufgehoben in the Fürsichsein of substance, which is reciprocal action within the system as a whole.

Here as elsewhere, McTaggart goes hopelessly astray.[23] He fails completely to understand the relation between substance and cause, as also between formal cause and determining cause (Cf. W.L.,II, pp. 223-227; Miller pp. 558-562), and the transition in each case from the former to the latter. His cavilling criticisms are based on a faulty, or at best shortsighted, analysis of causality (for instance, his objections to Hegel's examples of the identity of cause and effect), and compound new errors with some he has made earlier. As he has done previously, he objects here again to Hegel's transition from one category to another on the ground that it appears to revert to an earlier category, but the objection springs from his inability to grasp the nature of Aufhebung, as preserving and transforming as well as superseding and transcending what it has surpassed.

Reciprocity

Substance differentiates itself as accidents or attributes, which are its changing self-utterances. The permanent content is immanent in each and all of them, and the immanent identity appears as cause and effect. Immobile permanence is opposed to unceasing causal change. But substance is immanent as much in effect as in cause, and cause in producing effect simply realizes what is potential in itself, and so causes only itself. The effect is, therefore, as substantial as the cause and as much active as passive. Accordingly it reacts upon the cause and the causal relation becomes reciprocal.

The causal relation which is prima facie transitive, is in reality just as much symmetrical. For example, in the chemical reaction of sugar with sulphuric acid, the molecules of each compound ($C_{22}O_{11}$ and H_2SO_4) relate to those of the other as cause to effect and the relation is mutual and symmetrical -- the reaction is reciprocal. Hegel's examples are the interrelation of organs and processes in the living organism, and the interrelation of national character with form of government, where each is the cause as well as the effect of the other.[24] The action of the heart causes the circulation of the blood through the lungs, and the action of the lungs, in aerating the blood, regulates the rate of the heart-beat, which in turn controls the depth and the speed of breathing. But in truth it is the entire system and condition of the organism which determine the interdependent functionings of its organs. In the same way it is the state and activity of the social whole that determines and regulates the nature and functioning of its institutions. Thus, Hegel complains, to say that living organs, or social phenomena, are mutually cause and effect, explains nothing. The system, as one of reciprocal inter-determination of its parts, must be recognized as Concept if it is to become fully self-explanatory.

Once more, we have the immanent whole at work. The reciprocal causal relation is the manifestation of the organizing principle of the system, which governs all the differences and determines their interaction, so that each of them is indifferently cause or effect. It is now not that every effect becomes in its turn the cause of a further effect, but that in any causal coupling the terms are reciprocally cause and effect. This is so in three ways, or in three degrees: (1) the effect is as much determined by that which is acted on as by that which acts. A boulder falling from a cliff produces a different effect according as it falls on hard rock, on soft earth, or into water. (This does not contradict the identity of content in both cause and effect, as McTaggart maintains,[25] for momentum is conserved in all three cases). (2) The cause is modified by the effect, which now is just as much cause, as when an acid (e.g., H_2SO_4) acts upon a metal (say, copper) and both are changed to a gas (H_2) and a salt ($CuSO_4$). (3) The effect reverts as cause to re-establish the original cause, as in the chemical action of an enzyme or catalyst, and in such cases of physiological cyclical activity as instanced in the last paragraph.

Cause and effect are now no longer simply transient, and the infinite regress, both backwards and forwards, is no longer forced upon us. Cause has coalesced with effect to constitute an integral unity, which is the single content that has all along been the ground of the transitions and inter-relationships. Accordingly, Hegel tells us, reciprocity turns the endless causal chain back upon itself to constitute a self-determining totality, which is thus a true infinite. It is the self-maintaining whole that is truly causa sui.

Reciprocity, the pure interchange of self and other, is the unveiling of true necessity.[26] Necessity as embodied in substance and transmitted from cause to effect, is now explicitly revealed as reciprocal interaction of elements within a whole. The necessitation of effect by the cause is self-necessitation. It is its own cause and its own effect. What determines it is its own activity. The whole immanent in the cause is what provides it with its efficacy, and this is neither more nor less than the self-activity of the whole. Necessity and freedom once more transpire as two aspects of the same activity. But, in the last resort necessity is only truly freedom when it is understood, or brought to consciousness. 'The highest self-dependence of man is to know himself as wholly determined by the Absolute Idea, a state of mind and conduct which Spinoza calls amor intellectualis Dei.'27

From Essence to Concept

In the movement of the dialectic in the Doctrine of Essence the specification of the whole or system is presented over and over again as two correlated aspects reflected into each other. This is repeated in progressively more adequate forms: Identity and Difference, Ground and Consequent, Thing and its Properties, Whole and Part, Force and Expression, and so forth. All these two-fold categories are aufgehoben in and as Actuality, the mediated immediate, which again displays itself in further forms of the same correlation: Substance and accident, Cause and effect, and their sublation in reciprocal action. Here we are on the verge of the Concept, which has been immanent throughout and is now about to emerge in its true and fully explicit form.

In each of the dyads, the first is the unity of the prior couple, Ground of Identity and Difference, Existence of ground and consequent, Whole of Form and Content; and also the correlates in the pairs constitute triads of interreflecting dualities. Finally the two sides are revealed as one and the same content reflected back upon itself and constituting a single whole in both its phases, which at the same time embraces them both within itself.

As was noted above, the dialectical process changes its character as it proceeds and as its content becomes more concrete and complex. We have seen it transformed from transition in the doctrine of Being to reflection in the doctrine of Essence, and we are now to witness a further change to development in the doctrine of the Concept. Hegel frequently maintains that its course is 'necessary', and this claim is as frequently misunderstood to mean that it is rigid and unalterable. That it should be so is hardly likely, seeing that Hegel himself has varied it in the different versions of the logic which he wrote. These variations, however, could be attributed to growth in his insight into the mutual relation of the categories. But more important is the nature and meaning of necessity itself, which has now become clearer and is shortly to be still further elucidated. Necessity is of different kinds, depending on the degree of abstraction under which its object is envisaged. The more abstract the object, the more rigid the necessity; so that in the case of mere spatial relations (like that of the sides and angles of a triangle) it is more rigid than in the case of the relations between the working parts of a machine, where it is more rigid than in the case of those between the structure and functions of organs in a living body. Necessity, we have found, is the determination of the parts by the principle of organization of the whole; and as that principle becomes more concretely comprehensive, the structure becomes more complex and the necessity more flexible. It is, in fact, not just compatible, but really identical, with relevant variation -- that is, modification of relationships needful to maintain the unity and integrity of the whole. Accordingly, those who criticize Hegel for making transitions in the dialectic which are apparently arbitrary and are not strictly necessitated, are often misled by their unbending adherence to a conception of necessity derived from formal logic, which, as the creation of the understanding, is the most abstract sphere of all. In fact, the necessity which Hegel claims is that required by the self-determination and self-differentiation of the Concept.

The dialectic of Essence has now brought to view a world of Actuality, as a concrete whole of inseparably correlated moments. So it is for us, but it has yet to become so for itself. The totality, existing in itself and become also for itself (an und für sich) is der Begriff. But der Begriff has been immanent from the beginning and has been the underlying motif of the whole series of categories, which after all, as categories, are concepts -- differentiations of the Concept, its provisional definitions. The concept is the identity which differentiates itself and is identical in and with all its differences (the identity of identity and non-identity). It is the ultimate ground of all existence, the force which ubiquitously expresses itself (ultimately the Idea, embodying itself in -- or God working through -- Nature). It is the actuality which is rational and the rationality which is actual. It is the substance underlying all accidents, causa sui which is the cause of every effect, and which, as its own effect, is in thorough reciprocity with itself -- or in other words, is at home with itself in its other. In short, it is the essence of all existence. The Concept which has thus been immanent all along, now comes to light as what Being and Essence are in truth.

Properly speaking, therefore, the whole of the Logic is the doctrine of the Concept. But as the Zusatz to Section 159 makes clear, it could not begin with the Concept fully fledged. That would be to begin at the end of its self-development. Yet indeed we did begin with the Concept, for the Concept is the unity of Being and Essence, and to begin with it is to inquire into them -- to consider how Being and Essence can be thought and how they are related, or grasped together in one concept. To begin with the Concept requires that we begin with its moments, and these, in the first instance, are Being and Essence, which are, each at its own level the Concept an sich. The passage of Being into Essence and its reflection into itself as Essence, is the development of the Concept, which we must now follow on its home ground. For the dialectic of the Concept as such is development proper, and we shall not be surprised to discover that the moments we have so far examined reappear at the higher level in new guise.

The Concept proper is the concrete universal; that is, the universal that particularizes itself by its own inner dialectic. Hegel's

208

logic is the logic of this universal throughout its range. The logic of the understanding (formal logic), on the other hand, is the logic of the abstract universal, which is held apart from its particulars and receives them, as it were, from without, as fortuitous data. It may even be destined to be empty of particulars altogether, for it may be a non-instantiated concept, the null class. Such a logic is no genuine part of dialectical logic, although dialectical logic can account for its occurrence. If it is to be called logic at all, it is only by courtesy, for it is really one of the special (in our day, mathematical) sciences, and not a philosophical science -- not <u>Wissenschaft</u> in Hegel's usage of that word.

The transition from Essence to Concept is marked by the final identification of <u>Sein</u> and <u>Schein</u> (being and show)[28], or the reversion of the latter into the former. Throughout the dialectic of Essence the two moments, identity and difference, have reflected into each other, alternately playing the role of inner essence and outer show. Finally, in reciprocal action they reveal themselves as a single actual whole reflected into itself. The diremption is disclosed as self-diremption, and the showing as a self-revelation. But such an actuality, reflecting itself in itself, is precisely the description of a conscious being -- an immediate existent aware of itself, and thereby immediately of its own existence, hence reflecting and reflected into itself as its own object ('I'); and at the same time projecting itself (its own self-sentience) as an objective world (or Other) in perception. This perception is, on the one hand, the reflection (or showing) of the external world, and, on the other, (as sentience) of the organism in and to itself. As perception, it is also the product of the subject's reflection into and interpretation of the content of its own consciousness. The principle of this self-conscious being (<u>Fürsichsein</u>) is at once the principle of self-identity and wholeness (as we shall presently see more closely) as well as that of free activity, or self-differentiation. It is <u>der Begriff</u>, unveiling itself henceforth as identical with its other (its own differentiated content) in which it is ever immanent and 'at home' (<u>bei sich selbst</u>).

Hegel says, in Section 159, that this transition from Actuality to the Concept, from necessity to freedom, is the most difficult; because substantive actuality is to be seen as consisting solely in the identity of two substantive beings (cause and effect). This identity is achieved in thought (<u>der Begriff</u>) in which, Hegel says, this solidity (<u>Harte</u>) of actuality and (again playing on words) difficulty of transition are overcome and resolved. Here two substantive beings -- the sentient organism and its opposing environment -- are mutually cause and effect. The outcome of their reciprocal organic unity is self-awareness, the coming to consciousness of the object as subject. Indeed this transition is both the most mysterious in Nature and it is the most difficult to understand. How does a spatio-temporal pattern of electrical discharges in the brain become a feeling and an awareness? This is a problem unsolved, perhaps insoluble, by science. The neural-identity theory (so popular today) is no solution, only an ingenious way of ignoring the problem.[29] The difficulty is reflected in the dialectical move from Actuality to Concept. The transition from substance to attribute, from cause to effect and from action to reaction, is in each case the manifestation in its parts and elements of the pervasive whole; but in all of these the ground is hidden, submerged and blindly at work. Only when it becomes aware of itself is its activity, as free self-specification, visible and recognizable. But how does physical interaction become self-conscious? First it becomes organic, self-maintaining and self-activating, and the integration of this action upon itself somehow displays itself to itself as feeling or sentience. Substance thus becomes subject, which as self-identical synthesizes and organizes its experience as a single self-conscious whole. This, its spontaneous self-activity, is free, no longer blind but self-determined as consciously self-directed. Actuality has raised itself to Concept, and the opposition of organism to environment, as well as their identity in the organic relationship, is resolved in consciousness and thought, which 'shows' or illuminates both their difference and their identity. Being and show, reality and appearance, have become one in the consciousness of itself as subject which the object has gained through organic activity.

NOTES: Book II, Part II, Chapter 4

Chapter 4

1. Enz., Sections 142-159.

2. Cf. Enz., Section 141.

3. McTaggart's treatment of the Absolute in this section of the Greater Logic is typically confused and obtuse. It is totally misguided and worthless as either interpretation or criticism.

4. Cf. Enz., Section 142. Of course, the differences are not abolished (as McTaggart assumes). They are aufgehoben, preserved, while transcended and transformed.

5. I have argued elsewhere that this criticism of Spinoza is unjustified. See above pp. 144, 151, Bk. II, Pt. I, Ch. 3, n6.

6. Cf. Enz., Section 142 Zus.: '...das schlechthin Wirkende zugleich und auch Wirkliche,...'.

7. Cf. Leibniz, Monadology, 45; Meditationes de Cognitione, Veritate et Ideis, Gebhardt, IV, 424; New Essays Concerning Human Understanding, 504.

8. Op. cit., Ch. XIII, p. 479.

9. To say, as McTaggart does, that a four-angled triangle is a four-angled triangle and so is self-consistent (or self-identical) is nonsense. It is a contradiction in terms and so impossible even formally.

10. In the light of the above a great mass of contemporary discussion about possible worlds is seen to be founded in quicksands.

11. Cf. Enz., Section 146 Zus.

12. Enz., Section 145 Zus.

13. Cf. Process and Reality, (Cambridge, 1929), pp. 90ff. and 29-30.

14. Enz., Section 147.

15. Cf. my discussion in The Foundations of Metaphysics in Science, Ch. XXII.

16. Shakespeare, Julius Caesar, Act I, Sc. II, ll. 140-41.

17. Enz., Sections 150-155.

18. Cf. Kritik der reinen Vernunft, A 187, B 230: 'Daher ist alles, was sich verandert, bleibend...'.

19. Loc. cit.

20. Whitehead avoids the worst errors of this one-sidedness and, despite the insistence on process in his theory, his philosophy is much more than an uncompromising pluralism or transitionalism and has many affinities to Hegel's.

21. Cf. Enz., Section 151, Zus.

22. Cf. Thomas Aquinas, Summa Theologica, I, 945, A 7: 'Omnis effectus repraesentat aliqualiter causam suam.'

23. Cf. Commentary, Sections 166-178.

24. Cf. Enz., Section 156 Zus.

25. Cf. Commentary, p. 182.

26. See above, pp. 200ff.

27. Enz., Section 158 Zus.

28.   Cf. B. Lakebrink, _Kommentar zu Hegels Logik_, pp. 406ff.

29.   Cf. my 'The Neural-Identity Theory and the Person', _International Philosophical Quarterly_, Vol. IV, no. 4, 1966.

PART III

THE DOCTRINE OF THE CONCEPT

PART III

THE DOCTRINE OF THE CONCEPT

Chapter 1

The Concept of the Concept

The categories of Being passed over one into another; their relation to each other remained implicit until in Essence it was posited and set out (as we suggested) diagramatically. But neither was the transition nor the intro-reflection <u>for itself</u>. It was in the subject matter, but not for it -- only for us who were philosophizing. The transitions of Being occurred immediately, of their own movement, but were not aware of themselves as what they were. This is true both of nature and of spirit, for obviously natural forms are unaware of their own qualities and quantities, but neither is the ordinary consciousness (what Husserl calls 'the natural attitude') in its unreflective phase aware of the interdependence and the correlativity of these categories. In Essence, Being reflected into itself and showed, in this reflection, what inwardly it essentially was. But again this inwardness was not aware of itself as such, and the forth-shining of essence was only appearance. Substance differentiated itself and assumed different forms or accidents necessarily and reciprocally related one to another as cause and effect. But its phases showed forth these relationships and enacted them without knowing themselves to be such. Even scientific understanding, while it identifies causes and effects and discerns reciprocal action, and even describes natural events as 'phenomena', does not identify these relationships as the self-reflection and intro-reflection of being.

Ultimately all this is as it is and what it is only as apprehended by a self-conscious knowing subject, who is all this in himself -- a being, reflecting upon and into his own being -- and who is so <u>for</u> himself as well.

The understanding balks at this contention. Being, it declares, is what it is and does what it does apart from and independently of any knowing subject. But in saying so the understanding overlooks the fact that it is precisely <u>for the understanding</u> that being is thus allegedly independent. What the true essence of things is and how it appears outwardly, so the common consciousness maintains, is as it is whether <u>we</u> know it or not. Yet what appears can appear only to a consciousness, and that it is a veiled or hidden essence is an interpretative judgement. The stars are not themselves aware of their shining; it is only we who see them <u>for</u> whom they shine; and that their light is radiant energy emitted by nuclear fission or fusion is our interpretation. Of course it is not <u>merely</u> our interpretation, but without that it is what it is only <u>an sich.</u> It is only potentially its own truth or the awareness of itself, in which alone its meaning and essential nature is realized. Natural being does not wait for human consciousness in order to be. It exists in itself as the external manifestation of the Idea holding immanent within itself the principle of organization which, through it, develops to organism and self-awareness. But prior to the emergence of consciousness it is not and cannot be known to be the Idea in the form of other-being. For this it must have brought itself to awareness of itself as a conscious subject and in the first stages of its self-awareness the subject recognizes the external being of the natural world but sees it as an alien other and does not realize that it is its own prior becoming and self-generation. Nevertheless, it is only _for_ the percipient organism that external being is a world or an 'environment' enclosing and opposing its activities and its endeavours to know; and it is only for a conscious and thinking understanding that it is a world of nature subject to laws which express themselves in observable phenomena.

The transitions of being and the reflections of essence are thus posited (gestezt) only by and for a subject of consciousness, only as comprehended in thought by a consciousness which is aware of itself -- only by an _ego_, a being who can say 'I'. This is the Concept. It is the truth of Being and Essence; it is their unity aware of itself as real in and for itself. It has the immediacy of Being in which the reflective mediation of Essence is sublated. 'I think', 'I am', is an immediate self-evident self-awareness, and it is at the same time a reflection into self, and both the immediacy and the reflection are for itself.

Professor Charles Taylor has reprimanded Hegel for constantly 'taking a swipe at' Kant, but this allegation is belied by Hegel's praise of Kant in the Greater Logic,[1] where, as he introduces the Concept, he gives Kant credit for discovering it in his exposition of the original transcendental unity of apperception in the Transcendental Deduction. This 'transcendental unity' Hegel identifies as the Concept:

> It is one of the profoundest and most accurate insights to be found in the Critique of Reason that the _unity_ which consitutes the _essence of the concept_ is recognized as the _original-synthetic_ unity of _apperception_, as unity of the 'I think' or self-consciousness. (Loc. cit.).

It is, he says, 'one of the most profound principles for speculative development.'

The justice of this assessment of Kant is undeniable. The unity of apperception is the source and origin of the categories, into which it differentiates itself. They are _concepts_ to which objects must conform, and are each and every one a form of synthesis or principle of unification in which this original unity expresses itself. Without synthesis holding together the fleeting representations of sense, no apprehension of objects would be possible, and the primary condition of synthesis is that the elements cognized be objectified by a single identical subject, the I which can preface all its presentations with the rubric, 'I think...'. Such thinking unification of the manifold is the imposition upon it of the unity of the thinking subject specified into principles of order, or concepts, the indispensable condition of all objective knowledge. In other words, it is only as the nature of things, their being and essence (or relational content), come to consciousness in (and as) a unitary experience aware of itself as 'I', as the subject of the experience, that they become objectively actual. The world has being in and for itself only as an actually existing self-conscious knowing. As nature, it exists in itself but not for itself, until through the organic life and consciousness of human awareness it brings itself to this awareness of itself. And this being-in-and-for-itself is the Concept. This is why the ultimate integration of differences into a whole, or the ultimate whole differentiating itself as a world, is the Concept, or the self-conscious ego of Descartes, Kant and Fichte.

Let us for a moment return to Section 159 of the Encyclopaedia. Hegel writes,

> The Concept, in relation to Being and Essence, is defined (bestimmt) as Essence reverted into Being as simple immediacy, the show of essence has actuality by this means and its actuality, at the same time, is its free showing or shining in itself.

Essence is appearance or reflection, which given immediate being is the conscious ego -- cogito ergo sum -- an immediate existence which at the same time appears and is present in reflection to itself freely (not as a datum presented from elsewhere). Every sort of cognition involving immediate awareness is what Descartes meant by 'cogitatio' -- an immediately existing self-manifestation. Hence to think is to be immediately aware of oneself as existing. But to say of the concept (the self-unifying conscious subject -- cogito) that it exists (ergo sum) is the very least that one can say of it.

Professor Taylor seems only partially to understand Hegel's position at this point, which is crucial for the comprehension of his philosophy as a whole. Taylor notes Hegel's approval of Kant's thesis in the Transcendental Deduction, but he says that Hegel gives it a twist that would have horrified Kant (and it is not difficult to discern that it horrifies Professor Taylor)[2]. What might have horrified Kant, if Professor Taylor is right, however, is not quite what Hegel is driving at. For Kant, the objectivity bestowed upon all knowledge by the spontaneous activity of the subject in synthesizing is only epistemological. It is only a phenomenal objectivity as against the reality of things in themselves. Without the given manifold of sense, this knowledge would have no content, for 'concepts without intuition

216

are empty' supplying knowledge only with its form. For Hegel, Taylor reminds us, the objectivity is ontological and the content of intuition as well as its form are derivative from the Concept, or the self-conscious identity of the subject.[3] The conscious self, for Hegel, is the true reality, the truth of substance, the essence which shines forth in being and is manifested as the matter of intuition. The concept is the active principle underlying all reality and making it what it is. It develops the actual out of itself. So far, Taylor is not misrepresenting Hegel altogether, and how far such a doctrine would have horrified Kant is still a debatable point, depending upon Kant's later conception of noumena and things in themselves. But Taylor leaves his reader with the impression that Hegel's Concept is something merely subjective, so that Hegel is made to appear more of a subjectivist than Kant, who would indeed have rejected the thesis that the reality of things is derived from concepts. The concepts of the understanding, he maintained could be applied only in experience, and never to things in themselves. So long as the emphasis is on the understanding, Hegel largely agrees. Phenomena are but phenomena, and reality (for Kant but not for Hegel) remains apart in splendid isolation beyond the limits of the understanding. Hegel, Taylor implies, makes subjectivity the very being of the real, besides which there is nothing external whatsoever.

In fact, Kant is (as Hegel avers) subjectivist, because his thing in itself is a mere abstract posit, and phenomena are said to be only things as they appear to us. But for Hegel what appears to us and is conceptualized -- or rather, the Concept appearing to us as a systematized world -- is the truth of a reality out of which it has dialectically developed; and which, prior to its self-conscious emergence, is nevertheless real. At that level, however, it is the truth only implicitly. The insight that the Concept is the truth of Being and Essence -- is the real come to consciousness of itself -- is reached only at the end of the logical dialectic; and the logic itself, as the first phase of philosophical science (Wissenschaft), is a very advanced stage in the development of consciousness. It supervenes upon, and is the philosophical reflection upon, not just sense and intuition, but all experience, including common sense and scientific understanding. In the earlier forms of knowledge, the knowing subject confronts an objective world which it views as an external other alien to itself. This external other, however, is now seen to be nothing but the process, first as Nature and then as the content of experience, of the self-development of the self-conscious activity itself. It is an object identical with the subject the content of whose experience it is. But this recognition supervenes upon a long and elaborate series of lower phases (including inorganic and organic natural forms); and while the Concept is immanent in them and is in that sense the principle of their being and movement (their essence), it is not simply and abstractly identical with them, but is also, in more senses than one, different.

217

Kant's great discovery -- his Copernican revolution -- was that objects conform to concepts rather than vice versa. But what he failed in the end to admit was that this could be so only if the synthesizing and objectifying activity of thought really is the same principle as is manifested in the world of space and time, and actually does develop itself through a dialectical process, such as Hegel traces, up to the self-consciousness of the ego. In that case, the Concept must be recognized as the truth of Being, which is certainly not anything merely subjective, nor yet anything inaccessibly beyond consciousness. Nor does Hegel maintain that the real develops out of the subjective concept qua Hirngespinst. Nevertheless, the real world is the Idea in the form of other-being and externality, and its process is the process by which the Idea brings itself to itself in consciousness, its true and essential form.

If realism means belief in and affirmation of the solid actuality of the natural world, Hegel is as much a realist as, and effectively more so than, any other philosopher. It is from Nature that spirit develops itself, through the processes by which Nature becomes aware of itself in its organic product, the living being. Mankind is a natural species the members of which are at once aware of themselves and of the world, and of themselves as members in and products of nature. They have developed to this conscious capability through the natural process, so that nature becomes aware of itself in them. But none of this could be true unless Spirit were from the first immanent in Nature. Unless this were so no spirit could develop out of, or through, any natural process. Only because Nature itself is the self-manifestation in the form of externality of the Idea is this possible, and the natural processes are the dialectical activity of the Absolute in the media of space, time and matter. These are themselves manifestations of the infinite restlessness of the active Idea, which brings it through the natural processes to consciousness in the living organism, aware of itself and so capable of saying 'I', and of asserting its indubitable self-existence as cogito.

We know that this is so, and must be so, in so far as we know that we exist (as res cogitantes) as organisms which are products of nature; for if it were not so, no such self-conscious knowing subjects could ever emerge from the natural process. No dead existent, devoid of all order and dynamic self-integration tending towards the progressive establishment of its ultimate wholeness, could, simply by random movement of its parts, produce a living and consicous being. Accordingly, Nature must be the self-manifestation of Spirit, which must be immanent and active in natural processes, generating its own self-awareness out of the material matrix in which it is instant.

Spirit is the 'inner essence' (the 'soul') of material nature and its ultimate truth, in that, through its own dialectic, as the dialectic of Nature and of consciousness, which emerges in the course of its natural process, it becomes aware of itself as Idea, and of Nature as the self-manifestation of Idea in the form of external other-being. Thus the

218

Idea is Nature become conscious of itself as Spirit. Such a philosophical doctrine is at once realism and idealism: realism in its firm assertion of the external reality of material nature, and idealism in its equally firm assertion that the truth and dialectical outcome of material nature is spirit, which, as Idea, has been and eternally is immanent in all actuality.

It is not from any subjective concept that Nature is generated. On the contrary, subjectivity in the organism develops out of Nature. But this subjectivity is the truth of that from which it has emerged and which has become its object; is, through this development, identical with its object, and comes at the end of yet further dialectical 'self-enfoldment'[4] to the awareness of itself as so identical. In this ultimate outcome the Idea is revealed (or reveals itself) as both the source and the result of the entire dialectical scale, and for this reason Absolute Idealism is equally and at the same time Absolute Realism.

What would have horrified Kant, as Taylor alleges, would equally have horrified Hegel and is repeatedly repudiated by him in quite unmistakable terms. Yet it was Kant's very anxiety to keep things in themselves uncontaminated by the thinking of the understanding that led him, and after him Fichte, to confine himself within an inescapable circle of subjective appearances; and it was left to Schelling to insist upon the co-ordinate status in reality of Nature, and to Hegel to demonstrate that objectivity and truth in knowledge, dependent as they are on conceptualization, are equally dependent upon the fact that self-consciousness, spirit, and the Concept as truth, are the dialectical outcome (Resultat) of self-external Nature and its inwardization (Erinnerung) as feeling and experience.

In the Encyclopaedia (Section 160) Hegel opens the Doctrine of the Concept with the remark: 'Der Begriff ist das Freie als die für sie seiende substantielle Macht', which Wallace translates as 'the principle of freedom, the power of substance self-realized'. This is hardly literal, but both freedom and self-realization are involved, as in part we have already seen, in Being-for-self (die für sie seiende Macht). Freedom, especially, requires self-conscious determination, the paramount condition of wholeness and system in which differences are united. More than this, the differences are self-generating, or self-generated from and by the principle of unity -- that is, the identity of the self-conscious subject. This is the truth first seen, if not fully developed, by Kant, and worked out in detail by Fichte. It is this self-activity of the whole working in and through the self-conscious subject that is the essentially free activity; not an arbitrary, undetermined caprice, but an activity of self-determination by its own principle of order and generation. This is what Hegel means when he says that the Concept is that which is free.

Development

Because the Concept has developed out of Being and Essence, it transpires as what they have potentially been all along -- as what throughout their process has been immanent in them. For unless it were so the Concept could not have emerged from them. Precisely the same is true of Nature and spirit, and it is at this stage of the dialectic that we (ourselves manifestations of Spirit in a mature phase) begin to discover this truth in its explicit and self-conscious form. It is here in the Logic that the Concept emerges as what is immanent in Actuality and what therefore necessarily develops out of it.

This is the essential character of development. It is the peculiar process of the Concept, the explication of the implicit as the becoming manifest of what has hitherto been immanent. As in Being transition, and in Essence reflection, were the typical forms of dialectical progression, in the Concept the appropriate form is development. Transition and reflection were premonitions, but not yet transparent exemplifications of development, and only now, from the viewpoint of the Concept, can they be seen as forms or phases of the same process. Development is explicitly the actualization of the principle of wholeness potential and implicit in each of the parts or moments, so that each reveals itself as the whole, while it is still only one constituent moment, as each of the Leibnizian monads is a reflection of the whole universe while remaining only one of the innumerable constituents of the universe as a whole.

What is here being explained is the concept of the Concept. As we have seen, because the Concept is immanent in Being and Essence, their dialectic has been its dialectic -- its own self-development. So the whole of the Logic is, in a very important sense, the theory of the Concept. But now we are about to embark upon logic proper, in its most characteristic and appropriate form, the logic of logic, or the logic of philosophy (Wissenschaft). The doctrine of the Concept is the thinking study of thinking in its purest and most developed form.

We find, therefore, that from now on every category is self-referential. It is an instantiation of its own principle (the concrete universal) -- and that is the principle being explicated throughout the Logic, and especially in this section, the theory of the Concept proper. That is not just a doctrine of the Concept, not just a theory about it as an extraneous subject-matter; it is the Concept explicating itself, setting out its own logical and ontological structure. It is thought thinking itself in the form of the self-conscious ego.

From now on, every category is what the Logic as a whole is, and ipso facto what the Concept is. Each is the whole system, as it were, from one point of view; and so it is also one moment of the system. But each is a moment explicitly put as inseparable from and as implicating

220

every other moment, and as expressing the principle of wholeness which determines each moment to be what it is. And what each moment is, so the whole is.

For instance, we shall find that the Concept is universal (it is the universal) and this is also one of its moments, for the whole and its principle of order are universal, and that principle is universal to all the moments of the whole and to every element within it. Next we shall find that this universal differentiates itself into particulars, and each particular is also a concept and is universal in its own right. At the same time, the universal, as concrete, is and must be self-particulariz-ing. It has a particular aspect of its own -- it is differentiated, as well as self-identical. Further, every particular is a microcosm reflecting the totality, both particular and universal in one, and so is individual; and this too is what the totality is. These are each moments of the Concept, and each is the whole of the Concept, and the Concept is each and all of them, not simply as a collection or combination, but in essence and concept. This overlap of whole and part, of moment and concept, is true of every category which is to follow.

In the Greater Logic, when discussing Kant's procedure and comparing it with his own,[5] Hegel points out that Kant treats sense and intuition as the precursors of ideation (Vorstellung). This he says is a psychological rather than a logical description. Indeed, sense and intuition are precursors in consciousness of thought, and they were treated as such in the Phenomenology. Moreover, they do correspond to Being and Essence in specific ways. But they are concrete forms of consciousness of which being and essence are the logical, or categorial forms. Here, in the science of logic, we are not doing psychology, nor even phenomenology; we are concerned with the Concept as a logical principle, which does indeed exemplify and manifest itself, not only in psychological states and phases of development, but also in inorganic and organic nature. The task of Logic, however, is to consider the pure conceptual forms of the principle at work in these spheres. Such are the categories (or concepts) we have been discussing -- those of immediacy and of reflection, which correspond, respectively, to sense and intuition and to figurative thinking (symbolization) and abstraction. These are the phases of the Concept which precede its self-conscious phase, the principle of which (the ego) is rightly the principle of organization immanent in what has gone before, which realizes itself fully in speculative thought and in religion. Consequently, Hegel points out, Kant and those who remain at the level of the understanding, make the mistake of seeking concrete reality in the sensuous and perceptive manifolds instead of in the self-conscious principle of wholeness that determines the nature and detail of that manifold (Kant, even in spite of his progressive insights). Yet the Concept itself is relatively abstract until it has generated by its own self-specification its own object, and has united with it in the Idea.

Moments of the Concept as Idea

At first the Concept (as has just been intimated) presents itself as subjective. This is how it emerges in the history of modern philosophy, and how it appeared to Descartes, to the British Empiricists, even (in some respects) to Leibniz, and certainly to Kant and Fichte. It is primarily form -- knowledge, cogitatio. In the Greater Logic Hegel says that it is at first only implicitly the truth, only immediate and inner (cogito ergo sum), and so is opposed to a reality which falls outside it and outside of which it falls. In this subjective form it is Understanding (as it is for the Empiricists and for Kant), and its moments or determinations are taken to be fixed and isolated. But because they are really concepts, the unity of the whole -- the Concept proper -- is immanent in them and 'sets them dialectically in motion'[6], so that they coalesce into the totality which is objectively real.

The subjective content of knowledge is the scientific conception of the world as object. It is still concept because it is thought which has given it its form of objectivity -- as Husserl might say, it is intentional object, constituted as noema by the transcendental subject. Thus the subjectively known world 'passes over into determinate being,' and acquires 'a free determinate being of its own'. But this freedom, Hegel tells us, is only immediate. The concept is one with its object, but is so far only 'submerged' in it. It is its 'soul' or 'essence'.

When, as object, it becomes aware of this immanent subjectivity, and recognizes it as its own self, when it becomes, as object, aware of itself as subject, and conscious of their essential identity, it is the Idea, the unity of subjective and objective Concept -- the absolute, self-revealing truth. The main divisions of the theory of the concept are thus: Subjective Concept, Object, and Idea.

NOTES: Book II, Part III, Chapter 1

1.   Cf. W.L., II, p. 254; Miller, p. 584.

2.   Cf. Hegel, p. 297.

3.   If such a position might have horrified Kant, it certainly would not have horrified Fichte.

4.   I have borrowed this term from P. Teilhard de Chardin (cf. The Phenomenon of Man). It almost exactly fits the swelling, aufhebende course of the dialectic, which, while it unfolds the implications of the prior phases, gathers them up and recapitulates them at higher levels and in more developed forms in the later phases.

5.   W.L., II, pp. 255ff; Miller, pp. 586ff.

6. <u>W.L.</u>, II, p. 271; Miller, p. 592.

Chapter 2

The Subjective Concept

The Concept as Concept[1]

The Concept is the system or whole determining itself in thought; that is, the system conscious of itself as such, and so specifying itself in and through the thinking process. Thus it is the concrete universal, which is a self-differentiating whole, the system self-constituted as an individual totality. It is Concept, Spirit, the Absolute conscious of itself as subject. This is the transcendental ego of Kant and Fichte, and later of Husserl. In the philosophies of the first two it is seen as differentiating itself into specific forms or categories; in the former this self-specification is merely postulated, so that Hegel's reiterated complaint against Kant is that he failed to deduce the categories. But in Fichte's Wissenschaftslehre the process is set out in extenso as dialectical.

Each category is, first, one moment of the (transcendental) unity. It is, secondly, a universal and thus a specific form or exemplification of that unity, hence it is itself a concrete universal. Thirdly, it is as such also itself a system and so an individual whole. The universal differentiates itself into particulars, constructing a concrete system which is an individual. The concept is, therefore, at once universal, particular and individual, differentiating itself into overlapping species of which it is the genus.

'Specification' is perhaps a better word than 'differentiation', or 'particularization', because, under the influence of the understanding and its analytic philosophy, we tend to think of particulars as 'bare', as sheerly not universal, and so as having no specification of their own. But there are no bare particulars. Any such would be indefinable and indescribable, in fact, inconceivable. Bare particulars are the alleged unvarnished matter of intuition, devoid of all universal or conceptual qualification. They are therefore total abstractions, mere Dinge an sich. Every real particular is the exemplification of a universal and so has definable character, per genus et differentiam. It is thus a species, a specific example, of what it particularizes. Accordingly, having a specific character, it has a universal aspect of its own. A bare particular could exemplify nothing, nor could it be an instance of anything, except perhaps bare particularity. It has no character or quality and so, as we now know, can be nothing. It cannot even be mere being, for that is universal, and the bare nothingness of bare particularity lacks the universality also of mere nothing. If there could be a bare negative, it would be this; but we have seen that negativity always has a positive significance and thus always carries some universal implication. The particular, therefore, is the specific form of the principle of wholeness, structure or organization, which is universal to the system in which it is a particular. So it has the universal immanent in it, is both universal and particular at once, and so is individual.

Let us take a simple example from contemporary physics. A proton is a particular example of the universal, elementary particle; but it is no bare particular. It is specifiable as having a certain charge and mass; but not only so, it is also that specific elementary particle which combines with an electron to form a neutron, or holds an electron in orbit to constitute a hydrogen atom. In its own right, therefore, it is not only particular but also universal; and the individual proton which is the nucleus of a hydrogen atom has both these aspects of particularity and universality: it is differentiable as proton, hydrogen nucleus, hydrogen ion, and is the universal of all these.

The universal is system:

(1) it is a differentiated whole, organized on a principle which determines and integrates its elements (or moments, or differences, or specifications). It gives each of them its determinate character in relation to and in reciprocity with every other. This is precisely why each particular moment has the universal immanent in it.

(2) Each moment, being in inseparable and integral relation to every other, is in consequence the complement of every other. So each reflects into its other, opposes itself to it and unites with it as supplement to specify the universal further. This process requires explanation in more detail.

(a) An organized system cannot be posited all at once and, as it were, in a single act, because its varied differentiations have to be articulated. They must be run off, or spelled out. Positing means precisely this setting out (Setzen) in articulated detail.

(b) The differences must be specified in terms of one another. No single moment can be posited without involving the rest, which have been temporarily, in the positing of this one specifically, overtly omitted.

(c) Accordingly, the specification of the universal cannot take the form of mere addition or collection of similar units. It must be a development such as the whole dialectical movement in the Logic exemplifies. The process may be more suitably compared to the focussing of a projected transparency upon a screen than to the continuous accretion of indistinguishable items.

(d) Each moment is therefore a phase in a dialectical development. In each the whole is immanent, and as they are successively deployed the universal principle becomes more fully and more adequately manifested.

225

(e) Consequently each phase is a provisional version of the whole, and the successive phases rank as categories, each of which is a specific form of the universal, each being a more complete degree or gradation of realization of the whole.

(f) Yet each is opposed to its immediate predecessor and successor -- in fact, each is opposed to any and all of the rest. It is opposed to its successor in that it lacks what its successor provides and is so far not what the universal in its fulness demands (though at that specific stage it is exactly what the universal principle determines), and so it is not (yet) a true manifestation of the whole, whereas its successor, relatively speaking, is. It is opposed to its predecessor as having superseded, and so cancelled, it (er hat ihn aufgehoben). Yet they unite and become identified in a more concrete phase which is more truly whole, because each is complementary to the other, because they are mutually constitutive, as well as together constitutive of the whole.

(g) Therefore they overlap.

It follows that the Concept, or concrete universal, that is, the self-differentiating system, distinguishes within itself -- or better, expresses itself diversely as -- universal, particular and individual, which are overlapping moments such that each is at once itself and also both of the others -- each is itself, and is also the whole.

The process of self-differentiation of the concept is judgement; and here once again Hegel uses the etymology of the word Urteil to emphasize his thesis. Judgement is the original, primary partition of the concept. Kant had glimmerings of this truth in his recognition that the categories, as differentiations of the transcendental unity were the principles of judgement. The categories are principles of order or organization (synthesis), which is the unification of differences, and such a unification of differences is precisely what is expressed in judgement. In a single act of thought it distinguishes and identifies the subject and the predicate.

The Concept as Judgement[2]

After what has been said we shall expect the Concept to specify itself in various different ways. First we have seen that it is subjective, objective, and, in Idea, the unity of both. Secondly, as subjective primarily -- but also as objective -- it is universal, particular and individual. Its particular aspect is that of differentiation, and it differentiates itself into numerous concepts (categories, or universals). Its mode of differentiation is judgement, so that we may say with truth any of the following:

226

(1) The Concept differentiates itself into concepts (categories); (2) it differentiates itself as a judgement; (3) it differentiates into innumerably many judgements; or (4) the concepts into which it differentiates each develops into a judgement, or into many judgements. (5) The differentiations of the Concept are categories -- that is, specific concepts -- and judgement is the setting out of the relation between concepts. (6) 'The Concept is universal, particular and individual' -- this is a judgement in which the Concept is differentiated. (7) The Concept is a world, or system, inexhaustibly differentiated, and the exposition of the system in its detailed structure is expressed in (innumerably) many judgements. (8) The Concept is subjective, objective and ideal, and the subjective concept is constituted as concept expanding into judgement and syllogism.

In all these ways the judgement is the self-specification of the concept, and every one of the above statements is a judgement differentiating the Concept and illustrating how (and that) the mode of its differentiation is judgement. Judgement is the _ego_ articulating its experience as a systematic whole of interrelated elements, and so is its activity of thinking expressed in judgements ('I think..., 'I believe..., 'I assert...,' etc.). We shall return presently to discussion of this activity, but may notice meanwhile that what Hegel writes here under Subjective Concept is, like so much else, proleptic, and reappears in developed form and is further explicated under Idea, as cognition, and under Absolute Idea, as method.[3]

Traditional Formal Logic

The traditional text books divided the subject matter of Logic into three sections, headed 'Concept', 'Judgement', and 'Syllogism'. For them the Concept was that of the understanding, the abstract universal. It was thought of as a class concept, or common property.[4] Consequently, both judgement (or more usually, proposition) and syllogism were treated as loose conjunctions of concepts, or as expressing relations between classes, mutually exclusive, or partially or wholly coincident. These notions of concept and proposition are still current in modern symbolic logic, and today the calculus of classes is still a major branch of the discipline. Hegel protests against abstraction and refuses to tolerate the notion of an abstract common quality as adequate to the Concept. That he sees as a concrete system, and more than that, as a conscious experience. It is essentially an activity of organizing, or constructing in accordance with a principle of unity, an activity of self-differentiation by the principle of unity itself; and that activity is the activity of thought or judgement.

Traditional logic treats judgement as a linkage of concepts, and this is so far true that the judgement sets out differences which it simultaneously identifies. The subject and the predicate are explicitly distinguished from each other, and by the same act of thought, by the

227

assertion expressed in the copula, they are united and identified. But Hegel objects that there is only one concept involved, and in the judgement it differentiates itself into its particular moments, the unity and identity of which is what the copula asserts. In effect, he is saying that judgement is the self-development of the concept, which is apparent (as we should expect) even in common examples.

'A mammal is an animal that suckles its young'.

The predicate specifies the concept of the subject. In the Aristotelian definition this is more explicit, for it states first the genus (concept) and then the differentia (the specific character) of that which it defines.

In our everyday thinking we entertain a concept, which at first is vague, and seek to make it more definite. We look for, or elicit from it, the characteristics which specify it, and we express their relations to it and to one another in judgements predicating them of the subject; e.g., 'Light is electro-magnetic radiation within a specific range of wave-lengths.'

The empiricist, thinking at the level of the understanding, will say that we must discover the attributes of the subject from observation, assuming that sense-experience is given to us in the form of mutually independent percepts, independent likewise of thought and devoid of concepts. But Kant taught us the falsity of this assumption, and no theory of perception which does not acknowledge the operation of thought and the involvement of concepts, even in the apprehension of sensory qualities, has ever been made coherent. It is widely recognized by psychologists and should (after Kant) be immediately admitted by epistemologists, that every percept is a structured <u>Gestalt</u> -- a self-specified universal or whole, the structural principle of which determines the nature and qualities of its elements. Such a <u>Gestalt</u>, when described and explicated in thought, becomes a judgement. Thinkers like F.H. Bradley, Bernard Bosanquet, H.H. Joachim and Brand Blanshard have insistently maintained that perception is always and throughout implicit judgement -- in other words, it is the universal specifying itself in thought. We may, therefore, accept the empiricist's contention that the attributes of the subject must be discovered from observation, but with the proviso that observation itself is the self-specification in experience of the universal concept.

Another prejudice, against which Hegel inveighs, is the view that the subject of the judgement names some entity which exits independently in the outside world, and the judgement attaches to it an idea (the predicate) which is in our heads. He maintains that the force of the copula is to assert the objectivity of the entire differentiated unity of the concept. 'The rose <u>is</u> red' is not just our fantasy or concoction subjectively put together -- it is how the rose actually is.

'The picture is beautiful'. It is not just we who have attached a quality to it from the outside. In fact the relation of predicate to subject, or quality to substance, is no external attachment but an intrinsic self-differentiation which is expressing itself in the judgement.

The judgement is not a proposition,[5] if that means simply a form of words or a symbol, but is what the words mean in actual live thinking. So 'A carriage is passing' has to be the answer to a question, not just a 'statement' or 'sentence'.[6] It is a judgement, Hegel tells us, only if we were in doubt about the fact. To be a genuine judgement, 'The rose is red' must give expression to a discovery or to a poetic image ('My luve is like a red red rose').[7] As a mere form of words it is an empty husk in which logic (as Hegel conceives it) has little if any interest.

What the judgement affirms is that the individual is the universal. The subject is individual and the predicate universal. But without the latter the former is no more than a name the significance of which we begin to discover only from the predicate. That tells us what the subject is. In fact, the whole content of the thought is held in the predicate; or, perhaps more correctly, both subject and predicate contain the whole -- both are the entire concept, the concrete which, in the first, is put as a whole, and, in the second, is specified or differentiated. The judgement identifies the two, for they are indeed the same. The abstract judgement of the understanding professes merely to link an individual, as immediately perceived, with one or more abstract universals, otherwise indifferent to and independent of the perceptum. But in fact both are concrete contents. The individual subject is not just an immediately perceived object, but is a particular specification of a universal; and the universal predicate is no abstract quality, but is the individual system particularized in the subject. This is how they reveal themselves as they are developed in thought.[8] Both are in principle the concrete concept, and are therefore rightly identified by the copula.

The predicate, as designating only one characteristic of the subject, appears to be the narrower term; but as universal it can apply to other subjects, and it has a significance of its own under which this subject is subsumed. It seems therefore also to be the wider term. In truth the wider universal, even when alleged to be abstract, is a system of its particulars, of which the subject is one; and the individual, as in one instance particularizing the universal, implies the system which is specified in it. Only on these grounds is the identification justified which the copula effects. The further development of these implications produces the syllogism from the judgement, as we shall shortly see; and the progressive specification of the universal carries it from mere abstract similarity to the generic and specific definiteness of the concrete concept.[9]

To the understanding of all this the key is system. What we are dealing with is a world coming to consciousness and articulating itself in thought. The whole (the Concept) is implicit in every item, in every percept, and in every quality or character, and they are related to each other in accordance with the principle of order and unification that governs the whole. As these connexions explicate themselves in experience they are expressed in judgements, and the explicit judgement is only the overt expression of what is already implicit in sense and imagination. But here we are expressing in phenomenological terms what, in the Logic, Hegel contends is the concept differentiating itself as judgement.

Hegel next proceeds to the traditional classification of the judgement into its various kinds, commending Kant once again for demanding a systematic relationship between them. This, however, he postulated arbitrarily without demonstrating the dialectical connexions between the various forms. As set out by Kant, they do correspond to categories of Being, of Essence and of the Concept, 'the universal forms of the logical Idea'. These phases of the Idea are reflected in the forms of judgement as they unfold the various moments of the Concept. For the concept is the identity of Being and Essence, so that the unfolding of its moments recapitulates in judgemental form their categorial sequence. Accordingly, the types of judgement are ranged as an ascending scale (Stufenfolge) conforming to the universal dialectical pattern hitherto established.

There is, however, in this subsection an apparent departure from the usual tripartite division. The kinds of judgement fall into four groups: the judgement of quality, that of reflection, that of necessity, and finally the judgement of the concept (in the traditional classification: quality, quantity, relation and modality). But both the judgements of reflection and of necessity correspond to the categories of Essence, which are two-fold, and Hegel writes in the Zusatz to Section 171 of the Encyclopaedia that the second of these main types corresponds to the character of Essence as the phase of difference, and is accordingly doubled. Though it is not clear here which group, or groups, Hegel has in mind, the probability is that he is referring to the judgements of reflection and of necessity together, because there is no duplication in the former, although as judgement of reflection it does correspond to Essence. There is duplication in the latter, at least in the hypothetical and the disjunctive judgements. But the main duality is of reflection and necessity, the first corresponding to identity, difference and ground, and the second to substance, causation and reciprocity. The last three sublate and themselves reflect the intervening categories of existence, appearance and correlation, as we saw when discussing Essence. The triad of classes of judgement, therefore, may be taken as:

(1) The Judgement of Quality (Being),

(2) (a) Judgement of Reflection (Essence),
     (b) Judgement of Necessity

(3) The Judgement of the Concept (Concept).

(1) The Judgement of Quality[10] (Enz. Sections 172-173). Hegel calls this the immediate judgement and says that it is the judgement of determinate being, the finite which is a 'this-not-that'. So the sub-classes of judgement are positive and negative. Such judgements are judgements of perception (Wahrnehmung) and the universal in the predicate, with which the individual standing as subject is identified, is usually a sensible quality. The judgement states positively that the individual is (a particular case of) the universal, or negatively that it is not. However, as we know from our discussion of identity and difference (as well as of determinate being), the negative always has a positive significance and the positive always a negative bearing. 'The rose is red' implies that it is not yellow or blue, and 'The rose is not red' implies that it is of some other colour. The individual is, yet is not the whole of, the universal; it is one instance, but not the others. Conversely, the individual is concretely more than any abstract quality, and though it may have the quality stated, it cannot be wholly identified with it. Every statement about the finite subject, therefore, has both a positive and a negative aspect.

The attempt to deprive the negative judgement of all positive significance, or the positive of all negative reference, results in the absurd forms of the identical judgement and the so-called infinite judgement. 'The soul is the soul' tells us precisely nothing, nor does the equally nonsensical proposition, 'The lion is not a table'. (Compare Locke's examples: 'Sleep is not swift', the 'The soul is not square'). Of course, such propositions in special contexts may have sensible meaning. If a big-game hunter were to spread his lunch on the body of a lion he had just shot, somebody might properly object that 'a lion is not a table'. But here the proposition is not 'infinite'. It has a positive significance: a lion is an animal, alive or dead, and differs in important ways from a piece of household furniture.

In the Zusatz to Section 173, Hegel says that the distinction between the significantly negative and the infinite judgement is parallel to that between a civil action and a crime, or between illness and death. A civil action denies a particular right, but does not, like a crime, abrogate right as such. An illness is the disturbance of a single vital function, death the cessation of all vital functions whatsoever. But these analogies are not very instructive, for neither crime nor death have the sort of absurdity of the infinite judgement, and in each case the implicit denial is significant.

Qualitative judgements are commonly held to be true or false; but Hegel declares that they are at best correct or incorrect at the level of

231

finitude to which they apply. Truth is the whole, which these judgements (as finite) fail to exhaust. They are always as much false as true. So far as they represent a stage of the as yet undeveloped truth, they may be considered correct, but to attain truth in the full sense they must develop in form so as to explicate the whole to which the subject belongs. Here the form of the judgement fails to express the concrete nature of the subject, which is more than any single quality. Nor can it do justice to the predicate, which qualifies many other subjects besides. Subject and predicate are not identical as the copula asserts. In Hegel's view the judgements which express truth in its proper sense are what he calls judgements of the Concept,[11] which state what the subject is in its true character as it realizes itself (its concept) in the actualization of system in and for itself. Strictly, for Hegel, the subject is always, qua individual, the knowing subject, I, which is the concrete universal. Its content (or experience) is the world as a whole, and is only fragmentarily specified in qualitative judgements of perception, but the truth is the whole, which is belied by the fragmentariness of any such finite asseverations.

(2)(a) The Judgement of Reflection (Enz., Sections 174-175; W.L., II, pp. 326-335; Miller, pp. 643-650). The reflective judgement is one of relation and so corresponds to Essence, but it still falls short of the explication of the concrete system. Its varieties are the Singular, the Particular and the Universal judgement.

The singular judgement puts the individual into relation with an other, and the universality of the predicate signifies this relatedness. It is no longer immediate, as in the qualitative judgement, but is mediated through the relation: e.g., 'This herb is medicinal', 'This instrument is useful'. The quality ascribed to the subject depends on its relation to something else (the malady or the patient on whom the herb acts; the purpose for which the instrument is useful and the agent who uses it).

But the relation is not clearly explicated and is far from exhausting the concrete individuality of the subject. Consequently, the more concrete it is, the greater the variety of relations in which it stands, and the more such statements can be made about it. Hence common sense reasoning revels in this kind of judgement.

This singular relational judgement raises the individual above its merely immediate sensuous presentation (as having this or that perceptible quality), but the relation is external and, so to speak, tacked on from outside. It is therefore necessary to distinguish particular cases as positive and negative. For to regard all herbs (for instance) as medicinal could be dangerous. Thus we arrive at the particular judgement (Some S is P, Some S is not P), 'Some herbs are medicinal, others are not'. The individual is now being universalized, it becomes one of a class, related to another class (herbs and medicinal

232

substances). Not only is this herb, but others like it also are, medicinal; and if like cases are collected together we get the universal judgement of Allness: 'All plants of the genus <u>Digitalis</u> are medicinal'. The instances, however, have been collected from subjective, casual, experience, and are still only externally related. We have simply found each one that we have tested to be medicinal, we have not yet penetrated to the ground of the relationship. This is simply enumerative generalisation, the result of so-called enumerative induction. The judgement could be prompted by purely accidental similarities, or by inessential properties incidental to the generic character (e.g., 'All human beings have earlobes'). The basis of the judgement is still simply the individual as externally observed. When we penetrate to the ground of the relation in the systematic structure which determines the essential nature of the related items, the judgement becomes one of necessity. We shall then have discovered the necessary connexion that is the cause and basis of the constant conjunction we have observed. The form of expression then is no longer 'All Ss are Ps', but simply 'S is P' -- not 'All digitalis plants are medicinal', but '<u>Digitalis</u> is medicinal'.

(2)(b) <u>The Judgement of Necessity</u> (<u>Enz.</u>, Section 177; <u>W.L.</u>, II, pp. 335-344; Miller, 650-657). The first stage of the judgement of necessity is the <u>categorical judgement</u>, which is in effect the definition as prescribed by Aristotle, <u>per genus et differentiam</u>. The predicate, Hegel says, is the concrete universal, the genus, which contains the specific character as negative. This judgement is a specification of the universal founded upon the system which is here expressed in terms of classification. The necessity is at first latent. 'Gold is a metal' states the connexion as universal and necessary, but states it dogmatically, without revealing the underlying connexion which it nevertheless implies. In contrast to the singular qualitative judgement, what the categorical asserts is the substantive nature of the subject -- it expresses the category of substance. 'Gold is a metal' is necessarily true, because the metalic character of gold is essential to it. 'Gold is dear' is a conjunction dependent upon accidental circumstances, such as its scarcity, attractiveness as an ornament, use by human beings as currency, and the like. Nevertheless, the categorical judgement falls short, not only in failing to reveal the ground of the connexion between subject and predicate, but also because they are not mutually commensurate. Gold is indeed a metal, but so are copper, tin and silver. Gaius is a man, and that is essential to his being what he is, but he is also much else, and there are also other men.

So we proceed to unfold the universal further and to display first the grounds on which the categorical affirmation is made. The substantive nature (e.g., of gold) is further explicated in terms of the necessary connexions that relate its properties causally and determine its physico-chemical classification. This is more satisfactorily set out in the hypothetical judgement: 'If a substance is insoluble in aqua regia it must be gold', 'If the rainfall is excessive the crop will be spoiled'. This form of judgement corresponds to ground and consequent, or to cause and effect under Essence. The protasis of the hypothetical expresses the ground, or the causal determination, the consequent, or effect, of which is expressed in the apodasis. We are thus progressing in the discovery of systematic connexion, which in the categorical (substantive) judgement is still only implicit.

F.H. Bradley, in his Principles of Logic,[12] maintained that all necessary judgements are really hypothetical, because necessity rests upon conditions and these are stated in the hypothetical (or what later logicians have called 'conditional') form of proposition. Bertrand Russell, also, has maintained that every universal proposition is hypothetical. Its symbolic form is

$$(\underline{x}) \cdot \phi\underline{x} \supset \psi\underline{x}.,$$

of which a verbal example would be 'If anything is a mammal, it suckles its young'. For Russell, however, the connexion represented by $\supset$ is external. One must know in each instance whether $\phi\underline{x}$ is true when $\psi\underline{x}$ is the case before one can write $(\underline{x}) \cdot \phi\underline{x} \supset \psi\underline{x}$. The universality involved is therefore always enumerative and never really necessary. Bradley, on the other hand, would have insisted upon system as the ground of the universal connexion, and so is more nearly in agreement with Hegel, from whose Logic Bradley's is largely derived. What Hegel is urging is that the universal judgement develops, or expands, into the hypothetical, but he interposes the categorical (as distinct from the singular), which he regards as essentially a categorical statement of a universal connexion and as more substantial than the judgement of all-ness[13] -- τὸ καθόλου as opposed to τὸ κατά παντός in Aristotle's Posterior Analytics.

The full exposition of the system, put as a relation between the universal, or genus, and the inter-related gamut of its specific forms, is expressed in the disjunctive judgement: e.g., 'Number is either odd or even' (even and odd exhaust one aspect of number, and its other specifications dictate further disjunctions).

Here the disjunction is exclusive, for what is even is not odd, and the disjunctive is analysable again as two hypotheticals: 'If a number is even it is not odd', and 'If a number is not even it is odd'. So we cannot equate this disjunctive judgement outright with the disjunctive of contemporary logic:

$$\underline{p} \vee \underline{q},$$

which is not exclusive. But there is a sense in which the specification of the universal into mutually exclusive species is also inclusive of them all, for all are comprehended in one system. Nevertheless, 'either-or' expresses mutual otherness and the distinction essential to all articulated wholeness. It is the relation on which the understanding insists; but to insist upon it to the exclusion of the unity and interdependence of the disjuncts, is to overlook the universal which is being specified in the judgement. Hegel makes sure of the identity between the sides of the judgement by stating the full range of alternatives and by insisting that the particulars listed in the predicate correspond fully to the genus named in the subject.

'Colour is either red, or yellow, or blue.'

It is the reciprocal relations of the particulars which cement them in the unity of the universal, and this is what their disjunction as alternative exemplifications implies. Just as the hypothetical displays the causal links, so the exhaustive disjunction of particulars rests upon their reciprocal interconnexion. It is the hypothetical that develops into the disjunctive, thus the causal relation is aufgehoben and is intrinsic to the disjunction. Although Hegel does not stress the point, it should follow from what he has said of the categorical and hypothetical forms, that they give expression respectively to the categories of substance and causality, so the disjunctive judgement expresses reciprocity. The wave-lengths of light are so inter-related that, as their frequency increases, colour ranges progressively from red, through yellow, to blue. It is obvious, however, that these more deep-seated relations are not completely unveiled even in the disjunctive judgement, and further development in the syllogism is still required.

This is foreshadowed by Hegel's remark that in the disjunctive judgement subject and predicate have become fully identical (as well as explicitly differentiated).[14] The specific differentiation of the genus is (taken as a whole) the genus itself and both sides of the judgement have the same content. So, he says, the copula is the Concept itself.[15] This its true in two senses: (1) the genus is what the disjunction sets out. It is the same on both sides of the judgement, and what identifies subject and predicate is thus the genus itself. (2) Also, the genus in the last resort is the systematic connexion or principle of organization, and that is the concept, now set out explicitly and determined as totality.[16]

(3) The Judgement of the Concept (Enz., Sections 178-179; W.L., II, pp. 344-351; Miller, pp. 657-663). Before he proceeds to the syllogism Hegel interposes the judgement of the Concept, which completes this particular phase of the dialectic of subjective Begriff by providing a concluding triad. The judgement of quality or existence corresponds to Being, those of relation and necessity to Essence, and those of modality to the Concept. But Hegel here gives the modal forms an odd and somewhat arbitrary interpretation as judgements of

value. Whether or not modal forms are especially appropriate for the purpose, the insertion of value-judgement at this point is a healthy reminder that the nature of reality is not exhausted by statements of fact, however scientifically elaborated they may be. Moreover, the wholeness of the Concept is the ultimate criterion of value as it is of truth. Indeed, for Hegel, the criterion of truth is value. This coalescence of fact and value will be more clearly demonstrated at a later stage, but it is already implicit in the nature of the dialectic. The immanence of the whole at each stage is what impels it to the next. The inadequacy of each phase to the whole invokes its complement and generates a more complete phase, which is 'the truth of' its predecessor. It is this that the predecessor ought to have been but was not, so its truth is equally its completion and the actualization of its potentiality. Hence the criterion of value, of what ought to be, is also the criterion of truth, what things have it in them to become. It is upon this that what they are depends -- it is what they are in truth. For the truth is the whole, and anything less, in the symptoms of its inadequacy, reveals the degree of its falsity. In the last resort this criterion proves to be the fulfilment of self-conscious personality, in terms of which all human values are to be defined and assessed.

Why does Hegel identify the modal forms of judgement as the forms of value judgement? Nothing he actually says gives us any explanation. Earlier he rejected Kant's treatment of modality as merely subjective, and insisted upon the objectivity of contingency as much as of actuality. But Kant's view was that modality indicated the relation of the object to the knowing subject, that is, to the ego, and Hegel has identified the ego with the Concept, which is the whole become aware of itself; and that again is the criterion of truth and the standard of value. Judgements which express the relation of the object to the knowing subject, therefore, would precisely be judgements of value.[17]

As Hegel puts it: 'The judgement of the Concept has the concept, the totality, in simple form, as its content, the universal in its complete determination'.[18] Its first form is assertoric, in which the subject is individual and the predicate 'the reflection of the particular existent (Dasein) in its universal'. In other words, the predicate reveals the relationship of the particular phase represented by the individual subject to its universal, or ideal, completion (what it ought to be).

The assertoric judgement asserts a value judgement dogmatically: 'This action is good (bad)', 'This landscape is beautiful', etc. Hegel significantly includes as one of the possible predicates 'true', reinforcing what has been said above. He repeats that one would not say of anybody who asserted, 'This picture is red, green, and dusty' that he was a person of judgement. That requires a more penetrating discrimination, such as might be apparent in the judgement of a moralist on a course of action, or an art critic on the merits of the picture. Their judgements are judgements of value. After all, the man we habitually call a judge is the one officially appointed to decide upon guilt and innocence.

But a merely assertoric statement of value is palpably subjective, as Hegel implies by his remark that the assertoric form of judgement, though its claim to validity in its own right is commonly rejected by society, has been made the special and essential form of asseveration in philosophy by appeal to the principle of immediate intuition and belief -- an obvious allusion to Jacobi, whom he had criticized in the Introduction.[19] Intuitionism pronounces assertorically, giving 'hundreds upon hundreds of assurances' about reason, knowledge, thinking, and the rest.

Presumably Hegel is hinting here that self-awareness the thinking subject seeking to realize itself in and as its object, expresses its relation to it first in terms of feeling and intuition. So the first expression of value judgement is emotive. This is the dim sublated awareness, or intuition, of the totality which ultimately satisfies, but to which it is inadequate, and so immediately raises the question of its legitimacy. Is the judgement justified? Is the object good or true? Dogmatic assertion may be countered by equally dogmatic denial.

Thus the judgement becomes problematic -- it may be so or it may not. But 'may' and 'may not' depend on reasons, and the support of the original assertion (or of its denial) by reasons gives a necessary truth; so the problematic gives way to the apodictic. The essential reason for the value attributed to anything is its true nature as expressed in its genus, or to use language to which Hegel often resorts, its agreement with its concept. The example which Hegel gives is: This (immediate individual) house (genus), being of such and such construction (particular) is good (that is, conforms to what a house ought to be). The whole judgement, he says, is contained in each of the terms, the subject and the predicate. The nature of the subject is revealed as the mediating ground between individual and universal.

The conclusion to which we are led is that all genuine judgement is evaluative, that is, it grasps its subject in its total relationship to the complete system of the real, and ipso facto to the whole experience of the judging subject, or ego. That is why we say that it takes a person with great experience to judge soundly. This evaluation, mediated by the Concept as a whole, must next be set out (gesetzt) as syllogism.

The various traditional forms of judgement which formal logic had drawn from ordinary discourse and scientific exposition, and had classified according to their external forms, Hegel has set out as a developing scale. The qualitative judgement simply predicates an immediately perceived quality of a subject leaving the connexion unexplained. The reflective judgement develops the relationship of the

237

terms and discloses uniformities. It represents common sense explanation and an elementary stage in the development of science. This develops as an hypothesis which reveals the grounds of the relation and confirms itself as a systematic necessity. Finally, the modal forms penetrate to the holism involved in systematic structure, which grounds the judgement as a self-subsistent, self-generating ideal, the apodictic certainty of which is to be further developed in syllogistic form.

The judgment is a category of the subjective Concept, and one normally thinks of it as subjective activity. But Hegel has already protested against this attitude as one-sided. Judgment is just as much objective, as its copula declares. So we find him saying that all things are judgments (Section 167), as specifications of a universal. In particular he asserts that everything is a categorical judgement, for everything has a substantial nature which constitutes its permanent ground. This is no more than a reiteration of his contention throughout, that logic is just as much metaphysics. All things have a substantial basis, hence the category of substance; and the categorical judgment expresses at the level of Begriff what substance signified at the level of Wesen. The structure of the dialectic is such that what is potential at the lower stage is preserved, enhanced and elucidated, at the later. The actual substantial nature of things in the actual world is thus sublated in the higher phases of their evolution up to life and mind, and in consciousness is preserved as scientific and philosophic knowledge. Judgement, therefore, is the translation into conscious form of what pertains in the actual world. We shall find this characteristic of the dialectic persisting, and shall witness the same return of things upon themselves at later stages.

The Concept as Syllogism[20]

The syllogism is the concept set out as completely posited system, or unity of differences. It is therefore, Hegel says, rational. The rational is the explicitly differentiated and integrated system of the real -- the systematic and ordered. Reason, however, as usually discussed, is regarded in two distinct ways. While the syllogism is traditionally held to be the appropriate form of reasoning, there is also the conception of Reason as the intellectual intuition of supersensible and infinite objects. Each of these aspects is essential to reason, but in the historical treatment each has been taken abstractly to produce a distorted conception. In Hegel's day Kant and his successors stressed the intuitive contemplative aspect of reason, and Hegel complains that they seem to forget and to be ashamed of its syllogizing aspect. The opposite side is emphasized by the understanding for which reason is no more than raisonnement the deductive instrument of ratiocination. In our own day the various forms of contemporary empiricism represent the latter tendency, while the former appears as an offshoot of Existentialism (especially in Jaspers' work) and is prominent in Phenomenology. Hegel protests that the assumed infinite objects of contemplative reason are envisaged abstractly, as separated and held in isolation from the finite, and so themselves converted to finites. Whereas

> the infinity of these objects is not the empty abstraction from the finite and the contentless and indeterminate universal, but the fulfilled universal, the Concept which is determinate, and has its determinateness in itself in this genuine manner, that it differentiates itself within itself and is the unity of its intelligible and determinate differences. Only thus does reason raise itself above the finite, the conditioned, the sensible, or however it may otherwise be designated; and in this negativity it is essentially concrete (inhaltsvoll), for it is the unity of determinate extremes; but as such the rational is nothing but the syllogism.21

The infinity of reason is thus its 'infinite negativity' -- its unifying self-differentiation, or, what is the same thing, its dialectical self-development. This is why it is only as Resultat that the infinite is infinite and actual, and why the Absolute is inseparable from its process of self-development. And this too is precisely why, as actual it is rational, or in self-conscious realization, it is a syllogizing.

The concept as such is a unity or whole holding its moments sublated in itself. It differentiates itself in (and as) judgment, setting out the moments as terms in relation, the unity of which is immediately asserted in the copula but is not posited explicitly. This unity is therefore in one sense internalized, yet in another sense it is left (as it were) external to the judgment as a presupposed ground. In the syllogism this ground or unity of the extremes is explicitly posited as the middle term.

If we take Hegel's example of the apodictic judgement, we can see at once how it develops into a syllogism:

'This house, being thus and thus constructed, is good (or bad)'.

Making the ground into the middle term we get:

This house is thus and thus constructed.
Houses so constructed are good (or bad);
Therefore this house is good (or bad).

Just as the concept qua concept opens out into judgement, so judgement expands into inference.

We said above that the genuine judgement is always the answer to a question, and the answer is found by developing the implications of the question -- by developing its ground, or that from which it arose. What we explore is the structure of the reality implicit in the question, or the hypothesis which it suggests. This gives us the middle term through which we infer to the answer -- the conclusion of our inference. As judgement is the procedure by which the concept differentiates itself, so syllogism is that of unifying the differences in an all-embracing system. It is the gathering together (συλλογή) of the interrelated factors.

In his treatment of the syllogism Hegel, as ever, is at once criticizing the traditional logic of the understanding and developing his own theory of dialectical progression as the genuine movement of reason. The key to his argument throughout is that the former is based on the abstract universal and the latter is the self-development of the concrete. Hegel is pursuing a logic of genuine, live, operative thinking with a concrete content. He is not interested in the construction of a calculus with abstract symbols. So we find him complaining that the formal syllogisms of the traditional logic are based upon accidental and external linkages between the terms, and not upon genuine implication between concepts. The same looseness of connexion persists in modern symbolic logic, which reduces implication to a disjunction of truth-values determined independently of one another, so that it cannot be the means of discovery, but can only be used as a device for exposition.[22]

In a remark appended to his discussion of 'the Syllogism of Existence' in the Greater Logic,[23] Hegel expostulates against the abstractions of the formal logic, which takes the middle term as a separate and externally related link between the major and the minor terms. He is also contemptuous of the doctrine of the moods of the syllogism and of the juggling which results in grouping of valid moods under each figure. All this he dislikes because it treats the terms as mere ciphers and plays about with them mechanically, producing calculi, for which he has the most profound contempt of all. He brands Leibniz' idea of a <u>characteristica universalis</u> as an immature notion conceived in his youth, and the logical calculus invented by Plouquet he condemns as reducing all propositions to meaningless tautologies. To claim, as Ploucquet does, that such a calculus could enable one to teach a child logic as one would teach it arithmetic, so that it could reason as automatically as it can calculate, Hegel deplores as the poorest possible recommendation for any presentation of the science of logic.

Today it is precisely such formalizations of logic that hold the field and exclude all other claimants to the title. But the defects to which Hegel points can still be demonstrated. Formal logicians have never been able to give a satisfactory account of scientific method, nor of the principles of holistic structures. Dr. Wolf Mays has remarked prespicaciously that symbolic logic has nothing to do with thinking, which is not its concern.[24]

The traditional logic is criticized (1) for abstract instead of concrete thinking, (2) for treating judgements as propositions, (3) for operating, in consequence, with abstract and accidental connexions, instead of developing the intrinsic implications of concrete facts, and (4) for relapsing finally into petitio principii and infinite regress. Aristotle is praised for his achievement in discovering the figures of the syllogism and for elaborating the rules for its use, but equally for refraining, in the exposition of his own philosophy, from making use of it.

In this section Hegel seems to be putting new wine into old bottles, whereas Kant had put old wine into new. Kant accepted the traditional logic as finally complete, and then gave the doctrines of judgement and syllogism new forms in the Transcendental Analytic and the Transcendental Dialectic. Hegel rejects the traditional doctrine and adopts and develops transcendental into dialectical logic; but here he is, as least prima facie, casting the dialectic in traditional moulds, while concurrently denying their validity. This, however, is only a superficial appearance. In fact, what Hegel is doing is recasting the old theory of syllogism in dialectical form, so that in the end the genuine syllogism turns out to be the dialectical triad.

Reason, for Hegel, is no mere raisonnement or ratiocination. It is the constitutive reason operative in all rational conduct and theorizing, the genuine reasoning of practising scientists actually advancing the frontiers of knowledge, the reason inherent in morals and social order, and that which, in religious doctrine and ritual, is figuratively and symbolically represented. It is the reason more especially of philosophy, in which the concrete Concept, being explicit and aware of itself (an und für sich), specifies itself into moments each of which it recognizes as a necessary phase of the whole, and equally as containing the whole immanent in it. True thinking is not formally syllogistic in the traditional manner, neither in common inference nor in natural science, and even less so in philosophy (cf. Aristotle) -- it is dialectical. So the 'figures' of the syllogism in Hegel's hands are made to represent the reciprocal and mutually mediating relations of the primary moments of the Concept: the individual, the particular and the universal, as they function in the construction (or, better, self-development) of system.

The exact correlation between the Hegelian and the Aristotelian figures is difficult to trace, because individual, particular and universal, (I, P, U) in Hegel's expositon are terms, not judgements, and the relation between them does not seem to be tied to the position of the middle term in the premisses. The Hegelian syllogism is the dialectical triad, and, of course, I, P and U do form such a triad and are mutually implicated in such a way that each can mediate the other two, for, as we have seen, each is in principle the whole concept. Hegel gives as an example of syllogism (in Enz., Section 187, Zus.) the three major

241

branches of philosophy, Logic, Nature-philosophy and Philosophy of Spirit. He says that everything is a syllogism, just as everything is a judgment and everything a concept, for Concept specifies itself into judgment and syllogism, articulating the complete system of the Idea. In each case, once again, we find that the category under scrutiny is a provisional definition of the Absolute.

Under syllogism we have three divisions: the Qualitative Syllogism, the Syllogism of Reflection (the Inductive Syllogism), and the Syllogism of Necessity, corresponding once more to Being, Essence and Concept, and more nearly to the forms of judgement which we have just reviewed. There is, however, no Syllogism of the Concept corresponding to the modal judgement. The interpreter of Hegel is thus in a quandary. If hypothetical and disjunctive judgements are really judgements of essence, as they seem to be, for they are undoubtedly scientific judgements at the level of understanding, should not the hypothetical and disjuctive syllogisms also correspond to absolute correlation in Actuality? In that case there would be no syllogism especially appropriate to the Concept. The judgement of the concept was a value judgement; so one would expect some kind of deontic syllogism, under which, perhaps, Aristotle's practical syllogism might have fallen. But Hegel contemplates no special deontic logic. Perhaps this is because he regarded the whole of his logic as in principle deontic. Why, then, are we given a special class of deontic judgements? Are we really correct in alligning the judgement of necessity with Essence? The precise answer to these questions is not easy to come by. The apparent anomally seems to have something to do with the emergence of the Object as the result (Resultat) of the syllogism of necessity. For we shall find Object taking on a double sense, one antithetical to subject, and one as the final realization of subject. In the latter sense, Object, as value, becomes deontic and goes beyond the mere 'ought to be'. It does not cease to be a syllogism, which is sublated in it, and we rediscover both under Idea.

The Qualitative Syllogism[25]

The Qualitative Syllogism is the syllogism of Dasein, determinate being, and in the Greater Logic again is called the Syllogism of Existence. It is the immediate form of syllogism, the judgements in which are qualitative judgements. The first figure of the syllogism in the traditional logic (MP, SM: SP) Hegel criticizes as abstract and merely subjective. In it an individual is brought under a universal by means of an abstract particular. The perennial example is,

All men are mortal	(MP)
Socrates is a man	(SM)
Therefore, Socrates is mortal	(SP)

Hegel reverses the order of the premisses, but that makes no significant difference:

The rose is red	I
Red is a colour	P
Therefore, the rose is coloured	U

The general sense is: The individual, being particular is universal (I, P, U). The rose, being red, is coloured (or Socrates, being human, is mortal). But, of course, the individual is not merely particular, and not simply this particular; it has other characteristics. Nor is it sheerly universal, for the universal covers other particulars as well. But, Hegel complains, the syllogism of existence, as a syllogism of the understanding, leaves the moments standing abstractly over against one another in external relation. The subject is presented immediately, as an empirical object with innumerable particular qualities, any one of which might have been chosen as the middle term, and each would have brought it under a different abstract universal. So the result is contingent and one can 'prove' different conclusions with the same premisses, and sometimes, by choosing different, though equally legitimate, middle terms, one can demonstrate opposite conclusions. For instance, man, having a sensuous nature is amoral, but also, man, having a rational nature, is a moral being; or, planets, being associated with the sun, fall into it, but on the other hand, planets, having inertia, move centrifugally away from the sun. Moreover, because of the external linkage of individual, particular and universal, each premiss demands a proof of its own and we become involved in an infinite regress.

All this is criticism of the abstract form and use of the syllogism. But without the pedantry of setting out every inference syllogistically, we constantly infer in common thinking and (by implication) action. When we hear the creaking of footsteps[26] on the path in winter, we can infer to the fact that there has been frost in the night. Or when we make a claim in law on the ground of a legal title, we infer from a general principle to a particular case. The universal, qua principle of structure, specifies itself into particulars, each of which, as concrete, has both moments in itself. It can therefore mediate between the universal and the individual.

The external and the accidental character of the linkage between terms in the formal theory of the understanding is still reflected in the modern doctrine of formal implication.

$$\underline{x}\,(\,\phi\underline{x}\,\supset\,\psi\underline{x}\,)$$

is valid only if, on substitution for the variables, the corresponding propositions are both true, both false, or $\phi\underline{x}$ gives a false proposition (whatever the truth-value of the other). The connexion expressed by $\supset$ is entirely loose and contingent, and whether or not it holds depends solely upon the accidental conjunction of $\underline{x}$ with ϕ and with ψ. The whole expression is, therefore, at best a judgement of allness. But whether any of these relations obtain can be discovered only by inspection of every $\underline{x}$, and that is an infinite task unless we are dealing with an artificially limited range of objects (e.g., the books in a library). The contingency carries through to the transformation:

$$(\underline{x})\,.\,(\,\phi\underline{x}\,\supset\,\psi\underline{x}\,)\,.\,(\,\psi\underline{x}\,\supset\,\chi\underline{x}\,)\,:\,\supset\,:\quad(\underline{x})\,.\,(\,\phi\underline{x}\,\supset\,\chi\underline{x}\,)$$

The Aristotelian figures II and III are degenerate forms of the first figure, and in order to become 'scientific' they must be 'reduced' to the perfect figure (Fig. I). This, Hegel maintains, is due to the abstract connexion between the terms, which does not warrant the dialectical development of the first figure into the other two as it should properly proceed. If, on the other hand, the universal is seen as concrete concept, each of its moments is the whole and can serve to mediate between the others. The true concept of syllogism is a relation between differences mediated by a middle which is their unity.[27]

The individual having been universalized by the intermediation of the particular (in Hegel's first figure), it next becomes the middle uniting the other two, to give the second figure, U, I, P. The principle of structure, via the individual embodiment, indicates the particular exemplification. Then the particular, as specification of the universal, constitutes the individual system in conjunction with other particulars; thus the form of the third figure is P, U, I.

Suppose we have a graph in Analytic Geometry, such that when $\underline{x}$ = 2, $\underline{y}$ = 1; when $\underline{x}$ = 6, $\underline{y}$ = 3; $\underline{x}$ = 8, $\underline{y}$ = 4, and so on. We may conclude that the curve corresponds to the equation $\underline{x}$ = $2\underline{y}$. Here the individual is the curve, the universal the equation and the co-ordinates are the particulars. We have inferred in the form of the first figure, I, P, U.

The equation will then enable us to infer to values of other co-ordinates: if $\underline{x}$ = 4, $\underline{y}$ = 2; if $\underline{y}$ = 18, $\underline{x}$ = 36. We have now used figure II, U, I, P. If from such selected co-ordinates we construct the curve, we infer according to the third figure, P, U, I.

The second figure proves the minor premiss of the first, and the third proves the major. The first figure proves the major of the second and the third the minor. The second proves the major of the third and the first proves its minor. So the circle is complete and the reciprocal dependence of the moments is fully demonstrated. There is no infinite regress here in the demand for proof of each premiss in turn. The exposition has been fully worked out and the identity in difference of the moments in the concrete concept has become apparent.

Hegel illustrates this mutual mediation of the moments of the Concept in the syllogistic figures by the major triad of the Encyclopaedia, the Logical Idea, Nature, and Spirit. Each term functions in turn as middle and as one of the extremes. Thus Nature mediates between the Idea and Spirit , exhibiting the Idea in the form of externality and generating spirit out of itself as the awarenes of the Idea. In that capacity Spirit mediates between Nature and the Idea, which thus revealing itself as the substantial essence of both Nature and Spirit, mediates between them to form what Hegel calls the Absolute Syllogism.[28] From this it is clear what is meant when Hegel says that the Absolute is a syllogism; and, insofar as everything displays itself, whether in Nature, in Mind, or in Logic, dialectically as a triad of moments, everything is a syllogism.

As the three moments of the Concept have thus become interchangeable, their differences are aufgehoben and they have become mutually equal. The result is the 'quantitative syllogism': Things which are equal to the same thing are equal to one another. This, says Hegel, is regarded as an axiom in mathematics, but it is really a logical principle demonstrable through dialectical derivation from the Concept, as are all other so-called axioms. So Hegel demonstrates in an entirely different way what Frege and Russell have claimed to do, that mathematics is deducible in its entirety from pure logic.

This array of figures of the syllogism and the inferences they set out are circular and they reduce the moments to equality one with another, bringing about what is really the collapse of the immediate (or qualitative) syllogism. This is because the exposition of the self-differentiation of the concrete universal establishes the whole in evey part. So it develops further in the reflective syllogism, in which the individuality developed through particularity to universality is set out explicitly as the reflection into its other: the individual into the universal and the universal into the individual. In the immediate syllogism the terms at first posed as separate and abstract; but they proved themselves, through their very relatedness in the syllogism as it proceeded through the dialectic of its figures, to be mutually implicated. This mutual implication now shows itself explicitly in the syllogism of reflection in which the individual is treated at once as the particularization of the universal.[29]

The Syllogism of Reflection[30]

The individual and the universal reflect one into the other in the inductive syllogism, which develops through three stages: Allness, or

245

complete enumeration, Induction, or incomplete enumeration, and Analogy.

The defect of the syllogism of quality was that the mediating particular was only one of many and that each of the alternative possiblities could connect the subject with a different universal. The relation was external and might well be accidental. Now we seek to correct this by investigating all the cases in which the conjunction occurs to discover whether it is a universal connexion, seeking in this way to establish the major premiss of the first figure. This is done by using the individual instances as mediation.

Perfect Induction or complete enumeration, when it is possible, will give us what we require, but then the conclusion is included in the major premise, and the first figure commits <u>petitio principii</u>:

S_1 is P

S_2 is P

S_3 is P

"   All these S's are P, Therefore S_i is P.

"

S_n is P

S_i must have been included in our original list of what are merely immediate judgements, so that this phase of the syllogism corresponds to the first figure. The judgement of allness, in consequence, is itself immediate, that is to say, it is as contingent as any of the premises, even though we have exhausted the class, because the conjunction may still be merely accidental. If all the books now in this room were published in Britain, it does not necessarily follow that any book found in this room at any time will have been published in Britain; and to select one of those which was originally included in the enumeration is merely to repeat what we already know.

In most cases, however, and in those of greatest interest and importance, it is not practicable to examine all possible examples. If we then conclude universally from a number of favourable cases, the induction is incomplete and the risk is run of too hasty a conclusion (from too few examples). Moreover, we have no firm criterion by which to decide how many observations will be enough. An example would be:

Gold is a metal and conducts electricity,   ∴ All metals (tested)
Silver is a metal and conducts electricity,   conduct.
Iron is a metal and conducts electricity,

The individual as frequently observed serves as the middle term to unite the universal with the particular; and so the inductive syllogism falls under the second figure (U, I, P). The individual is taken concretely, not merely as immediately presented and abstract, but as an instance of the universal, so that when we have examined a number of examples we feel entitled to conclude that the particular under investigation (in the above case, conductivity) belongs to the universal or proximate genus. From this we proceed to:

Copper is a metal, therefore copper conducts electricity.

But copper may not have been tested and might, for all we can tell, be an exception.

Accordingly, we are thrown back upon analogy, which argues that if a certain substantial number of instances have a certain property, others like them, as yet unexamined, will probably also have that property. This gives partial justification to the above conclusion about copper.

While analogy is also liable to abuse, if drawn too hastily or on specious similarities, it can be a fruitful stepping-stone to scientific discovery, if used with care and circumspection. If the observed conjunction is frequent and the observation meticulously made, further investigation of a more systematic nature may disclose evidence of connexion which cannot be overthrown simply by listing further individual cases. As Hegel implies at the end of the Zusatz to Section 190 in the Encyclopaedia, when the evidence is diverse in character but through interlocking implications consitututes a self-sustaining system, the conclusion to necessary connexion is virtually invincible. The presence of life on earth is not just due to its being a celestial body, but to its having the right kind of atmosphere, the right kind of hydrosphere, the appropriate range of temperatures and climatic conditions, etc., and the interlocking of all these conditions relevant to the nature of living activity. The body of evidence available about the moon shows these conditions lacking; not only, therefore, may we not conclude from analogy that, because the moon is a celestial body it harbours life, but we are forced by the systematic nature of the evidence to conclude the contrary.

In the Syllogism of Reflection the universal is linked to the particular through the mediation of the individual. It is thus an expansion of the second figure of the Qualitative Syllogism. More obviously still, it is an elaboration (as we should expect) of the Judgement of Reflection, interrelating the three types of judgement into which that is specified in the process of constructing a concrete system. That concrete system now emerges in the forms of the Syllogism of Necessity. Analogy gives us the premonition of, and a more systematic form of scientific inference develops, the systematic

247

inter-connexions. It is this system which has been lurking in the background all along and has been gradually coming to light in the forms of judgement and syllogism hitherto examined.[31]

The Syllogism of Necessity[32]

As the reflective syllogism corresponds to the reflective judgement, and so to Essence, so the syllogism of necessity corresponds to the judgement of necessity. But here we remain in doubt whether this is the sublation and development of the categories of Actuality, of substance, cause and reciprocity, or somehow expresses the Concept as the value-judgement was shown to do. There is some ground for alligning this final type of syllogism both with Actuality and with Concept; and we must not forget that Actuality (which is Essence on the verge of becoming Concept) covers the modal categories as well as those of absolute correlation. Both sets of categories are rooted in the concrete universal, as self-specifying system, and that is what is being elaborated in the syllogism of necessity. Hegel emphasizes this unfolding of the self-sublating and self-mediating system in his exposition, but he gives no hint of any correspondence between the syllogism of necessity and the judgement of the Concept; and he alligns the former only with the third figure of the qualitative syllogism, in which the universal is the middle term, as he relates the reflective judgement to the second figure.

The exposition in the Encyclopaedia is too condensed to offer us much guidance and we must help ourselves out by following that of the Greater Logic, where he goes into more detail. Corresponding to the judgement of necessity, this phase of the syllogism has three forms: categorical, hypothetical and disjunctive, and each is obviously the development of the parallel form of judgement.

The Categorical Syllogism

To understand this section we must, once again, keep in mind the conception of the universal as a system immanent in each of its different specific forms (or moments) and uniting them all into the whole which is its very self. The two aspects of unity and difference confronting one another especially in the judgement of reflection, are now explicitly seen to be identical and their difference is aufgehoben. The system, or Concept, thus negates its own negation (its specific differences) in its Being-for-self (or ideality), which unites its determinations, the phases through which it has developed. The process of mediation culminates in its own cancellation, and the resolution of the oppositions it contained issues in its own union with its other, which is no other than itself.[33]

In the syllogism of reflection the middle term was the individual, which expanded to universality. Formally treated (as it is by the understanding) this was first only a judgement of allness; but we saw how the approach was made to systematic interconnexion of diverse specifications, true universality, in which the relation between the terms is securely rooted. This concrete universality Hegel identifies as the genus. The categorical judgement was distinguished, by its foundation in this genus, from the singular judgement. It asserted no mere casual association of subject and predicate ('The picture is dusty'), but an essential inherence of attribute in substance. It had the force, therefore, of definition in the Aristotelian sense, expressing, Hegel says, 'the universal nature of the fact, the genus'. Now this substantial judgement is taken as the premiss to the categorical syllogism, and in it develops the substantive connexion as its middle term. This middle is 'the objective universal, which contains the entire determination of the distinguished extremes'.[34] In consequence, the connexion established is necessary, being intrinsic to the interlocking structure of the universal system.

The first figure of the syllogism of quality linked an immediately given individual with an abstract universal by means of an abstract particular. It was a syllogism of mere inherence, for which the categorical syllogism is liable to be mistaken by superifical thinking. The difference, however, is that already explained: in the categorical syllogism the minor establishes the specific character of the subject and the middle connects this with the genus to give us an universal interlock. So the defects of the syllogisms of quality and reflection are eliminated. The premisses are not contingent and they do not require separate proof.

This is the true purport of the Aristotelian 'perfect figure'.[35] The middle term states the essential nature of the subject and links it with the universal in which that essential nature is rooted. To this extent it is objective rather than subjective, for the structure of the whole is immanent in the moments (the major and minor terms) and is expressed in the relation. But it is subjective so far as the subject is only one specific form of the genus, and there are others; so that there is an element of arbitrariness as to which specific form is chosen. Moreover, the structural relations expressed in the middle term are not exhaustive, so that the subject could have been subsumed under a different genus. Accordingly the connexion established, though necessary, is only hypothetical, and the categorical grows into the hypothetical syllogism.

The Hypothetical Syllogism[36]

The hypothetical judgement affirms a connexion between terms without asserting their immediate occurrence or existence. The connexion is necessary and is founded in the structure of the actual; but whether the connected features actually occur or not is not stated (If A is, B is; but we are not told whether A is). The hypothetical syllogism links the immediately presented individual through this connexion to a predicate, as follows:

If $\underline{A}$ is, $\underline{B}$ is.

$\underline{A}$ is;

therefore, $\underline{B}$ is.

The middle term $\underline{A}$ is the immediate existent individual, but it is enmeshed in the structure of the real, in the conditions out of which it arises -- what Hegel calls the objective universality which is the mediating factor in the categorical syllogism. This structure is being further elaborated in the hypothetical syllogism, and the middle term $\underline{A}$ identifies and fixes one point in this structure, the ordering principle of which immediately necessitates the existence of the other, $\underline{B}$. Strictly, the status of $\underline{B}$ is the same as that of $\underline{A}$ -- their 'absolute content is the same' -- they both specify the same underlying fact of structure which makes their mutual connexion necessary.

Hegel remarks that condition and conditioned could as well be ground and consequent as cause and effect, once again drawing attention to the fact that the necessary connexion is not just a link between two singular events or objects but is the network of structural relations in the system to which they belong and within which they are distinguished. The $\underline{A}$ and the $\underline{B}$, accordingly, overlap and merge into the unity of the whole -- an identical content in which their difference is sublated. The mediation of the syllogism is an identity which differentiates itself and constitutes itself out of its differences as one single whole. This now explicates itself further as the Disjunctive Syllogism.

The Disjunctive Syllogism[37]

Here the mean is the explicated system, the universal particularized as individual, the Concept as totality. The system contains its differentiations as discriminated species:

$\underline{A}$ is $\underline{B}$ or $\underline{C}$ or $\underline{D}$.

Each is determined by all the rest and, as such, manifests the universal principle of structure.

If $\underline{A}$ is $\underline{B}$, it is not $\underline{C}$ or $\underline{D}$; if it is not $\underline{B}$ it is either $\underline{C}$ or $\underline{D}$.

and so for each disjunct.

250

Hence, $\underline{A}$ is $\underline{B}$ or $\underline{C}$ or $\underline{D}$;

$\underline{A}$ is $\underline{B}$;

therefore $\underline{A}$ is not $\underline{C}$ or $\underline{D}$;

and $\underline{A}$ is $\underline{B}$ or $\underline{C}$ or $\underline{D}$;

$\underline{A}$ is not $\underline{C}$ nor $\underline{D}$,

therefore $\underline{A}$ is $\underline{B}$.

$\underline{A}$ is the subject throughout, it is the organizing principle specifying itself in alternative possibilities which exclude one another, so making the system determinate. The totality which grounds the entire relationship is one and the same. The only important difference between the alternatives is, then, one of point of view. Together they constitute the totality of the Concept, which is the mediating basis, but also both extremes. The whole expresses itself in each of the parts, and the parts constitute the whole. The inner necessity of the hypothetical syllogism is now posited or explicated as the pregnant or objective universal actively differentiating itself. It is no longer an external form imposed on an indifferent content, no longer a fortuitous content subsumed under an indifferent form. It is the universal content self-specified. The difference between mean and extremes has been aufgehoben; it has sublated itself and is transformed into Object.[38]

In this way, Hegel tells us, the formalism of the syllogistic process and the subjectivity of the Concept in judgement and inference have been overcome. Formality and subjectivity consisted in the abstract character of the terms, whether middle or extreme, their treatment as separate and as (in varying degrees) externally linked. The process through which the Concept has gone has progressively internalized the relations and made the content more concrete. This Hegel calls the process (through the different types of syllogism as stages) of the fulfilment, or concretion, of the middle term.[39]

The Concept first divided itself in judgement positing its differentiations as distinct determinations over against one another. In the syllogism it opposes itself to these differences, but, as it develops, the differences (in which it has all along been immanent) are equated with the inner unity and shown to be identical to it. The figures of the immediate, or qualitative, syllogism, each in turn shows one moment of the Concept as middle term. The implication is that the Concept ought to be the mediating influence as an organic whole. The syllogism of reflection gathers together externally the determinate differences of the extremes and foreshadows their intrinsic interdependence. The syllogism of necessity reveals this, turning upon the totality of the

Concept as a simple yet differentiated unity containing the extremes in itself and expressing itself in them.

Thus made concrete, the Concept has become an objective determinate whole. It is objective in that it is universal and necessary -- Kant's criteria of objectivity -- and also in that it is stable and concrete, not subject to whimsical change or arbitrary stipulation. It is proof against the abstracting of the understanding, which thinks apart of things that go together, as well as against the vagaries of the imagination, which associates at random. It is a stable, self-maintaining whole, and as such it is the objectively real.[40]

The Subjective Concept was introduced as the truth of Being and Essence. It is their unity become aware of itself as subjectivity. Its forms are the activity of the thinking ego -- judgement and inference, through which it differentiates itself and unites its diverse contents into a concrete whole. This, in the last resort, is its objective world -- the actual world of its experience.

NOTES: Book II, Part III, Chapter 2

1. Enz., Sections 163-165; W.L., II, pp. 273-300; Miller, pp. 600-622.

2. Enz., Sections 166-180; W.L., II, pp. 301-350; Miller, pp. 622-663.

3. Cf. Enz., Sections 223 et seq. and 236 et seq.

4. McTaggart, with his inveterate tendency to think on the level of the understanding, confuses Hegel's concrete universal with the common property. In consequence, he confessedly fails to grasp the transition from Essence to Concept and misconstrues the relations between necessity and freedom, as well as between reciprocity and universality, and between universal and particular. His treatment of 'universal notion', 'particular notion' and 'individual' is entirely unHegelian; so it is not surprising that he goes altogether astray in his attempts to assess what Hegel does with judgement and syllogism.

5. Cf. Enz., Section 167.

6. Cf. R.G. Collingwood, An Autobiography, Ch. V, on question and answer and propositional logic.

7. Robert Burns.

8. Cf. Enz., Section 169 and Zus.

9. Enz., Section 171.

10.   The name of this category in the Greater Logic is The Judgement of Existence.   Cf. W.L., II, p. 311, Das Urteil des Daseins; Miller, p. 630.

11.   See below, and cf. Enz., Sections 178-180.

12.   Book I, Ch. VII, Sections 7-11.

13.   Cf. Bernard Bosanquet, Logic, Book I, Ch. V.

14.   Enz., Section 177 Zus.; W.L., II, pp. 339-344; Miller, pp. 654-657.

15.   Cf. W.L., II, p. 344; Miller, p. 657.

16.   Cf. Enz., Section 177.

17.   McTaggart is as completely oblivious of all this as he is of the nature of Aufhebung and its effects; so Hegel's transition from Disjunctive Judgement to the Judgement of the Concept, as well as the significance of the latter are lost on him, and he sees the interposition of this triad only as error.

18.   Enz., Section 178.

19.   See above, Bk. I, Pt. II, Ch. 4; Enz., Sections 61-78.

20.   Enz., Sections 181-192; W.L., II, pp. 351-401; Miller, pp. 664-704.

21.   W.L., II, p. 353; Miller, p. 665.

22.   Accordingly, in contemporary philosophy of science, 'the context of discovery' is kept firmly separate from 'the context of justification'.

23.   W.L., II, pp. 374-380; Miller, pp. 681-686.

24.   Cf. The British Journal for the Philosophy of Science, II, 1951, p. 249 and Philosophy, XXVII, 1952, pp. 158-59.

25.   Enz., Sections 183-189; W.L., II, pp. 351-380, Der Schluss des Daseins, Miller, pp. 664ff.

26.   The carriage wheels of Hegel's example are no longer with us.

27.   Cf. Enz., Section 185.

28.   The order of the terms in the various figures seems to be more or less immaterial, as each can always be replaced by either of the other two.

29.   McTaggart's treatment of this section of the Logic is as misguided as ever, owing to his inability to see the difference between the concrete and the abstract universal. He tries to equate Hegel's figures of the syllogism with those of the traditional logic, which cannot be done, and he fails to understand Hegel's criticism of formal logic in consequence.

30.   Enz., Section 190; W.L., II, pp. 380-390; Miller, pp. 686-695.

31.   Here, as elsewhere, McTaggart fails to see that Hegel is demonstrating, via the adapted forms of the traditional logic, the development in thought of the objective system of the real. So he objects to the transition from the Syllogism of Reflection to that of Necessity (Commentary Section 225) on the ground that Hegel uses the term 'universal' in different senses. Of course, he does not; the universal for him is always the concrete system. This failure on McTaggart's part vitiates the whole of his Commentary and nowhere more than in his discussion on the Syllogism (Sections 213-231).

32.   Enz., Sections 191-192; W.L., II, pp. 391-401; Miller, pp. 695-704.

33.   Enz., Section 192.

34.   W.L., II, p. 391; Miller, p. 695.

35.   E.g., All rational beings are moral agents.
       Men are rational beings. Therefore men are moral agents.

36.   W.L., II, pp. 395-398; Miller, pp. 698-701.

37.   W.L., II, pp. 398-401; Miller, pp. 701-704.

38.   Cf. Enz., Section 193.

39.   W.L., II, p. 400; Miller, p. 703.

40.   Cf. Geistesphilosophie, Enz., Section 398: 'But the self-awareness (Fürsichsein) of the waking soul concretely conceived is consciousness and understanding, and the world of the intelligent consciousness is something different from a collage of mere images (Vorstellungen) and pictures. These as such hang together for the most part externally in unintelligent fashion, according to the so-called law of association, with which indeed categories here and there can be mixed. In the waking state, however, man behaves essentially as a concrete ego, an intellect; through this intelligence, perception (Anschauung) stands before him as a concrete whole of features in which every member, each point, takes its place determined by and with all the others at the same time. So the content has its confirmation, not from the mere subjective representation and distinction of facts as external to the person, but

through the concrete coherence in which each part stands with all parts of this complex.'

Chapter 3

Objectivity

Object, properly so-called, is correlative to subject. It is what Husserl identifies as 'intentional object' -- what a subject of consciousness intends (or subtends). We ordinarily think of object as what exists independent of thought or consciousness, but we have seen that existence is a category of Essence, a concept of the understanding. Likewise, actuality is said to be 'objective', meaning that it is independent of thinking, but again we have found that actuality is only adequately conceived as the concrete whole when it becomes aware of itself as such in the Concept. Object, for Hegel, is thus a category higher than any of those below the level of Concept. It is the Concept in its objective phase, or the object of developed consciousness, something far more sophisticated than any merely presented Gegenstand of sense-perception, which is variable, self-contradictory and often illusory. It is for that reason that Plato, Descartes and many other philosophers who are inclined towards rationalism, have denied that sense-perception can reveal to us the truth about reality. They regard the truly real (or 'objective') as the object of the intellect -- the Platonic Idea, or, for Descartes, what we clearly and distinctly understand. In short, it is what is not subject to the vagaries of sensation and fancy, but has a stability and solidarity which is the same for all subjects and for every consciousness; that is, it is universal and necessary, and therefore, as Kant averred, objective.

This object is, as Hegel says,[1] the unconditioned whole, the Absolute Object, God. It is Spinoza's Substantia-sive-Natura, and it specifies itself as a world of objects, -- or, in Spinoza's language, infinite things in infinite ways (modes) follow from it of necessity. But as object it is never separable from subject. According to Spinoza, the Idea of God, the primary product of the Infinite intellect, is identical in Substance with facies totius universi (the face of the whole universe) and is the same thing (res) as its corresponding infinite mode in every other Attribute.

Object, fully developed, then, is the Concept objectified, the answering antithesis to the subjective Concept, while at the same time it is what the subjective Concept has developed into. In it the phases of the subjective concept are sublated, cancelled and absorbed.

Hegel protests against the customary assumption that thought is a mere form, acquiring its filling from an external source. Concept, judgement and syllogism were treated in the school logic as Elementarlehre, the theory of the elements of subjective thinking -- its forms. This was then followed by Methodenlehre, the theory of the method by which the content externally supplied was to be dealt with. This dualism Hegel rejects, and he deplores 'the thoughtless procedure which summarily picks up the determinations of subjectivity and objectivity without investigating their origins'. Both subject and object, he declares, are categories of thought and are rooted in the universal, self-determining concept (the concrete universal) whose development we have traced through Being and Essence. Consequently, the forms of the Subjective Concept are no mere framework into which to fit an alien content. They are that content itself as it has developed dialectically:

> ...die Subjectivität ist es selbst, welche, als dialektisch, ihre Schranke durchbricht und durch den Schluss sich zur Objectivität erschliesst. (Enz., Section 192 Zus.). ('...it is subjectivity itself which, as dialectical, breaks through its bounds and by way of the syllogism opens out into objectivity.')

What this means may be explained in terms of three parallel and yet interdependent processes:

(1) Sentience and sensation (what in the Geistesphilosophie Hegel calls Empfindung, and what in the Phänomenologie appears as the slightly later stage of sense-certainty -- die sinnliche Gewissheit) are both of them at best subjective. Strictly Empfindung is neither subjective nor objective, because it is prior to the distinction between them. It is the mere feeling of the organism-in-relation-to-its environment, as one felt mass (to use Bradley's term) in which no clear distinctions are made. We discover in the Geistesphilosophie that this Empfindung is the inwardizing (Erinnerung) of Nature, in which the organism has developed, and of the natural influences which impinge upon it (e.g., climate, terrain, seasonal changes and diurnal alternations). By its own activity of self-differentiation, the immanence in it of the 'absolute restlessness' of the Idea, distinctions are made and relations established between the differences (of quality and the like) which it contains, held as it were in suspension, the aufgehobene processes of Nature. This activity of distinguishing and relating is, in essence, thought, and its effect is the discrimination of objects within 'the manifold of sense'. It is the process of what Kant called synthesis and the application of the schematized categories to objects of perception. This process, we have already learned, both from Kant and from Hegel (not to mention Fichte and Schelling), is judgement. In its course objects are distinguished, ordered and correlated to constitute an external world set over against the knowing subject. The world is held, at this stage, to be independent of thought -- and in some sense it is, so far as thought is abstract and 'merely subjective' -- but strictly it cannot be independent of thought, except as Ding an sich, which being merely an sich, is mere being, or alternatively mere nothing, the most subjective of all concepts. What we have been tracing is a process of judgement and inference, through

which 'subjectivity' (having emerged from sentience) 'breaks through its own bounds and opens itself out to objectivity'.

(2) So described, however, the process is foreshortened. Common sense and perception, which develop in this way, are not adequate to understanding, and give rise to perplexities which force the ordinary consciousness on to more developed 'syllogizing' in science. The understanding thus constructs a systematic world picture, which ranks par excellence as objective knowledge. It is what Sir Karl Popper lists as his 'third world'. The objective world is then what science reveals by analysis of data derived from observation and by the construction of theories. Once again, therefore, it is true to say that 'subjectivity itself, as dialectical, breaks through its bounds by way of syllogism to objectivity.'

(3) Subjective activity is 'merely subjective' so far as it is imperfect, vacillating and incomplete. Our awareness of the shortcomings of our representations (and consequently of our actions) leads us to set before ourselves an ideal or objective, not only for our conduct, but concomitantly and as a prior condition, for our observation and theorizing. This is the object in its ideal form 'in accordance with its concept'. Apart from thinking and concept it is nothing, and regarded as independent of thought it is a bare abstraction (of all things the most dependent upon thought) -- a mere Jenseits, an ought-to-be that never is, or once more a Ding an sich. But ranking as the ideal object and aim of both thinking and acting, it is eminently a product of thought and one attained through judgement and inference, in fact, through the dialectical procedure established in the logic of the Concept, by which 'subjectivity itself, as dialectical, has burst through its bounds and by means of the syllogism has opened itself out to objectivity.'

In the last resort, the Object is what can be rationally regarded as objectively real. What, after all, do we mean by the thing as it really is in itself, in its real internal constitution, or essence, other than the most complete, coherent and concrete conception of it that we can attain. The real world is either something totally unknown, and so, to us, as good as nothing, or else, and more plausibly, the best and most coherent idea of it that we can form by considering and rationally ordering all the available evidence. What the world is really like is the best that science and philosophy can reveal to us, and as Hegel presents it, that is a dialectical development through which Nature generates organic beings, in whom it develops further to self-conscious mind, the content of whose awareness is the real become aware of itself, and continuously making itself more concrete and more self-sufficient through the same dialectical urge towards absolute wholeness. It is this concretion and nothing else that is the hall-mark of objectivity. It is as Resultat that the real reveals itself, and not as abstract initial datum.

The Ontological Proof of the Existence of God[2]

The transition from Subjective Concept to Object is, according to Hegel, the basis of the Ontological Argument for the existence of God. He constantly recurs to this matter from various angles and in numerous contexts. It is especially the form in which Anselm states the proof to which he refers here, and the contention that the idea of God cannot exist in the intellect alone, because it is the idea of 'that than which a greater is inconceivable', and we can conceive of something greater than what is merely subjective.

Hegel's thesis is that what is conceived as fully concrete is ipso facto objective. It cannot be, or remain, 'merely subjective' in the abstract and imperfect sense of that phrase, for it has become perfected (in the Spinozistic sense of 'complete') and is not just imperfect, partial and disconnected Vorstellung. But he points out also that the Ontological Proof fails in that its quasi-syllogistic form is no more than abstract and formal and does not set forth the dialectical development of the content. Thus it omits and overlooks the essential difference between subject and object in asserting their identity. The difference, however, is also relevant and is what Guanilo and later critics rely on in their opposition to the argument. Nevertheless, this difference is only relevant in the case of finite concepts and finite objects, to which Anselm's reasoning (as he expressly states) does not apply. If it is understood as attributing finite, phenomenal, sensuously perceptible existence to God, of course it is unsound and is vulnerable to the criticism. But any such interpretation would be absurd, for the claim is not that God exists as a phenomenon, as finite perceptible things exist, but that He is the infinite Being than which a greater cannot be conceived, the absolute Object or object as Absolute.

The conception of such an absolute object, however, is only possible and legitimate as having developed dialectically from Nature, through finite experience and intelligence to the point we have now reached. And it could have done so only if the absolute Idea were immanent throughout the process, as well in Nature and natural forms as in human consciousness and experience both of nature and of self. It is this immanence of the Absolute and nothing else which drives the dialectic, and it is only because it comes to consciousness in (and as) our minds that religion can rightly claim that man is created in the image of God. It is, likewise, for this reason alone that man has any idea of God or of an absolute object. Having brought itself thus to consciousness as realized Concept, it cannot be derogated as 'mere idea' or a purely subjective imagination. It is the concretely self-realized object. But it is so only as the fruition of the dialectical process, without which, or in ignorance and disregard of which, it is a mere idea, a mere abstraction, cut loose from its roots in the actuality which is the truth an sich, the truth which is actual and must exist. But the reality of this truth and its essence is only fully actualized in its awareness of itself, so that it has to bring itself to consciousness and realize itself as concept, which as self-differentiating universal is its own object, and as object is eminently real.

This is Hegel's position, which is set out again and more fully in the Religionsphilosophie, where he contends that, in order to reach this transition from subjective conception to absolute Object, the Concept must have developed itself, through its differentiating moments to a concrete and self-complete Idea, which, being in and for itself, is absolute and truly infinite. Only as such can it be fully real, and only to such an Idea is the Ontological Proof relevant. The transition at this point in the Logic, from subjective to objective Concept is still only a prefiguring of this final consummation.

In the Greater Logic he expresses the same idea by saying that God is only known through his works and in his activity. His works are his self-manifestation in the world of Nature,

'The heavens declare the glory of God.'

Nature is the idea in the form of other-being,[3] and Nature raises itself to Spirit through the consciousness of man.[4] Thus the transition from subjective to objective concept is at once the logical foundation of the Ontological Proof and of the doctrine of Creation. We shall see the position return and the whole movement repeated at the end of the Logic.

We are told further, in the Zusatz to Section 194 of the Encyclopaedia, that the conception of God as Object and no more (i.e., as set over against subject) is the viewpoint of superstition and slavish fear. The conception must develop itself to the point at which God's self-manifestation is in truth made through the subjectivity of man in Christ, and in the redemption of sinful humanity. This is the realization of man's unity, or atonement, with God -- the conception of God as love, revealing himself to mankind and redeeming humanity through that self-revelation in his Son, and so overcoming the opposition between subject and object.

What has here been summarized in the guise of religion is the same process as that of the overcoming in science and philosophy (Wissenschaft) of the externality and alienity of external nature, by which we find in it only ourselves; or conversely, the process by which we lead the object back to the subjectivity that is our own inner consciousness and knowledge.

In this way, Hegel says, we can see how stultifying it is to hold subject and object apart in fixed and abstract opposition. For the Concept, without any need of external matter, objectivizes itself by its own peculiar dialectic, and the object is no static and processless block,

260

but is an activity which moves itself similarly on to the Idea. This is Hegel's interpretation on the one hand, of God's creativity and self-manifestation in Nature and History, and, on the other hand, of Nature's evolution, by its own process, to finite spirit, which consummates itself in religion and philosophy. This major antithesis of Nature to Spirit is reflected in the objectification of human experience in knowledge and moral action, which is just as much a subjectification of the objective world and the subjection of it to Spirit.

Subdivisions of the Objective Concept

The object of developed consciousness is (1) the object of knowledge, and (2) the object of desire and action. The two aspects are not separable, for as object of knowledge it is the aim of the activity of learning and research, and unless it is known it cannot be an object of desire. The root of Socrates' doctrine that virtue is knowledge lies here. This object is the self-consciously self-differentiated whole, the concrete universal, sublated in and realized as Concept and now objectified. As such, it is opposed (entgegengesetzt) to subject, which is nevertheless involved and aufgehoben in it, as we shall presently see more convincingly.

The Object is a return to immediacy, but, as we are now well aware, it is an immediacy sublating mediation. It is something directly presented as Gegenstand, but at the same time it is interpreted and systematized as a world, the immediate apprehension of any part of which is implicitly mediated by its context in the whole. The differences implicit in the immediate whole and the unity implicit in the differences are thus in conflict. So Hegel says that the object is the absolute contradiction between the complete independence of the many and their equally total dependence, in the interlacing of their differences. He interprets Leibniz' Monadology as an expression of this contradiction, for there each monad is a simple and independent immediate object, yet it holds within itself an idealized representation of the whole universe of monads, differing among themselves in their varying degrees of development. Each has thus the whole sublated in itself. For the Monad of monads, however, and in consequence of the Pre-established Harmony, each is internally related to, and so wholly dependent for its own character and status upon, every other.[5]

In similar manner, the diversity of the whole (as has occurred so often before at lower levels in the dialectic) breaks up into independent, apparently atomic elements, each of which presents itself as an object in its own right. But it can do so only because it is dependent on its place in the world and its systematic relations to all other objects,which are thus implicit in its seeming independence.

We must constantly bear in mind that, although the Concept in its fully developed form is the philosophical concept, it has degrees or stages in its self-realization. The concepts of the understanding are examples of these, and the understanding also universalizes and objectifies its content, even if abstractly. So it conceives the objective world as a world external to itself, and made up of objects mutually in external relation. Implicitly, however, it is a unitary world and is systematically structured. The concept is expressed and is immanent in it, though not at first in the most appropriate form. Consequently, there are different levels of interpretation and the Object presents itself with different degrees of concretion. The first stage is atomistic, on the level of interpretation typical of naive perception. It corresponds roughly to Being but not entirely, for just as in sound common sense naive perception overlaps with understanding, so this phase of objectivity involves both immediate existence and causal relation. The objective world, at this level, is a vast mechanism, as it came to be conceived in the science of the seventeenth century. The second stage is a development of the first corresponding to Essence. The merely external relations of the parts of the mechanical world are conditioned by a ground and evoke the demand for explanation in terms of more internal and intimate relations. The consequent properties are not simply additive but are rooted in a more integral unity. This is the phase of Chemism; but that ultimately comes to comprise a still more overt holism and self-maintenance. The object now reveals itself as an organism, in which the parts or members are not only internally related but are mutually means and ends, and the whole is at once objective and is the determinant of the objective nature of the parts. This is Teleology in the proper meaning of the word. Hegel says, with justice, that it is the union of mechanism and chemism, for both are involved in it. The determinant whole is at once self-sustaining and self-differentiated. The object, here, is reverting to subject, as self-determining and self-aware, its perpetual activity directed to its own self-realization. So it leads to the Idea.

Mechanism, Chemism and Teleology are all of them at once forms of actuality -- of the self-specifying universal -- and also ways of conceiving the world. As the former they are phases in the dialectic of Nature, and they appear again in the Naturphilosophie; as the latter they are Denkbestimmungen, metaphysical concepts characterizing types of metaphysical theory. They are different styles of world-view, or concepts of Nature.

Mechanism[6]

In some sense, Mechanism is a recurrence of pure Being, and in some sense of Being-for-self, though now, of course, sublating the whole dialectical process of Essence and of subjectivity. It is, in one aspect, the Being of Parmenides over again, the one, uncreated and indestructible, excluding difference and change, through and through solid and uniform, containing no element of non-being. All non-being is other and external to it. So it is, as it were, in the first instance, a vast atom in an infinite void -- the Parmenidean sphere. This Parmenidean One was earlier invoked as corresponding first to pure Being and then to Being-for-self. But this is only one aspect of the mechanistic object -- its monadic aspect -- and as we were told before,[7] it reverts to or evokes its opposite, the Many.

The One relates to its other, the Void, as to another one, each is uniform, featureless and undivided, and is distinguished from the other by nothing except negation and opposition. Just as Being and Nothing became one something in opposition to another something, and the One of Being-for-self proliferated into atomic ones, now the monadic object does likewise and becomes an aggregation of objects. In the history of philosophy the Parmenidean One proliferated into the atoms of Leukippus and Democritus, each atom being one, indestructible, uncreated and indivisible, like the original Being.

Hegel prefers to compare the mechanistic world with Leibniz' universe of monads, presumably because he wishes to stress the sublation of the many in each one and the implicit mediation of the immediate. He says that atoms are not objects, meaning presumably that they are not, as objects are, correlative to subjects, whereas the monads reflect one another, each and all, and are therefore inter-related as subject and object. Here, however, Hegel seems deliberately to be overlooking Leibniz' emphasis on the teleological character of the monads and their appetition, which would make them more suitable examples of organism, as they are viewed by Leibniz himself. Undoubtedly Hegel's intention is to keep before us the conceptual mediation of the Object, which is certainly important and must not be lost to sight, but the mechanistic world is, nevertheless, a world of atomism, in which 'material points' are externally related one to another and are centres of forces acting upon one another in accordance with the distances between the points and the masses centred on them. But in the first instance we are presented with an aggregate of externally related simple bodies, in which anything of a qualitative nature is merely apparent and all change of whatever kind is reduced to the movement, combination and rearrangement of atomic units. Even that movement itself is the consequence of the external relations between the atoms, whether attraction and repulsion, or impact and rebound.

This level of objectivity Hegel calls 'formal mechanism'.

Taken as a merely immediate object, the mechanical world is only an aggregate, a universe describable as 'everything there is'; and its parts are equally immediate objects mutually indifferent and indifferent to their common aggregation (the 'whole' they constitute). Their determination is therefore self-external, and that is true of each as it is of all. It involves an infinte regress: each is determined from without by another, and that again by another, ad infinitum. As merely mechanical the object has no self-determination and is ultimately inexplicable. This is typically what determinism is -- determination from without, which is, in the last resort, no determination, because it still requires further determination from without. Accordingly, it is tantamount to indeterminateness, and Hegel says that the object is 'in the first instance indeterminate',[8] its determinateness (as Concept) being mere multiplicity -- relationless manifoldness.

The mechanistic object is the whole of nature as a mechanical system throughout. It is the universe of Laplace. If all things are ultimately atoms obeying mechanical laws, there is just one all-embracing mechanical system, in terms of which everything should be finally explicable. It is a self-specified system, because its forces are derived from the spatial position and masses of the bodies contained in it, and they are all-pervasive and comprehensive. But they are such that each particle is (or seems to be) intrinsically independent of them. They impinge from without: the vires impressae of Newton. Hence the objectified concept is, on this level, not for itself, but only in itself.

Mechanism is obviously a world-view, a conception or theory of Nature, a metaphysic. But it is concept as object. It is the way objective Nature is conceived, and conceived essentially as objective, unadulterated by subjectivity -- purely material. As Hegel says, '...in its immediacy it is the Concept only implicitly (an sich), and has it as subjective at first outside it.'[9]

It is nevertheless a real aspect or level of Nature itself. There are material bodies in external relations, moved by impact, exerting and subject to pressure, moved also by forces varying with mass and inversely with distance; and, as Hegel points out, there are even mechanical forms of living and conscious activity. This is undeniably the case, for living processes are wholly dependent on 'mechanisms' of various kinds, tensions, pressures, feed-back servo-mechanisms (not that Hegel knew of these) and quantitative equilibria. Instinctive behaviour is often, even predominantly mechanical, as Fabre never tired of demonstrating. Habit is the mechanical repetition of practised action, and we often derogate artistic performances as stiff and merely mechanical.

Mechanism is thus at once both a category of thought and a form of objective reality, the Concept become object. But it is not a category adequate to cover every aspect of reality. Organic and psychological facts lie beyond its scope. It is not even adequate to all physical phenomena, as Hegel points out. Light, heat, magnetism and electricity are not mechanical principles. In saying this Hegel is far in advance of his time. He wrote when these forms of physical phenomena were explained in crassly material terms and scientists spoke of heat and electricity as fluid substances. We observed above, where he was dealing with the thing and its properties, and with form and matter, that he had already recognized the futility of such attempts to materialize the forces under scrutiny. Yet much later in the nineteenth century physicists were still trying to envisage electro-magnetic phenomena, including light, in mechanistic images. Lord Kelvin refused to be satisfied with any explanation of physical process unless it could be presented in the form of a mechanical model. The persistent failure to explain electro-magnetic phenomena mechanistically was just what led at the turn of the century to the abandonment of mechanism in physics with the advent of Planck and Einstein and the theories of quanta and of relativity.

The mechanistic attitude in science and in other disciplines today, even though it is no longer current in physics, its original home and breeding-ground, still persists. Hegel is therefore justified in including it as a category of objectivity (even apart from the additional reasons given above). Moreover, it is, as we have seen, an aspect of all objective reality. But in modern sciences there is a persistent tendency towards holism, a tendency which permeates the chemism typical of the subsequent phase and unites with organism to give a universal teleonomy, which Hegel anticipated and to which we shall presently return.

In truth, the mutual independence of atomic parts of the mechanical world is spurious. So likewise is that of the incidence of forces. Bodies are supposed to move under the influence of gravity, and this is dependent upon distance and mass. In consequence, the forces are pervasive throughout space, and every body must exert some effect, however slight, on every other. Thus even in their supposed separation they are mutually interdependent.

The conception of gravitation develops itself in terms of centres of gravity, and Hegel observes that, while each body has its own centre, apparently irrespective of every other, when it gravitates towards another body it is (as he says) referred to a centre outside itself (abstract centre). It becomes part of a gravitational system (for instance the solar system) which has its own (absolute) centre -- and this may be, as it is in the case of double stars, outside any or all of the gravitating bodies. Then every body has its centre in an other. This interdependence in mechanism Hegel calls differenter Mechanismus, translated by Wallace as 'mechanism with affinity', a relative mechanism referring to an other. Hegel gives as examples, gravitation (Fall), appetite, social impulse (herd instinct). It is (1) correlated with the first figure of the syllogism (I,P,U), the central body (relative centre) being the middle term linking the gravitating satellites with the relative centre as individuating unity. Hegel expands this into the other two figures: (2) the mediation of the dependent bodies between absolute and relative centres (U,I,P; it is the disposition of the bodies that determines the position of both of these centres), and (3) the mediation of the absolute centre between the relative centre and the

265

gravitating bodies (P,U,I). The parallel example is (a) the social process by which the individual with his personal needs and efforts to fulfil them contributes to the economic intercourse of the civil society (die Bürgerliche Gesellschaft) which gives rise to law and government (I,P,U). (b) Alternatively, the activity of the individual mediates between the administration and particular personal requirements (U,I,P), and (c) likewise it is the state and social order which guarantees, and so mediates between the economic process and the fulfilment of the individual person (P,U,I).

In this way Hegel indicates how the moments of the subjective concept are aufgehoben, preserved and realized, in the Object.[10] It is only in the system as a whole that the individuality and action (or movement) of the parts is determinate and actual. It is now a system, no longer a mere aggregate, though still as yet a mechanical system -- what Hegel calls 'Absolute Mechanism'.

The reciprocal action of bodies in absolute mechanism and their dependence upon relations one to another for their stability bring out their mutual affinities or biasses, which are now emphasized and developed further as Chemism.

Chemism[11]

The nature of the chemical object is constituted by an immanent bias or affinity towards others. Its properties are its chemical affinities. Its constant tendency, therefore, is to unite with its other, in which union it finds its true individuality. The interdependence of mechanical bodies still leaves them, at least apparently, free to move in separation from one another; but chemical action by its very nature is concerted interaction between two or more substances, involving their mutual biasses or affinities, which leave none of them free to act independently.

A philosophy of nature would trace in detail the transformation of mechanical into chemical activity and the corresponding transmutation of the relationships involved. Here we are concerned primarily with the logical relation between simple self-identity and identity in and through difference as the categories of Essence are aufgehoben and exemplified in mechanism and chemism respectively. Chemism is the reflective moment of the object corresponding to Essence. The mutually interdependent entities are still seen as separable, and in combination they simply neutralize one another. In the product the specific properties of the interagents are cancelled (aufgehoben) -- not 'merged', as Wallace here translates that word.[12] Hegel is clearly thinking in this context of the reaction of an acid with an alkali to form a neutral salt or base. This again is capable of separation into and return to the biassed reagents. But the chemical compound once formed has properties which are not the properties of either of the

266

reagents taken separately. These have been cancelled and something entirely new, though not entirely unrelated and independent, has emerged.

The reflective character of chemism consists, also, in the fact that the various chemical substances have the nature and properties that pertain to them by virtue of their affinities to, or reflection in, others. But the chemical compound is a unity which is still only immediate, although more intimate than the mechanical mixture. It is not yet 'for itself'. It becomes so only when the unity becomes an end or purpose, when the system of interacting substances and processes spontaneously maintains and reproduces itself by its own ebullition; that is, when the chemical process becomes organic metabolism.

In chemism, and even in mechanism, teleology is already implicit. The interlock of mechanical parts and the forces cementing the mechanical system together, and the mutual affinities of chemical substances producing their concerted interaction, are premonitions of teleology. In mechanism the bodies derive their stable identity from their interdependence, and in chemism their individuality. In mechanism this is realized in the mechanical system set out and integrated as a whole; in chemism, the 'neutral' compound holds in suspension the properties of the component elements. These are halting steps towards the Being-for-self that supports subjectivity, a return which is being effected throughout the dialectic of the Object. The externalized structure of the Concept is progressively being reabsorbed and made internal to itself, or self-sustaining. This is more successfully achieved when the mechanical and chemical processes unite in a self-maintaining system, which preserves its integrity under diverse conditions and circumstances by using the very laws and forces of mechanism and chemism as means to its own subsistence as end (Zweck). Such a system is organic and teleological, and it brings us to the third and final level of objectivity.

Teleology[13]

The crude and naive attribution of deliberate purpose, the pursuit of a preconceived goal, to natural processes, or of planned subservience of inanimate objects to human ends, is rejected emphatically by Hegel as a thoughtless and stupid interpretation of Teleology.[14] The key to the understanding of this category is, as ever, the concept of wholeness. Teleology, properly understood, is the self-maintenance of the whole through its determination and direction of its own members or moments. As thus self-sustaining, the whole is end or aim (Zweck), and that again is the persistence and self-generation of the whole through its own process. Purposiveness is expressed in the mutual relation of the parts as ends and means, which is also the mutual relation of the parts to the whole; for the activity of the whole is directed to the maintenance of the parts and the perpetuation of the processes that sustain them; and the concerted effect of these processes and of the functions performed by the parts is the self-maintenance of the whole. Such processes are teleological, and explanation of parts in terms of whole is teleological explanation. Human purpose marks an advanced stage in the development of such processes, which in truth lies far beyond the level of natural teleology. And divine purpose is the immanence of the Absolute and infinite Whole in the finite, what we shall revert to below under the guise of 'the cunning of Reason'. In human purpose the principle of teleology is preserved, aufgehoben, but now become self-conscious and deliberate. Its ultimate and ideal realization coincides with divine purpose: that is, the redemption of mankind through atonement with God.

It is clear that teleology appears on at least three different levels: (1) the teleology of living, organic activity, (2) the conscious teleology of human conduct, and (3) the teleology of the Idea realizing itself through the dialectical process of Nature and Spirit. In his discussion Hegel does not always make these distinctions explicit but speaks of the first two simply as finite purpose, and refers to the third somewhat obliquely as 'the cunning of reason' and as the eternally realized Absolute Good.[15] The fundamental principle of all three is, however, the same, the whole, which is the Truth and the Absolute Good in one, along with its immanence in its own moments at every level. It is obvious, therefore, that to attribute conscious purposiveness to the organic processes of nature is a category-mistake, and it is clearly recognized as such by Hegel.

Zweck is object in the sense of purpose or design; that is, the organic whole as the aim or objective of its own activity of self-determination and self-generation. It is subjective so far as it is unrealized goal in the process of objectifying itself through means which have already been realized and are objectively to hand. As such it is merely ideal and opposes itself to the present reality, the abolition of which is what the effort to realize the ideal seeks. So Hegel says that 'the end or purpose is the Concept emerged into free existence by means of the negation of the immediate objectivity.' (Enz. Section 204.) It seeks to supersede the latter in order to realize itself in ideal form (as Idea).

Further, Zweck is objective as real self-actualizing potency and as actually immanent in the activity of realization, which is the endeavour to remove and nullify (aufheben) the contradiction between what is presently at hand and the ideal objective. This is essentially what the Concept is -- self-actualizing activity -- what Hegel frequently refers to as 'infinite restlessness' -- objectifying itself as a reality. Thus Zweck is both subjective and objective at the same time, and so is precursor of the Idea, which is the unity of subject and object, the self-actualized, or realized end.

Hegel draws attention here to the contrast between efficient and final causation. The first is blind and external, a compulsion which is nevertheless fortuitous and contingent (as we saw earlier[16]). The second is not blind because it is determined to a preconceived end and (in its fully developed form) is self-consciously designed, its necessity is self-enforced and its compulsion self-imposed. It is a potency realizing itself by its own nisus. Thus in final causation the moving principle is not an external cause but is the very self of that which is moved. The end, Hegel says, in being attained, 'has only closed with itself and sustained itself.'[17]

The proximate example of teleology is appetite in living beings. It is the feeling of contradiciton inherent in the finite and its urge towards fulfilment. Its impulse is towards negation of the opposition between subjective want and objective insufficiency, and its satisfaction is the reconciliation of these two poles, making apparent the insufficiency of either of them, the one-sidedness of each, and giving assurance of the necessity of their unification.

But this is only one example of finite teleology, and is to be distinguished from the infinite teleology of the Absolute Idea. Finite purposes regard the immediate object(s) merely as means, and value them simply as 'useful'. Moreover, the object as the end of finite purpose at once becomes a means to some further purpose (so that we commonly ask about any projected activity, 'What is its use?'), and this leads to an infinite regress. Here we have the outlook of Utilitarianism, and also the senseless evaluation of natural things as means to human purposes.[18] It is the failure to get beyond finite teleology, or to see the immanence in it of the truly infinite. For finite purpose is limited to the imposition of an external form on a pre-existing material found ready to hand (as means). It is not the self-generation and self-determination in and for itself of the absolute whole, but only a phase in the process of that self-generation, in which infinite teleology is at most implicit (an sich).

Again Hegel asserts that teleological relationships are syllogistic, and as, for him, the syllogism is the dialectical triad, we can see how the various factors fit together. The subjective aim unites with the objective fulfilment through the mediation of the activity (an objectification of subjective feeling) and the objective means made instrumental to subjectivity. Thus we have (1) the aim, (2) appropriation of the means, (3) the fulfilment. The first Hegel identifies with the universal in the form of self-sustaining (für sich seiender) Concept. This is the totality of the Concept subjectively grasped. It is entirely general, the end as self-realization, or in Kantian terms as the good will. The second consists in the specification of this general aim in particular purposes. The third is the realization of these purposes, in which the universal is actualized and the self fulfilled. In this, he says, the universal returns upon, and closes with, itself.[19] One must recall that the universal is the Concept, which in principle is the self-conscious ego or self, and what we are dealing with here is that aspect of the ego as practical in which it realizes itself purposively. Its dynamic is, as always, the dialectic, now become conscious of itself and so felt as appetite and desire, and operative as action.

As is his wont, Hegel again expoits the ambiguity of common words. Here it is that of entschliessen (to resolve or decide, as well as to conclude from inference) and of urteilen (to partition, or to judge, as well as to evaluate). The individual evaluates (urteilt) means and ends, and resolves (entschliesst) to act, and in these functions the Concept (the ego) partitions itself and again closes with itself (schliesst sich mit sich selbst zusammen). In so doing it constructs a syllogism (Schluss) in which the universal is united (zusammenschliesst) with the self-realizing individual, through the mediation of the particular.

This is the first syllogism of teleology, corresponding to the subjective purpose unrealized. The process through which realization is effected is a direction outward of the subjective activity of the agent, in his rejection of the opposition of subjective desire and objective presentation, both as equally inadequate moments, in the endeavour to reconcile them in a coherent (zusammengeschlossenen) totality.[20]

So we are led to the second syllogism. The middle term is the combined activity and means, the activity as the power of the concept (or individual) subjecting the object to itself. The domination of the means by the power of the subject is the first premiss of the syllogism. It also, Hegel says, becomes the middle term, which contains the conclusion implicitly in itself. We may unravel all this as the mediation by the individual of the universal with the particular -- the adaptation of the means to the purpose (or end) by the activity of the agent. The second syllogism corresponds to the carrying out of the purpose.

The third syllogism is its realization. For this the activated means must be mediated by the aim or purpose with the final goal or objective; that is, they must be made means to it through assimilation to the universal aim. The means are consumed in the process and the end is at once realized through them, yet is not reduced to their level, but remains, as it were, aloof while maintaining itself through their ministration. This, Hegel says, is 'the cunning of reason'.[21]

All three syllogisms have the same content. It is the concrete universal which is realizing itself through the teleological process, and is, in its satisfaction, the unity of subject and object -- the realized end. Of this Hegel says that it is the free Concept, in which the one-sidedness of both subject and object is overcome and both attain completion.

In the Zusatz to Section 208 he tells us that the immediate empowering of the means is exemplified in the objective embodiment of living animals. The soul is the dynamic directly objectified in the body, which it then uses as means to the realization of its ends through its activity. Of the cunning of reason we shall say more anon, it is the way in which particular interests and purposes conspire, without the intention of the individual agents, to the realization of a wider and a higher end than they envisage.

Purpose is always the endeavour to fulfil a design; it is the nisus to a whole of some sort, and ultimately to the absolute whole. Its underlying principle is always the self-realization of the absolute Idea in and as an actual world. Natural processes realize wholes, as it were, by accident. They arise out of apparently random processes without any deliberate purposiveness. This is one example of the cunning of reason. Those living processes which are teleological in themselves (the instinctive behaviour of living creatures satisfying their own appetitive urges) generate wholes (like eco-systems, the tendency to which in nature Hegel seems to have sensed without the knowledge that we now have of the organismic interrelation of species in biocoenoses). These go beyond and are not envisaged in the finite ends of the individual creatures. So it is also with men, whose purposes and interests combine in the realization of social ends not deliberately planned, which include but go far beyond the conscious intentions of the persons acting. This process reaches its fulfilment in man's final awareness of his own membership in and union with the ultimate totality. This is the end of religion and of philosophy. It is what Spinoza identified as the knowledge and love of God -- amor intellectualis Dei -- the attainment of which is blessedness. In this we become apprised of the fact that the Absolute Whole which is the Truth and the Good is eternally realized, and that the contradiction between what is and what ought to be, felt in us as desire and will, is a sort of illusion. Our constant striving to improve our lot and to remedy ills is incident upon our finite status and is characteristic of finite purposiveness. Hegel says that the fulfilment of the infinite purpose is the removal of the illusion that it is not already fulfilled. He writes,

> The God, the absolute good, fulfils itself eternally in the world, and the result is that it is already fulfilled in and for itself and does not need to wait upon our efforts.[22]

This assertion is two-edged. The Absolute realizes itself eternally in (and as) the world through the very nisus of the finite towards the whole. The infinite purpose is to bring that perpetual nisus to satisfaction, and it does so when the illusion is removed that the whole is unrealized. It is eternally fulfilled, therefore, only because and by virtue of the fact that it is ceaselessly and unremittingly in process of realizing itself through the endeavour of the finite, in which the whole is immanent. Good is realized only in the continuous overcoming of

271

evil; truth only in the persistent rectification of error. Moral virtue is the unceasing resistance to temptation, and the acquisition of knowledge is the persistent search for truth.

> To travel hopefully is better than to arrive, and the true success is to labour.[23]

The whole realises itself only through the continuous development of its moments into the complete totality.

In finite purpose external means are used to gain an external end, by the imposition on the presented object of a subjectively devised form. But the ultimate fulfilment of finite purpose is the realization that its own process is the fulfilment of the infinite. The opposition between form and content then evaporates, as does that between end and process. We shall return to this identification of opposites under Idea, where the unity of the process in its consummation, and the immanence of the end in the process, is finally revealed. But it is already exemplified in teleology, and especially in human morality, the end of which turns out to be nothing more nor less than the good life, the exercise of the good will, the practice of virtue, which is an end in itself. It is a sustained moral activity, which is nothing other than the constant striving to make things better and to preserve the achievements already gained. As the White Queen said to Alice in Looking-glass Land, one must run hard in order to stay in the same place. In politics, the price of liberty is eternal vigilance and the constant battle to preserve acknowledged rights. In religion, redemption and blessedness are not static conditions of beatification, but are an unrelenting strife against sin and finitude -- a constant process of sublation. The eternal and infinite nature of God is his eternal self-manifestation in Nature, in life and in human personality.

The Cunning of Reason

'Die Vernunft is ebenso listig als machtig (Reason is as cunning as it is powerful)', Hegel writes,[24] and, especially for the use he has made of this doctrine in the philosophy of history, he has been most frequently and most adversely criticized. But the criticism is for the most part due to, perhaps excusable, misunderstanding. The cunning of reason is the pervading influence of the whole, and the governance by the whole of every detail that contributes to its wholeness. Such a whole, Hegel has told us from the outset, is a result, the outcome of a long and complex development, the culmination of a series of phases or degrees of increasing perfection. It cannot itself be whole and perfect except as such, and is only abstractly conceived (or rather, merely imagined) as a separate and rounded off perfection divorced from the process through which it generates itself. The lower, imperfect, forms are therefore integral to it and are necessary phases in the process of perfection without which it cannot be absolute and whole. And as they

272

are necessary to it, so it is immanent in them and realizes itself through them. Apart from the whole they are nothing -- or at best abstractions which contradict themselves and one another; yet in the whole these conflicts are reconciled and the moments combine harmoniously to fulfil the concrete self-completion of the totality. Hegel says that the cunning of reason consists in its mediating activity, and this works in two directions at once, in that the finite mediates the fulfilment of the infinite and the whole regulates and co-ordinates the contingent activity of the finite. Thus what is finite, imperfect, haphazard and apparently disorderly, cannot be absolutely so, for, in the first place, to be anything at all it must have immanent in it the principle of the whole (which is a principle of order and organization)[25]. In the second place, contingency and disorder are imperfections incident upon finitude, which is a necessary moment in the generation of the perfect, in which it is sublated and which is the determinant throughout of the generative process.

Thus we find random physical processes producing ordered effects, determined by the energy system as a whole -- and in the last resort, by the whole system of the physical world.[26] In the living organism, chemical processes and accidental effects from the environment are adjusted and adapted to the metabolic system and the needs of the organism, and accommodated to its persistent urge to self-maintenance: for example, the absorption of energy from sunlight and its use by the chlorophyl in plant cells to synthesize vitamins, and the accommodation to the organic wholeness of the genome of accidental mutations in the genes. In human society the persistent endeavour of the community towards a common good (what Rousseau calls the General Will, and Bosanquet the 'real will' of the community) is achieved, if only in approximation, through partial and limited individual strivings for personal benefits, the immediate aims of which do not coincide with the common interest, but which, as corrected and adjusted through discussion and criticism in the legal and political processes, tend in the long run towards its realization. The process can in some cases be virtually automatic, as in the mutual adjustments of economic supply and demand.

The cunning of reason is the same notion as that of divine providence, and is the idea that underlies the religious teaching that 'all things work together for good'. This is because evil is always and only an incident of finitude, and in the finite the infinite is immanent. Without that immanence the finite is nothing. Hence the positive factors in all evil acts and occurrences are not evil, only the negative and self-contradictory. And even these, as we have seen, are the stimulants to progress and the resolution of the conflicts, for the finite phases upon which they are incident are essential phases and integral moments in the dialectical process which is the self-generation, and is throughout governed by the determining principle, of the whole.

273

As Augustine and Aquinas taught, God created a whole which is perfect, and the perfection of which requires the inclusion in it of every degree of goodness, not only the highest, but also the very least; not only the incorruptible, but also the corruptible. And Spinoza likewise declared: '...He did not lack material for the creation of every degree of perfection from the highest even to the lowest.'[27] In the ultimate consummation all the imperfections of the lesser and lower phases are aufgehoben -- they are cancelled and vanish. And the process through which the consummation is reached is one of constant overcoming of evil.

The power of reason is its explicit drive, für sich, towards self-completion, a drive powered by the immanent dialectical activity of the Idea. The cunning of reason is (as it were) the quasi-automatic precipitation of the Idea from accidental ingredients, in which, however, it is in fact implicit, and for that reason. The latter is just the implicit reflection of the former. There is nothing more mysterious about the cunning of reason than this prevailing influence of the universal Concept, the active principle of organization immanent in the finite, assimilating even fortuitous and random material, which is fortuitous and random only because of its finitude, and is assimilable because its very finitude is determined by and is a manifestation of the principle of holism which makes it what it is.

NOTES: Book II, Part III, Chapter 3

1. Cf. Enz., Section 193.

2. Enz., Section 193.

3. Cf. Enz., Section 247.

4. Cf. Enz., Section 247, Zus.: 'Die Natur is aber nur an sich die Idee,...der Gott bleibt aber nicht versteinert und verstorben, sondern die Steine schreien und heben sich zum Geiste auf.' (Nature, however, is the Idea only implicitly...but God does not remain stony and dead, the stones cry out and raise themselves to Spirit.)

5. Cf. Enz., Section 194.

6. Enz., Sections 195-199; W.L., II, pp. 409-428; Miller, pp. 711-726.

7. Cf. pp. 115-119, above.

8. Cf. W.L., II, p. 411; Miller, p. 712.

9. Cf. Enz., Section 195. 'Denselben als subjectiven ausser ihm' is the observing scientist.

10.   The inclusion of the example from social process is relevant in that Hegel treats society and social morality as <u>Objective</u> Spirit.

11.   <u>Enz</u>., Sections 200-203; <u>W.L.</u>, II, pp. 428-436; Miller, 727-733.

12.   Cf. <u>Enz</u>., Section 202.

13.   <u>Enz</u>., Sections 204-212; <u>W.L.</u>, II, pp. 436-461; Miller, pp. 734-754.

14.   Cf. <u>Enz</u>., Section 205, <u>Zus</u>.

15.   So extraordinary a combination of partial insight and total error as McTaggart achieves in his treatment of Teleology is difficult to credit.   He recognizes, in a somewhat ham-handed manner the distinction between the popular notion of teleology and the Hegelian (derived from Kant).   But he fails to grasp the dialectical movement within the category, in which human finite purposiveness is a phase of the total infinite teleology, subsequent to and developed from organic teleology.   The different phases and aspects of purpose in which means and end are variously distinguished and identified are quite lost on McTaggart, whose treatment of the whole topic is abstract and artificial and a mere caricature of Hegel's. (see <u>Commentary</u>, Sections 525-261).

16.   Pp. 172, 186, 200 above.

17.   <u>Enz</u>., Section 204:   '...<u>sich nur mit sich zusammengeschlossen und erhalten hat</u>.'

18.   Cf. <u>Enz</u>., Section 205 <u>Zus</u>.

19.   Cf. <u>Enz</u>., Section 206, <u>Zus</u>.

20.   Cf. <u>Enz</u>., Section 207.

21.   Cf. <u>Enz</u>., Section 209.

22.   <u>Enz</u>., Section 212, <u>Zus</u>.

23.   Robert Louis Stevenson, last line of 'El Dorado' in <u>Virginibus Puerisque</u>.

24.   <u>Enz</u>., Section 209, <u>Zus</u>.

25.   Cf. my discussion of randomness and order in Ch. XXII of <u>The Foundations of Metaphysics in Science</u>, p. 463.

26.   Cf. Sir Arthur Eddington's discussion in The Philosophy of Physical Science (Cambridge, 1939), New Pathways in Science (Cambridge, 1935) and The Expanding Universe (Cambridge, 1933); and D.W. Sciama, The Unity of the Universe (New York, 1961).

27.   Cf. Spinoza, Ethics, Pt. I, Appendix; Augustine, Enchiridion, XI; Aquinas, Summa Theologica, I, Q 2, a 3, and Q 48, a 2.

Chapter 4

The Idea

The Idea is not just my idea; it is no mere Vorstellung in my head. On the contrary it is the Object aware of itself as truth. Till now every category has been a provisional definition of the Absolute, but the Idea, Hegel tells us, is the absolute definition -- it is what the Absolute is in and for itself -- and no longer provisional. This definition, however, applies to the Idea as such, or eminently to the absolute Idea, which is the absolute truth, not only of Idea, but of everything, because it is absolute. For the Idea has phases of its own, although they are not unqualifiedly new but are the aufgehobene moments of prior development raised to a higher plane of reality. We have already learnt that the end of the dialectical development is not separable from its process of becoming, but coalesces and unites with it, and this union of end and process is the Idea.

Consequently, it is the union of subject and object, the consummating phase of the Concept. It is the unity of body and soul, the objective manifestation of reality along with the subjective feeling and awareness of it. It is the ultimate identification of the finite with the infinite.[1]

These descriptions, especially the last, the understanding finds self-contradictory, but that is because it is mere understanding, which sticks at the level of difference and cannot get beyond the divergence of the moments which it mistakes for independent realities. But they are not independent. Each and every one of them is finite, and as such belongs to, and demands completion in, a wider whole -- hence the contradiction involved in holding them apart as independent. This wider whole is the total system of the real, now posited in its ideal phase as complete in and for itself. Only as seen in this whole, as one of its moments, as determined by its universal principle of structure, is any finite properly comprehended. This is why the Idea is the truth of every finite individual and every finite phase, and why the individual entity taken by itself and as if self-dependent (das Einzelne für sich)[2] fails to correspond to its concept. But apparently separate and independent finites, when taken together and assimilated in accordance with the principle of organization which is universal to the whole, supplement one another and harmonize in the unity of the system. This unity is the Idea, and it includes the differences sublated in itself, for it specifies itself in them and has developed through them and the progressive reconciliations of their contradictory oppositions, whose contradictions it cancels out, while it holds the moments transformed (aufgehoben) within its unified wholeness. The differences between the moments, as we are now well aware, because they depend on and define one another in their mutual supplementation, are at the same time an identity; and this identity in difference is now explicit and self-aware in the Idea.

277

The proof that the Idea is the truth is no longer to be sought in further argument.[3] It has already been given in the prior dialectical unfolding. The proof is the dialectical process out of which the Idea has emerged as the truth of everything that has preceded; and we shall presently find that what has preceded is ever-present in what has emerged, so that the Idea is its own proof and its own self-evidencing.

Hegel protests that we must not imagine finite and infinite, subjective and objective, merely to neutralize one another in the unity of the Idea. While the Idea is the whole system, which gives character, meaning and existence itself to every partial element, it is the universal substance activating the finite moments, working in and through them as process and activity, which impels them onward to self-realization in and as self-consciousness. It is, therefore, also subject; and its subjectivity includes and yet exceeds its objectivity. Its infinite phase comprehends and transfigures all its finite phases. As Hegel puts it,

> ...in the negative unity of the Idea, the infinite overreaches (übergreift) the finite, thought overreaches being, subjective overreaches objective. (Enz. Secton 215).

The real substantiality is subjectivity -- not the abstract one-sided subjectivity envisaged by the understanding (any more than its separated, one-sided, other-worldly notion of the infinite). Subject is the truth of substance and so transcends (übergreift) what is just object, although it is at the same time and always immanent in it.

It would, similarly, be a grave mistake to regard the Idea as a fixed or static identification of the opposites mentioned above, as it would be so to imagine any other identity of opposites in the dialectical series. We saw at the very outset that the identity of Being and Nothing was Becoming, and now the Idea is (as Spinoza says of it) 'not a dumb picture on a tablet', but is essentially activity, 'infinite restlessness'. It is itself process, eternally active. It is no mere end-stage or stopping point, but is the whole process and the entire gamut of its moments held together in one whole. The Idea is thus the entire Logic, and everything Hegel says of it is a description of the Logic as such.

The Idea is the truth of the Concept and so of subject and object in unison. This is the conformity of the object to its concept (as well as the reverse). It is thus 'the thinking study of things', the grasp of things in the form of their concept and the grasp of the Concept as the outcome and self-development of the thing (die Sache). And this is the description of the Logic.

278

It is the concrete, self-specified universal. The Concept specifies itself as a scale of categories dialectically related; and that scale is the Logic as a whole -- which is the Idea.

The Idea, as Reason, is the standing critique of the understanding from the vantage point of the Concept, yet it is also a development from the understanding and holds the understanding in itself as one of its moments. This again is a description of Logic as such.

The Idea is the free and realized Concept, the truth of all abstract and inadequate categories and the completion of all partial forms. Such is the Logic in its entirety. It is the <u>aufgehobene</u> process, the logical dialectic -- the ideal phase of the dialectic of experience in general.

The idea is, finally, the world come to consciousness as ideal, in and as the embodied mind -- the true union of object with subject: that is, Life.

The peculiar moments of the Idea are Life, Cognition and Will, and the Absolute Idea. The first is the immediate phase -- the Idea in being --, the second is the phase of reflection and mediation, or difference, which typically splits into two interdependent forms, theoretical and practical. The activity of theoretical and practical reason re-establishes the unity in the Absolute and brings the Logic to its conclusion -- the last step reverting to the first.[4]

Life[5]

Life is consciousness embodied and thus it is the objectified subject (Concept). It is subject and object in one as living organism. This unity is realized and expressed in several ways. First, the Concept is soul to the organism as body. It is its life, the universal principle uniting it as an organic system. On the other hand, the body particularizes this universal in its limbs and organs, which, though mutually differentiated, are functionally interlinked and related reciprocally as ends and means. So they are all integrants in a single individual -- the living organism. But its unity, which is its life, is soul, the sentience of the body in and as one, which, as sentient, permeates its physical being and is merely immediate. In Hegel's words, it is not yet free Being-for-self.[6] This somewhat obscure remark will presently become clearer, but we can see immediately how sentience represents the organic unity of the body in its functional differentiation. What we have still to explain is how this unity constitutes a subjective microcosm of the objective macrocosm, the Concept being the universal principle of both.

Hegel says the the living being is a syllogism of which the elements are themselves syllogisms, a system constituted of systems which unite in a single process of concrescence (Zusammenschliessens) of the organism with itself. Its specific functionings are sensibility, irritability (excitability or stimulability), and reproduction. Through these functions life proliferates and differentiates as Species (Gattung). The species is the universal in re; but in re it is only an sich, not yet for itself. However, in its inner aspect, it is Empfindung or sentience, and this is the inwardizing of external nature, the feeling of the body which is the product of natural evolution and upon which all natural influences impinge and are registered in feeling. Empfindung marks the emergence from nature of soul, which is the felt body, subject and object undistinguished and in one.[7] Bodily sensation (the 'lived body') is at one and the same time the registration in feeling of all the external effects upon the organism from organic and inorganic nature. It is thus the inwardization of nature in life, as soul. Thus the microcosm, which is the felt body is equally the focus of the macrocosm of Nature, and both epitomize (though each differently) the concrete universal. Concurrently feeling is the organism's self-appraisal and its appraisal of its other (the inorganic), that is, of what it lacks -- its wants and needs. it feels itself in its appetites, and they inform it of what it lacks. Its irritability impels it toward the means of supplying its needs in external nature, which it then assimilates in its effort to unify subject and object and become whole. But even at its inorganic level Nature is life in posse, it is virtually (an sich) what life is in actuality. So in its assimilation and dominion over the inorganic, life (Idea) unites only with itself -- or finds itself in its other. This is scientifically correct, for what the living organism consumes and converts into its own substance is the very material from which it has evolved and out of which it has grown.

From sensation soul advances to consciousness, and the living organism becomes overtly aware both of self and of other. In man this involves awareness of himself as man -- i.e., as species. Thus Gattung becomes für sich and is raised to universality (Allgemeinheit), which, as we now know, is in principle the ego, as Concept. Man is conscious of himself as individual organism and at the same time, in the same cognitive act, as species; and he is equally conscious of the world in his consciousness of others and of the environment he shares with them. In this way, through its teleology, sentience and self-awareness in man, life is, as Hegel says in the Greater Logic, the universality pervading the objectivity of nature.[8]

The logical idea of life (we are told in the Greater Logic) is not one derived from psychology or anthropology, even though these sciences are presupposed by Logic (as we saw at the outset). By the empirical sciences life is studied as an external object presented for observation. But logically life is the Concept itself (the ego, the identity of the self-conscious subject) embodied in being and reflecting into itself in its awareness of its other, as essence. So Hegel says that it presupposes logically only what is presupposed by the pure Concept, namely, Being and Essence.

The reproduction of individual organisms generates the species, but the survival of the species entails the death of the individual. Hegel says (in Encyclopaedia, Section 221, Zusatz) that the living being dies because it is the contradiction between the universal and the immediately existent individual. 'Im Tode erweist sich die Gattung als die Macht über das unmittelbar Einzelne.'9 The species, as universal, has actuality only in the individuals, but then only through their reproduction and proliferation; and it is a biological fact that sexual reproduction, which preserves and passes on reproductive cells, the germ-plasm, requires the aging and decay of somatic cells, so that the individual organism eventually dies. Death is the price of the survival (and equally of the evolution) of the species. But the species is relatively immortal, and the universal or concept which it embodies, when brought to consciousness, is immortal in very truth.

> For death takes toll
> Of beauty, courage, youth,
> Of all but truth.
> (John Masefield)

The Concept is brought to consciousness, as we have just observed, through sentience, which is at once bodily feeling and the registration in the organism of all the skyey influences composing the universe of Nature. Sentience is raised to consciousness in the distinction of self from not-self and the emergent awareness of the ego as the universal and original transcendental unity of apperception. In this advance from sensation to consciousness the living organism becomes aware of itself in becoming aware of its other, and in human consciousness this leads to an awareness of oneself as human; that is, as species. This then is how the Gattung becomes für sich; and its universality both is, and is consciously grasped as, universality, as I, which is Concept.

Had McTaggart not grossly misrepresented and misunderstood this phase of the dialectic of Idea, it might not have been necessary to say anything further; but he confuses the species (Gattung) with the abstract universal,10 or common property, which is never what Hegel means by it. It is the actual existent specific population, the concrete universal immanent and actual in its particulars. For Hegel the Concept is always concrete; but he does recognize abstraction involved in conscious ratiocination, especially by the understanding, which always conceives universals as abstract. In the transition from Life to Cognition, this difference is indicated.11 Gattung, species, is a concrete universal, but when it consciously becomes für sich, it is abstracted as the aspect of 'pure identity' distinct from the process by which it has been brought to consciousness, and from the diversity implicit in it. As such it is 'simple equality with self', I = I, the Concept as such. As sense develops to understanding the universal is entertained as abstract, and we have seen how Kant regarded the unity of apperception, in the first instance, as an analytic (abstract) identity. This is characteristic of reflective consciousness, and what marks the transition to Cognition is the emergence of self-awareness -- of self as universal and as species.

The Idea of Cognition[12]

The consciousness of self and other is obviously cognition, which is the second phase of the Idea. In principle it is the conscious unity of subject and object, though not at first the explicit recognition of that unity in self-consciousness. At first the Idea as object is taken to be external to its subjectivity, and the form assumed by cognition is that of the understanding, developing its knowledge by analytic and synthetic methods. Here we retrace our steps over ground already traversed under Essence and Subjective Concept, both of which are, however, retained aufgehoben in Idea.

In cognition the initial unity of subject and object can be seen first in the instinctive identification of the qualitative content of our sensuous perception, while we recognize that it is our subjective sensuous awareness, with an objective world in space and time. This is Anschauung, perceptual intuition, in which the Idea makes itself its own object, 'repelling itself as a totality from itself, and thus, in the first place, presupposing itself as an external universe.'[13] This self-diremption of the Idea Hegel refers to as its first judgement (Urteil).

The correlation of the two aspects of the Idea constitutes the reflective and finite stage of knowledge, which in its more sophisticated and scientific form is, as was said earlier, regarded as eminently objective, yet is concurrently acknowledged to be our subjective construction, and is, as Kant demonstrated, the imposition upon the sensuous content of concepts, universals or categories, which are specific forms of the universal Concept that is the unity of apperception. But in the forms of ordinary observation and science, the forms comprehended by the understanding, the separation of subject from object is still maintained. Their identity is in these forms only an sich,[14] but is not yet für sich. It is the absolute conviction of reason in science that it has the ability to make the identity actual 'and to raise its certainty to truth'; but this conviction is implicit and is not yet self-consciously for itself.

This is one way in which reason seeks to overcome the one-sidedness of the moments of the Idea, in this case, the one-sidedness of its subjectivity. The second judgement is the urge to overcome the one-sidedness of the objective moment, which is seen as merely contingent and finite (as it typically is in the reflective stage of knowledge), and the endeavour is to bring it into conformity with the subjective unity. This is now taken as the 'objective' or aim in purposive activity. So there are two drives: one towards the realization of the truth, and the other towards the realization of the good. The duality is the direct consequence of the reflective character of the correlation between the subjective and the objective moments at a stage where their identity is only implicit.

Cognition proper

As the etymology of the word makes plain, cognition is knowledge, and Hegel sets it out as method of exposition, analytic and synthetic, or inductive and deductive. Here again he is criticizing as well as expounding. The methods are those of the understanding, of the empirical and the exact sciences, and while they are given their due rank as stages in the development of knowledge, their shortcomings are also recognized and exposed. They typify a necessary and important phase in the dialectic of cognition, but are not the highest nor the final form of truth.

The distinguishing, within the felt unity of subjective experience of objects in a perceived world is characterized by Hegel as judgement, the internal differentiation of the universal. This first takes the form of acceptance or assimilation, of the material content of experience as a given datum. A second judgement consists in the self-diremption of the self-conscious ego into self and not-self. This is what Fichte presents as the positing by the ego of itself as opposed to the non-ego, and what Husserl later came to describe as the constitution of the intentional object by the transcendental subject. Thus the Idea has itself for object (Gegenstand), itself as universal -- or the Concept as object. In Hegel's words it 'exists free for itself'. It is free because it is not determined from without by another. Its other is itself and so it is its own determination.

The distinction of the extremes in these 'judgements' is the reflective relationship of essence, which presupposes the identity of the correlates, and the nisus of reason is to sublate the difference and establish the unity as the truth of the moments; and the two interdependent ways in which it does so are its theoretical and practical activities. The first is knowledge (Erkennen) and the second will.

The first phase in the development of knowledge is the differentiation of objects and the systematic interrelation of them as a world, the second is the extrusion of this world as 'external' from the subject as 'internal', leaving the latter as a 'blank tablet' to receive its 'ideas' from outside.[15] But the knowledge which takes the object for granted as a given datum is only the finite science of the understanding, which contradicts the assumption of the externality of the data by its own act of constitution, the assimilation of the content of experience

283

under categories. To the understanding with its finite outlook the infinite truth of the Idea appears only as an unattainable ideal. Yet even its finite knowledge remains under the sovereignty of the Concept expressing itself in the categories, and regulated (as Kant maintained) by ideas of reason.

Under the second heading of 'cognition' in the Encyclopaedia,[16] Hegel seems to have collated a number of critical notes on the current methods of the science and philosophy of his day, as well as of the past, without producing any very coherent picture of the way they fit into the account of knowledge he has already given. Clearly here he is criticizing rather than expounding, and what he is criticizing are procedures of the understanding. But it is only dimly apparent how these procedures follow from the general nature of the understanding or what their logical relation is to the speculative method of philosophical reason.

The analytic method proceeds from the individual to the abstract universal. Its starting point is an assumed given, which it analyses into abstract qualities, and these it elevates to abstract universality. It is essentially the inductive method of the empiricist tradition. Hegel complains that it destroys the wholeness and integrity of the concrete by its dissection, and so fails to achieve the desired goal of knowledge.

The synthetic method begins from the definition derived by means of analysis and proceeds from it through division and classification, to theorems which it demonstrates deductively (or by 'construction'). The definitions as well as the classifications are based on abstract qualities and tend therefore to be more or less arbitrary. Sometimes rival definitions are offered, when the definiendum is a concrete subject rich in characteristics, because it is difficult then to decide which aspect should be chosen as its hall-mark. Similarly, classification can be superficial and otiose unless it is based on the essential nature of the objects concerned. Demostrative proof, along with the definition above mentioned, is most suited, and succeeds best, in the abstract sciences, like geometry and algebra. But none of these methods is appropriate to philosophy, because they rest dogmatically on unexamined assumptions, and when they are used by philosophers they produce at best excessive formalism (as in the case of Spinoza), or at worst execrable pedantry (as in the case of Wolff). In other sciences than geometry the strict continuity of deduction tends to break down because the concrete nature of the subject-matter presents obstacles to the understanding. These are commonly overcome by making breaks in the strict reasoning and then papering over the gaps by appeal to arbitrary assumptions or the capricious introduction of extraneous material.

The transition from cognition to will[17] in the Encyclopaedia seems unnecessarily obscure and inadequate -- unnecessarily, because one would have expected Hegel to demostrate their intimate interdependence, of which what he writes elsewhere shows him to be fully aware. After all, knowing is not just observing and ratiocinating. It is not mere theory, but also involves practice, as the experimentation of the natural sciences testifies. More than this, knowledge, both every-day and scientific, is applied in the practical pursuits of living, and theory becomes, or is itself, just as much technology. Knowledge, as well as skill, is acquired by practice, and successful practice is impossible without knowledge. Morality is the fruit of reflection as well as of custom, and without insight and wisdom it must fail of its objective. Hence cognition is implicitly and becomes explicitly volition. Knowledge, it has been said, is for the sake of action.

What Hegel does say at this point is that the process from the assumed tabula rasa of Empiricism to objective knowledge (as for Kant) is the progressive assimilation of the allegedly external datum, sensuously perceived, to the subjective certainty of the ideal. But as the ideal remains beyond the limits of cognitive achievement, the theoretical endeavour to impose it upon the material of knowledge is transposed into the practical effort to impose it upon the recalcitrant, immediately presented, actuality in the midst of which the subject finds himself. This is the position of Kant and Fichte, whose viewpoint is here being presented. Quite clearly, Hegel has them in mind, and he refers to them explicitly in the Zusatz to Section 234. Precisely because the ideal of unifying subject and object was, in Fichte's view, theoretically unattainable, he contended that the very task of attaining ultimate truth is imposed upon the understanding by practical reason and is a practical imperative.

Volition

'The subjective Idea, as simple content, determined in and for itself, is the Good.' (Enz., Section 233).

This cryptic statement is difficult to interpret, and the sentences which follow in this section do not elucidate it. But it may be taken to mean that the fulfilment of the Idea, as self-activating spirit, in its own self-knowledge, is the Good. It is subjective in as much as it is enjoyed contemplation of the infinite whole, νόησις νοήσεως. One is also put in mind of Plato's Idea of the Good, and of Spinoza's teaching that the highest good for man is the perfection of the intellect, which is achieved only in the knowledge and love of God, the amor intellectualis Dei. This is really the Absolute Idea, but here it is considered simply as the object of desire and the ultimate goal of all finite endeavour. As truth, under cognition, was provisionally regarded as merely theoretical, so here good is taken simply as the practical end. It is, moreover, also subjective as motive of action, the good conceived as the realization of the rational ideal -- the Kantian good will.

285

Initially good is the end (Zweck) which ought to be brought about by moral effort and practical action, the agency of which is will. And the nisus of will runs in the opposite direction to that of cognition, in that will seeks to determine the world according to its own (subjective) aim, whereas cognition seeks to conform its knowledge to the world. Finite will, on the one hand, takes the immediatey presented state of affairs to be of no (or of scant) value (hat einerseits die Gewissheit der Nichtigkeit des vorausgestzten Objects), and, on the other hand, acknowledges its aim, the good, to be a subjective ideal in contrast to the presupposed subsistence of the presented object. And this subjectivity is indispensable to it, for if the good were actual and not only ideal (what ought to be but is not), effort and volition would become unnecessary and will would be altogether abrogated. Accordingly, the implication of finite will is that its end should never be realized. Consequently, it is self-contradictory, for its own activation presupposes the opposite. Its finitude is the source of this internal conflict, the resolution of which can only be gained by passing to a higher dialectical phase. This is the position represented by the ethical theories of Kant and Fichte, according to which the self-fulfilment of human rational nature is impossible for finite agents, for it requires endless striving, ad infinitum, for its accomplishment. Kant uses this implication as a ground for belief in immortality. But Hegel resolves the contradiciton by uniting the end with the process, the goal with the endeavour to attain it, and by identifying the realization of the Ideal with the continuing activity of its becoming.

For the appearance of insufficiency and the impossibility of fulfilment is, as we saw earlier,[18] an illusion. The end is in truth eternally realized in its perpetual struggle to realize itself. Sound moral theory finally recognizes the Good to be the good life, the constant endeavour of the good will, the unceasing striving to overcome evil, the continuing and unfailing love of one's neighbour, which does not consist in any single act or any final state of affairs but is an established disposition of mind and will and a persistent on-going activity. This goes hand in hand with the recognition of the identity of this activity with the knowledge and love of God ('What ye do unto the least of these, ye do it unto me')[19] and the atonement of finite and infinite in the contemplation of this truth.

In this consummation practical and theoretical reunite. The realization of the end as Idea is at once the attainment of truth and the actualization of value. The goal of practical endeavour is seen as the apprehension of the truth that the Idea is actual in the objective world. In this way the one-sidedness and the finitude of the merely theoretical as well as that of the purely practical are overcome and both attain their objective in the Absolute Idea.

Cognition and Volition as treated here have not been simply a repetition of, on the one hand, the subjective Concept, and, on the

286

other, the teleological Object. They are both of them activities of the living unity of subject and object which is Idea. Because this unity is actualized in them, they display themselves as the truth of the earlier categories, in which they were anticipated, and which are now recapitulated in more concrete and aufgehobene realization.

Throughout these sections we see Hegel, as before, following the dialectic along its self-prescribing course, and in so doing criticizing the inadequacy of the forms in which it has manifested itself historically. The inadequacies of the understanding and the frustrations of finite willing are neither more nor less than incidents of their finitude, which marks them nevertheless as necessary moments in the dialectical process through which the Absolute Idea incessantly realizes itself. In the history of mankind and of human thought these inadequate forms have been expressed and are transcended only in the contemplation of the Infinite and Absolute as it occurs in Art, Religion and Philosophy, and even there only in their most highly developed forms. For, as we are shortly to reaffirm, the Absolute is no static, fixed and separable perfection detachable from the process of its self-generation, and in these ultimate phases of the self-realization of Spirit dialectic is still alive and in process.

The Absolute Idea

The unity of the subjective with the objective Idea, of the practical with the theoretical, is the Concept of the Idea -- the concept of which the object is the Idea, and the idea of which is the Object. In other words, the Object or whole, come to consciousness of itself (Concept) as Idea, is the Absolute. It is the absolute self-awareness, the thought which thinks itself. This is the final philosophical speculative phase of knowledge and thought, at which both theory and practice aim, and to which they lead, uniting in this self-identity to consummate the self-conscious oneness of life as objective subject.

This is the infinite whole -- truly infinite, not as endlessly extensive nor forever beyond the finite, but as self-subsistently whole and all-inclusive, sublating the finite in its transcendent unity and consolidating its truth and value. If so, the critic asks, how can we (and Hegel), who are finite, know that it is so? How can the finite encompass the infinite and the absolute? The answer is that we could know nothing at all, indeed we could have not the slightest inkling of the nature or the being of the Absolute, if it were not immanent in us (as finite beings). Our knowledge is the immanence of it in us and is at every stage implicitly knowledge of it. To know the infinite and how it becomes infinite is not necessarily to know it absolutely as it knows itself. Our knowledge is one of its major moments: life as cognizant, the Concept emerging and actualizing itself in the Object. To become aware of ourselves fully is, therefore, to become aware ipso facto of the infinity immanent within us, and to be aware of that is to know that it transcends our finitude, supports our being, constitutes the truth of our knowledge, and effects our redemption from the short-coming and evil which our finitude entails.

This is the contradiciton between finite and infinite which the Absolute Idea absorbs and resolves; and it is this that is expressed by art, religion and philosophy, each in its own peculiar form. Critics, like Kierkegaard, therefore, who deride Hegel because he professed to comprehend the Absolute, are misguided, and are blinded by the restriction imposed upon thought and insight by the understanding. Their criticism fails completely to grasp the nature and principle of the dialectic, and to appreciate the significance of Aufhebung.

Nor is Hegel's professed knowledge of the Absolute anything exorbitant or inordinately presumptuous. As we are about to find, it does not exceed what he has already thus far established. The highest claim that he makes, both here and at the end of the Geistesphilosophie, is no more than that made by Aristotle in the Metaphysics, whom Hegel explicitly quotes. It is the assurance that God, the infinite and absolute being, is the pure form of the world, pure activity, the realization of all that, in the world and in us, is merely potential -- He is absolute self-knowledge.

Another misconception that must be avoided is that, because the Logic culminates in the Absolute Idea, it has said the last word that Wissenschaft has to offer. As we shall presently see, it is the last word in one sense only, but by its very finality it proves also to be the first. Yet it is the first aufgehoben and transformed, mediated and raised to a higher plane. It therefore burgeons out into further philosophical sciences, in a manner shortly to be explained.

In the Greater Logic Hegel writes of the theoretical and the practical Idea:

> Each of these by itself is still one-sided, holding in itself the genuine Idea only as a sought-for beyond and an unattainable goal, each, therefore, is a synthesis of striving which both has, but also has not, the Idea in it...[21]

The object of the intellect in science and philosophy is to comprehend the world and our place in it. In such knowledge we seek intellectual satisfaction. But this is not sufficient by itself, for its urge is inspired by the need to understand our own place and destiny in the scheme of things, and to conduct our lives in accordance with the conception that we form of that destiny. If we do not find ourselves in harmony with the universe; if it appears to us as a blind, physical mechanism, indifferent to our 'immortal longings' -- a world into which we have been fortuitously 'thrown' -- we are frustrated and become despondent,

288

and our intellectual accomplishment conflicts with our practical aspiration. This, in the main, is the situation in which the science and philosophy of the understanding lands us, abandoning us either to despair or to a blind faith in some supernatural salvation through the inscrutible will of a hidden and unknowable divinity. The aim of our practical endeavour is equally the pretext for our intellectual search, and neither can be fully satisfied unless by the same goal. Yet, though we pursue this ultimately common end, our finite efforts fail to reach it. Their ideal is the union of intellect and will and would be their common satisfaction. That is what the absolute Idea actually is; but while they thus have it in them, they also do not, because they come short. 'Each of them by itself is still one-sided, holding in itself the genuine Idea only as a sought-for beyond and unattainable goal.'

Kant's thesis was that the Idea, in consequence, was only an ideal, remaining subjective, the actuality of which is at best a postulate of practical reason. It remains, for him, wholly transcendent, as a perpetual 'ought to be', of which we can never say with intellectual assurance that it is.

But if we have followed consistently the course of the dialectic, we must be convinced that this cannot possibly be the case. As we have already been told, it is too late at this stage to ask for a proof that (as Hegel has it) 'the absolute Idea alone is being, imperishable life, self-knowing truth, and all truth.'[22] We do not now have to cast about for special reasons why we should believe that the Absolute is actual and real. For the whole course of the dialectic has proved and produced this result, and we have reached it precisely by developing the implications and potentialities of what we took initially to be immediate certainty and reality. It is only because the absolute Idea is immanent in our consciousness that it becomes the ideal of our intellectual and practical drives and expresses itself in them; and it could not be so immanent if it were not the actual whole of which they are essential moments. Both its immanence and its transcendence are conditions jointly of its being conceived as an ideal.

Moreover, we do attain it in some degree, so far as we experience practical and intellectual satisfaction in art, religion and philosophy, the content of all of which is the same, namely, the absolute Idea. The business of philosophy, Hegel tells us, is to cognize the absolute Idea in the various shapes that it takes: the modes of its existence as Nature and Spirit, and the forms of its self-apprehension in art and religion. Philosophy has the same object and content as these, but the form of its cognition is self-conscious thought (the Concept itself) and it is, therefore, the purest and the highest form. And as self-apprehension is the peculiar and most fully adequate mode of existence of the Idea -- what gives it 'a determinate being appropriate to itself' -- it is philosophy. In short, form and content coincide, and in the absolute Idea they are one and the same.

The content therefore is thought thinking itself, and so it is the whole range of its own Denkbestimmungen in its complete self-unfolding. The whole content of the Logic is concentrated and integrates in the absolute Idea. The entire scale of its moments and phases is grasped as one transparent unity, in the light of which every element, each phase, each category or specific difference, receives its true significance; and without this illumination any isolated category or element is falsified, if not left entirely meaningless. In Spinoza's terminology the absolute Idea is that through which everything is and is conceived, and without which nothing can be or be conceived.

In this luminous totality there is no transition. Its becoming and its mediation are wholly sublated. It is a timeless analytic-synthetic discursus. Yet this has been a feature of every unification of opposites since the first, in which we saw 'being does not pass over, but has passed over, into nothing and nothing into being.' In the absolute Idea all the categories sind übergegangen. So the Idea is once more immediate, all its mediation being suspended within it. It is the timeless flash of insight of which Plato writes in the Seventh Letter -- the insight in which all connexions are revealed at once, like the 'Aha! erlebnis' that the Würzburg psychologists found characteristic of thinking when all the disconnected bits and pieces of a problem suddenly cohere in the mind of the thinker and reveal its solution.[23] It is like the new vision which dawns unheralded after deep thought upon a vital question. It casts a fresh light upon everything that was previously familiar but lacked the significance that it now gains. It is Plato's synoptic vision of all time and all existence, which bursts upon the philosopher at a certain juncture in his reflections, supervening upon the dialogue in the soul. It is the scientia intuitiva which Spinoza ranks as the highest form of knowing, immediate in its intuitiveness but discursive in its comprehension of the total context of its object. It is what Schelling called intellectual intuition. This new light suffuses the whole content of the Logic which is now revealed as the total content as well as the characteristic form of the Logical Idea.[24]

In Chapters XIX and XX of his Study of Hegel's Logic, G.R. Mure calls in question the possibility of 'a simple and final philosophy of the Absolute, a flawless dialectic,' in which finite and infinite unite and are reconciled in a luminous, transitionless whole, such as is finally claimed in Hegel's conclusion. His critique, however, does not question this possibility in principle. Rather he asserts (with Hegel) its inevitability (Cf. op. cit., Ch. XIX, 5.01, 5.1, 5.11). What he questions explicitly is whether, in human experience, oppositions such as space and the supra-spatial, time and eternity, the empirical and the a priori can completely coincide, or if they persist as an insuperable obstacle to the final consummation. He argues closely and cogently for the latter alternative -- and for human experience, surely he is right. Because human experience is finite experience, and in the Hegelian system is at most a superior phase in the dialectic of Absolute Spirit, not its consummation. Nevertheless, that consummation is immanent in it, and unless it were, human experience would not be what it is, would not display the contradictions that it does, and could not attain the level of insight that Hegel attributes to it and that his own philosophy evinces. The claim is not that human experience and philosophical insight are absolute, for only the Absolute itself could deploy a 'flawless dialectic' as a unique, processless, act of self-illumination. But the position is inescapable that, human experience being what it is, the actuality of this consummation cannot in the final issue be denied or doubted, because it is and must be immanent in human aspirations for those aspirations to have the character and significance they do.

However, we must repeat and insist that, in calling the absolute consummation processless, we are not denying that it is discursive. It is always, eternally and ineradicably activity. Of this Mure has no doubt. But activity is discursion, which preserves, in the whole that it comprehends, the detail of its diversity and the moment (though not the transience) of its developmental progression. Hegel loses no opportunity and never fails to insist upon this indispensable necessity of the dialectic. The announcement, however triumphant, of the unity of the opposites, is always one-sided. Their opposition is as essential to the whole as is their identity. It is just this fact that is meant by sublation (Aufheben), and yet it is just this indispensable preservation of the moment of difference that Mure's argument seems to overlook, in its persistent effort to demonstrate the ultimate impossibility of what he repeatedly refers to as total sublation in a 'flawless dialectic'.

Mure demonstrates with admirable lucidity the paradox inherent in spatial perception, which requires necessarily the localization in space, relative to the perceived object, of the knowing subject, without whom there can be no 'here' nor 'there' nor dimensionality. Yet in this very localization, the presence of the subject, as subject of the Erlebnis, is what gives unity, system and wholeness to the perception and its characteristic self-internality. Thus, almost incredibly, the supra-spatial character of the apperception must itself be located in the space perceived. No degree of idealization of the spatial object can wholly overcome this self-contradictory character of the perceptual synthesis.

Further, the very nature of space itself, being essentially self-externality, excludes system, and yet demands it. The self-externality persists even in the interconnexion of elements, for complete concentration and interpenetration would annihilate extensity. But this is the very nature of spatial (or any form of) system -- that it is unity in and through difference. The absence of system in sheer self-externality is the dissipation of extensity itself. Total externality of relations abolishes relation altogether. Consequently, self-externality requires interconnexion in order to be self-external; just as concentration and interpenetration requires diversity in order to unify.

Were it otherwise there could be no whole, neither system nor dialectic, and Aufheben would be meaningless.

The localization of the subject in perception, however, is precisely the manifestation, at the level of developed organism, of the immanence of spirit in nature. It is incident upon a particular phase of the dialectic, through which the Idea, immanent in Nature as a whole, brings itself to consciousness, through the living organization of the organism. Nature is erinnert as sentience, which is ordered in the synthesis of its manifold diversity by the activity of the finite subject. Because it is thus emergent in the spatio-temporal, material, organism, and precisely as so emergent, spirit is finite; but because it is the immanence in the finite of Absolute Spirit, the activity of which is essentially ideal and eternal, the finite subject transcends its own localization in its own perception of it, sublates it in successive degrees of idealization, and ultimately in its comprehensive envisioning of the whole system dialectically issuing as Absolute Spirit.

This idealization, however, cannot at any stage relinquish the moment of difference in its progressive unification of itself as its own object, and of its object as itself. The difference is indeed sublated, but that means preserved and transformed as well as cancelled, not totally abolished.

With like elegance, Mure displays the progressive sublation of the transience of self-annihilating time, as it advances towards development and approaches eternity, recovering thereby das ruhige Nebeneinander of space, and becoming the medium of duration in its very transience. Yet in this advance, Mure argues, both time and space persist and are integral even to the eternal and the supra-spatial.

Similarly in human judging and inferring there is temporal movement which cannot be eliminated. Perception is prior to, while it is also simultaneous with, imagination and both are presupposed, at once temporally and logically, in judgement, which similarly precedes and is nevertheless retained in the inference developed from and drawn out of it as premiss. Paradoxically the sequence is at once temporal and logical (and, as logical, atemporal or eternal). Still, in its logical aspect the presuppositional relationship parallels the temporal and neither are wholly transcended. Thus, says Mure, 'we appear bound to conclude that the spatio-temporal moment cannot be sublated wholly in a flawless dialectic, if that dialectic is in any sense to express human experience.'[25]

Surely, however, the persistence in development of temporal sequence is resolved in the Aufhebung, in the developed product, of the process itself -- the sublation of its mediation, not utterly sublimated, but absorbed and preserved, even in its sequential relations. If this were not so, development would not be development, of which the very definition is its sublation of its own process. Eternity is a mere empty abstraction without time, as duration is without succession. Time (Plato told us)[26] is the moving image of eternity, which again is duration sub specie aeternitatis. And Hegel says both, 'Die Zeit ist der Begriff selbst, der da ist...deswegen erscheint der Geist notwendig in der Zeit, und er erscheint solange in der Zeit als er nicht seinen reinen Begriff erfasst, d.h. nicht die Zeit tilgt.'[27] and, 'Aber die Zeit selbst ist in ihrem begriff ewig.'[28] The sublation of time in eternity must preserve the moment of difference which is the element of succession, if only because succession itself is the resolution of the contradiction between the mutual incompatibility and the mutual interdependence of the successive phases (infancy excludes maturity, but only by sublating development from childhood does the adult mature). The negation of negation, which Aufheben effects, is not the total submersion or suppression of the first negation, but is its development. The opposites which are reconciled are, in the reconciliation, still preserved. This is no less true of process and end than of any other opposition.

What then is Mure really demanding as total sublation? How should the spatio-temporal moment be 'wholly sublated'? If that meant 'absorbed and superseded without trace', spatio-temporality would cease to be a moment altogether. How then could the dialectic be flawless -- or how could there be any dialectic at all? Neither dialectic nor its product is flawed by difference. Without that its unity is not flawless but eviscerated; it is in fact destroyed. A flawless dialectic properly understood is one in which difference is completely aufgehoben without loss, and so completely retained, while transfigured in this retention to unity and wholeness.

If this must be true of wholeness and dialectic in general, it must be true of Absolute Spirit, as of the absolute Idea. It could much less fail to be true of human experience, which is inevitably finite, as inherent in a natural organism, inevitably spatio-temporal. What, in human experience, is aufgehoben is never finally sublated, its dialectic is never quite flawless, the understanding is never wholly transcended. Human reason is but the prefiguration of divine reason, the immanence of which in human experience is, nevertheless, the guarantee of truth as the genuine goal of human knowledge and of the validity and vitality of the dialectic.

In principle the same reply is appropriate to Mure's very complex yet careful argument in the next chapter for the ineradicable persistence of the empirical throughout the dialectic, and its failure to unite it completely with the a priori, or fully to sublate the opposition between them. The argument is very subtle and intricate, so that to do it adequate justice would require too long a digression. It would also require some anticipation of what is to be said presently about the transition from the Idea to Nature. Of the crucial importance of this transition in Hegel's philosophy Mure is clearly and acutely aware, and in paragraphs 5.3 and 5.4 he states succinctly the true principle of Hegel's view. But his central contention seems to be that the logic itself is to the end 'tainted' by the empirical because the categories of pure thought can neither be divorced from their embodiment in the Begriffsbestimmungen of Nature and Concrete Spirit, nor yet wholly and satisfactorily identified with them. The philosophy of Nature is confessedly dependent upon the empirical sciences for its content, and they are not only empirical but are the product and exercise of the understanding; nor are their theories complete or final. Therefore their sublation in philosophic thought can never be total and they cannot be wholly reduced to pure Denkbestimmungen. Much the same is true of Geistesphilosophie, Rechtsphilosophie and the philosophy of History. All this Hegel not merely admits but insists. Mure quotes several passages which make Hegel's disclaimer of finality in these spheres so obvious as to silence all cavil concerning his philosophical arrogance.[29] But if this is acknowledged, and the Logic is recognized as the system of absolute knowing, in which concrete spirit finds its culminating activity, the Logic is tainted with the contingency and empiricism of the other philosophical sciences which it can never wholly shed.

The dependence on empirical science of Naturphilosophie is declared and unavoidable, for the philosophy of Nature is nothing other than the interpretation of the results of the empirical sciences, and of the world-view they provide, in the light of the conclusion of the Logic as the identity of subject and object. The other philosophical sciences are in like case, as they are reflection upon human action and human history. Hegel's thesis is that the Idea manifests and embodies itself both in Nature and History, bringing itself, with them, to consciousness, through their process, as subject and object in one. This unity in the final outcome is the Absolute, but it is not absolute in the course of the process nor in our finite consciousness. Nevertheless it is the immanence of the Absolute in both that makes us capable of the awareness of the necessity of the consummation and its implication in our experience.

Science and history are empirical because mankind is not omniscient. The contingent, provisional and empirical character of the sciences, of political action and of historical knowledge are necessary features of finite being. They cannot therefore be wholly transcended in finite experience. But the dialectic of finite experience and knowledge is such that it implies and requires the ultimate transcendence of the merely empirical in the Absolute. Even so, the Absolute is no mere Jenseits. There is no pure and unadulterated a priori apart from all a posteriori content. The unity of the Absolute qua Absolute must be differentiated; for it is not so much transcendent beyond the empirical, as the perfect union of the empirical (which from the beginning is never pure, or crassly hyletic) with the rational.

The Logic is that phase of human thought in which finite experience of the world and of human affairs becomes aware of itself as the self-awareness of the world through human experience, as well as of the dialectical process by which this awareness is brought about. It is thus the thinking study of things, in and as dialectical, in pure categorial, form. In it the contingent and empirical aspect is not lost, but is thought. It is seen to be implicit thought (an sich), become self-aware (für sich). The empirical is aufgehoben, but not utterly volatilized away. If it were, the absolute Idea would not be the concrete, but at best an abstract, universal.

What Mure seems to be requiring of human experience is that it should cease to be human, and of the Absolute, that it should transcend beyond the finite and cease to be concrete. Yet he knows full well, and knows that Hegel knew, that this is a futile and self-defeating demand, for absolute knowing must be at once both a priori and a posteriori, both form and content, both subject and object, both end and process; and the 'flawlessness' of its dialectic consists precisely in the fact that nothing of the finite, the contingent and the empirical, is lost in its ultimate Aufheben, not that it is dissolved away in a contentless and unmediated transcendence.

It follows that the end must overlap with the process, not partially but altogether. It is the process held in suspension, recapitulated but all at once, as Mozart said he experienced a symphony once he had ordered and united its themes as a single structure.

So Hegel declines to 'declaim senselessly' (Gehaltlos deklamieren) about the absolute Idea, and simply goes back over the whole ground and course of the logical movement, now showing all the moments in their mutual relation and interdependence as a single whole brought to complete awareness of itself as its differentiations (its other).

Method

The method of Logic (or of any science) is its formal aspect. In the case of logic it can be set out diagrammatically in several different ways:

(1)   as a movement from immediate to the mediated and thence to the mediated immediate sublating mediacy;

(2)   as a movement from the implicit (an sich) to the explicit (für sich), and thence to the self-conscious totality (an und für sich);

(3)   as a movement from identity to differentiation, and thence to identity in and through difference;

(4)   as a movement from universal to specification or particularization, and thence to the self-specified concrete individual;

(5)   as a process from intuition (perception) to reflection, and thence to rational comprehension (intellectual intuition); or, finally,

(6)   as transition from being, through essence, to the concept.

In the Encyclopaedia, Hegel recalls the moments as this major triad, Being, Essence and Concept. But now we see Being as the Concept implicit, the immediate universal which differentiates itself (urteilt sich). It is the concrete self-differentiating universal which is implicitly, and becomes explicitly, Concept, through its own reflection into itself as Essence. We now see why the immediacy of Being and its showing in Essence is only seeming -- a Schein which is sublated and abolished in the self-consciousness of the Concept. At the same time it becomes apparent that these categories and the method of their exposition are only forms in which the content of the absolute Idea is presented. These categories are the self-specification of the Idea and together as a whole they constitute it. Content and form are one and the same.

In the Greater Logic, perhaps because here Hegel had separated, as 'Subjective Logic', the doctrine of the Concept from the doctrines of Being and Essence, as 'Objective Logic', the recapitulation is made in terms of the moments of the Concept: universality, particularity and individuality. Here Hegel gives more emphasis to, and speaks more at length about, dialectic, covering what, in the Encyclopaedia, is treated mostly in the Introduction (Sections 79-82, Wallace's Ch. VI). Here once again he expatiates on the nature and importance of Aufheben, the preservation and absorption in its other of what has been cancelled by negation and superseded in the mutual identification of opposites.

> To hold fast to the positive in its negative, to the content of the presupposition in the result, is the most important feature in rational cognition; at the same time only the simplest reflection is required to persuade one of the absolute truth and necessity of this requirement, and so far as examples of proof are concerned, the whole Logic consists thereof.[30]

He also points out that the triadic structure of the dialectic is only 'the superficial and external side' of it. What is important is the nature and function of negation as 'self-sublating contradiction' (der sich aufhebende Widerspruch), the negativity which restores the initial immediacy or simple universality -- that is to say, the negation of the first negation, which sublates the contradiction and, in reconciling the opposites, reconstitutes the universal and restores its immediacy.

296

The dialectical unity could just as well be a quadruplicity, or a duality, as a triplicity; and one must never overlook its essential unity. (a) First, immediacy is negated and sublated in a differentiated and mediate phase, and this is re-united, through negation of the negation, with its other, in a differentiated unity or a mediated immediacy. So we have triplicity. Or (b), secondly, we may consider the second phase to be the negation of the first immediacy, and the third to be the negation of the negation; then the final reconciliation will be a fourth, to make a quadruplicity. Or thirdly (c), the first phase is undifferentiated immediate identity, and the second is differentiated unity, giving a duality. Or finally (d), we take the whole movement in one as a single differentiated unity, the triad as minimum rationale, what in the very first instance we found it to be.

Indeed the Hegelian dialectic (whatever may be said of the Fichtean) is no procrustean bed prescribing fixed thesis, antithesis and synthesis. Of course these terms have appropriate applications, but what corresponds to each may very well change with point of view, and Hegel is far from always holding rigidly to the same trichotomies. He recognizes that the schema can be used in this formal and unintelligent fashion, and he accuses unnamed contemporaries of such abuse:

> Formalism has, it is true, also taken possession of triplicity and adhered to its empty schema; the shallow ineptitude and barrenness of modern philosophic construction so-called, that consists in nothing but fastening this formal schema on to everything without concept and immanent determination and using it as an external arrangement, has made the form tedious and given it an evil reputation.[31]

But misuse by others does not detract from Hegel's insistence on the proper significance and logical interdependence of the moments, and we know well enough by now that the form and relationship of the antitheses develops with the dialectic, becoming subtler and more complex as it proceeds.

The Problems of Error and Evil

The apprehension in absolute Idea of the totality in one processless act of analytic-synthetic discursion is of paramount importance for the solution of two of the most difficult and persistent of metaphysical problems. The problem of error and the problem of evil are not really two; they are the same problem in two aspects, one in the context of knowledge and the other in that of practice. Plato wrestled with the first in the Meno and in the Theaetetus and the Sophist, and he recognized its intimate connexion with negation. The second has a long history going back (if one omits the Book of Job) to Augustine and Aquinas.[32]

297

A complete and satisfactory discussion of these problems would fill a large volume. All that can be done here is to indicate how the solution is held in the Hegelian dialectic and in the concept of the Idea.[33]

If knowledge is the truth, and what is not true is false, if the truth is cognition of the real, and what is not real is nothing, then cognition of the false, or error, must be impossible, for cognition can derive no content from the non-existent. Or, if knowledge is of truth and error is mere opinion about what is real, how are we to distinguish one from the other? As Plato argues in the Theatetus, opinion could not be mere confusion, for we cannot confuse something we know with something else that we also know, nor with something we do not know, least of all could we confuse two things of which we knew neither. Or again, if error were a lack of correspondence between our ideas and reality, and the sole medium of our knowledge of reality is our ideas, how can we ever discover whether or when the latter correspond to the former.

To these difficulties the Hegelian may find a solution by insisting that truth and error are relative features in the dialectic, error being relative abstraction and truth relative concretion. He would deny that truth and error are mutually exclusive any more than being and nothing, and he would deny that truth depends on correspondence between ideas and any external, unknowable Ding an sich, but would declare it to be the whole which is absolutely concrete. So far all might be well, but the problem is not yet solved. If the whole is the truth and the abstracta are moments in the whole, are they not preserved and perpetuated as error? If the truth is generated through the dialectical process and the end is not separable from the course of its development, does not the truth itself become infected with error? Even if we do separate end from process, considering the latter a necessary but not a sufficient condition of the former, we are still committed to the occurrence of the process, fraught as it is with errors of differing degree. So the total reality must involve ineradicable error -- and we are asserting that it is this totality which is the truth. Here then is a final contradiction and one that seems to resist all attempts at reconciliation of the opposites.

In this last form the problem of error is translated into the problem of evil, if only because error is itself a form of evil. Further, as Socrates and Plato insisted, error is the root of all moral delinquency.[34] But that is not all, because, it will be maintained, evil is not confined to human immorality, however deplorable that may be, but extends to natural disasters and includes the widespread suffering among the lower animals, as well as among men, for which no rational pretext or justification can be found.

That all such evils occur nobody would wish to dispute, and to argue that they are merely apparent and unreal would seem both stupid

298

and callous. To any who have suffered evil its reality is manifest. But what problem does it really present? Could we not, perhaps, simply say that evil is a fact, that it brooks no final remedy, and that the world is a vale of tears from which there is no escape? Such a view need not be unmitigated pessimism, for one might still point to forms of compensation and some means of consolation. But no such resignation can satisfy the Hegelian philosopher, for Hegel has maintained that the real is the rational and the rational the real. He has also identified truth with value, so that the absolute Idea is as much the object of desire as it is the ideal of reason. Yet he denies that it is <u>ein Jenseits,</u> or an unrealized ideal. It is said to be eternally complete and actual, good throughout and fully realized. How then is this rational whole to accommodate the irrationality of error and evil? The lower reaches of the dialectic which fall short of the Idea are nevertheless essential to it. They are phases and constituents which cannot be argued away. They are its moments, which are <u>aufgehoben,</u> preserved in and incorporated into its wholeness. Can it then escape contamination, and if so how?

Once more the key to the solution of the problem is the proper understanding of <u>Aufheben.</u> The reality of evil and error are certainly not altogether to be denied, at least in one sense. They occur, they actually make themselves felt in experience. But experience is itself dialectical, and in another sense they are, as Hegel frequently asserts, null and void (<u>nichtig</u>). That they are real in some sense is established by the fact that differentiation is an indispensable aspect and a necessary phase of the totality. The Concept is particular as well as universal and individual; and differentiation, particularity, involves negation and opposition. Except as particularized the universal is an empty abstraction, and is neither true nor good. Perfection in the full and proper sense of the word is concretion and that certainly does and must include difference, negation and contradiction. There is thus a necessary sense in which these features are actual. Moreover, it is these features which in themselves are evil and error, or upon which evil and error are incident, for negation and difference are characteristic of the finite, and the finite is what is deficient, what comes short of the whole, and so is abstract, is in some degree false and likewise evil. But these finite features (or differentiations) are not <u>in themselves</u> real or self-subsistent. Their claim to be so is spurious. Their stability and subsistence (<u>Bestehen</u>) consists only in their being moments in a whole which transcends their finite limitations. Pain and suffering are but the way in which contradiction and deficiency are felt, and are, however intense and unconscionable, always the incidents of finitude. Moreover, pain is not identical with evil any more than pleasure is identical with good. It is our attitude and response to suffering that is good or bad, not the pain itself. We may overcome it and rise superior to it, or we may succumb to it, and whichever we do depends upon the degree of our finitude and the extent to which we can transcend it. The evil and error reside in the degree of our failure, but

299

in our success they disappear. In the Absolute all finitude is transcended, although it is still a necessary moment. Yet, as moment, it is not self-subsistent and is real only as supplemented and aufgehoben.

In the absolute Idea the conflicts and contradictions of the finite differences are aufgehoben. Their positive contributions are retained but their contradictions and clashes are cancelled and transfigured; for the positive contents are mutually interdependent and each contributes something essential. As such, as moments, they are good, not evil, true, not false, so long as their dependence and momentary character is not overlooked. In the larger whole their differences complement one another and their oppositions and contradictions are reconciled, their abstractness is filled out and made concrete, and their shortcoming is supplemented and removed. It is only from the point of view of the finite that our vision is disoriented and the evil pains and frustrates. When seen from the viewpoint and in the light of the whole, the positive contribution of each element alone is illuminated and the shadows vanish. The partiality, abstraction, falsity and deficiency of the finite is then recognized as mere seeming (Schein). Error and evil, the incidents of abstraction and finitude, are abrogated and only the positive contribution proves to be substantial. But this transcendent vision transfiguring the finite supervenes only at the end of the dialectical progress, where it occurs all at once and, as Hegel avers, without process. The differences are not eliminated, but now are affirmed in mutual harmony. The Idea is still judgement (Urteil), still involves distinction, but it tolerates no separation of its moments. And in their mutual dependence and ultimate unity they are not in conflict but belong together, supplement and support one another and shed the one-sidedness which afflicts them in finite separation. The complete, concrete, timeless and single totality of the absolute Idea abolishes this finitude, while it transforms it and transmogrifies the finite contents in their union.

Two points must be remembered: error and evil are incident upon the finite, which being finite comes to be and passes away in time, so they are essentially temporal; whereas the absolute Idea, in which all finites are sublated and unified, comprehends all time and is the eternal concept in which all time is superseded. Secondly, the Idea is one single unity in which all differences are united self-consciously and in a single intuition as one whole. In it the defectiveness of the finite moments has vanished and is wholly surmounted. The prophet Habakkuk proclaims of God, 'Thine eyes are too pure to behold evil', for God is the infinite and eternal being in whom evil has evaporated in the transfiguration of the finite into glory.

What has vanished is only the seeming and the apparent ill, not the substantive content of the actual differentiations. They appear as error and are felt as evil only when regarded as self-subsistent in their separateness and mutual isolation. As moments of the whole they are features of its own self-positing and are both necessary and real. They are necessary because without them the Absolute would not be absolute and perfection would be less than perfect. A god who does not create is not omnipotent; and one who creates cannot but create finite creatures. And as his creation is the manifestation of his own nature (his power) it must comprise every degree of finitude, in the words of Augustine and Spinoza, 'from the highest to the lowest'; and where there is finitude there is of necessity the possibility and the actuality of evil. But they are seen and felt as such only from the viewpoint of the finite, and what is evil to us, who see only 'through a glass darkly' is transfigured and abolished in the infinite totality. The existence of evil in the world is thus no obstacle to belief in the reality of an infinite God, infinite in both power and goodness, as has been alleged by those who rest agnosticism or atheism on the ineradicable obtrusion of evil upon our consciousness and its undeniable occurrence in fact.

Can this sort of argument dispose of the excruciating evils that oppress so many of us and arise so repeatedly in human history? It can so long as we remember, first, that our experience is finite experience, in which we do not grasp things in the context of the absolute whole; and, secondly, that the degree of intensity of pain and the enormity of evil is proportional to the degree of this finitude. Does the anguish and frustration that is undoubtedly experienced then count for nothing in the whole which comprehends all finite aspects? That whole, we must not forget, is infinite and eternal, whereas anguish and frustration belong only to the finite as finite. In the whole the finite is sublated becoming a moment and losing its apparent (and illusory) self-subsistence. Anguish and frustration are passions, whereas the Absolute is pure activity. Even in our own finitude we are capable of transcending and overcoming the deepest anguish and the most acute distress, an achievement which we acclaim as the virtue of courage and which transforms the evil into triumphant victory. It is the blinkered view of the understanding, which persists in isolating its objects, that creates evil and which then, seeing it as such, deprecates it. But all this is left behind and cancelled, while the true content is transfigured and transformed, in the rational grasp of the absolute Idea. Here then the anguish and frustration do count for nothing, they are null and void (nichtig); here there is no error, for the necessity of the finite moments is set in its rightful perspective and they rank as legitimate differences within the transcending unity. Passion and pain are transcended likewise, for neither in itself is evil, but only the response which is made to them by finite minds. Seen in their true context, as features of a transcendent and transfiguring whole, they no longer corrupt, frustrate, or debilitate.

Evil and error, we may therefore conclude, are only incidents upon finite being, and are progressively overcome in the course of the dialectic, which as process is sublated in the absolute Idea, and is transfigured so as to illuminate not only the positive content of the finite moments but also their distorting isolation; and in that illumination both the error and the illusion of evil are eliminated.

Transition to Nature

The absolute Idea has now transpired as the complete truth of Being, and reveals itself as its ultimate substance and true essence. It is what was all along immanent in it and what Being implicitly was from the start. We have reached the Idea by developing this implication in Being, so in this regard Being is the presupposition of the Idea. That it is so is of special importance for what is to follow. On the other hand, however, as the Idea is really what Being in essence is, the Idea is presupposed by being, and that too is important for the sequel. The dialectic has brought us full circle, at the end we are also at the beginnning, for the absolute Idea recovers the immediacy lost in its self-differentiation in Being and Essence. Yet the immediacy is achieved by sublating the mediating moments in the unitary intuition which is equally discursive thought. It is, therefore, no purely abstract immediacy, but is the concrete immediacy of the perceived world, an immediate which is also a completely schematized (or gesetztes) universe. The Being to which we have returned in the absolute Idea is the entire external world in its systematic completeness, the world of Nature, as the Idea in the form of other-being, or self-externality, of which Hegel says that it is not only external to the Idea but also external to itself -- spread out in space and time. This too is the Idea an sich: 'The external world is implicitly the truth, for the truth is actual and must exist.'

The Idea is presupposed and immanent in Nature and evolves through its processes in a fresh return to itself as life and consciousness. The dialectical circle, therefore, does not close upon itself finally in the Logic, but coils above itself into a new circle, and that again into a third, the circle of self-conscious spirit. But the whole system does return upon itself in absolute Spirit, which is the whole in possession of itself as Idea, not only as at home with itself in its other, but also aware of itself as such.

At the end of the Logic Hegel declares that,

The absolute freedom of the Idea is that it not only passes over into life, nor as finite cognition allows life to appear in itself, but in its own absolute truth resolves to release freely from itself the moment of its particularity, or of the first determination and other-being, the immediate Idea as its reflected image, itself as Nature.[35]

This statement, with the 'resolve' that it announces, is one of the most controversial and oft-debated issues in Hegel scholarship. The

302

inveterate idealists say that it is, and on Hegel's own showing can only be, illegitimate. For the absolute Idea is the complete and self-fulfilled whole. All its phases have been traversed in the Logic, which is also ontology. Hegel has given us the entire theory here of both being and knowledge; so beyond the Idea there can be nothing further, either in thought or in reality. Nothing is left wanting, for the Idea is the final and all-inclusive self-awareness of the whole, and is its substance and essential being. How can it now (in the words of the Greater Logic) 'freely release itself, absolutely sure of itself and resting secure in itself' as Nature? The realist merely dismisses the whole enterprise of philosophy of nature as futile pretension. Legitimate knowledge of the world, he contends, is to be obtained only through empirical science. Philosophy can make no pronouncements upon it which supersede those of the natural sciences and any attempt to dictate what these sciences will or should discuss is grossly inept. Benedetto Croce, in his book, What is Living and What is Dead in the Philosophy of Hegel adopts both of these attitudes. He alleges with the idealist that Hegel's philosophy of nature is a mistake, and with the realist condemns it as a concoction of borrowed material, spurious both as philosophy and as science.

The last allegation we need not discuss here,[36] but we must consider the issue of transition from Idea to Nature, because it is crucial for Hegel's system as a whole and fundamental to his entire philosophical position.

We must begin by making a distinction clear, which, if overlooked, may lead to confusion. The Idea is a principle or Denkbestimmung, which, in Hegel's view manifests itself in and as Nature, and is, therefore, as much a principle of actuality as of thought; and the passages we have quoted refer to that doctrine. Idealistic objectors to the transition from logic to philosophy of nature should not wish to object to this, unless they wish to imply that really there is no nature, but only idea; and that would be just the sort of subjectivism that Hegel utterly rejected. The question then simply is whether the whole philosophical theory of reality has been exhausted by the Logic, or whether Hegel is justified in going on to a philosophy of nature which he claims to be a necessary further dialectical step from the absolute Idea.

The Logic is what in the Phenomenology was called pure or absolute knowing, and this is now quite evidently the absolute Idea. It is the final insight of a clearly self-conscious mind into the identity of subject and object in knowledge, as well as of cognition and will in action. It is, accordingly, a specially high level of self-consciousness attained after reflection upon the lower levels of experience, all of which are in some degree self-conscious, and in fact are nothing else but degrees of self-consciousness. Naive perception is a primitive form of self-awareness, for it involves distinction of self from not-self and confrontation by the self of the object as external. This projection and externalization of sentience as a world of objects is shared by both common sense and science as understanding, for which the subject is conceived as separate from and as set over against the world which is its object (Gegenstand). The world likewise is conceived as independently real and unaffected by the knowing subject. This is the attitude of the realist, who declares that 'knowing makes no difference to the known.'

Scientific understanding is reflection upon common sense, and the empiricist philosophy of the understanding, which affirms the position of Realism, is a further stage of reflection. As such, they are all degrees of self-consciousness each reflecting upon the one that precedes. But so also is perceptual knowledge, in a degree, reflective. It is a reflection upon immediate, pure, sentience and has the same form of dialectical relation to that as the more advanced phases of science and philosophy have to common sense.

It is yet a further stage of self-reflection that takes us beyond the attitudes of naive and scientific realism. This stage is represented by the transcendental idealism of Kant and Fichte, which demonstrates the dependence of objective knowledge upon the spontaneous synthesizing activity of the knowing subject. But deference is still paid to externality, first by postulating an unknown thing in itself, from which the sensuous manifold synthesized is alleged to originate, and secondly by attributing the object to an inexplicable Anstoss which stimulates the postulation by the ego of itself in relation to a non-ego. In Fichte idealism is virtually total. The self-conscious ego is the source of all experience and equally of its opposited objects. But the ego turns out to be an absolute Ego which is not to be identified with the finitely experienced self of the empirical subject. Yet it is this finite self which says 'I', is aware of its own finitude and its distance from the absolute Ego, and no clear method of distinguishing the two is brought to light.

In this idealism we reach the degree of self-consciousness at which the subject recognizes its own immanence in its object, a recognition that leads it further to see the development of its object in perception and reflection as its own self-development. Subject and object are then explicitly identified; but to reach the fully fledged theory of this identity we need to follow the dialectic of the entire logic which brings us to the concept of the Idea, or the Idea as concept. It is then fully established that the Concept is as much object as subject, and the Idea as much subject as object, with the proviso that subject over-reaches object in as much as it is conscious of the identity, as object qua object is not. But the object from which we started was the external world, and the subject from which idealism set out was the ego cogitans, and the dialectic which led to the realization that the latter was immanent in the former began from naive and immediate perception of the object as independently existing. In this conception the thinking mind appears as a finite subject embodied in a finite organism which is a part and a product of nature.

Now it is a principle of the dialectic that what results from its process is the truth of that from which it began, and that it can be so only because it is already present implicitly in its beginnings. In that case the world of common sense and of science must be 'the truth of' immediate sentience and must be implicit in it, and sentience is felt as the bodily sensation of the finite organism which experiences itself as a part and a product of nature. In this organic sentience self-conscious subjectivity has been shown to be immanent but the demonstration of this immanence has required the whole course of reflection upon common experience, in its successive stages of self-conscious returns upon itself, both in the Phenomenology and in the Logic. It is only at the end of the doctrine of the Concept that we finally become aware of the immanence of the absolute Idea in immediate being. Not to common sense, nor to empirical science, nor yet in phenomenology, has this been explicitly disclosed. Accordingly a further advance in self-consciousness demands a return to the concept of Nature, to work out in detail the sense in which the Idea is immanent in all natural forms and in Nature as a whole. This will require a new philosophical science, setting forth the dialectic of Nature, in which mind and consciousness develop themselves through the very natural processes revealed by empirical science, and which that science presents (for the most part unwittingly) as an evolutionary process, developing life from the inorganic and self-consciousness from life.

We move then from the absolute Idea back to Nature, which, as Being, was presupposed in the beginning, and we study it now, not empirically, as the natural sciences do, observing and analysing its phenomena, but, with the help of their findings, disclosing the dialectical relationships of its various phases, physical, chemical and biological, as a scale of forms leading up to the sentient organism in which consciousness awakens. Here the whole of nature is inwardized (erinnert) in sentience and brought to consciousness. It is subjectivized within the organism, a being existing and determining its own activity in its own conscious self-differentiating thought.

As Hegel puts it at the end of the Greater Logic:

But this next resolve of the pure Idea to determine itself as external Idea posits thereby only the mediation out of which the Concept raises itself as free existence returned into itself from externality, fulfils its emancipation through its own self [-consciousness] (durch sich) in the Philosophy (Wissenschaft) of Spirit, and finds the highest concept of itself in the Science of Logic as [culminating] in the self-conscious pure Concept.[37]

305

A reconciliation of idealism with realism has thus been accomplished by declaring Nature, in its immediate and subsistent being, to be the self-manifestation, or self-embodiment, of the Idea in the form of other-being and self-externality.[38] But the full recognition of this relation of nature to mind has been reached only at the end of a long dialectical process of increasing self-awareness in which the thinking consciousness has repeatedly turned back upon itself in successive phases of reflection upon its prior levels. Hence the philosophy of Nature is related to the Logic as a further degree of self-consciousness, at which the mind sees the external forms of nature as the stages of its own self-evolution (die Vermittlung, aus welche sich der Begriff als freie, aus der Äusserlichkeit in sich gegangene Existenz emporhebt). The self-external, spatio-temporal manifestation of the Idea, impelling itself through the range of natural forms, from physical to organic, to the emergence of Spirit as self-conscious personality, eventually achieves satisfaction through the institutions of social order, and its ultimate self-fulfilment in the transcendent visions of art, religion and philosophy. The last of these comprises the all-comprehending syllogism of the philosophical sciences, of which the Logic has set out the dialectical schema.[39]

NOTES: Book II, Part III, Chapter 4

1. Cf. Enz., Section 214.

2. Enz., Section 213.

3. Cf. Enz., Section 213, Zus.

4. McTaggart's opening remarks on the Idea, to the effect that it is the complete coincidence of unity and difference (see Commentary, Section 263) are in the main sound. But he relapses almost at once into error in his assertion that the 'dialectic deals only with a priori conceptions and we cannot acquire by it any knowledge of the different characteristics of Individuals which -- for us at any rate -- can only be known empirically.' The common accusation of Hegel, originally made by Krug, that he professed to deduce a priori what could only be learned from experience is no more than a misconception of the nature of dialectic. That is not a priori deduction in any formal sense. It is the self-development of the content (or subject matter) in which empirical knowledge is itself a phase (or moment). It is presupposed, not acquired, by logic and is sublated in the Concept and Idea.

What follows in McTaggart's discussion of Life is a texture of confusions, misunderstandings, and misinterpretations, detailed criticism of which would be digressive and unfruitful. The statement that Hegel did not regard the world as a single organism composed of organisms is a misrepresentation which ignores the Naturphilosophie (especially Enz., Sections 337-338).

5.   Enz., Sections 216-222; W.L., II, pp. 469-487; Miller, pp. 761-774.

6.   Enz., Section 216 Zus.

7.   Cf. above, pp. 54 and 257. Cf. also, Merleau-Ponty's doctrine in The Phenomenology of Perception.

8.   W.L., II, p. 472; Miller, p. 763.

9.   'In death the species reveals itself as the power over the immediate individual'.

10.   Cf. Commentary, Section 274.

11.   Cf. W.L., II, pp. 487ff; Miller, pp. 774ff.

12.   Enz., Section 223-235; W.L., II, pp. 487-548; Miller, pp. 775-823.

13.   Enz., Section 223.

14.   Enz., Section 225.

15.   Enz., Section 226, Zus.

16.   Enz., Sections 227-231.

17.   Enz., Section 232.

18.   Cf. p. 271f. above; Enz., Section 212, Zus.

19.   Matt. 25, 40-45.

20.   Enz., Sections 236-243; W.L., II, pp. 548-571; Miller, pp. 824-844.

21.   W.L., II, p. 548f.; Miller, p. 824.

22.   W.L., II, p. 549; Miller, p. 824.

23.   Cf. my Foundations of Metaphysics in Science (London, 1965), p. 434.

24.   McTaggart is as far from understanding Hegel's conclusion and the meaning of absolute Idea as he is of so much else in the Logic. He even says, in Section 294, 'To discuss the dialectic method would...be beyond the object...proposed...in this book.' Yet the book professes to be a commentary on the logic, which essentially is the theory and practice in

one of dialectical method. However, McTaggart concludes on a conciliatory note, saying that 'Hegel has penetrated further into the true nature of reality than any philosopher before or after him.' Like the schoolmaster to whom Mure compares him, he ends by giving the pupil an encouraging pat on the back saying, in effect, 'Well, my boy, in spite of all the mistakes you have made, you are still top of the class.'

25. Op. cit., p. 313.

26. Timaeus, 37d.

27. Phänomenologie, VIII (Hoffmeister, p. 558; Suhrkamp, p. 554; Miller's translation, Oxford, 1977, p. 487; Baillie's translation, London and New York, 1966, p. 800): 'Time is the Concept itself, as it exists...for this reason Spirit necessarily appears in time, and it appears in time just so long as it does not grasp its pure concept, that is, does not extinguish time.'

28. Enz., Section 258, Zus.: 'But time itself is in its concept eternal.'

29. Cf. loc. cit., p. 324f.

30. W.L., II, p. 561; Miller, p. 834.

31. W.L., II, p. 565; Miller, p. 837.

32. Cf. my Aquinas Lecture, The Problem of Evil (Marquette University Press, 1977).

33. For fuller discussion see, besides the lecture cited above, Revelation through Reason (Yale University Press, 1958, Allen and Unwin, London, 1958), Ch. 6; Salvation from Despair (Martinus Nijhoff, The Hague, 1973), pp. 152-159; and Atheism and Theism (Tulane University Press, 1977), Ch. VI.

34. Cf. Meno, Phaedo, Gorgias, etc.

35. Enz., Section 243.

36. I have discussed it elsewhere. Cf. Nature, Mind and Modern Science (London, 1954), Ch. XII, v; 'Hegel and the Natural Sciences' in Beyond Epistemology (Nijhoff, The Hague, 1974), Editor, F. G. Weiss.

37. W.L., II, p. 573; Miller, p. 843-44.

38. In religious imagery the resolve of the Idea 'to release the moment of its particularity, or of its first determination and other-being,...freely out of itself as Nature', is the cretaion of the world by

God. The Logic, we have been told, is 'the presentation of God in his eternal essence before the creation of nature and the finite spirit.'

39. Cf., Enz., Section 18: 'The differences of the separate philosophical sciences are simply the determinations of the Idea itself, and it is this alone that presents itself in these different aspects (Elementen). In Nature it is not anything other than the Idea which is to be discerned, but there the Idea is in the form of externality; so also in Spirit it is the same Idea, as existing for itself and become absolute (an und für sich).'

POSTSCRIPT

POSTSCRIPT

IS HEGELIANISM TENABLE TODAY?

Unless Hegel's Logic were at the same time a metaphysic it would be a monstrous structure of paradoxes produced, no doubt, by a genius of incredible ingenuity and fertility, but without cogency, consistency, or plausibility. If the world is a concrete self-sustaining whole, it will necessarily have a dialectical structure; if reality is a dialectical process in and through which spirit expresses itself and brings itself to consciousness, then the Logic is the thinking phase and study of that dialectical process, which reveals its structure and expresses its truth. But if the protasis of this hypothetical can justifiably be denied, the apodasis collapses and the Logic must appear as the fantastic brain-child of an almost incredible paranoia. Yet, if we accept the protasis, are we not begging the fundamental question? Is Hegel not, after all, making one enormous, unwarranted initial assumption, which his system can be said to prove only if it is initially assumed, namely, that the universe is an absolute whole manifesting itself in and as a dialectical process in Nature and Mind, of which the Logic gives us the structure and dynamic principles? Is it not this question-begging assumption which is really focussed and implicit in his final claim, which I have just attempted to defend, that the absolute Idea goes over into and expresses itself in the form of other-being, as Nature?

How can this question be settled?

It seems to me that there is only one way consonant with philosophical integrity and impartiality, and to this I shall presently turn.

It is of course possible to say with Charles Taylor that, however impressive Hegel's system may be and despite its relevance in significant ways to the problem of our time, his conclusion is no longer viable and his central thesis is dead, because our civilization has reverted to the outlook of the Enlightenment, 'rationalized' by its increasingly technological and industrial development. The advance of modern science has broken the bounds of Hegel's system and the synthesis which he sought between human freedom and natural determinism for which the Romantic age longed.[1] Whatever Professor Taylor may mean by this assessment of modern science, his judgement is sociological and historical rather than philosophical. It does not address itself directly to the philosophical cogency (or otherwise) of Hegel's 'central thesis' but merely to the general attitude towards it taken by contemporary thinkers. As to the impact upon Hegel's system of the advance of modern science, to me Taylor's contention appears simply false. The demonstration of its falsity I had already attempted long before Professor Taylor wrote his admirable account of Hegel's philosophy.

311

I have claimed in The Foundations of Metaphysics in Science to show, by a detailed review of contemporary scientific theories, that they do in fact present a world-picture which is dialectical in form, in which the universe is shown to be a self-contained whole, which expresses itself in dialectically related phases developing from physical through chemical and organic forms to self-conscious mind. Unless this whole theoretical structure is to be abandoned, we cannot say that contemporary science makes the principles of Hegel's system untenable or forbids modern philosophy to attend to them.

One might also contend that to the analytic bent of the modern mind Hegel's holism is uncongenial and that after the logical discoveries of Russell and Wittgenstein nobody can take it seriously. That would be rank dogmatism and could be shown to be untrue. So far as the history of 20th Century Empiricism (from Russell and Moore to the present day) is simply a reversion to what Hegel called the thinking of the understanding, the judgment could as well and with as much justification be reversed. One could pronounce with equal pontifical authority that modern analytic thought was a throwback to the eighteenth century and the recurrence to an outlook the failure, futility and implicit falsehood of which Hegel had long since exposed. Some such thesis I long ago attempted to argue (I hope without pontificating) and to demonstrate historically in Nature, Mind and Modern Science.

A third reaction to Hegel is one that attributes to him a virtually blasphemous claim to have attained the ultimate truth and to have encompassed 'the eternal essence of God before the creation of nature and finite spirit'. The claim has been attributed to him even of being himself the incarnate divinity who brings the history of philosophy, and with it history itself to its destined end. This interpretation has appealed, at least to Kojève, as both true and attractive, while to others (following Kierkegaard) it is ridiculous and repulsive. What I have said in the commentary above should contribute somewhat towards showing that the interpretation is misguided and mistaken, and that to accept Kojève's conclusion would wreck the whole structure of the Hegelian dialectic,[2] because it would restrict to one finite and phenomenal existent that transcendent totality without which there could be no dialectic nor any finite phenomenal existents. It would also contradict the nature of human consciousness and experience as Hegel describes and analyses them, and would nullify the tension which he recognizes between the finite and the infinite, itself a manifestation of the dialectical drive. It would also distort and degrade that content which Hegel declares is identical in art, religion and philosophy, so that they could not have the essential character that is claimed for them, as the atonement of human nature with the divine. Where the infinite and eternal is that in which everything has its being and through which alone anything is conceivable, to reduce the Absolute to the level of the finite is to destroy the finite and to subvert reason. In the light of Hegel's philosophy it therefore becomes unthinkable that he should have intended any such reduction or could have made any such claim as Kojève attributes to him.

But adopting attitudes to Hegel's system or making facile and dogmatic pronouncements about it are both unphilosophical. The only genuinely philosophical way to address the question stated above, whether indeed the world is the sort of dialectical whole which Hegel postulates, is to consider it on its merits and that can be done in three possible ways: (1) one may defend it dialectically as Hegel himself does. That defence the whole of the foregoing volume has reviewed and it is what is now being called in question. (2) One could reassess the conclusions of contemporary science and judge of their conformity or otherwise to Hegel's thesis. That I have done elsewhere.[3] (3) One may presume the truth of the contrary and then develop the consequences of that assumption and see where they lead.

The assumption will be that the universe is not a self-contained, systematically organized whole. If it is not, it cannot be dialectically ordered for, as we saw above, dialectic is nothing more nor less than the self-explication and self-differentiation of such a whole.[4] Further, if it is not a self-complete totality, no part of it can be ordered, or even partially ordered, because order implies an organizing principle and that implies completion, so that any partial order bespeaks total order and will of necessity develop it dialectically. That this is so follows from these considerations: A whole to be genuinely whole must be organized, otherwise it is at best a mere congeries of diverse elements, and even that is a whole of a rudimentary kind. But the kind of whole which our provisional assumption excludes is an organized system fully self-realized. Now a partially ordered structure occurring in a disordered congeries is only distinguishable as 'partially ordered' if the principle of order can be identified, and any such principle (a) is realized only in the completely ordered system, and (b) determines the place and function in it of all the parts. Therefore, unless it is somehow fully actualized no parts, as ordered, can be determined or exist in orderly relation. If then some partial order is distinguishable, it must of necessity imply the deficient parts of the system and will, dialectically develop them, and so generate the totality.

If this is denied the status of the alleged 'partial order' becomes dubious. If it is real it must rest upon some actual ordering principle in the real, which would subvert our assumption. Yet we may not allege that it is 'apparent' for that would make it dependent on how we viewed it and, for the moment, we are considering the nature of a universe apart from any relation to a knowing consciousness, if only because it is assumed not to be a whole, and in relation to consciousness it can only be viewed as a whole of some sort (as Kant demonstrated).

Alternatively, it might be alleged that the 'partial order' could occur 'accidentally.' But in that case it would not be genuine order.

The notion of accidental order emerging in a sea of disorder always feeds upon the assumption of a submerged order in that sea, for what could be so ordered, except elements with some prior structure -- particles, molecules, or some such coherent units? Without distinguishably structured parts there can, in fact, be neither order nor disorder. Shuffling a pack of faceless cards will produce neither, whether by accident or by design.[5] Accordingly any degree of order must imply a principle of structure which again implies completion and wholeness. Even if nothing beyond a spatial pattern is envisaged, that immediately involves the whole system of spatial relations required by the spatial manifold -- and the same is true of time.

Objection, however, may be raised that we are being too extreme. Why could the universe not be in the main a chaotic sea of energy (or what you will) with scattered islands of ordered matter, as, in fact, astronomically it appears to be? And how would that entail any sort of Hegelian dialectic?

At once it is apparent that this suggestion gives away the anti-Hegelian case. Of what is the chaotic sea to be composed? Energy is wave activity -- a form of order and structure, which should be forbidden by our initial hypothesis. If it is admitted, it will at once give rise to dialectical development, wave-packets and standing waves will arise and these will constitute structured particles, with 'charges' and the like. Then they will combine to form atoms and these again will combine to produce molecules. At once we are on the evolutionary ladder and in the ascent organisms with sentience will emerge and we shall have consciousness on our hands, explicable, if at all, only dialectically.

Why only dialectically? Might all this not be explicable as the result of random activity? Clearly not if the primordial activity is wave-motion; and if it is not that, where are we to begin? If it is wave-motion it involves periodicity and regularity, it bespeaks some principle of order; and if it spontaneously issues in an ascending scale of increasing organizations, principles of order must necessarily be invoked. What, indeed, could be substituted as the matrix of chaos, if energy is rejected? Democritean atoms? -- but they are the crystalizations of Parmenidean Being, which is a whole and so defeats our purpose. And what is to be the law of their movement, and how could it be divorced from the ordered manifold of space and time? If principles of order, a whole is immediately and necessarily posited and will inevitably (as has been shown) develop itself dialectically. Moreover, no whole is properly realized unless and until it is grasped by a conscious subject and becomes 'for itself'. This is why the emergence of conscious mind from unconscious matter can be explained only dialectically.

314

Further, to return to the suggested hypothesis of ordered islands in a sea of chaos, how are the islands to be related one to another? They must be somehow related, and clearly their relation cannot be sheerly random, for at least it must be spatial, and then we at once have a spatial whole. Also, presumably, it must be physical, and that brings us back to energy, waves, particles, and the rest -- a physical system pervading the whole physical world. Again, how could islands of ordered matter be formed if there were no principle of order implicit in the presumed chaos? Their very formation requires such a principle and physicists and cosmologists tell us that there is just such a principle inherent in space-time itself, which is a structured manifold dictating in its own nature the very laws of motion which determine the form, movement and agglomerations of matter.

'God', said Einstein, 'does not play at dice';[6] by which presumably he meant that nature has immanent in it an organizing principle determining its diverse phenomena; and those who declare that Einstein might be wrong and point to alleged evidence against him are those who most assiduously labour to reveal the principles of order governing the stocastical material they claim to have discovered. This is the inveterate bent of scientists, without which there could be no science.

But our objector will persist. Could the universe nevertheless be a whole of sorts without the need to postulate immanence of the Idea dialectically generating, in the consciousness of man, its own self-knowledge and absolute self-determination? This half-hearted middle course will not serve, because it will only return us to the dialectic. What sort of whole is to be contemplated? Will it include human consciousness? -- as surely it must, for the actual existence of our own consciousness is the one thing we cannot deny. And, if so, what coherent account can we give either of the whole or of consciousness? If consciousness is to enter at all into the natural world, as a product of evolution or as in some other way ingredient, the natural world must be such as could generate it, or such as in some way to harbour its presence. If it is a product of evolution, there must be potentially present in nature that which eventually emerges as human intelligence. And however we conceive the whole that we take the universe to be, we cannot exclude from it our own experience of it, for whatever we say or think, even if we contradict ourselves, is evidence of our own awareness.

So our initial hypothesis commits us to an extremism short of which we must abandon it altogether. The universe, we must assume, unless it is to be dialectical in form, must in reality be utterly and unmitigatedly chaotic. If it is not ordered it cannot be a whole, for any whole involves order and structure, and any sort of order involves wholeness. The only alternative, therefore, is sheer chaos, and our assumption must be that the world is in truth and in itself utterly chaotic throughout, for if any degree of order is anywhere admitted it will permeate the whole and reestablish the system.

This should be a discouraging and disconcerting consequence of the initial assumption, but need not lead immediately to its abandonment. The world we experience is certainly not what the assumption requires, much less so is the world of the empirical sciences, nor could it possibly be, because such a world must be in principle intelligible, and the presumed chaos would render science impossible and any scientific research futile. Nevertheless, it could be (and has been) argued that the world might be sheer chaos although it appears to us as an ordered system, because our minds impose upon the manifold of sense (as we experience it) categorical principles of order, as Kant alleged. Our science then would be purely phenomenal and the real world 'in itself' could be quite otherwise. To fulfil the requirement of our initial assumption, however, the real world must be quite otherwise, and no alleged ignorance of things in themselves may allow of the possibility of an unknown order, whether 'corresponding to' our experience or not.

But no such hypothesis can be consistently maintained; we must assume either that our minds are part and product of the world or that they are not, and it is admitted that our minds impose an order upon our experience, and therefore that our thinking is an ordering activity. In that case, our minds could not be parts of, or members in, a really chaotic world, for that has been taken as entirely devoid of order and as containing no ordering principle. From such chaos, we have concluded, no order or ordering activity could emerge, even by accident. If it were to emerge at all, it could do so only if the principle of order were already potential or implicitly contained in that from which the ordering activity emerged. If our thinking activity is to be part of the world, the world must be such as could produce it, and a sheerly chaotic world could not.

Yet this is exactly what the above hypothesis assumes. We are alleged to experience a manifold of sense on which our intellects impose an order. The tacit assumption is that we are organisms existing somehow in the world and processing its effects upon us as sensation. But, under the restriction imposed by the initial assumption, and by the proposal itself that is being made by our imagined objector, no such presuppositions are legitimate.

We are then thrown back upon the Cartesian alternative that our thinking and the physical world are two utterly separate and different beings, two 'substances' each dependent for their existence only upon itself. For we may not allege, with Descartes, that they might both have been created by God, as that would reintroduce into our conception of the world, apart from our minds, an ordering principle and would destroy our initial assumption. Descartes's view of a supreme and perfect Being creating a dual world of Extension and Thought leads directly, as the history of philosophy gives evidence, through Spinoza's Substance to Hegel's Absolute. Once admit the creative immanence in the world of an infinite and perfect being and you have all the makings of a dialectical universe. The duality of substances demands reconciliation in the unity of the infinite being such as it finds in Spinoza's Deus sive Natura, and in Leibniz' universe of monads, each reflecting all the others and harmonized by the thinking activity (actus purus) of the Monad of monads. From there we go to Kant's Ideal of Reason, the inevitable expression in idea of the unity of the ego, which is necessarily immanent in and regulative of all experience; and so to Fichte's Absolute Ego and to the Absolutes of Schelling and Hegel, in the last of whom the inconsistencies of the earlier theories are ironed out by the movement of the dialectic.

One may, of course, decline to follow out the course traversed by the history of philosophy. One may wish to stop at any one of these historical positions, or adopt some variant of it. Perhaps Leibniz' theory will appeal, and some adaptation of it brought up to date in the light of modern science might prove acceptable. Whitehead developed just such a metaphysic. But of course no such doctrine would be consonant with the presuppositions demanded by our imagined opponent. Whiteheadian philosophy is far from contemplating a chaotic universe ordered only ideally by human thinking. It presumes a cosmic process of integrative activity directed by principles of order systematized in God's Primordial Nature, and it leads in part explicitly and in part by implication to the conception of a dialectical process generating conscious subjects, which (as we remarked earlier) has much in common with Hegel's.

Alternatively, one might opt for some form of neo-Kantianism; and it is just such a view the consequences of which we are now considering: one that regards our knowledge of an ordered world as purely phenomenal and as incommensurable with whatever the world might be 'in itself'. And that we have just found to be incoherent. Neo-Fichteanism would have to establish some way of avoiding development into Hegelianism, if the latter is to be rejected; and even if it could, it would still, presumably, be dialectical in form, as in Fichte's own Wissenschaftslehre. As Fichte insisted, to be aware of itself the ego must be both subject and object, and must therefore limit itself by a non-ego, creating in its own being a self-contradiction which, unless it can be resolved in a higher synthesis, wrecks and dissolves it altogether. But if the contradiction is resolved in a higher synthesis a dialectical process is instituted and we are on our way back to Hegel.

If one were to prefer a more Husserlian version of transcendental idealism one would have to refute interpretations such as that of André de Muralt, who presents Husserl's phenomenology as a dialectical

317

system, seeds of which it undoubtedly has in it, many of them cultivated and brought to fruition by Merleau-Ponty.[7]

If we are to show that any and every form of Hegelianism is unviable, however, we must avoid precisely the outcome to which any of these doctrines point. Human knowledge may not be conceived as a dialectical system of any kind, for if it is true of the world it will commit us to a dialectical theory of the real; and if it is assumed not to be true of the world, it ceases to be knowledge at all. If we postulate a chaotic world set over against a systematized experience in minds which somehow impose principles of order upon their sentient contents, we must also hold that the minds are not parts or products of the world; and that not only makes their very existence and possession of sentient experience inexplicable, but also forces upon us the conclusion that our experience is not 'of the world' at all -- not of the real (chaotic) world -- but only of an apparent world, wholly subjective to us. And that is tantamount to saying that our alleged and much vaunted science is, after all, not knowledge, not science, but mere illusion.

This is not simply a distasteful conclusion, it is utterly incoherent. For confined as we are to the sort of experience we have, which is not of a chaotic reality, there could be no pretext for us to assume the existence of any such alleged reality and no grounds whatever for the hypothesis being entertained. Moreover our experience is of a world, not only ordered, but one of which we are ourselves members and to which we belong in the form of organic bodies. It is only through the medium of our felt bodies that we are in any way aware of a surrounding environment and only in such an environment that we are aware of other organic bodies and so of other minds. If all this is merely subjective and illusory appearance (for according to the assumption made, it is not how the world really is), each of us is condemned to solipsism, and talk of others, or of our minds in the plural, ceases to be legitimate. At the same time, as my body becomes illusory, my mind, in contrast to yours or to what is not my mind but only its object, becomes part of the illusion. I as an individual become unidentifiable even by myself, and the whole conception of experience, which, to be an experience requires an identifiable subject, collapses.

The consequences of our anti-Hegelian hypothesis, therefore, either plunge us into an abyss of incoherence and confusion or lead us back to a Hegelian universe of dialectical progression.

Does this mean that we are constrained to swallow Hegel, hook, line and sinker? If we could put the question to him Hegel would probably answer, 'Yes and No.' No, because if we did, we should be adopting the dialectical system as something fixed and unalterable for all time; and that, by its very nature it is not. The absolute Idea is absolute restlessness, perpetual activity and movement. The whole must, to be whole, ceaselessly differentiate itself. Spirit is eternal

318

activity, and the system cannot be accepted unless it is put to work and unless it continually develops. If accepted the dialectic must reveal itself as the principle for the solution of new problems. It will be seen also as the source of new conflicts, the resolution of which must be sought by its means. If the Hegelian logic is to be adopted it can be only as a living principle of thought, not as a dead, fixed and finished framework.

But if its living force and the inevitability of its progressive impulse is admitted we have accepted it, and, despite, ourselves, are committed to it. We can then see, in the history of post-Hegelian thought, the dialectic continuing, generating its opposites and its syntheses: Marxism, Fascism, Social Democracy; Existentialism, Phenomenology, and Merleau-Ponty's dialectical reconciliation of the two; Positivism, Linguistics and the later philosophy of Wittgenstein, with its Hegelian overtones; the Empiricism of Carnap and Reichenbach, the reaction against them of Popper and then the synthetic doctrines of Lakatós, Kuhn and Feyerabend.

Science has now provided us with material for a new philosophy of nature and the social sciences with more for a new philosophy of mind. This material is eminently holistic and any sound philosophical account of it will be dialectical, if not explicitly, at least in general tendency. Susanne Langer's great work, Mind, An Essay on Human Feeling,[8] is a case in point. Her dominant concepts, though derivative more directly from Cassirer and Whitehead, are (not surprisingly) in principle Hegelian -- notwithstanding that she may emphatically reject that judgment -- and the material with which she works and which she interprets is what contemporary sciences provide.

Our conclusion is that Hegelianism, if rightly understood, is tenable, and the common contempt and repudiation to which, in many quarters, it has been subjected are almost invariably based upon misunderstanding and misinterpretation, when they are not the consequence of sheer ignorance. The present commentary is aimed at the removal of the latter and dissipation of the former. If I can persuade the reader at least to approach Hegel, in the future, with an open mind, I shall count myself to have succeeded.

NOTES: Postscript

1.   Cf. Hegel, Ch. XX.

2.   Cf. 'Some Marxist Interpretations of the Phenomenology,' Presidential Address to the Hegel Society of America, 1978, Method & Speculation in Hegel's Phenomenology,   ed. M. Westphal, Humanities Press (New Jersey, 1982).

3.   Cf. op. cit., and 'Hegel's Naturphilosophie Updated' in The Owl of Minerva Vol. 10, 1979 (Address to the Internationale Hegelverein at the Weltkongress der Philosophie, 1978).

4.   Cf. Bk. I, Ch. III, above.

5.   Incidentally, this inescapable condition, that even disorder implies structured entities which are shuffled or randomly agitate themselves, actually destroys the initial assumption. For any such entities could be structured only if some principle of order were inherent in the matrix which produced them. In truth disorder is always parasitic upon order and never the other way round.

6.   Letter to Max Born, see Albert Einstein, Philosopher-Scientist, ed. P. Schilpp, New York, 1949-51, p. 176; and Giorgio Santillana, 'Einstein' in Reflections on Men and Ideas (M.I.T. Press, Cambridge, Mass., 1968), p. 272.

7.   Cf. André de Muralt, The Idea of Phenomenology: Husserlian Exemplarism, Trans. by G.L. Breckon (Northwestern Univ. Press, 1974); and also M. Merleau-Ponty, The Structure of Behaviour, Phenomenology of Perception, and Sense and Non-sense.

8.   Johns Hopkins Press, Chapel Hill, N.J. (Vol. I, 1967, Vol. II, 1972, Vol. III, 1983).

SELECT BIBLIOGRAPHY

SELECT BIBLIOGRAPHY

1. Hegel's Works.

Gesammelte Werke, Herausgegeben von Friedrich Hogemann und Walter Jaeschke, Felix Meiner Verlag, Hamburg, 1981.

Werke, 1832-1845, 18 vols., edited by P. Marheinke, J. Schulze, L. Henning, E. Gans, H. Hotho, L. Michelet and F. Forster, Berlin, Duncker und Humboldt, 1840-47.

Sämtliche Werke, Jubiläumsausgabe, 20 vols., ed. Hermann Glockner, Stuttgart, 1927-1934, reprinted 1964.

Sämtliche Werke, Kritische Ausgabe, Georg Lasson, Johannes Hoffmeister, Felix Meiner Verlag, Hamburg, 1911-1955; succeeded by other editors.

Werke, in zwänzig Banden, Theorie Werkausgabe, SuhrkampVerlag, Frankfurt-am-Main, Redaktion Eva Moldenhauer und Karl Markus Michel, 1971-78.

Differenz des Fichte'schen und Schelling'schen Systems,ed. G. Lasson, Leipzig 1928.

Glauben und Wissen, ed. G. Lasson, Leipzig, 1928.

2. English Translations.

The Science of Logic, Trans. W.H. Johnson and L.G. Struthers, 2 vols., London, 1929.

Hegel's Science of Logic, Trans. A.V. Miller, London, 1959.

The Logic of Hegel, Trans. William Wallace, Oxford, at the Clarendon Press, 1892; Revised by A.V. Miller, with foreword by J.N. Findlay, 1975.

The Phenomenology of Mind, Trans. Sir James Baillie, London, 1910, revised, 1931, Reprinted, 1955, 1961, 1964, 1966.

Hegel's Phenomenology of Spirit, Trans. A.V. Miller, with Analysis of text and foreword by J.N. Findlay, Oxford, 1977.

Hegel, the Difference between Fichte's and Schelling's System of Philosophy, Trans. by H.S. Harris and Walter Cerf, State University of New York Press, New York, 1977.

Hegel, Faith and Knowledge, Trans. Walter Cerf and H.S. Harris, State University of New York Press, New York, 1977.

Hegel's Philosophy of Nature, Trans. A.V. Miller with Foreword by J.N. Findlay, Oxford, 1970.

Hegel's Philosophy of Mind, Trans. William Wallace, Oxford at the Clarendon Press, 1894. Revised with translation of the Zusatze by A.V. Miller and foreword by J.N. Findlay, 1971.

Hegel's Philosophy of Nature, Trans. Michael John Petry, 3 vols., London, 1970.

Hegel's Lectures on the History of Philosophy, Trans. E.S. Haldane and F.H. Simsom, 3 vols., London, 1892, reprinted, 1955, 1963, 1968.

Hegel's Philosophy of Right, Trans. T.M. Knox, Oxford, 1942, 1949, 1953.

Lectures on the Philosophy of World History, Introduction, Reason in History, by G.W.F. Hegel, Trans. H.B. Nisbet, with an Introduction by Duncan Forbes, Cambridge, 1975.

Lectures on the Philosophy of History by G.W.F. Hegel, Trans. J. Sibree, London, 1881.

3.   Commentaries on the Logic.

Harris, W.T., Hegel's Logic, Chicago, 1895, New York, 1969.

Hyppolite, J., Logique et Existence, Essai sur la Logique de Hegel, Paris, 1953.

McTaggart, J.M.E., A Commentary on Hegel's Logic, Cambridge 1896, New York, 1964.

Mure, G.R.G., A Study of Hegel's Logic, Oxford, 1950.

Lakebrink, Bernhard, Kommentar zu Hegel's 'Logik', Band I: Sein und Wesen, Freiburg/München, 1979. (Band II had not appeared, at time of writing).

Léonard, A Commentaire Litéral de la Logique de Hegel, Paris-Louvain, 1974.

Noel, Georges, La Logique de Hegel, Paris 1897.

Trendelenburg, Adolf, Die Logische Frage in Hegels System, Leipzig, 1843.

Wahl, Jean, La Logique de Hegel comme Phenomenologie, Paris, 1965.

Weil, E., Logique de la Philosophie, Paris, 1967.

4. Other Works on Hegel.

Caird, E., Hegel, London, 1883.

Findlay, J.N., Hegel, A Reexamination, London, 1958.

Günther, Gotthard, Gründzuge einer neuen Theorie des Denkens in Hegels Logik, Hamburg, 1933.

Kaufmann, Walter, Hegel, A Reinterpretation, Garden City, New York, 1965.

Litt, Theodor, Hegel: Versuch einer Kritischen Erneuerung, Heidelburg, 1953.

McTaggart, J.M.E., Studies in Hegelian Dialectic, Cambridge, 1896, New York, 1964.

Müller, Gustav E., Dialectic, New York, 1953.

Mure, G.R.G., An Introduction to Hegel, Oxford, 1940., The Philosopy of Hegel, Oxford, 1965.

Stace, W.T., The Philosophy of Hegel, London, 1924, Dubuque, Iowa, 1967.

Taylor, Charles, Hegel, Cambridge, 1975.

Wallace, William, The Logic of Hegel, Prolegomena, Oxford, 1894.

5. Collections of Essays.

The Legacy of Hegel, eds. Algozin, K.W., O'Malley, J.J., Kainz, H.P., and Rice, L.C., The Hague, 1973.

Lauer, Quentin, Essays in Hegelian Dialectic, New York, 1977.

Gergoire, Franz, Études Hegeliennes, Louvain and Paris, 1958.

Hegel, ed. MacIntyre, A., New York, 1972.

324

New Studies in Hegel's Philosophy, ed. Steinkraus W. E., New York, 1971.

Art and Logic in Hegel's Philosophy, eds. Steinkraus, W.E. and Schmitz, K.L., Atlantic Heights, New Jersey, 1980.

Hegel's Social and Political Thought, ed. Verene, D.P., Atlantic Heights, New Jersey, 1980.

Hegel in Comparative Literature, eds. Weiss, F.G., and Paolucci, A., New York, 1970.

Method and Speculation in Hegel's Phenomenology, ed. Westphal, M., New York, 1982.

Beyond Epistemology, ed. Weiss, F.G., The Hague, 1974.

A

Absolute, 10, 30, 32, 36n6, 55, 57, 65ff., 70, 91n3, 143, 150, 156, 161, 182, 185f., 189f., 192, 218, 239, 242, 259, 268, 271, 277, 287, 289ff., 294, 300, 312, 316f
   definition of, 97, 108, 158
   Idea, see Idea
   syllogism, see Syllogism

Accident, 203

Actuality, 182, 188, 189-212, 242, 248

Addition, 130

Alexander, S., 21

Algebra, 131

Alice through the Looking-glass, 272

Alteration, 105-108

Analogy, 246f.

Anaxagoras, 146

Anaximander, 146

Anaximenes, 97, 124, 146

Anselm, 10, 259

Ansichsein, see Being-in-itself

Anstoss, 72, 304

Anzahl, see Sum

Appearance, 67, 72, 154, 156ff., 174, 181-188, 202

Apperception, 65, 68, 215f.

Aquinas, Thomas, 10, 91n4, 274, 297
   Summa Theologica, 91n4, 211n22, 276n27

Aristotle, 3, 10, 21, 25, 41, 54, 78f, 87, 95, 97, 106f., 115, 124f., 128, 140, 172, 176f., 181, 190, 191, 204, 228, 233, 241f., 244, 249
De Anima, 140
Metaphysics, 288
Nichomachean Ethics, 140
Posterior Analytics, 234

Armstrong, D.N., 62

Art, 287ff., 306, 312

Atheism, 71

Atomism, 117, 263, 314
Logical, 62

Attraction, 115-119, 263

Aufheben, 31f., 81, 205, 253n17, 288, 292f., 295f., 299

Augustine, 10, 274, 297, 301
Enchiridion, 276n27

Ayer, A.J., 10
Language, Truth and Logic, 141n13
The Problem of Knowledge, 62, 73n4

B

Becoming, 95ff., 120
moments of, 99f.

Begriff, see Concept

Being, 87ff., 93f., 101, 120, 125, 129, 155ff., 161, 170, 175, 182, 187, 189f., 208, 214, 216, 220f., 230, 262f., 278, 280f., 296, 302
determinate (Dasein), 100-107, 129, 136, 148, 164, 166, 190, 231, 242
Doctrine of 93-151, 153, 207
for other (Sein für Anderes), 103-105
for self (Fürsichsein), 107, 109-120, 126, 138f., 166, 189, 205, 209, 267
in itself (Ansichsein), 103f., 106

Bergmann, G., 8
Realism, 18n10

Bergson, H., 21, 108, 161, 204

Berkeley, G., 48, 59, 61ff., 158, 178, 190

327

Berzelius, J.J., 143

Blanshard, B., 228
 Reason and Belief, 192

Body, 50, 54, 277

Born, M., 320n6

Bosanquet, B., 228, 273
 Logic, 253n13

Bradley, F.H., 228
 Principles of Logic, 234

Braithwaite, R.B.
 Scientific Explanation, 179n19

Buddhism, 97, 162

Burnet, J.
 Early Greek Philosophy, 151nn9-10

Butler, J., 38

C

Calculation, 126, 130f.

Camus, A., 14

Carnap, R., 319

Cassirer, E., 319

Category, 12, 29, 64, 75, 128, 132, 153f., 157, 215, 221, 226, 230, 282
 empty of content, 67

Causality, 67, 188n4, 200, 202f., 235. See also Cause and Effect
 efficient, 172, 200, 269
 final, 172, 269

Causa sui, 205f., 208

Cause and Effect, 205, 206, 208, 214, 234, 250. See also Causality

Chance, 194, 198

Change, 96f., 105

Chemism, 262, 266f.

Christianity, 76, 186, 201f.

Cognition, 282-285

Collingwood, R.G., 43
An Autobiography, 252n6
An Essay on Philosophical Method, 19n17

Concept, vii, 3f., 10, 12, 23f., 26, 29, 32f., 39, 44f., 52f., 64, 67, 77, 80,
    86, 88, 90, 97ff., 104, 108, 110, 113f., 127, 129, 131, 155ff., 161,
    171, 173, 175, 182, 185, 187, 189, 198f., 201ff., 206ff., 212, 215f.,
    227, 248, 251, 274, 287, 296, 299, 304
Doctrine of, vii, 79, 144, 153f., 173, 214-306
Judgement of, see Judgement
Objective, see Objectivity
subjective, 224-255, 282

Condition, 174, 190, 199

Consciousness, 80, 86, 190, 207, 209, 238, 280, 294, 302, 312. See also
    Self-consciousness

Content, 172, 183, 185, 272, 296

Contingency, 194-198, 273

Copula, 228f., 232, 235, 238f.

Correlation, 184-188
    absolute, 202-207, 248

Cosmology, 52, 54f., 68

Croce, B.
    What is Living and What is Dead in the Philosophy of Hegel, 303

D

Darwin, C., 20

Dasein, see also Being determinate, 101

da Vinci, L., 39

Death, 281

Deduction, 284

Einstein, A., 143, 265, 315

Empedocles, 117

Empfindung, 196, 257, 280. See also Feeling, and Sensation

Empiricism, 13, 38, 47, 53, 59-63, 72, 154, 164, 202, 222, 228, 238, 294, 319
Epistemology, 3

Equality, 128

Equilibrium, dynamic, 99f., 107

Essence, 98, 101, 108, 110, 119, 142n33, 145, 150f., 154, 161-178, 189, 208, 214, 216, 220f., 230, 232, 234, 248, 256, 262, 266, 283, 296, 302
Doctrine of, 16, 49, 77, 153-212, 280f.

Eudaemonism, 71

Evil, 55, 272ff., 297-302

Excluded Middle, 166f.

Existence, 154, 161-178, 174ff., 185, 189f., 208, 256

Existentialism, 177, 239, 319

Experience, 12

Expertise, 78f.,

Explanation, 171, 173, 186, 268

Extension, 50, 17, 181f.

F

Fabre, J.H., 264

Faith, 75f.

Feeling, 40, 209f.
lure for, 196f.

Feyerabend, P.K., 319

Fichte, J.G., viii, 5, 47ff., 51, 65, 72, 89, 109, 112f., 137f., 161, 216, 219, 222, 222n3, 224, 257, 283, 285f., 297, 304, 317
Wissenschaftslehre, 5, 36n8, 224, 317

Findlay, J.N., x
Hegel, A Reexamination, xinl

Finite, 40, 49, 103-107, 186, 268, 277, 286, 312

Force and expression, 185f.

Form, 134, 172, 176ff., 183, 185, 191, 196

Freedom, 41f., 75, 196, 200f., 207, 209, 219

Frege, G., 8, 38, 134, 143, 245
'Function and Concept', 45n4
Grundlagen der Arithmetik, 18n10, 141n20

Fürsichsein, see Being for self

G

Gattung, see Species

Geist, 55. See also Spirit and Mind

Genus, 224, 233, 235, 247, 249

Gestalt, 228

God, 9f., 25, 50ff., 54, 56, 60f., 66, 68, 71, 75ff., 80, 89, 97, 143, 158, 181f., 186, 189f., 192, 196f., 201f., 208, 256, 259f., 268, 271f., 274, 285, 288, 300, 301, 315
as Truth, 10f.
proof of existence, 56f., 69f., 76f. See also Ontological

Goethe, J.W. von, 17, 73n6, 187

Good, 55, 268, 271f., 285f.
Idea of, 177, 285

Gorgias, 41

Gravity, 147f., 172

Ground, 158f., 161, 169, 170-174, 185, 190, 202, 208, 233, 234, 250

Guanilo, 259

Hegel, G.W.F. - cont.
Religionsphilosophie, 74n17, 74n18, 260

Hegelianism, 311-320

Heisenberg, W., Physics and Philosophy, 45n6

Heraclitus, 97f., 108, 117, 146, 204

Hinduism, 145

History, 187, 261
Philosophy of, 201, 294

Hobbes, T., 61, 135
Leviathan, 141n22

Hume, D., 3, 37, 40, 48, 59, 61ff., 69, 202f.
An Enquiry into Human Understanding, 73n3
A Treatise of Human Nature, 45n1, 73n4

Husserl, E., 5, 214, 222, 224, 256, 317
Formal and Transcendental Logic, 5

I

I, see Ego

Idea, 24f., 29f., 34, 54, 65, 67, 70f., 90, 98, 107, 113, 154, 156, 176f.,
    190f., 202, 208, 215, 218, 221f., 242, 245, 259f., 268f., 271f., 274,
    277-306, 311, 315
Absolute, 81, 104, 110, 119, 177, 197, 207, 269, 285f., 287-297, 301f.,
    318

Idealism, 113f., 219, 303f., 306
Objective, 65
Subjective, 12, 65, 114, 181

Ideality, 111, 119

Identity, 38, 71, 95f., 98, 100, 104, 158f., 161-163, 184, 187, 197, 208,
    231, 277, 295
Law of, 162, 166f.

Immediacy, 47, 49, 75-81, 85-90, 93, 155f., 174, 221, 267, 290, 295,
    296f., 302

Individual, 221, 224f., 229, 237, 241f., 296, 299

335

Logic, 3-19, 20-26
  bifurcation of, 4f.
  deontic, 242
  formal, 7, 48, 153f., 169, 208f., 227, 240, 242
  Hegel's conception of, 3-19
  main divisions of, 90
  objective, 6

M

Magnitude, 124f.
  extensive, 132
  intensive, 132, 134

Maimonides, M., 10

Manifestation (Offenbarung), 158, 190

Mathematics, 125, 131, 144, 153, 245

Marx, K., 21f., 34

Marxism, 319

Materialism, 60, 62, 125, 135

Matter, 124, 127, 135, 172, 176ff., 185, 218

Mays, W., 240f., 253n24

Measure, 107, 134, 140, 143-151, 156
  standard of, 143, 147

Mechanism, 262-266, 267

Mediation, 155, 174, 290, 295

Mendeljeff, G., 143

Merleau-Ponty, M., 54, 317, 319
  Sense and Non-sense, 320n7
  The Phenomenology of Perception, 307n7, 320n7
  The Structure of Behaviour, 320n7

Metaphysics, 3, 7, 54, 56, 68, 97, 157, 204, 238, 311

Method, 42, 187, 284, 295-297

Mill, J.S., 173f.
  A System of Logic, 179n18

337

Mind, 55, 311

Minkowski, H., 143

Modality, 191-202, 236

Molière, 172

Monad, 85, 116, 118f., 220, 263, 317

Morality, 125f., 272, 285

Motion, 135, 146ff.

Mozart, W.A., 295

Multiplication, 130

Mure, G.R., viii, x, 103, 106, 290-295
A Study of Hegel's Logic, xin4, 159n1, 188n2, 290-295

McTaggart, J.M.E., viif., 19n15, 97, 109, 114f., 131f., 134, 144, 149,
159, 160n3, 205, 210nn3, 4, 211n9, 252n4, 253n17, 254n29, 257n15,
281, 306n4, 307n24
Commentary on Hegel's Logic, viii, 19n15, 36n10, 120n9, 141n15,
142n34, 151n4, 160n7, 179n21, 211nn23, 25, 254n31, 275n15, 306n4,
307n10
The Nature of Existence, 141n16

N

Nature, 12, 20, 21f., 25, 29, 34, 55, 57, 65, 67, 85, 104, 185, 187, 197,
202, 208f., 214, 217ff., 245, 259f., 262, 280, 289, 292ff., 302-306,
311
Philosophy of, 22, 25, 29, 59, 70, 242, 294

Necessity, 60, 64, 198-202, 203, 206, 247, 249ff.
judgement of, see Judgement

Negation, 40, 56, 72, 96, 101ff., 105f., 122n21, 136, 163f., 169, 239, 293,
296f.

Newton, Sir I., 44, 59

Neitzsche, F., 14

Nothing, 94f., 120, 125, 263, 278

Noumena, 217

338

Number, 128, 129-132, 148

O

Objectivity, 16, 47, 64, 192, 216, 219, 228, 242, <u>256-276</u>, 287, 304

Offenbarung, see Manifestation

One, 85, 110, 114, 115-119, 126, 128f.

One and Many, 115-119, 263

Ontological Proof, 56f., 69f., 76f., 192f., 259ff.

Ontology, 52f.

Opposition, 165, 167, 169

Other, 103, 107, 120, 136

Organism, 176, 262f., 265, 279

Organization, see System

Ought, 109, 201, 236, 242, 258, 286

P

Pantheism, 56, 71, 144

Parmenides, 41, 97f., 110, 117, 129, 262f., 314

Particular, 39ff., 144, 221, 224ff., 241ff., 296, 299

Pascal, B., 38

Perception, 9, 40, 60, 62, 65, 67, 75, 79, 85, 111, 135, 153, 191, 209,
228, 231, 257f., 262, 282, 291f., 296, 303

Phenomena, 64, 67, 154, 157, 178, 181ff., 214

Phenomenology, 25, 153, 177, 221, 230, 239, 305, 317, 319

Philosophy, 5, 12ff., 220, 241, 271, 287ff., 303, 305f., 312
Critical, 63-72, 154
History of, 50
Mediaeval, 47f., 54, 154, 177

Physicalism, 62

Physics, 125f., 134f., 198, 224, 264f.
  quantum, 126, 198, 265

Pilate, Pontius, 15

Pitcher, G., 62

Planck, M., 265

Plato, 8, 10, 24, 41f., 44, 79, 96, 134, 139, 176f., 191, 204, 256, 285, 293, 297f.
  Epistles, 290
  Gorgias, 308n34
  Meno, 297, 308n34
  Parmenides, 24, 41, 262
  Phaedo, 55, 120n7, 179n17, 308n34
  Republic, 45n7, 120n7, 177
  Sophist, 42, 101, 177, 297
  Theaetetus, 41f., 297f.
  Theory of Forms, 41
  Theory of knowledge, 44
  Timaeus, 177

Plotinus, 110

Ploucquet, G., 240

Pneumatology, 53

Politics, 125f., 266

Popper, Sir K., 258, 319

Positivism, 62

Possibility, 192ff.

Pre-established Harmony, 123n44, 251

Principia Mathematica, 7. See also Russell, B.

Probability, 18n2, 194

Properties, 174f., 185

Proposition, 227, 241
  judgement not a, 229

Protagoras, 41

Providence, 186, 198, 201, 273

Psychology, 52f., 75, 125, 221, 280

Purpose (Zweck), 196, 268ff.

Pythagoras, 144

Q

Quality, 93-120, 124, 143, 149f., 175. See also Judgement of Quality
primary, 119, 174
secondary, 119, 175

Quantity, 107, 118f., 124-140, 149f.
continuous, 126f.
determinate. See Quantum
discrete, 126f.

Quantum, 120, 127ff., 132, 137f.
specific, 147

Quine, W.V.O., 8, 108
From a Logical Point of View, 122n30
Methods of Logic, 18n8
Word and Object, 18n10

R

Raisonnement, 12, 38, 43, 238, 241

Ratio, 138-140, 142n34, 144f.

Rationalism, 13, 38ff., 47, 60, 63, 72, 256

Realism, 113f., 218f., 303f., 306

Reality, 104, 154

Reason, 4, 16, 38, 42-45, 67, 72, 75, 238f., 241, 279, 282f., 293
cunning of, 198, 268, 270, 272-274
dialectic of, 67
Ideas of, 65, 284
Ideal of, 190, 317
practical, 71, 185, 289
sufficient, 170f., 173
theoretical, 71

Reciprocity, 202, 205ff., 208, 235

Reflection, 161, 184, 187, 192, 221, 230, 245, 296. See also Judgement of Reflection

Reichenbach, H., 319
The Rise of Scientific Philosophy, 141n13

Reinhold, K.L., 14, 87

Relation, 162, 165, 262

Religion, 76, 80, 125f., 158, 259, 271, 273, 287ff., 306, 312
Philosophy of, 201

Repulsion, 115-119, 126, 263

Right, Philosophy of, xi, 13, 34, 294

Rousseau, J.J., 273

Rule, 147

Russell, Bertrand, 7f., 62, 234, 245, 312
Our Knowledge of the External World, 122n30
and Whitehead: Principia Mathematica, 7

Ryle, G., 79, 91n2
The Concept of Mind, 82n6

S

Santillana, G., Reflections on Men and Ideas, 320n6

Sartre, J-P., 94

Scepticism, 41, 81, 193

Sciama, D.W., The Unity of the Universe, 276n26

Schein, 156, 158f., 181, 209, 296, 300

Schelling, F.W.J. von, viii, 5, 13, 17, 47, 50, 55, 89, 91n3, 161, 190, 219, 257, 290, 317

Schilpp, P., Albert Einstein, Philosopher Scientist, 320n6

Schleiermacher, F.E.D., 48

Schrödinger, E., 'Our Conception of Matter', What is Life? and Other Essays, 120n12

342

Science, 39. See also Wissenschaft

Sein für Anderes. See Being for other

Self-awareness, 9, 215. See also Self-consciousness

Self-consciousness, 29, 85, 89, 112, 189, 196, 200, 201, 209f., 216, 221, 236, 239, 268

Self-specification, 44f., 224, 226, 262

Sensation, 65, 135, 221, 228, 230, 279, 281, 292, 304. See also Empfindung

Smart, J.J.C., 62

Socrates, 41, 55, 251, 298

Solar System, 112, 146

Solipsism, 318

Something, 103, 106f., 120, 175. See also Other

Sophistry, 41, 171, 193

Soul, 50f., 54, 60, 68, 277, 280

Space, 127, 137, 146f., 218, 291f., 302

Species (Gattung), 224, 280f.

Specification, 224f. See also Self-specification

Specific heat, 147

Spencer, H., 20f.

Spinoza, B de, 10, 12, 47, 50, 71, 77, 81, 89, 127, 139, 144, 151n6, 161, 181f., 190, 195, 202, 204f., 207, 210n5, 256, 271, 278, 284f., 289f., 301, 316f.
  Epistles, 19n16, 108, 122n21, 188n5
  Ethics, 19n16, 89, 141n6, 276n27
  Short Treatise, 77

Spirit, 28, 54, 65, 67, 85, 104, 113, 214, 218, 220, 245, 287, 289, 294, 302
  Absolute, 21, 36, 70, 76, 87, 104, 163, 202, 290, 292
  Philosophy of, 25, 29, 70, 242, 294

Stace, W.T., 97
The Philosophy of Hegel, 120n9

Stevenson, R.L., Virginibus Puerisque, 179n10, 275n23

Stoicism, 201

Subjectivity, 16, 64, 201, 242, 257

Substance, 71, 127, 145, 161, 174f., 181f., 188n4, 190, 202-204, 214,
    233, 235, 249

Sum (Anzahl), 129, 132, 137

Syllogism, 227, 235, 237f., 238-252, 269f., 279, 306
    absolute, 245
    categorical, 248ff.
    disjunctive, 250-252
    hypothetical, 249ff.
    of necessity, 242, 248-252
    of reflection, 242, 245-248
    qualitative, 242-245
    quantitative, 245

Synthesis, 65, 226

System, 14, 27-36, 44, 111, 125, 157, 161, 167ff., 193f., 202, 224ff., 230,
    233f., 238, 241, 248, 250, 266, 313f.

T

Taylor, C., x, 63, 106f., 119, 122n27, 123n43, 215ff., 311
    Hegel, 36n11, 123n44

Teilhard de Chardin, P., The Phenomenon of Man, 222n4

Teleology, 125f., 172, 186, 198, 200, 262, 263, 265, 267-272, 275n15

Thales, 113

Theology, 52, 56, 69, 97

Thing, 174f., 185
    in itself, 52, 64f., 67f., 72, 73n12, 128, 175, 177f., 190, 216f., 219,
    224, 257f., 298, 304, 316

Thought, 50, 71, 181f., 227
    determination. See Denkbistimmung

Tiglathpileser, 162f

344

Time, 127, 137, 146, 218, 292f., 302

Trendelenburg, A., 96

Truth, 9f., 15, 18n12, 27f., 36n6, 47, 62, 70, 86, 105, 154, 183, 191, 193, 202, 217f., 222, 232, 236, 259, 268, 271, 277f., 281, 283, 286, 302

U

Unconditioned, 67, 200

Understanding, 4, 7, 9, 16, 37-40, 50, 55f., 63f., 69, 72, 81, 90, 96f., 102, 108f., 128, 131, 153f., 157, 161, 164, 168, 176ff., 184, 191f., 202f., 208, 214, 221f., 227ff., 235, 238, 240, 242ff., 249, 252, 256, 262, 277ff., 281f., 287ff., 293, 301, 312

Unity, 100, 129
  of subject and object, 277

Universal, 17, 39ff., 43, 66, 96, 144, 176, 186, 221, 224ff., 228f., 235, 237, 241ff., 248, 251f., 279, 296, 299
  abstract, 37, 227, 281, 295
  concrete, 29, 40, 42-5, 70, 86, 105, 139, 220, 224f., 232f., 244, 248f., 261, 270, 280f., 295

Universality, 60, 64, 280, 296

Urmson, J.O., Philosophical Analysis, 73n5

Utilitarianism, 269

V

Value, 236

Verification principle, 62

Vernon, M.D., The Psychology of Perception, 82n6

Vienna Circle, 62

Void, 97, 116f., 263

Volition, 285-287. See also Will

Vorstellung, 12, 23, 36n3, 178, 182, 221, 259

von Haller, A., Unvollkommenen Gedicht über die Ewigkeit, 142n28

W

Wallace, W., xi, 77, 188n8, 266

Warnock, G.J., English Philosophy since 1900, 73n5

Whitehead, A.N., 21, 108, 122n31, 196f., 204, 211n20, 317, 319
and Russell, Principia Mathematica, see Russell.
Process and Reality, 211n13
The Concept of Nature, 26n6

Whole, 28, 35, 36n6, 43, 90, 104, 110, 113, 116, 125, 127, 155, 161,
184f., 186, 189f., 198, 206, 209f., 221, 224ff., 230, 232, 235f., 238,
241, 249ff., 262, 265, 268f., 271f., 274, 287, 313
and Part, 184f.

Will, 201, 283. See also Volition
free, 196
General, 273
good, 270, 285
rational, 71

Wissenschaft, 5, 13, 24f., 27-36, 47, 86, 153, 209, 217, 220, 260, 288,
305

Wissenschaftslehre, 5. See also Fichte

Wittgenstein, L., 7f., 15, 108, 126, 312, 319
Philosophical Investigations, 73n5
Tractatus Logico-Philosophicus, 7, 18n6, 36n5, 45n5, 62, 122n30

Wolff, C., 47, 50, 284

X Y Z

Zeno, 41, 108, 128

Zweck, see Purpose